Southern
Steam Sunset

by
John H. Bird MA (Oxon)

RUNPAST PUBLISHING

Dedication

This book is for Marian, Peter and Matthew

© John H. Bird 1997

Published by Runpast Publishing, 10 Kingscote Grove, Cheltenham, Gloucestershire GL51 6JX

Printed in England by The Amadeus Press Ltd., Huddersfield

ISBN 1 870754 42 5

Southern Steam Sunset is a revised, enlarged and combined edition of *Southern Steam Surrender* and *Southern Steam Specials* (both out of print) by the same author, with much new information and many new photographs.

Above: A pair of Standard 4-6-0s blasting up-grade through the beautiful Dorset countryside on March 27th 1967. The location is the cutting between the two tunnels at Upwey, and the train is the 16.46 from Weymouth to Waterloo. Locomotives Nos. 75075 and 73043 are doing battle with one of the steepest climbs on what was the Southern's last remaining steam worked route. *Author*

Preceding page: The dying days of Southern Steam are recalled as 'West Country' No. 34004 *Yeovil* passes Beaulieu Road on June 10th 1967 with the 08.46 Bournemouth-Waterloo train. *Author*

Contents

List of Tables

Preface

The summer of 1967 was a sad one indeed: steam train operations in the South of England came to an end and I had to come to terms with the resulting void in my life. Thirty years later, my memories of those days in the mid-1960s are as fresh as ever. I was fortunate enough to witness and take part in those last years of steam on the Southern Region and the experience left an indelible impression on my then adolescent mind. Even now, I still dream occasionally that steam didn't really die and that all I have to do is go down to the nearest station and things will be as they ever were …

Perhaps this is because one of my last memories of Southern steam from 1967 is of being woken at night by the sound of a train in distress. It was about 1.00am and although the railway line was a mile from my home, I was dragged from the land of slumber by the slow and faltering beat of a steam engine's exhaust, as a locomotive battled unsuccessfully with the uphill stretch through Netley station. Time and again the train stopped, paused for breath, and then tried the ascent once more.

Each time, I weighed up the odds of leaping from bed, grabbing some clothes, and cycling to the station to witness this dramatic spectacle. I was torn between the warmth of my bed, and the knowledge that this was probably the last ever steam train I would see at my nearest station. For this was the penultimate night before all steam traction was banished from the tracks of Southern England and as far as I was aware there were no more steam trains scheduled to pass through Netley. I had thought I had seen the very last one two days before, now it seemed I was going to miss the true history maker. To my everlasting shame the attractions of sleep won the victory, although the steam locomotive's battle with the gradient continued for what seemed like ten or fifteen minutes, time enough to have reached the station and seen with my own eyes what was taking place. Sadly, I never found out what that train was doing there in the middle of the night, why it had got stuck and where it was going to.

In fact, that isn't quite true. Twenty years later I was giving a talk about the end of Southern steam to a small group of railwaymen. I was describing my nocturnal experiences and the struggling steam engine on that July night in some detail, when one of the audience, Mr Len Witt, spoke up and amazed me. "I was the driver of that train", he asserted. "We were pulling a long load of wagons bound for Redbridge, and we got stuck on the bank up to Netley. I remember it well. We kept setting back, and having another go. I think it took us about twenty minutes to get through the station". I found it hard to believe what he had to say. During the passage of two decades, I had come to think that maybe the whole experience had been a dream. It was strangely reassuring to discover that I had been experiencing reality after all!

This book is full of such memories, my own and those who were in control of events. I could not have written it without the assistance of the many railwaymen and enthusiasts who responded to my pleas for assistance. They have thrown open their homes and their recollections to my requests for information, and I hope that the result is a book which pays tribute to the last years of Southern steam and to all those who were involved in making it happen. I trust that it adequately conveys something of the thrill, excitement, but also the sadness of those momentous days.

In many ways, the chapters that follow could well be described as the product of a misspent youth. In the company of hundreds, even thousands of other boys and men, I fell in love with steam engines, and followed them with dedication and ardour. None of this would have been possible without the support and encouragement of my parents, who perhaps regretted on occasion the willingness with which they aided and abetted me in my quest for steam. This book owes a great deal to them, so I am pleased to begin by saying "Thank you, mum and dad!"

John Bird
Alton, March 1997

Introduction

On Sunday July 9th 1967 'Merchant Navy' class No. 35030 *Elder Dempster Lines* rolled into Waterloo station, London, pulling eight green carriages, loaded with an assortment of holiday-makers, Sunday trippers and above all, dozens of railway enthusiasts. This was the very last steam operated passenger train on the Southern Region of British Railways, and its arrival in London brought to an end a way of transport which dated back to the 1830s.

Yet just ten years earlier, Waterloo station was alive with the sounds and smells of living steam. Most of the South's railway lines at that time saw regular daily steam workings, and in many areas steam dominated completely. Many of the locomotives then in use were of considerable antiquity, while alongside there were others newly built! In the short space of a decade those engines, old and new, were swept away, as steam surrendered to electric and diesel motive power as part of a major transport revolution.

"Southern Steam Sunset" is a detailed record of Southern steam from those glory days of virtual supremacy in the mid-1950s, until its complete eclipse in the summer of 1967. It focuses in particular on the last eighteen months of steam operation, from January 1st 1966, when hundreds, maybe even thousands, of enthusiasts gathered daily to ride behind and photograph the dying remnants of a once proud fleet of steam engines. For the men who operated the trains those were days of mixed emotions. For some of them the impending end of a lifetime's pattern of working was a threat, for others the prospect of a cleaner, more straightforward future beckoned attractively. This book tells their story, as well as providing a definitive account of the final years of Southern Steam.

Few students of railway history would have expected that the Southern Region would be the last on British Railways to operate steam express trains. The Southern Railway, its predecessor before Nationalisation, had been the pioneer of *electric* railways in this country, and by the 1930s had already developed an extensive network around London, using such modern traction. With further diesel-isation and electrification programmes launched in the 1950s, as described in the following chapters, the likelihood of steam surviving in the South seemed remote. Yet, survive it did, primarily on the main route from Waterloo to Weymouth and to a lesser extent on the line to Salisbury and in one or two other isolated pockets. Steam expresses still pounded the tracks of the Southern several years after they had disappeared in most other parts of the country. Although a few steam passenger trains did survive in Lancashire until 1968, in terms of number and importance they could not compare to 'Britain's last steam main line'.

So it fell to the most unlikely region to claim the distinction of running the last high speed passenger trains in Britain, and indeed the last steam branch lines as well! Happily steam working continued right up to the very last day before the new electric services were fully implemented, hence the historic arrival of Bulleid pacific No. 35030 at Waterloo on July 9th, 1967 working the 14.07 from Weymouth, with driver Ray Hardy on the footplate.

So ended the one hundred and nineteen year reign of steam at Waterloo. The station had been opened originally on July 11th 1848 to provide the terminus in the capital for the London and Southampton Railway. When that line had started working in May 1838, the trains had only travelled as far as Nine Elms, 1¼ miles to the west. Nine Elms eventually became the site of the London and South Western Railway's main locomotive works, later transferred to Eastleigh, and also one of the main motive power depots, which survived to the very end of steam.

The use of steam locomotives was reasonably extensive during the final eighteen months or so before full electric services were introduced. Inevitably though, steam became more elusive as time passed and more electric and diesel trains were brought into use. In particular, Sundays were almost steamless during 1967 and even on weekdays and Saturdays, it was useful to have a good knowledge of the Working Timetable and rosters to be sure of steam haulage. Nevertheless, just one month before its final disappearance, steam power was still much in evidence. For example, in just 4 hours on Saturday June 10th, eleven west-bound steam hauled passenger trains were observed passing Beaulieu Road station in the New Forest.

For most enthusiasts, the last months of Southern steam were largely about the locomotives in action. Some engines were so run-down that they could not be coaxed to keep time, even by the most experienced drivers, but others in the hands of exuberant crewmen, gave exhilarating performances, the like of which had rarely been seen before. A devoted band of followers, many teenagers and young men, became obsessed with the thrill of high-speed steam in action. They travelled extensively on these 'last flings', sometimes outnumbering ordinary passengers. Recording speeds and station passing times became a way of life, and a community of like-minded fanatics grew up, riding up and down the Southern at all hours of the day and night.

Others concentrated on recording the scene with their cameras, and few unusual workings or dramatic sights eluded the lens of some cameraman. But there was more to photograph than just trains in action, for the steam railway had a whole range of features which have now been swept away, but were an essential part of the Southern ethos. These included the stations, with their green and white enamel nameboards, and 'targets' mounted on gas or electric lamps. These were already giving way to the black and white plastic signs of the new British Rail corporate image. At some platform ends and marshalling yards the water columns stood to attention, awaiting the call to duty from a thirsty locomotive. They were swept away with indecent haste within days of steam disappearing, as if their remaining was an un-wanted reminder of the dead. However, the large water tanks which had supplied them remained as a longer-lasting epitaph. Favourite haunts of photographers were the engine sheds with their symbolic images of ash and smoke and fire, and latterly also, the rusting hulks of withdrawn locomotives.

Most steam hauled trains were composed of green-liveried carriages, many built to the designs of Bulleid in the late 1940s. These were comfortable, well-styled vehicles, mellowed by natural wood interiors and silvered components such as hand-rails and grab-handles. They presented a homely and relaxing atmosphere for travel, compared to the all-pervading plastic worlds of later decades. Most of the expresses were provided with restaurant and buffet cars, offering a full-scale service of breakfasts, lunches and dinners. Now the electric trains cover the route so quickly that such lavish meal provision is deemed unnecessary.

The Bournemouth line even boasted the opulence of Pullman travel, as the 'Bournemouth Belle' made its daily return journey, setting out from Waterloo at 12.30 and returning in the evening. This too ended with the advent of electric services, although it had been largely diesel hauled anyway during 1967.

Although the emphasis of this book is on steam on the Weymouth and Salisbury lines, steam also operated from other depots at Guildford, Basingstoke, Southampton Docks, and for a time, Feltham. This meant that steam worked trains were also to be seen on some of the cross-country routes straddling the Southern's South Western division, and on some freight workings as well. Until its closure in March 1966, Bournemouth was the southern terminus of the Somerset and Dorset line to Bath, and that took SR steam engines off into Western territory, and sent the last WR steam engines southwards to the Bournemouth area. The branch lines to Swanage and Lymington were steam worked during part of this time, and the little used line from Clapham to Kensington had daily steam passenger workings right up to the final weekend of steam.

By 1966 steam was unwelcome on the Central and Eastern divisions of the Southern Region which were almost entirely electrified. Nevertheless it did manage to make sporadic incursions into forbidden territory, mainly in the form of railtours for enthusiasts. SR steam also penetrated the Western Region's diesel defences, from which it was officially banned at the end of 1965. In the London area, inter-change of passenger and freight workings sometimes took steam onto other regions as well. In the far extremes of east and west, at Ashford, and Meldon Quarry near Okehampton, departmental engines shunted in little islands of steam working far away from the mainstream. The Isle of Wight fitted that description literally of course. Its fleet of class '02' tank engines dating back to 1889, remained hard at work until the end of 1966, when electrification caught up with them as well.

Apart from the Southern's own steam locomotives, there were a number of notable visitors from other regions, coming from as far afield as Scotland. These included the famous *Flying Scotsman* and *Blue Peter* working rail tours, as well as non-descript freight engines sent to Eastleigh Works for repair, and then 'borrowed' by the Southern for a while.

All in all, the period from 1957 to 1967 was an exciting time for devotees of steam in the South, whatever their particular focus of interest. As the years and months passed by, the enjoyment was given a sharpened edge by the sad knowledge that it was all about to come to an abrupt end in the summer of 1967. How different the picture had seemed in the carefree steam-filled days of ten years before ...

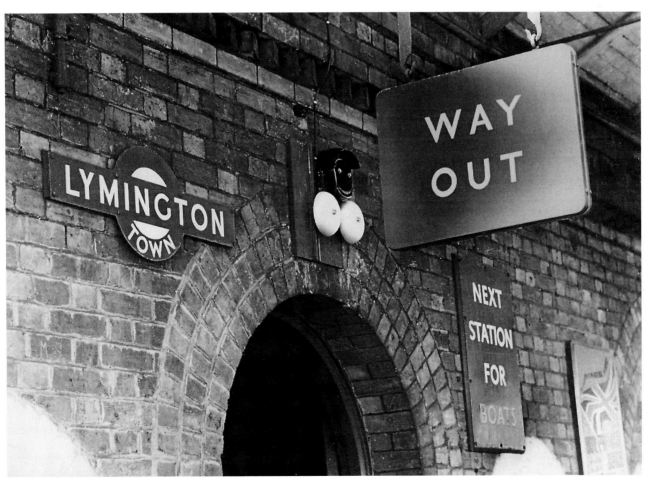

Green enamel signs were a vital ingredient in the Southern ethos. They are seen in force at Lymington Town.   *Author*

At the end of 1960 the steam shed at Ramsgate in Kent was closed to make way for electrification works, leading to the creation of a temporary locomotive stabling facility nearby at Margate. In this interesting view taken on February 4th 1961, can be seen the variety of motive power to be found at this time of transition. The 'D1' 4-4-0 was a Maunsell rebuild of a 1902 constructed 'D' class locomotive, next to it is a BR Standard 2-6-2T built in the 1950s, and further beyond a member of the 'Schools' class dating from the inter-war period. Alongside on the right are two new diesels, a BRCW Type '3', of a type which was to survive on the Southern for nearly forty years, and next to it a Derby/Sulzer Type '2' diesel, one of a number loaned to the Southern during this interim period.

S. C. Nash

Chapter One

Southern Steam's BR Heyday 1957-1963

Nationally and internationally, 1957 was indeed a momentous year. The Russians shocked the Western world by putting the first artificial satellite, Sputnik 1, into space. The six original members of the 'Common Market' met in Rome to sign the founding Treaty, and Bill Haley and the Comets arrived for their British tour, which would put rock'n'roll firmly on the map. Their first journey in this country was in the hands of the Southern Region, on board the 'Daily Mirror Bill Haley Special' from Southampton Docks to Waterloo, specially chartered by the newspaper, and hauled by Bulleid 'West Country' pacific No. 34020 *Seaton*.

Meanwhile, at the other end of the country, in July 1957, Prime Minister Harold Macmillan, was addressing a Tory party rally in Bradford. It was there that he uttered his unforgettable phrase "Most of our people have never had it so good". He was referring to the economic situation, the growing prosperity of post-war Britain. However, looking back from forty years later, his remarks could be aptly applied to the opportunities available for steam railway enthusiasts of the day! Those fortunate souls were able to enjoy a railway system which was still virtually at its greatest extent, before the fall of the infamous 'Beeching Axe' which was to sever so much route mileage in the early years of the next decade. Above all, steam power was still holding glorious sway on most of Britain's railways, but not, sadly, for much longer. 'Supermac's' immortal words came ten years to the month before the complete extinction of steam railway operation in the South of England, but what a momentous decade it would prove to be!

At the beginning of 1957, the Southern Region was part of the then nationalised British Railways system, and had complete responsibility for railway services from Kent through Sussex and Surrey to Hampshire and the Isle of Wight. In Dorset, Wiltshire, Devon and Cornwall it shared provision with the Western Region. Broadly speaking its territory was the same as that of the former Southern Railway company, which it had replaced on January 1st 1948 when Britain's railways passed into public ownership. However, until 1958, the Southern Region also had control of the former Somerset and Dorset railway between Bournemouth and Bath. Much of that route was taken over by the Western Region in that year, but in exchange the Southern received the Weymouth to Yeovil line and there were several other adjustments.

Although its predecessor private companies had been pioneers of electrified railways, as far back as 1909, a remarkable amount of the Southern Region's traffic was still steam worked at the beginning of 1957. The exceptions were the many inner and outer suburban services emanating from the main London termini at Waterloo, Victoria, Charing Cross, Cannon Street and London Bridge. These had been progressively electrified in the years leading up to the outbreak of World War II. On the other hand, the only main lines *not* steam worked were those from Waterloo to Portsmouth via Guildford, Victoria to Portsmouth via Horsham, and Victoria to Brighton via Haywards Heath, each of which had each been turned over to electric traction in the 1930s. All the other main arteries, as well as the cross-country routes, apart from the Sussex coast line between Portsmouth and Eastbourne and Hastings, were steam worked.

The result of all this was that if you wanted to set out from London for such varied locations as Ramsgate, Dover, Folkestone, Hastings, Southampton, Salisbury, Bournemouth, Weymouth, Exeter, Plymouth, Ilfracombe, Bude or even the full 259¾ mile expedition to Padstow, you would certainly travel behind steam power. Furthermore, apart from a handful of diesel shunters, which admittedly had been growing in number in the previous few years, and also a few workings by the Southern's three electric locomotives, all freight traffic throughout the Region was still steam powered.

Unrebuilt 'Merchant Navy' class No. 35007 *Aberdeen Commonwealth* photographed to advantage as it pulls away from Andover Junction with a West of England line train.
S.C. Nash

Top: Towards the end of its life, former PDSWJR 0-6-2T No. 30757 *Earl of Mount Edgcumbe* is seen at Eastleigh mpd, with the as yet unrebuilt 'Merchant Navy' No. 35028 *Clan Line* alongside, and also visible to the right is Urie 'H15' No. 30487, which like the tank engine was condemned during 1957. *G. R. Siviour*

Above: Before the introduction of 'Hampshire' diesel units, many local services in the Southampton area were worked by 'M7' class 0-4-4Ts, with trains of ancient LSWR carriages. Such a formation is seen at Marchwood on the Fawley branch, in the care of No. 30378 in May 1957. The line had very few passenger trains, mostly timed for the convenience of workers at the oil refinery and other installations, but oil traffic was heavy and regular. *C. L. Caddy collection*

Left: The local fire brigade are seen in action alongside 'Battle of Britain' class No. 34057 *Biggin Hill* at Hamble on May 22nd 1961, after it had caught fire while working from Brighton to Bournemouth. A Standard '4' 2-6-0 passes by gingerly on the down line with a Portsmouth-bound working. *P. Fagin*

To operate these many services, the Southern had a total of 1,444 steam locomotives* allocated to its various engine sheds in the summer of 1957; ten years later, nearly all of these had gone and there were just a few survivors left to face withdrawal. Clearly there was still an enormous amount for the steam locomotive lover to savour in 1957. There were sixty nine different designs, still in existence, displaying enormous variety. On the one hand there were those classes which had acquired great scarcity value because they had just a few survivors, such as the '757', 'C14', 'H2' and 'N15x' breeds, all to be withdrawn in the very near future. At the other extreme, there were the elderly 'M7' class tanks which, despite dating back to 1897, still comprised an amazing one hundred and two class members.

Rather more glamorous, and certainly far more modern, were the even more numerous one hundred and ten 'West Country' and 'Battle of Britain' 4-6-2s, all built since 1945, and designed by O.V.S. Bulleid, the last Chief Mechanical Engineer of the Southern Railway. Like their larger but very similar counterparts, the thirty 'Merchant Navy' pacifics, built between 1941 and 1949, they were well known for their distinctive appearance, and novel design aspects. Their air-smoothed casing, a form of streamlining, led to their being known variously as 'spam cans' or 'streaks'. Their innovative features were not always appreciated by train crews or shed fitters, although particular depots seemed to cope very well and apparently the men of Exmouth Junction shed thought very highly of their fleet of unmodified Bulleids. While they certainly had a voracious appetite for coal, they were remarkably speedy and powerful when running well. A particular Achilles heel was the chain-driven valve gear, which was located in an oil bath, slung between the frames. Wear of the chain links sometimes led to spectacular failures, and the large amount of oil presented a fire hazard, when leaks seeped upwards to the hot boiler region.

One well-recorded fire occurred between Hamble Halt and Netley on May 22nd 1961, when 'Battle of Britain' No. 34057 *Biggin Hill* came to grief on a Brighton to Bournemouth West passenger working. The Hamble fire brigade was called out, and I recall cycling along the path beside the railway to find a foam engulfed engine standing at the head of its train. It was later removed and parked ignominiously in Netley goods yard by Standard class '4' 2-6-0 No. 76019, sent light engine down the 'wrong' line from St. Denys. However, it wasn't so much their tendency to spontaneously combust, but the sheer high running costs, which led to the momentous decision to redesign the Bulleid pacifics.

It is remarkable, with hindsight, that an extensive rebuilding programme of these locomotives was authorised when dieselisation and electrification were already on the agenda, both nationally and in the South. It would suggest that the many reported design faults were matters of serious concern. The modifying of Bulleid's larger pacifics, the 'Merchant Navy' class, had already begun before 1957. The first, No. 35018 *British India Line*, had been dealt with in February 1956 and five others had been completed during the year. Nevertheless, there were still two dozen in their original condition at the beginning of 1957, working on both the Western and Eastern flanks of the Southern Region. The rebuilding of the 'light pacifics' was agreed soon after, and 'West Country' No. 34005 *Barnstaple* was outshopped in its new guise from Eastleigh Works at the end of June 1957.

A further 59 locomotives were to follow until the last,

No. 34104 *Bere Alston*, was released in May 1961. The remaining fifty were to remain in their unmodified condition until withdrawal, it finally being recognised that there could be no economic justification for rebuilding machines that were to be redundant in less than five years time.

I have three or four cherished childhood memories of Southern steam that date back to 1957. They are dominated by an unforgettable image of the last surviving Atlantic (4-4-2) No. 32424 *Beachy Head*, which occasionally worked the Bournemouth to Brighton through train. This stopped at my local station, Netley at 15.18* each afternoon, and made a big impression on a six year old, with an already well-developed fascination for steam engines. I think it was the beautiful curved nameplate carried on one of its wheel splashers that used to catch my eye, as I read out aloud those magic words - BEACHY HEAD. No. 32424 was the last one of a class designed by D. Earle Marsh for the London Brighton and South Coast Railway (LBSCR) in 1911, and the last of its wheel arrangement still in service anywhere in England. In its heyday it worked the one hour Pullman trains between Victoria and Brighton, but now this handsome Edwardian survivor was eking out its final months before withdrawal in 1958. It was just one example of the veteran locomotives which were still in regular use at the time.

My next main childhood railway memories are of two even older survivors, this time from the Victorian age. The first is my much beloved father, born in 1900 and still active as I write. After retiring from the Army at the end of World War II, he took up the post of booking clerk at Netley station. On alternate Sundays he worked a twelve hour shift, and I often spent the afternoon in his office. It was a magical environment, the walls lined with racks of little-used tickets, ready printed to destinations all over the country. I was fascinated by their seemingly endless variety, yet most were covered with dust and probably undisturbed for twenty years or more. My father would be sitting as his sloping Southern-green painted wooden desk, puffing on his hand-rolled cigarette of A1 tobacco. He always seemed to be wrestling with the mathematical complexities of the "Cross-cast", a challenge which resided in the rows and columns of his enormous ticket sales ledgers, and all the while the gas lights sang away overhead.

Sometimes my father allowed me to issue the tickets, which was a great joy as it allowed me to use the ticket stamping machine to apply the date to the reverse ends of each ticket. Unfortunately, Netley seemed to have very few passengers on whom I could practise my sales techniques, for it was then a very sparse Sunday service. But by mid-afternoon, the whole station seemed to come to life, following one short ring of the platform bell by the signalman. I would run out onto the platform and enjoy an enormous thrill as a 'T9' class 4-4-0, (of a similar vintage to my dad) rolled in from Fareham. It would be trailing an equally ancient collection of London and South Western Railway carriages, on its way to Southampton Central with the afternoon 'stopper'. I used to run alongside the engine to the end of the platform, and then smile endearingly up at the driver and fireman, hoping desperately that they might invite me up onto the footplate of their open cab. Sadly it never happened, but those were certainly days of bliss as I stood and stared, and then watched the train disappear on the upgrade to Sholing, listening to its fading sounds long after it had disappeared from sight.

---

* Although the use of the 24-hour clock in railway timetables did not begin until the mid-1960s, all times in this book are based on that system for the sake of uniformity.

* see Appendix One

Above: No sign of the author standing on the up platform at Netley on this occasion, but this is the working which I remember so well, the Bournemouth to Brighton through train, which called at the station at 15.18. My recollections are only of 'H2' class No. 32424 *Beachy Head* but on this occasion in 1956 the locomotive was the next in sequence, No. 32425 *Trevose Head*, leading a mix of four Maunsell and Bulleid designed carriages. Note the distinctive headcode for this working and the lower quadrant signal on the left which controlled access to the Netley Hospital branch.

G. R. Siviour

Below: The very essence of my Sunday afternoon recollections from 1957, is evident in this charming view of 'T9' class 4-4-0 No. 30732 departing from Swanwick with a train of matching LSWR rolling stock. Its destination is Portsmouth, as clearly indicated by the two discs carried on the smokebox, and it has probably originated from Southampton Terminus station.

G. R. Siviour

"Tubby" (to the rear of the photograph!) and the author, a six year old with a well developed fascination for steam engines and impeccable taste in choice of shorts, photographed at Southampton Town Quay in 1957. No. 30588, a 'C14' 0-4-0T, was still performing there on a regular basis when the photograph was taken.

Mrs. Joan E. S. Bird

My third recollection from 1957, concerns the area near the Town Quay in Southampton, where various small tank engines fussed about with wagons and passed by hauling freight trips between the Old and New Docks. Whenever my mother took me shopping to town, I always asked her to stop off at the Town Quay on the way home, just so that I could watch the antics of one engine in particular, which I christened "Tubby". This was a 'C14', one of a class originally built as 2-2-0Ts in 1906, for use in a rail-motor arrangement, being semi-permanently coupled to single carriages. Some were rebuilt in 1913 as tiny 0-4-0T engines, being under twenty feet long, and my favourite, No. 30588, was the last to survive in ordinary service. It looked small enough to be picked up by hand and put into my mother's shopping bag and taken home! On one occasion, I persuaded her to bring the old box camera to photograph "Tubby", but she insisted on including me in the picture, thereby cutting the top off its chimney, which I recall making me very cross at the time!

Elsewhere on the Southern there were plenty of other old-timers at work, some of which were to survive several more years and will be mentioned later. Many others only had a short time left however. These included the ancient 'E1' class 0-6-0Ts, designed by William Stroudley and built from 1874 onwards. There were only five left at the beginning of 1957, but I often used to see one in action around Southampton Docks while stopping to watch 'Tubby'. However, there were also four based on the Isle of Wight, numbered not surprisingly Nos. 1, 2, 3 and 4! It was on a visit to the Island, probably in 1959 or 1960, with my long-suffering mother, that I had my one and only experience of 'driving' a steam engine. I cannot recall now which of the 'E1s' I had the honour of controlling, nor indeed whether it happened at Newport or Ryde. But I do know that the driver welcomed me on to the footplate and took me for a ride up to the end of the sidings. Then he asked me if I would like to drive it myself, and so with great difficulty I pushed the big black regulator across a little, and off we went. He also introduced me to the brass brake handle, but I was in rather a panic because I was far too small to see out of the cab window, and had no idea when to make the engine stop! Anyway, with the kindly man's help we drew up right beside where my mother was waiting at the platform, and I had acquired another treasured memory, the sort that any little boy would have longed for at the time.

There were a number of other 0-6-0Ts around in the late 1950s, the remnants of the smaller engines of the Southern railway's constituent companies prior to grouping in 1923.

The 'E1s', and the modified 0-6-2T version, the 'E1/Rs' which were to be found at work in the Exeter area, originated on the LBSCR. So too, did the ten members of the 'E2' class, although they were not of such great age. They worked out their lives shunting and on local freights around the ports of Dover and Southampton, and also in the London suburbs. The contribution of the South Eastern and Chatham Railway (SECR) to this tank engine progeny included the minute 'P' class engines, which looked hardly strong enough to move themselves, let alone any sort of load, and were mainly to be found on light shunting duties at the eastern end of the SR. Rather more robust were the nine 'R1' tanks, a number of which spent their days at Folkestone, working full pelt to drag heavy boat trains up the short line from the Harbour to the main line. Very similar in size, and to some extent in appearance, were the 'G6' 0-6-0Ts of the old London and South Western Railway (LSWR) which were to be found dotted about the main centres of their former company's territory, carrying out station pilot and shunting work.

Most of these tank engines dated from well before 1900, but the Southern also had an excellent collection of efficient modern steam locomotives, many constructed during the preceding fifteen years, and some still arriving from the builders as 1957 commenced. The most recent arrivals were those built to the new British Railways 'Standard' designs, but their arrival was bound to hasten the demise of the older engines. Ironically, the new locomotives' life spans would be judged simply in years, not decades, like their predecessors. This was not because of any lack of suitability, but because the very idea of using steam locomotives on Britain's railways became anathema as the 1960s dawned.

The old privately-owned Southern Railway had been toying with more electrification in its final ten years of existence, intending to start with the Sevenoaks-Hastings route just before World War II. Not surprisingly the international situation postponed the plans, but even during the War years the Southern's management was busy planning ahead. In 1946, Sir Eustace Missenden had announced that the Board had approved plans for the future which advocated ridding the Southern of all steam working east of a line from Reading to Portsmouth, with diesel traction for freight traffic and on subsidiary routes. However, Nationalisation swiftly loomed, delaying any such expensive decisions. Nevertheless, the British Railways Modernisation Plan of 1955 revived much of the Southern's post-War strategy, so it was just a matter of time until steam's domination was seriously attacked.

The BR Standard '2MT' 2-6-2Ts had a brief career on the Southern, and were fairly regular performers on local passenger services in Kent until electrification. No. 84026 is seen in Folkestone Warren in 1960 with a train from Maidstone East. *Mike Esau*

Even so, as already hinted, it was a time of considerable confusion nationally, as regards the future traction policy for Britain's railways. While the first diesel and electric prototypes were being ordered, the railway workshops were still busy turning out new steam locomotives, some of which would eventually see no more than four or five years use before being scrapped. Thus, in the early months of 1957, the Southern's Brighton locomotive works was busy completing what proved to be its last order to build steam locomotives, the BR Standard class '4' 2-6-4Ts. The very last to be delivered was No. 80154 which emerged on March 20th. Meanwhile, other Standard tank locomotives, class '2' 2-6-2Ts, in the No. 84000 series, continued to be delivered to the Southern from Darlington Works until June 1957. Yet, ironically, at the Southern Region's Eastleigh Works, the first diesel-electric multiple units for service on the Southern Region were also taking shape. Unit No. 1001 made its debut on a test run on January 17th, and by the time No. 80154 was in steam for the first time, several of the new diesel units had made their way to the east of the region for familiarisation trials. From the start of the summer timetable they took up regular service between Hastings and Cannon Street and Charing Cross, displacing much of the steam passenger operation on the route. Their introduction undermined the celebrated 'Schools' class 4-4-0s, built specially for the line in the 1930s, because of the need for unusually narrow rolling stock due to the restricted width of some of its tunnels. By 1958, the new diesels were in almost complete command and the steam engine siding and turntable at Hastings had been taken out of use, a foretaste of what was to become a regular occurrence over the next ten years as steam gave way area by area.

One of the stations served by the new Hastings diesels was Robertsbridge, junction for the former Kent and East Sussex light railway, a fascinating rural railway in the traditions of "Oh, Mr. Porter!" It had been closed to passenger traffic in 1954, but still saw occasional hop pickers' specials in the late summer each year, wending their way up to Bodiam and Northiam. These were powered by the octogenarian LBSCR 'A1x' 0-6-0Ts, the only locomotives able to use the line, for which purpose three were based at St. Leonards shed. One of these was used to power the daily early morning pick up goods to Tenterden Town station, returning thence to Battle, by early afternoon. Diesel shunters took over this duty from the 'Terrier' tanks in 1957, but for a few more years Cockneys were still occasionally transported through the hop-fields behind steam.

The 'Hastings' diesel units were followed very quickly by similar but shorter two-coach units for service in Hampshire, which brought an end to local steam working between Portsmouth and Southampton. This caused a major reduction in the use of steam engines at Netley, bringing to an early end my Sunday afternoon joys. On September 15th 1957, Eastleigh depot provided the power for the last normal steam working, Standard class '4' 2-6-0 No. 76015, hauling the 22.26 service from Portsmouth. From the following day, the diesels took over almost all the stopping and semi-fast services, apart from those working through to Bristol and beyond.

It was intended originally that the diesels would also operate the Romsey to Andover and the Alton branch services, and new intensive schedules had been drawn up. However insufficient units were available initially, and so the steam relics from the turn of the century had a two month final fling in the meanwhile! Eastleigh's ex-LSWR 'T9' 4-4-0s and 'M7' 0-4-4Ts took the brunt of the workings, until a full diesel service was implemented on November 4th. So, as 1957 drew to a close, steam had virtually disappeared from local passenger services in several parts of Hampshire, and on a key route through Sussex into Kent.

Meanwhile, the future steam-free operation of the main Kent coast lines was being heralded by the unloading of electric conductor rails beside the track between Gillingham and Canterbury during the summer of 1957. The next step in implementing the BR Modernisation plan, the Kent Coast electrification, was underway! As part of this process, some sections of the route were quadrupled and the rebuilding of stations and lengthening of platforms ready for twelve-coach electric train formations was also being commenced. Electric multiple units of the '4-CEP' and '4-BEP' variety were soon being turned out by Eastleigh works at the rate of three a fortnight, well in advance of electrification. They were then stored on the Haywards Heath-Horsted Keynes branch in readiness for the 1959 start of services, but that did not mean that steam operation was in decline yet, even though its days were clearly numbered.

Left: 'Hastings' demu No. 1005 is photographed on a test run to Andover near Chandlers Ford, soon after delivery from Eastleigh Works on March 26th 1957. *Les Elsey*

Middle: One of the last regular steam workings over the Hastings line, this Saturdays only up train climbing Hildenborough bank, has a Pullman car amongst its formation of distinctive narrow-bodied stock. The locomotive working hard is 'Schools' class No. 30925 *Cheltenham* and the date is April 1958. *G. R. Siviour*

Bottom: 'A1x' No. 32678 at Robertsbridge with the coaching stock of a hop-pickers train bound for Northiam on the Kent and East Sussex railway in September 1957. *Mike Esau*

13

In fact steam was still to be seen in profusion, enjoying its final fling on the Kent Coast, between 1957 and 1959. Unmodified and modified Bulleid pacifics, and Standard '5' 4-6-0s were putting in splendid performances on such famous trains as the "Golden Arrow", the "Night Ferry" and the "Man of Kent", as well as the other regular passenger services and boat trains. Stewarts Lane shed (73A) provided the motive power for many of these workings, including the Southern's only two Standard 'Britannia' class 4-6-2s, Nos. 70004 *William Shakespeare* and 70014 *Iron Duke*, which were used on prestige Kent services until being transferred away in May 1958.

Despite having plenty of modern locomotives, it was remarkable that the Southern continued to employ pre-War 4-4-0s and 2-6-0s on so many of its passenger workings in Kent. For example, 'L' class No. 31766 was seen on the down "Kentish Belle" on August 30th 1958, the last summer of operation of that all-Pullman working from Victoria to Ramsgate. That was certainly unusual, but appearances on secondary workings by any of the 'L', 'L1', 'D1' or 'E1' breeds were certainly to be expected, and were a source of pleasure to enthusiasts. Also prevalent on passenger services were the more modern 'Schools' class 4-4-0s, always very competent performers, while the 'King Arthur' class 4-6-0s were also to be frequently seen. The various Southern 2-6-0s, particularly of classes 'N', 'N1' and 'U1', took a major share of passenger workings, while local services on the main lines were often the preserve of 'Ivatt' or Standard 2-6-2Ts. On some local and most branch line workings, the 'H' class 0-4-4Ts, designed by Wainwright and introduced back in 1904, were very prominent. They powered services such as those from Paddock Wood to Hawkhurst, Gravesend to Allhallows-on-Sea and Dunton Green to Westerham. Usually paired with very elderly push-pull sets, they maintained an unforgettable link with the past and all that was best about English country branch lines, while that very world was about to be destroyed by the ravages of railway reshaping under Dr. Beeching.

In connection with the modernisation programme, a number of electric and diesel locomotives were on order, to ensure steam would be largely eliminated from freight as well as passenger working over the next few years. The first of 15 Derby-Sulzer diesel locomotives was scheduled to arrive in the first week of December 1958, deputising on loan for the Southern's own BRCW/Sulzers, which did not materialise until January 1960. Also appearing at about the same time was the first of the Doncaster-built electric locomotives, to be numbered in the E5000 series. Meanwhile the retraining of drivers was underway at a training school at Stewarts Lane depot, where a large electric and diesel shed was being built. By the end of 1958 the steam depot at Gillingham was being adapted to a future role as a diesel depot, and its turntable had been removed. As a result steam locomotives had to travel to Hoo Junction to turn. The pace of change was relentless and Stage One of the Kent electrification was completed in 1959. That meant the start of electric services throughout between Victoria, Gillingham and Ramsgate and Faversham to Dover, which eliminated steam from most regular workings on those lines. Trial electric running from Ramsgate began on June 1st 1959, the 'Night Ferry' went over to electric haulage a week later and June 15th was the date for full electric services to start. The final steam workings were by 'WC' No. 34001 *Exeter* on the 20.35 to Ramsgate and by 'L1' 4-4-0 No. 31753 on the 20.52 to Dover, as night fell on June 14th 1959.

A beautiful portrait of 'Britannia' No. 70014 *Iron Duke* at Stewarts Lane shed, fully decked out, prior to working the down "Golden Arrow" from Victoria, on October 20th 1957.
R. C. Riley

Left: One of the twenty-one members of the infrequently photographed 'U1' class, No. 31892, is seen at Sole Street on the 10.36 Broadstairs to Victoria on July 26th 1958. *Peter Harrod*

Below: Class 'E1' 4-4-0 No. 31506 is seen on the 13.10 Sandwich to Victoria passenger train climbing Sole Street bank on the same day. *Peter Harrod*

Bottom: The last day of steam services before inauguration of the first phase of the Kent Coast electrification scheme, and 'L1' No. 31753 is leaving Victoria in the dusk with the 20.52 to Dover on June 14th 1959. Its place in history as the last official steam train is marked by a wreath on the smokebox door. *Mike Esau*

'N15' class No. 30451 *Sir Lamorak* (who sounds as though he should have been a train-spotter in the court of King Arthur) pulls away from Farnborough with the 09.56 Basingstoke to Waterloo on February 2nd 1962, six months before final withdrawal. *Peter Harrod*

It was not only on the lines into Kent that the Southern's steam locomotives had been showing their paces in the late 1950s. In the summer of 1957, the decision was taken to accelerate the schedules of a number of Bournemouth line expresses, so that they would reach that town in two hours from Waterloo station, including the enforced stop for water at Southampton Central. Thus trains such as the 10.30 Waterloo-Weymouth were timed to reach Southampton in 81 minutes for the 79¼ miles, just outside the 60 mph average which was considered to be the pinnacle of steam performance at the time. In fact the 'Merchant Navies' allocated to these trains were well capable of knocking five or six minutes off the schedule, but the Southern authorities probably thought it advisable to leave a margin for unexpected delays. Bulleid's light pacifics were often found on these expresses, and certainly on the semi-fast workings to Bournemouth and Weymouth. The 'King Arthur' and 'Lord Nelson' 4-6-0s were also stately performers down the line to Bournemouth, although the particular niche for the latter was the haulage of Southampton Docks boat trains.

Many such trains operated to and from Waterloo, for Southampton Docks was still a major passenger and freight gateway at the time, generating almost 3,000 freight workings a year and well over a hundred "Ocean Liner Expresses" in any single month. Some of these were all-Pullman affairs, and others conveyed one or more Pullman cars in their formations. Apart from the international travellers from America, Australia and South Africa and other parts of the Commonwealth, the passengers for the Channel Islands and the French ferries had to be catered for. This required the provision of further regular boat trains. Eastleigh shed provided much of the motive power for the Southampton

Docks workings and as well as the 4-6-0s already mentioned, the 'Schools' class were also associated with these glamorous trains, as well as the inevitable 'Bulleids' and occasional Standard locomotives. As mentioned later in the book, steam hauled boat trains continued to operate until the very last day of Southern steam in July 1967.

As well as these boat trains, and those operated to the Kent ports, such as the 'Golden Arrow', there were also regular workings to Newhaven to connect with the ferry service to Dieppe. These were mainly worked by the Southern's mini-fleet of three Bulleid/Raworth designed electric locomotives, but steam was often pressed into service to substitute or to power additional workings, and this continued well into the 1960s.

The other key port was Weymouth, but in 1957 it still belonged to the Western Region, and its railway needs were mainly served by trains to and from Paddington. However, the Southern Region's operating area was considerably amended in 1958, gaining and losing parts of its territory in exchanges with the Western Region. The former GWR route from Yeovil Pen Mill through to Weymouth, and the branch from Maiden Newton to Bridport were taken over by the Southern, so that the engine sheds at Weymouth (becoming 71G), sub-shed at Bridport, and also Yeovil (now recoded 71H) passed into the hands of the rival region. Thus the Southern now had a fleet of WR locomotives under its wing, although those at Weymouth were to be gradually transferred away or withdrawn, so that by 1963, only a handful remained among the SR and Standard types then dominating. Nevertheless, WR locomotives continued to work into Weymouth from Yeovil and beyond, on freight and van trains, as well as some long distance passenger workings until 1965. Local services to Yeovil had been largely dieselised in 1959 however.

The change of greatest significance as a result of this demarcation change between SR and WR was the handing over of most of the Somerset and Dorset Railway to the WR, which arguably led to its eventual closure in 1966. The two main engine sheds at Templecombe and Bath, and the smaller sheds at Radstock and Highbridge became Western property. Bath Green Park was recoded to 82F and Templecombe to 82G, in the Western series of shed codes, while Highbridge lost its separate identity, and like Radstock became a subshed of 82F. However this meant few changes in motive power in the short term, apart from the appearance of one or two GWR pannier tanks, and the transfer away of the line's two ex-LMSR 'Black 5s' in exchange for WR Standard class '5s'.

The other main territorial change concerned the former Midland and South West Junction Railway (MSWJR) line, which linked the LSWR at Andover with the Midland Railway at Cheltenham, and passed through GWR territory all the way. The southernmost section from Grafton had been in Southern hands until 1958, but the whole line was operated on a joint basis with the Western right through to closure in 1961. It had a very infrequent service, never living up to the hopes of its original promoters, and passing through countryside which for the most part is still virtually deserted at the end of the 20th century. However, it did bring WR 2-6-0s and 'Manor' 4-6-0s to Southampton Terminus on a through working, while Southern 2-6-0s (either class 'U' or 'Standards') wandered fairly aimlessly up to Cheltenham. It was a beautiful unspoilt part of England, but over the weekend of September 9th/10th 1961 its railway quietly died.

Left: These untypically looking Southern locomotives were actually under SR control until the transfer of most of the Somerset and Dorset Railway to the Western region in 1958. Until that time Sentinel 0-4-0T No. 47191 and Fowler '3F' 0-6-0T No. 47465 would have been seen carrying 71G shed plates, because Radstock, where this photograph was taken, was a sub-shed of the Southern controlled depot at Bath Green Park. *Peter Harrod*

Below: An interesting view of class 'U' No. 31806 leaving Stockbridge with a train of three ex-GWR carriages on a through Southampton Terminus to Cheltenham service in March 1957. Having traversed the Romsey to Andover line it will then follow the route of the MSWJR via Swindon Town to its destination. *G. R. Siviour*

Left: A perfect portrait of the Brighton Works shunter DS377, which was actually numbered 377S, photographed at Brighton shed. *R.C. Riley*

Below: It was difficult to photograph the famous 'Lancing Belle' as its daily journey in each direction was made from directly out of the sunlight. The regular pairing of two 'E4' 0-6-2Ts is seen passing Portslade and West Hove heading for Brighton on March 10th 1963, the locomotives being Nos. 32503 and 32468.
Edwin Wilmshurst

Bottom: The last freight train to travel on the Newhaven West Quay branch, hauled by 'A1x' No. 32678, crosses the heavily restricted Swing Bridge on August 10th 1963. *R.C. Riley*

A picturesque scene on the Horsham to Brighton line, with 'E4' No. 32512 passing a period signal at Itchingfield Junction. *John Scrace*

In contrast to that sleepy cross-country route, the area around Brighton managed to remain a hive of steam activity in the late 1950s. This was really quite astonishing, since the Sussex resort was the terminus of a main line electrified in 1933, and at the mid-point of a coastal route connected to the 'juice' between 1935 and 1938. Even more amazingly, it still saw a large number of old LBSCR engines, dating back to World War I and long before, in active service. Its depot housed 65 steam engines drawn from a dozen different classes in mid-1957, and the nearby works was also very active in repairing steam locomotives, although it had built its last engine during 1957 as already mentioned. The Works had its own shunter, class 'A1x' No. DS377, of striking appearance, recalling the days of the LBSCR. It had been specially repainted in Stroudley yellow livery back in 1947, lettered BRIGHTON WORKS on its side tanks and fitted with a copper-capped chimney. It was hard at work each day until the Works closed in 1959, when it returned to normal service as No. 32635, but otherwise in unchanged livery.

Pre-grouping memories were also evoked at Brighton every evening by the return of the "Lancing Belle", a set of ancient carriages, often hauled by two 'E4' class 0-6-2Ts, which brought back some of the employees from the Lancing Carriage Works, a few miles west along the coast. At that location, two more 'A1xs', Nos. DS680 and DS681, were to be found as service locomotives, built in 1875, and yet still hard at work over eighty years later. Brighton shed also supplied another 'A1x' for steam heating and miscellaneous shunting duties at Newhaven. This task continued until as late as 1963 and included working the daily goods down the West Quay branch. This involved crossing a heavily restricted swing bridge over the river Ouse, for which the lightweight LBSCR veterans were alone suitable. The line closed in 1963, which dispensed with the need for the aging 'A1x' class to be retained. No. 32678 worked the last trip on August 10th, to clear the remaining wagons. It departed for Brighton eight days later, with various chalked inscriptions and carrying a wreath marking the occasion. The departure of the Terrier tank also brought about the end of Newhaven's four road engine shed, which had been a sub-shed of Brighton.

Other interesting workings abounded around Brighton, such as the employment of the handsome ex-LBSCR 'K' class 2-6-0s. These were normally assigned to heavy freight duties up the main line to destinations such as Norwood yard, London and to local goods trips to places as diverse as Beeding, Chichester, Rye, Newhaven and Tunbridge Wells West. However, on Summer Saturdays their lives sometimes became rather more interesting when they were turned out to work some of the inter-regional passenger trips to and from the Sussex coast. Thus a pair of 'Ks' could on occasions be seen at Eastbourne, one bringing in the through train from Wolverhampton Low Level and the other waiting to take it on to Hastings after reversal. Likewise, for example, on August 2nd 1958 it was possible to see Nos. 32342 and 32344 well off the Southern at Willesden Junction, handing over to LMR locomotives, as their trains continued to the Midlands. 'Schools' class locomotives from Brighton depot also took a hand in such workings. In the same way, various LMR and ER 4-6-0 locomotives would work right through to the South Coast, a pattern destined to continue until 1965, by which time native SR steam operation in the area was negligible. However the appearance of class '4F' 0-6-0 No. 44043 at Brighton on an excursion from Luton on July 31st 1958 was certainly extraordinary!

There was other steam activity to be seen at Brighton on a regular basis. Two steam departures left every hour, one for Horsham and the other for the Uckfield line. In the late 1950s, 'M7' 0-4-4Ts shared these duties with 'H' class tanks, as well as the ubiquitous 'E4' 0-6-2Ts and also various ex-LMSR and Standard tank engines. Push-pull working ceased on the Steyning line to Horsham on March 5th 1961, but although the 'Hs', and later the 'M7s', faded away as a result, the pattern of steam operation remained much as before otherwise. In spring 1962, there were still five 'E4s' active at Brighton, which also kept two of the fast disappearing 'E6' class, Nos. 32417 and 32418, active as shed pilots and in excellent external condition.

Apart from these local workings, Brighton enjoyed daily main line steam activity in the shape of the through services to Bournemouth, Plymouth and Cardiff. The employment of No. 32424 *Beachy Head* on the Bournemouth turn was described earlier. Its final recorded fling between the seaside resorts was on December 20th 1957, after which it was stored. Sadly its final duty of all was soon to come when on April 13th 1958 it worked an empty stock train from Lancing Works to Micheldever Sidings. It then moved on to Eastleigh Works for scrapping. Even before the disappearance of the 'H2's, Brighton's small collection of unrebuilt Bulleid pacifics were also regular performers on the Brighton to Bournemouth/ Cardiff/ Plymouth services, Nos. 34039 and 34045-48 being the locomotives in question, although there were changes in the allocation in later years. I well remember 'Battle of Britain' No. 34055 *Fighter Pilot* rushing downhill through Netley on a regular basis in the early 1960s heading for Fareham and thence Brighton, with the through train from Plymouth. 'Schools' class 4-4-0s and 'L' class 4-4-0s had also played their part, especially on the Bournemouth turn, until they faded from the scene during the early 1960s.

Top: A pair of 'K' class 'Moguls' meet at Southeram Junction, near Lewes, on August 8th 1959. No. 32344 is in charge of an up Newhaven freight and No. 32345 is hauling the 11.05 Walsall to Hastings through train.   *S. C. Nash*

Left: A general view of Brighton shed taken in 1962 before the mass elimination of ex-LBSCR motive power at the end of that year. Class 'E6' No. 32417 is in the forefront, retained for various shed pilot duties, while an 'A1X' 0-6-0T is visible in the left background with a short line of locomotive coal wagons. The anachronistic presence of a large steam depot in this electrified stronghold is emphasised by the conductor rails in the foreground.   *G. R. Siviour*

Bottom: Double-domed 'C2x' No. 32535 was one of the last three members of the class to survive into the springtime of 1962. However it is seen here in August 1959, powering the 09.02 Hove to Three Bridges freight near Horsham.
    John Scrace

Above: Class 'C' 0-6-0 No. 31068 at Beckenham Junction on August 16th 1958 with an engineers' train of cable drums. *P. J. Lynch*

Below: The 'W' class 2-6-4Ts did not often stray from their familiar haunts, but a heavy fall of snow at Oxted is the setting for No. 31925 with a pick-up freight from Norwood Junction in 1962 . *G. R. Siviour*

At the other end of the Brighton main line, the London area also saw a number of ex-LBSCR engines at work, notably the 0-6-0 class 'C2X' goods locomotives, as well as similar survivors of the old SECR, the 'C' class. These operated from the large, sprawling engine shed at Bricklayers Arms and also from that at Norwood Junction, working freight and empty stock trains to all sorts of destinations in the London suburbs and beyond. They were also to be found on similar duties into Kent from Stewarts Lane and Hither Green depots. These last two depots, as well as Norwood Junction, also gave extensive employment to the 'W' class 2-6-4Ts, particularly on inter-regional freight exchange trips to the London marshalling yards of the Eastern, Western and London Midland regions. However, unlike the 0-6-0 freight engines, the 'Ws' were never allowed to work passenger trains, due to safety concerns dating back to an accident in the 1920s that involved a locomotive of the same wheel arrangement.

The impact of dieselisation and electrification was soon to diminish the role of all these locomotives, as predicted by the Locomotive Condemnation Programme for 1960, published in the RCTS's *Railway Observer*. It recorded 206 engines to be scrapped during the next three years, including the planned elimination of all remaining 'L' and 'T9' 4-4-0s, and the scrapping of no less than 26 class 'C' and 19 class 'C2X' 0-6-0s. Also planned for extinction were the veteran SECR 'O1s', the LSWR '0415' Radial tanks on the Lyme Regis branch, and the '0298' Beattie Well Tanks at Wadebridge in Cornwall. Rather surprising was the attached comment that "the 'Lord Nelson' 4-6-0s are expected to have a further life of fifteen years..."; the last of the class was actually withdrawn just two years later, after what seems to have been a rather rapid change of policy!

Despite the impact of phase 1 of the electrification programme in 1959, parts of Kent retained full steam activity for two more years at least. Ashford, like Brighton, was a rail centre well worth visiting by the enthusiast in 1960. The locomotive and carriage works continued to be busy with general repairs to a wide variety of locomotives including the famous 'Schools' class and various examples of the SR 2-6-0s of classes 'N' and 'U'. I remember visiting Ashford station, and also touring the engine shed in June of that year and being overawed at the sight of 'Schools' No. 30912 *Downside* beautifully turned out after overhaul, in lined green livery. I also saw No. 30928 *Stowe* on a passenger working, several 'N' class passing on freights, class 'U' No. 31806 also in ex-works condition and an 'H' arriving on a local passenger working. However, many changes were afoot locally, that would see steam largely eliminated within a few months. At the end of 1960, the steam depot at Ramsgate was demolished to make way for extensions to the electric multiple unit sheds. This resulted, rather oddly, in the creation of a new locomotive stabling facility at Margate. About eight engines were in future accommodated overnight in sidings near the turntable. At the same time, the end had already come for the 'R1' 0-6-0Ts on the Folkestone Harbour branch. Class '57xx' No. 9700, borrowed from the WR, had been at Folkestone in October 1958 on trial and following its success, other members of the class took over from Southern locomotives during the summer of 1959.

To my great regret I never did see the famous Folkestone four engine boat train spectaculars, using the 'R1s', or indeed the replacement pannier tanks. However, I did manage to make a visit to nearby Dover shed specially to see the 'O1' class 0-6-0s before they too were all scrapped. I had seen many photographs of these goods engines and was fascinated by their elderly appearance. The outside springs on the tenders, in particular, as

well as their open cabs, gave them the look of locomotives even more ancient than they actually were. There were only two left in service when I went to Dover, and since their main duty in recent years had been working coal trains from Tilmanstone colliery on the old East Kent railway, there was no guarantee that I would actually see one of them. However, I was in luck, because my first glimpse on arrival was of that familiar tender protruding from the end of the shed, which could belong to none other than an 'O1'. In fact it proved to be No. 31065, in steam, but very badly positioned for photography, being mostly in darkness inside the shed. That disappointment was compensated for by seeing 'West County' No. 34100 *Appledore* being serviced, before working the "Golden Arrow" up to London. How magnificent it looked, decked out with all the regalia, flags, golden arrows and headboards! It seemed dreadfully sad that in a few months, steam haulage of this romantic train would be no more, and that virtually all operations from London into Kent would have passed into the anonymity of electric and diesel traction.

The Kent Coast project was subsequently completed by stages through to the summer of 1961, causing further decline of steam operation to follow in its wake. Steam working of freight duties on the All Hallows branch, particularly the oil trains from the refinery on the Isle of Grain, ceased on February 4th 1961, with 'Q1s' Nos. 33035 and 33040 operating on the last day. Local services between Ramsgate and Dover were quietly transferred from steam to electric working on January 2nd 1961, displacing a number of Standard tank locomotives. The third rail was energised between Dover and Folkestone (and Harbour) and between Sevenoaks and Pluckley on May 1st, and then between Maidstone West and Paddock Wood fourteen days later. The line between Folkestone Central and Ashford followed on May 24th. Then the Pluckley-Ashford section was made live a few days later. Consequently, from June 12th 1961 electric working was able to commence between London and Folkestone, Dover, and Ramsgate via Tonbridge and between Paddock Wood and Maidstone East.

The last weekend of steam working saw 'West Country' No. 34100 *Appledore* make its final run on the 'Golden Arrow' on June 11th. From the following day electric locomotives took charge, and likewise the 'Night Ferry' passed out of steam control. That weekend also saw the end of two famous branch lines. June 10th was closure day for the picturesque Paddock Wood to Hawkhurst branch. 'C' class No. 31588, took charge from the usual 'H' class tank engines and worked a specially increased five coach formation. The remaining section of the Kent and East Sussex railway was also closed at the same time, and like the Hawkhurst branch, was visited by an LCGB railtour on June 11th to commemorate the event in style.

However, steam operation continued on the Westerham and All Hallows branches for a further few months. In each case, 'H' class engines and push-pull sets survived until the end. The last day for services from Dunton Green through Brasted to Westerham came on October 28th. Tank engine No. 31518 operated the service until early afternoon, when a seven coach set hauled by class 'E1' No. 31739 took its place. A 'Q1' No. 33029 was also used, working alternately with the 4-4-0, and having the honour of hauling the last train, the 20.30 from Westerham. Members of the 'H' class also continued to work the push-pull passenger service from Gravesend to All Hallows, until services were withdrawn during the first weekend of December. Again, the last day was marked in suitable style, this time by the use of another class 'C' 0-6-0, No. 31689, which was turned out for the final workings with a seven carriage train.

On the main lines, electric operation with multiple units and electric locomotives, had been introduced about a year

Above: A pair of class 'R1' 0-6-0Ts stand idle in a siding at Folkestone Junction shed in 1959, while beyond two of the WR pannier tank replacements are seen in steam. The leading Southern engine is No. 31010, which owes its unusually squat appearance to the need to comply with restricted clearances when it worked over the Canterbury to Whitstable line.   *Mike Esau*

Below: A superb setting for a superb portrait of 'O1' class 0-6-0 No. 31434 marshalling continental ferry wagons at the Harbour, while Dover Castle stands guard on the horizon.   *Peter Harrod*

ahead of schedule, so it was initially a case of electric traction running in steam timings. It was not until the summer of 1962 that the full electric timetable was introduced, leaving steam activity most unwelcome. The engine shed at Dover closed from October 1961, but the other remaining steam depots which had been involved in steam workings into Kent, only faded away gradually over the following two years.

In the far West, at the other geographical extreme of the SR, there was no sign of anything as alien as electrification between 1957 and 1961. However, it was a period when the once numerous range of locomotives of LSWR origin slipped quietly from the scene. Four of the eleven remaining little 'B4' class 0-4-0Ts were based at Plymouth Friary shed in January 1957, and for a year or more, they continued their traditional duties, until replaced by diesel shunters. These activities included working the busy Cattewater Harbour freight branch, and the nearby Turnchapel line with its light goods trains conveying coal and timber. The Southern's own passenger foothold in Plymouth, the Friary terminus, was closed on September 15th 1958, and all passenger workings transferred to the rival WR station at North Road. As the Friary site was to be converted to a new freight concentration depot, alternative carriage sidings had to be provided for SR trains.

These were brought into use at Mount Gould Junction, where an ex-LSWR 'O2' class 0-4-4T often found employment as carriage shunter. The 'O2s' also worked freight trips to the Admiralty dockyard at Keyham, and the twice weekly goods to Stonehouse Pool, once the scene of the LSWR's attempt to win the Ocean Liner traffic from the GWR. There were also some two dozen 'M7s' based in the West Country, including two which survived at Plymouth until late 1962. One of their latter assignment's was the daily 17.30 Plymouth to Brentor passenger trip. Other LSWR steam power still extant at this time took the form of the dwindling ranks of the 'T9' class 4-4-0s, universally known as 'Greyhounds'. This was a highly appropriate nickname for they put up many a spritely performance, reaching speeds in the 70 mph region on suitable downgrades. The North Cornwall line was one of their last strongholds, where they remained active until the summer of 1961. They were popular with footplatemen, pulling the light loads of three or four carriages with relative comfort and riding smoothly over the many curved sections. They were often to be seen at Okehampton, waiting to set out for points west, their serene good looks bringing dignity and beauty to the railway scene.

When their passenger turns took them through Wadebridge, on the Padstow line, the 'T9s' frequently rubbed shoulders with the remarkable class '0298' Beattie 2-4-0WTs. These little gems of Victoriana, although much rebuilt, were three survivors from the 1870s, originally built to work suburban trains out of London. Out of a once numerous class, this famous trio had been pensioned off to the far west, where they maintained a charmed existence working china clay traffic on the Wenford Bridge line, and even the odd lightweight passenger duty to Padstow. Remarkably, they still remained at work in the early summer of 1962. When I visited Wadebridge during a family holiday to Cornwall in 1961, I found No. 30586 shunting the station yard, and No. 30587 sitting inside the small wooden engine shed. The interior was wreathed with the most overwhelming sulphurous smoke cloud, but that did not detract from my pleasure at finally seeing these much sought-after examples of 19th century engineering.

However on April 12th 1962, a stranger appeared in the form of a WR 0-6-0PT, No. 1368. It had been displaced from its former work hauling the Channel Island boat trains along Weymouth Quay by the introduction of diesel shunters. Now it was here to receive what was to prove a successful trial to find a replacement for the LSWR engines. The other two members of its class were hauled down to Cornwall in June, and they soon replaced their illustrious predecessors. By the end of August 1962, Nos. 30585/6 had reached Yeovil Town shed, while No. 30587 remained to work brakevan specials to Wenford Bridge in September 1962. After that final fling in the South West, late September saw all three congregated at Eastleigh, but there was a last chance for glory when Nos. 30585/7 returned to the London area in December to work a suburban rail tour, which was so popular that it had to be repeated.

The Beattie Well-tanks long-lived and self-assured tenure of office at Wadebridge was exactly mirrored by the story of three more LSWR veterans. These were the Adams Radial tank engines, known more prosaically as the '0415' class 4-4-2Ts, which monopolised operations on the Axminster to Lyme Regis branch. The trio, Nos. 30582, 30583 and 30584, based at Exmouth Junction, had resisted all attempts to find alternative steam power, that could cope with the sharp curves and steep gradients of this fascinating branch and yet not exceed the line's severe weight restrictions. For example, the Southern had experimented in November 1958 with a WR '14xx' 0-4-2T, No. 1462, but the interloper failed miserably, giving the Adams tank engines a further two years of activity.

I have treasured memories of a journey I made behind No. 30583 to Lyme Regis in 1960. It was a dreadfully wet day, which made the lack of shelter on the branch platform at Axminster particularly noticeable! However it was well worth a drenching to ride in the single composite carriage, lacking any other passengers except the guard, as the train swept back and forth along that switchback route, changing directions abruptly as the curves dictated. Summer Saturdays were a special feature of the line, when two of the '0415s' would join forces to work the through coaches to Waterloo which would be attached or detached from main-line trains at Axminster. The operation of this line must have been one of the most photographed per route mile of any in the country. Sadly, it could not last for ever, and to everyone's distress, except perhaps those responsible for the upkeep of the eighty year old machines, 'Ivatt' No. 41297 was tested successfully on the branch on September 18th 1960. By the end of February 1961 No. 41292 was to be seen in occasional use on the branch, leading to the final withdrawal of all three of the graceful 4-4-2Ts by the summer. Even one of the Standard '2' 2-6-2Ts appeared, No. 84021 to be precise, now that the LSWR engines had stepped aside. The 'Ivatts' themselves were not to last very long, as they were replaced by a single unit diesel car on November 4th 1963.

Although they were not LSWR in origin, mention must be made of the four ex-LBSCR class 'E/1R' 0-6-2Ts which were to be found in Devon. They had been moved West in the days of the Southern Railway, and were usually to be found working at Exeter as 'banking' engines between St. Davids and Central stations. When they were finally withdrawn in 1959, their place was taken by the heavyweight class 'Z' 0-8-0Ts, designed by Maunsell and introduced in 1929. These great beasts could sometimes be seen working in pairs, slogging away at the rear of the heavier up trains as they did battle with the short but demanding 1 in 37 incline. On a visit to Exeter St. Davids in 1962 I photographed the combined efforts of four locomotives, including three of the 'Zs', together with the train engine, a class 'N' 2-6-0, getting to grips with the afternoon ballast train

Top: The beauties of the Devon landscape are complemented by 'T9' class 4-4-0 No. 30709 and its short train of Maunsell-designed coaching stock, which are seen approaching Maddaford Moor as the 17.51 Okehampton to Padstow passenger service on May 8th 1961. *S. C. Nash*

Left: One of the most enchanting locations on the Wenford Bridge line was in Pencarrow Woods where locomotives could take water from the simple facilities. Here '0298' No. 30585 is pausing for refreshment on its way from Wadebridge on July 19th 1960. *R. C. Riley*

Bottom: The sun spotlights the venerable styling of '0415' class No. 30582 as it draws away from Axminster with a two coach train for Lyme Regis in 1958. *Mike Esau*

Top: Class 'E1/R' tank engine No. 32697 is providing rear end assistance to an up train on July 19th 1958 at Exeter St. Davids. *R.C. Riley*

Left: As well as acting as banking engines, the class 'Z' 0-8-0Ts at Exeter found employment on local shunting duties. No. 30953 is seen performing that role at Exmouth Junction on July 15th 1959. *Peter Harrod*

Bottom: A sad farewell to once familiar haunts as the last two 4-4-0s of the 'D1' and 'E1' classes are specially steamed to haul an extra empty stock train from Stewarts Lane to Sevenoaks, en route to Ashford for scrapping. The pair, Nos. 31749 and 31067, are seen passing Knockholt on November 4th 1961, in external condition that appears to be far too good for imminent condemnation to be permissible. *S. C. Nash*

from Meldon Quarry, near Okehampton. However, the 'Zs' did not last anywhere near as long as the 'E/1Rs', as on September 25th 1962, 'W' 2-6-4T No. 31924 made the first appearance of its class in the West Country and was soon engaged on clearance tests. The object was to replace the 0-8-0Ts after their short-lived command of the banking duties, now that they were in need of reboilering. The 'W' tank proved reasonably successful, and so classmate No. 31921 followed, allowing the condemnation of the entire 'Z' class by the end of the year.

Other newcomers to the area in the summer of 1962 were ten Standard class '4' 2-6-4Ts transferred from Tonbridge to Exmouth Junction as a result of completion of the Kent electrification. They found various forms of employment, such as the Halwill-Launceston Sunday shuttles, Exeter to Plymouth passenger services, the Meldon Quarry ballast trains and also the Exmouth branch. Further changes saw the handing over of the Plymouth to Tavistock North stopping trains to WR diesels of the D63xx class from November 5th 1962, replacing the 'Ivatt' tanks, foreshadowing the impending WR takeover of the remains of the Southern's empire in the West. This left limited work for Plymouth Friary's 'Ivatts', two of which were sub-shedded at Callington for the Bere Alston branch and one for shunting at Laira carriage sidings.

As shown by the transfer of the 'Standards', the Kent electrification had an inevitable knock-on effect throughout the Southern's steam collection. While the more modern machines could be transferred westwards, for the old stalwarts time had run out, both in Kent itself, and in the areas which would now receive an influx of newer engines. The sole operating 'D1' 4-4-0 at Eastleigh, which had eked out an existence on local parcels turns together with the last few Hampshire based 'T9s', was condemned at the beginning of April 1961. Later in the year, on November 6th 1961, there was a last poignant run by a 'D1' and an 'E1', when 4-4-0s Nos. 31749 and 31067 worked an engineers special from Bat and Ball to Tonbridge, and then ran light to Ashford for scrapping. This left just two Eastern section 4-4-0s in stock, class 'L' No. 31768 and class 'L1' No. 31786, of which the latter lasted longest, until the spring of 1962. It had been transferred to the Western section at Nine Elms and was active on light duties in the London area until its condemnation. A number of Bulleid pacifics and 'Schools' class 4-4-0s found themselves moved away from the South East, several of the latter turning up on Waterloo-Basingstoke-Salisbury turns. However, Southern electrification schemes could not be blamed for the regular use of No. 30925 *Cheltenham* on a diagram between Marylebone and Banbury on the Great Central line between May 17th and 22nd, 1962, which arose after railtour duty from Nottingham!

As well as the 'Schools' class, another interesting performer in Hampshire by 1962 was the preserved class 'T9' No. 120, bringing back its elegant looks to the byways after an absence of over a year. There had been several changes of mind over which 'T9' would be saved, but circumstances eventually dictated that it would be No. 30120. It entered Eastleigh Works and was outshopped in LSWR green livery. It was working a roster at the end of March 1962 which included the Portsmouth-Fareham portion of the Brighton-Plymouth train, and the Meon valley goods from Fareham to Droxford. Nearby, the last regular freight working took place on the short branch from Botley to Bishops Waltham on April 27th 1962. 'Ivatt' 2 2-6-2T No. 41328 performed the honours as another little portion of the railway network disappeared. It was reassuring that the LSWR 'M7s' were still soldiering away, push and pull style, on the Lymington and Swanage branch lines, as well as along the Bournemouth West-Ringwood-

Brockenhurst trail, right through to the end of 1963 and beyond. However, the long tradition of 'M7s' dragging eleven, twelve or even thirteen coach empty stock trains between Clapham Junction yard and Waterloo seemed to be drawing to a close, as ten Standard class '3' 2-6-2Ts were transferred to Nine Elms in November 1962. However the 'M7s' and also ex-LBSCR 'E4s' were still at work at Christmas 1962, together with the odd WR pannier tank.

The period 1961-1962 did see the extinction of some other classes normally found on the Western section, no doubt also enabled by transfers of locomotives from Kent. Thus surplus, the last ex-LSWR 'H15' 4-6-0s and 'G6' 0-6-0Ts (apart from the Meldon Quarry shunter No. DS682) were removed from service. The 'Lord Nelsons' so recently assured a long future were rapidly falling by the wayside. No. 30863 *Lord Rodney* made a last visit to the Dover main line on February 3rd 1962 when it worked the 11.20 freight from Hither Green to Tonbridge and then ran light to Ashford for scrapping, to be joined by No. 30852 *Sir Walter Raleigh*, a week later. Their withdrawal left just six 'Nelsons'. The first 'USA' tank No. 30063, perished also, coinciding with the arrival of fourteen new 275 h.p. Ruston Paxman diesel shunters in Southampton Docks. They were intended to replace the fleet of USA tanks as well as the handful of 'E2' 0-6-0Ts, hitherto handling most work in the Docks. However, even when the entire class was delivered enough work remained to keep several 'USAs' employed, and that was to continue to the very end of Southern steam.

Salisbury shed's last two 'King Arthurs' were withdrawn in the summer of 1962, although a few remained active for a few more months at Basingstoke and Eastleigh depots. By the end of September only two were left, and the last, No. 30770 *Sir Prianius* was withdrawn by the year end. The last few 'Lord Nelson' 4-6-0s also survived for the summer, and were to be seen on some top link work, as well as freight duties. The last two were condemned in October 1962, being Nos. 30861 *Lord Anson* and 30862 *Lord Collingwood*. However the 'Schools' 4-4-0s transferred away from Kent, were hard at work for most of the year, particularly on the Lymington Pier services, and also on a number of Exeter line turns and reliefs. A batch of Type 3 diesels were now surplus on the Eastern division, following introduction of the full electrification timetable, and they were transferred to Western division, to be seen on freight and passenger workings, including Southampton Docks boat trains. However the employment of diesels on passenger workings ceased from the autumn of 1962 as they were not equipped to steam heat the carriages. Nevertheless, the need for steam locomotives was declining rapidly.

Steam's tenure of some local services in parts of Sussex was also seriously challenged in 1962. The first of the SR's new demus for the Oxted line, unit No. 1301, was seen on test between Eastleigh and Alton on March 14th. A further eighteen were eventually delivered for service. Initially, however, they were used to launch the extended Hampshire area diesel scheme in the summer of 1962, taking in the Reading-Southampton Terminus services. This followed the dieselisation of Portsmouth-Reading services, which had commenced on May 1st 1961, using WR diesel units. Later in the summer of 1962, five new purpose built 'Berkshire' versions of the 'Hampshire' demus were delivered from Eastleigh carriage works, releasing the Oxted units for their intended destination. There they were used to replace most of the peak hour steam trains from East Grinstead, Tunbridge Wells West and Brighton to London Bridge and Victoria. They were also scheduled to displace many steam services along the

Above: The Bishops Waltham branch did not generate much traffic and this seems particularly true in this view taken in April 1962, shortly before closure, as Ivatt class '2' 2-6-2T No. 41328 returns down the single track towards Botley.   *G. R. Siviour*

Below: Class 'H' 0-4-4T No. 31263 is seen near Worth hauling the 11.08 Three Bridges to East Grinstead service on May 26th 1963. These were some of the last push-pull operated services in the country and No. 31263 is credited with the final such working on the line on January 4th 1964.   *S. C. Nash*

'Cuckoo Line' to Eastbourne in the off-peak period, however they were not sufficient in number to remove steam completely. Another precursor of steam decline was the news that the first electro-diesel locomotive, No. E6001, had been completed at Eastleigh in January 1962. It was soon seen making trial runs to Basingstoke on February 5th, and it was joined by five others. The flexibility of the new locomotives, able to work on and off the live rail, would soon be appreciated.

Quite apart from the changing circumstances on the Southern, it seemed that a ritual slaughter of steam had been called for throughout Britain, to be completed by the end of 1962. The Western had condemned some 169 locomotives at the end of the summer service, whilst 302 LMR steam locomotives were withdrawn during November and December. It was to be no different on the Southern, which extinguished a number of classes at a stroke by the end of the year. Apart from the 'King Arthurs' and 'Lord Nelsons' already mentioned, the last fifteen 'Schools' 4-4-0s went for scrap in the last weeks of 1962, completing the rout of ex-Southern named passenger locomotives. The ex LSWR '700' class 0-6-0s were also eliminated, the last two, Nos. 30316 and 30695, having been acting as shunters in Eastleigh works yard. There were also a variety of tank engine classes obliterated to join the Exeter 'Z's in extinction. These were the five 'H16' 4-6-2Ts, the two remaining 'G16' 4-8-0Ts, the last 'E6' 0-6-2Ts and the mainland 'O2' 0-4-4Ts, of which the last two Nos. 30199/30225 had been based at Eastleigh and included shunting at Redbridge sleeper depot in their portfolio of local duties. The small class of six 'N1' 2-6-0s was also withdrawn from Stewarts Lane shed in November. However, for many, the biggest shock was the destruction of the entire class of ex-LBSCR 'K' class 2-6-0s which went from an unscathed seventeen members in the autumn of 1962 to non-existence by the New Year. Their place was taken by 'N' class 2-6-0s transferred from the West Country.

Evidently there were accounting reasons for this wholesale scaling down of steam stock, which coincided with the replacement of the British Transport Commission by the British Railways Board at the beginning of 1963. Thus at 30th December 1962 the Southern had a total of just 565 steam locomotives left in normal stock, of which 386 were of Southern origin. The scale of the changes of the last five years was shown by the increase in non-steam locomotives to 285, notably the 98 Type 3 Bo-Bos diesel-electrics and the eventual 24 new E5000 type electrics. The inevitable result of the locomotive condemnations was a sudden accumulation of locomotives awaiting scrapping, which were to be seen lined up in sidings at Brighton, Fratton, Hove and Eastleigh. Many of these were eventually sold off to private scrap-merchants and it took over a year to clear the backlog.

Despite all this gloom and doom for steam enthusiasts, it must not be forgotten that steam was still putting in excellent work on the main lines out of Waterloo. In the 1961-2 Southern timetable there were four runs timed at 60+ mph for steam, between Waterloo and Sidmouth Junction, being stages of the up and down "Atlantic Coast Express", which was allowed an overall 178 minutes between Waterloo and Exeter Central. This compared favourably with the rival Western Region 'Cornish Riviera Express' between Paddington and Exeter St Davids which was allowed only six minutes less, despite the supposed benefits of diesel haulage. Few would have realised that the end of Southern steam passenger working was less than five years away. Certainly not the renowned commentator, Cecil J. Allen, who when writing in *Modern Railways* in September 1962 said:

"It is pleasant to realise that steam is still likely to remain in command over the principal main lines of the Western District for a considerable time to come... and that the SR still has enginemen prepared to make the most of their charges..."

This quote should be read in the context of an article celebrating the power and speed of the rebuilt Bulleid pacifics and wondering why services on the Exeter and Bournemouth lines were not further speeded up. At the time of his article, the "Bournemouth Belle" had not joined the ranks of the two-hour expresses, although it was soon to do so.

Elsewhere, on the Southern, a new order was already taking shape. Three British Railways Standard '9F' 2-10-0s, the first to be based on the Southern, had arrived at Eastleigh to take over working of the Fawley to Bromford Bridge oil tank trains. They had arrived at the beginning of 1961 and the engines concerned were Nos. 92205/92206 and 92231. With their new motive power, these heavy trains were soon rerouted over the Winchester-Newbury-Didcot line, en route to Birmingham, rather than the former circuitous journey via Bristol. This brought new life to the D.N.&S. route which had lost its sparse passenger service from March 7th 1960, the last down train, the previous Saturday, being hauled by 'T9' No. 30120, in its pre-preservation days. On the Fawley branch itself, the oil trains had recently been taken over by the 'H16' 4-6-2Ts, transferred from Feltham to Eastleigh. They replaced Standard '3' tanks, which were not powerful enough. Tender locomotives were banned from the line as there were no turning facilities and tender-first running was ruled out due to visibility problems with the many 'open' level crossings. The 'H16s' did not last very long in this role, neither did the '9Fs' on the long-distance haulage. In April 1962 the first Type 3 diesels began to take over over the Fawley-Bromford Bridge trains and although the '9Fs' remained in use into 1963, it was through taking over workings such as the sugar beet trains from Eastleigh to Didcot.

Without doubt, the event with the greatest significance for the future of Southern steam was the announcement in mid-September 1962 of further boundary changes between the BR regions, which were to have far reaching consequences. The rather unexpected news was that with effect from January 1st 1963 the SR main line to Plymouth, and all its associated branches from a point west of Wilton South, just beyond Salisbury, would become WR property. The Somerset and Dorset line, which had been entirely in SR hands in 1957, was now to remain Southern for the last few miles from Blandford Forum southwards only, and a similar change would be made to the Yeovil-Weymouth line, with everything north of Dorchester passing to the Western. The decline of the Somerset and Dorset, which this transfer predicated, was symbolised by the transfer away of the famous "Pines Express" at the end of the summer 1962 timetable. The last steam locomotive to be built for British Railways, Standard '9F' No. 92220 *Evening Star* headed the last S&D journey of the "Pines" on September 8th 1962.

The regional boundary changes also brought about a change of locomotive ownership, with 149 SR-based locomotives passing into WR hands with the transfer of the sheds at Exmouth Junction, Yeovil Town, Barnstaple and Wadebridge. The Southern's Exmouth Junction motive power district (72 series) was thus abandoned, and the sole remaining Southern controlled shed in that group, Salisbury (72B) was recoded 70E in the Nine Elms sector. The result was the strange sight of Bulleid pacifics, and others, wearing WR shedcode plates.

Top: One of the Maunsell built 'H15' 4-6-0s No. 30521 hurries through Surbiton with the 14.54 Waterloo to Basingstoke passenger train on September 21st 1960.   *Peter Harrod*

Middle: The noble looking 'Lord Nelsons' were down to two survivors by the autumn of 1962 and they did not survive to see the year out. Photographer Peter Harrod was unable to believe his luck when what proved to be the last two members of the class passed his vantage point in quick succession on June 1st 1962. No. 30861 *Lord Anson* was on a traditional duty, an evening boat train to Southampton Eastern Docks and is seen passing Berrylands. Within a few minutes No. 30862 *Lord Collingwood* also appeared, this time on the 19.05 Nine Elms to Portsmouth mixed freight train.   *Peter Harrod*

Left: Another named class of 4-6-0s to disappear in 1962 were the 'King Arthurs'. The last to see regular service was No. 30770 *Sir Prianius*, photographed at Waterloo on October 29th 1962 with the 13.54 service to Basingstoke.

John Scrace

Above: Performing a typical duty for the class, 'H16' No. 30518 is seen at Clapham Junction with a van train on October 16th 1959.   *John Scrace*

Below: Following the mass condemnation of steam locomotives at the end of 1962, many were dumped in sidings around the region, until they could be dealt with by the scrapyards. One such location was at Hove, where about a dozen faced their wintry destiny on January 6th 1963. From left to right are 'E6' No. 32418, 'E4' No. 32479, 'E6' No. 32417, 'Ks' Nos. 32342 and 32341 and 'Schools' No. 30923 *Bradfield*.   *Edwin Wilmshurst*

Above: Although its engine shed was probably the smallest and flimsiest in Britain, it still dwarfed 'B4' class 0-4-0T No. 30102, performing its normal role as yard shunter at Winchester. The sharp curves which necessitated its use can be seen clearly in this view from May 7th 1962. *Peter Harrod*

Below: Hayling Island sunset spotlights diminutive 'A1x' 0-6-0T No. 32650 as it crosses Langston bridge on its way to Havant in the final hours of operation of this antiquated branch line. November 2nd 1963. *Mike Esau*

All these changes seemed very strange at the time, although no more bizarre than the fact that my local Football League team, Southampton, actually managed to reach the semi-finals of the FA cup in 1963! For a Second Division team that was some achievement, and their progress through the rounds had led to increasing demands for supporters excursions to the away fixtures. The climax came on April 27th, when over a dozen specials had to be laid on to convey the Saints fans to Villa Park, Birmingham for the showdown between the Southern minnows and the mighty Manchester United! This was a unique spectacle, as Southampton Central station had to deal with three or four thousand red and white bedecked fanatics, and fourteen steam hauled excursions, all in the space of about two hours. I spent a fascinating time watching the manoeuvres, which seemed to be carried out with extraordinary efficiency, born of years of practice with boat train extras. The invasion of the Midlands was under way, and fourteen Bulleid pacifics set off in quick succession, bringing a rare spectacle to enthusiasts at various locations in the Birmingham suburbs and points thereto. It was an event never to be repeated, by which I refer, of course, to the role of the steam trains, and not Southampton's footballing achievements!

One other footnote to 1963 was the end of the class 'B4' tank engines. No. 30089 had idled away at Guildford for the previous four years as shed pilot, while Nos. 30096 and 30102, the other two survivors, alternated in performing the last remaining duty for a 'B4', as yard shunter at Winchester City. Their lives came to an end on October 7th 1963, when the work was taken over by a diesel shunter, and so a tiny black steam engine would no longer nestle inside what must have the smallest and flimsiest engine shed in the country, an open-ended corrugated iron assembly which looked more like a domestic garage!

Within a month, the equally small and rather more famous 'Terriers', the ex-LBSCR 'A1x' class 0-6-0Ts would also figure no more in the life of the Southern Region. The last domain, in which they held unchallenged domination, was the four and a half mile branch line from Havant to Hayling Island. Its main engineering feature was the 1,000 feet-long timber trestle bridge crossing to the island at Langston, which was as flimsy in appearance as the insubstantial locomotives that rode gingerly across it. There was an intensive service in the summer, with up to two trains an hour in each direction. The eighty year old engines had to be worked very smartly with their trains of two or three carriages, if punctuality was to be maintained.

Closure proposals for the line were issued at the end of 1962, but the process was drawn out until November 1963. The last day of normal working was Saturday, November 2nd, when the winter service was increased from lunch time onwards to cater for the many enthusiasts and local people who came to pay their last respects. Two trains an hour left Havant that afternoon, one non-stop, the other calling at the intermediate stations at Langston and North Hayling. Two three coach formations were used, with No. 32650 working in the morning, to be joined by Nos. 32662 and 32670 for the afternoon. The former, although rather scruffy in appearance, carried a large wreath on the top half of the smokebox door.

Many passengers packed the trains as the sun set over Langston Harbour, and the end drew near. The remaining supplies of tickets, luggage labels, handbills and other souvenirs were duly bought or 'acquired'. When the time came for the last ordinary train, the two coaching sets were coupled together to provide a six coach formation, a rarity on the line. 'Terriers' Nos. 32662 and 32650 took charge, with the latter trailing at the Havant end. I was one of the many passengers packed into the train, and during the brief stop at Hayling Island (allowed only five minutes) I jumped down to the track from my place in the front carriage, which was way beyond the end of the platform, to attempt a flash photograph. I just managed to scramble back on board before departure, as the 20.56 with No. 32650 now leading, set off noisily on the return to Havant. The local newspaper's report of the occasion said:

"Passengers joined hands and sang Auld Lang Syne in the guard's van of the last 'Hayling Billy' on Saturday night as it steamed, with whistle sounding continuously, round the last bend to Havant station... People thronged fences and gates and other vantage points. Curtains were drawn back, windows thrown open, and even tape recorders were produced to catch the last familiar and very distinctive sounds."

After this passionate, but largely local farewell to a distinctive part of the local scene, the following day's brilliant winter sunshine spotlighted the enthusiasts' salute to the Hayling Island branch. The LCGB had organised a suitable farewell occasion, combining a main line tour of various interesting Hampshire and Sussex byways, with a final trip down the Hayling branch. A separate five coach train set was provided, four BR compartment seconds and a Maunsell brake composite, hauled up from Fratton by two immaculate 'A1xs', Nos. 32636 and 32670. It was hard to believe that the motive power had a combined age of 182 years! Complicated shunting operations at Havant put the two engines at the extremities of the train, each facing chimney outwards, for the benefit of photographers.

Hundreds of cameramen lined the route, signal posts being especially popular vantage points. Photographic stops were made at Langston and North Hayling, and of course at the terminus. Crowds thronged the platform and goods yard, before it fell silent for ever. Then guard Fred Morris waved his flag at Hayling for the last time, and No. 32670 led the entourage back to Havant, truly saying farewell to a delightful relic of the 19th century. Their final duty done, the two 'Terriers' and their carriages paused briefly for more photographs and then returned to Fratton shed and immediate withdrawal.

With the closure of the Hayling Island branch, it was literally the end of the line for its diminutive 'A1x' tank engines. I felt a sense of change in the air, for it seemed to me that a Golden Era was coming to an end. Apart from a handful of 'M7' and 'H' class 0-4-4Ts, and a similar number of 'Urie' designed 'S15' 4-6-0s, there were now no other survivors from the pre-Grouping companies left in Southern mainland service. Branch lines and Victorian steam engines were clearly not destined to be a part of the decade which was to become known as the Swinging Sixties. It was now a world of transistor radios, and the Beatles. As their distinctive choruses of "Yeah! Yeah! Yeah!" belted across the air-waves, it was clear that Britain was experiencing a revolution in music, fashion and all manner of public and private values. Somehow, the decline of steam, a solid and dependable feature of this country for the previous 130 years, seemed entirely in keeping with the spirit of the Age.

Chapter Two

Southern Steam Decline 1964-1965

"The times they are a-changin'..." was certainly a suitable theme for the mid-Sixties, and the summer of 1964 was undoubtedly the last taste for lovers of of the old order on the Southern Region. Within a few months the steam expresses to the West of England would have ceased for ever, and the contraction and eventual closure of much of the Southern's empire in Devon and Cornwall would have begun. For the time being there remained a good variety of Southern classes left in action, although it has to be said that some of the more interesting survivors passed from the scene in the earlier months of the year. Nevertheless, there was still plenty of Southern steam to be sampled if you happened to be in the right place.

Peter Turnbull, was a young and devoted enthusiast at the time. He had left school and was waiting to start his first job, which commenced in October 1964. In the interim he was able to spend all his time at the lineside, enjoying Southern Steam's last parade in the sunshine. He recalls:

"I spent much time at Raynes Park and at places like Basingstoke. As I recollect, it was still 100% steam that summer. The locomotives were in general clean and well cared for and on Summer Saturdays you could see an endless stream of up West of England expresses pulled by unmodifieds from Exmouth Junction. There were still so many obscure workings to be found, performed by steam, all over the South Western Division. I feel very fortunate to have been around that summer..."

The Southern Region's timetable for Summer 1964 provides a fascinating insight into the sort of activities that young Peter, and many others, were able to enjoy. In its one thousand and thirty two green bound pages, the Southern and all its offerings were laid bare. Among the introductory pink pages, headed "Southern at your Service", one can read of many diverse aspects which are now little more than memories. Pride of place might go to the description of the Southern's Pullman services, not just the "Bournemouth Belle" which remained steam worked, but also the electric "Brighton Belle", and the individual Pullman cars within ordinary electric trains that ran between London and the Sussex coast. The fact that so many passenger trains offered "Attractive refreshment facilities" is also mentioned. How different an age the Sixties seem to have been in retrospect, when a Table d'hote luncheon was available on a variety of Southern services and could be purchased for just 13s. 6d. (67½p) while a Full Breakfast cost 10s 0d (50p). For those, such as most railway enthusiasts, who could not afford, or chose not, to visit the restaurant or buffet cars, there was always the option of the now long-forgotten "Packed Meals in handy carrier bags". For the princely sum of 2s 6d (12½p) they provided the traveller with nothing less than the much-ridiculed British Transport Catering Cheese Sandwich, together with a Sausage Roll, a Packet of Biscuits and Fruit, and were said to be available on request at "all station refreshment rooms"!

Other services mentioned in the timetable which clearly belong to a different era, include special ticket arrangements for those going to scout camps, the possibility of the "transfer of complete farms including implements and livestock", and "all the fun of a camping holiday without any of the bother" in a Pullman holiday coach. Also advertised is a short-lived experiment that was still in progress in 1964, the Surbiton to Okehampton car/carrier service. This ran on summer Saturdays, giving the opportunity to avoid the notorious traffic jams of the West Country, at a cost of £17 return for a driver and car, and £4 13s 0d for additional passengers. It was certainly not cheap, but it did allow the increasing number of car owners the opportunity to get from outer London to Devon in little more than four hours.

The Southern's many shipping routes and connecting passenger services are also described, not least the "Golden Arrow" and "Night Ferry", which by 1964 were of course electrically worked. However steam still held sway on the Waterloo to Southampton Docks boat trains for the sailings to St. Malo in France, and to Weymouth for other sailings to St. Malo, and also services to Guernsey and Jersey. The 08.10 Channel Island boat train from Waterloo was shown as conveying a restaurant car, and completing its three and a half hour journey on the quay side at Weymouth, in time for the 12.30 sailing.

However, for many, the most nostalgia-laden pages of the timetable must be those which lie between pages 442 and 465, the renowned Table 35. There can be found, in its final glory, the LSWR main line to Exeter and Devon and Cornwall, about to be butchered at the hands of the Western Region. Browsing through the many columns which encompass this last summer of steam operation and full passenger services, one can relive interesting imaginary journeys. One such was the 10.00 from Okehampton to Padstow, which with its fourteen intermediate stops, took two and a quarter hours over its 62¼ mile journey, visiting such delightful locations as Maddaford Moor Halt and Egloskerry. Sadly, by the summer of 1964, a number of rural workings such as these had already been taken over by Western Region diesel locomotives and multiple units, but there was still a healthy preponderance of steam working. It was a similar picture for the branch lines radiating from the Salisbury to Exeter section, some also now diesel worked, but still serving Yeovil Town, Lyme Regis, Seaton, Sidmouth, Budleigh Salterton and Exmouth.

The real glamour though belonged to the main line expresses, working from Waterloo to Exeter Central and then on to Plymouth via Okehampton and Bere Alston, the old LSWR route which was soon to be abandoned. These lengthy green-liveried corridor trains, complete with restaurant cars, still included through portions to places such as Barnstaple Junction and Ilfracombe, and in some cases on Saturdays only, to Sidmouth, Exmouth, Torrington, Bude or Padstow. The most distinguished of these was of course the "Atlantic Coast Express", departing from Waterloo at 11.00 on weekdays, and as two separate trains, at 10.35 and 11.00 on summer Saturdays. The importance of the route can be seen in the fact that on a typical summer Saturday in 1964, Salisbury station handled no less than eight west bound steam hauled passenger services between 10.30 and 12.45, heading down the Exeter line.

Following the takeover by the Western of all former SR territory west of Wilton South at the beginning of 1963, the reign of Southern steam on the Waterloo-West of England line, and its associated branches, was inevitably doomed. In the 'Beeching-era' it was the conventional wisdom to eliminate competing routes, and so the Southern's line to Exeter lost out, and was indeed fortunate to escape the fate of complete closure. Instead, the Western decided to reduce it to secondary status, close many stations, and single the track, while steam was to give way to Western Region diesel locomotives and multiple units on the little that remained. Nearly all of the network of Southern branch lines in the West, as well as the central section of the former main line between Exeter and Plymouth was proposed for closure in press notices published on August 20th 1964.

One sign of the loss of Southern control could be seen daily at Exeter Central, where the task of 'banking' trains up the formidable climb from St. Davids station, had been taken over by ex-GWR pannier tanks at the end of 1963, bringing to an end the short reign of the 'W' class 2-6-4Ts, and their various Southern predecessors. After a period of trial running for crew-training, the WR diesel hydraulic locomotives ('Warships') began work on the Waterloo-Exeter line from August 17th 1964, initially taking over three return workings. As a result the up "Atlantic Coast Express" (12.30 from Exeter) made its last steam weekday run on Friday August 14th. Unrebuilt 'Battle of Britain' No. 34084 253 Squadron brought five coaches up from Bude, but unfortunately stalled on the climb from Exeter St. Davids to Exeter Central. It was rescued by 'Ivatt' tank No. 41321, and this caused a 12 minute late restart from Exeter Central, now with 'Merchant Navy' No. 35013 Blue Funnel in charge of the combined twelve coach train. Any hopes of a spectacular last steam thrash were dashed when the train was halted en route at Honiton Incline signal box, to be warned that the down 09.00 from Waterloo had failed to appear and to look out for any problems. It transpired that No. 35019 French Line CGT on the 09.00 had also stalled, causing severe disruption to following services,

until it too was rescued by a tank engine. The net result for the up "ACE" was an inglorious 38 minute late arrival at Waterloo.

However, the down "ACE" and a number of other main line services remained steam worked until the very end of the summer 1964 timetable, and there were many examples of spectacular steam working. Friday, September 4th was seen by many as the last day of fast Exeter steam services, the Saturday workings being rather more convoluted. I joined many other enthusiasts, who crowded on to the final run of the down weekday "Atlantic Coast Express" at Waterloo. The engine was 'Merchant Navy' No. 35022 Holland America Line and it was turned out in beautiful condition, complete with the train headboard, which had been rarely used during the previous year. The run to Exeter was thrilling, with thirteen crowded carriages, in one of which I spent the entire journey standing in a corridor, eyes fixed to the lineside flashing past, looking out for the mileposts to record the train's speed. The 500 tons or so of train presented no problem to Driver Sibley and his fireman, as we reached Salisbury in just over 78 minutes, despite a frustrating prolonged slowing before Clapham Junction for signals, which must have cost three minutes on our journey time. Restarting from Salisbury after taking water, and now with Driver Turner in charge, we went storming on to the next stop at Sidmouth Junction, completed inside schedule in some $73\frac{1}{4}$ minutes, with a top speed, by my timing, of around 88 mph. Then it was the short sprint down through Broad Clyst before we came to rest in Exeter Central after an exhilarating $171\frac{3}{4}$ mile journey from London.

At Exeter, the "ACE" divided, and the Padstow portion was taken forward by unrebuilt 'West Country' No. 34015 Exmouth, its passengers facing a further three hours of travelling before completing the remaining eighty-eight miles.

Descending Templecombe bank on the last weekend of steam operation, unrebuilt Bulleid pacifics Nos. 34079 141 Squadron and 34106 Lydford are working the 08.25 Plymouth to Waterloo on September 5th 1964.
                                                                                                              Author

For some unaccountable reason, in my excitement at the occasion, I had forgotten to take a historic photograph of No. 35022 proudly displaying its headboard, before No. 34015 took its place. Probably it was because I was thinking ahead to my next ride, on the 14.30 back towards Waterloo. I planned to catch this as far as Axminster, along with many other timing compatriots. It proved to be a lively run, showing how much faster these trains could have been scheduled, as we knocked a total of about seven minutes off the timetabled point to point times.

At Axminster there was a convenient twenty minute gap before the arrival of the Brighton-Plymouth through train. This seemed to be a regular unmodified Bulleid pacific turn, and sure enough 'Battle of Britain' No. 34079 *141 Squadron* rolled in for the non-stop twenty seven mile journey back to Exeter. The schedule of 34 minutes would seem generous on paper, but it included the climb to Honiton, seven miles mainly at a gradient of 1 in 80. It turned out to be a competent, if unexceptional run, completed in 32 minutes 49 seconds, with a minimum speed of 31 mph at the summit coming out of Honiton Tunnel, and a maximum of just under 80 mph before Sidmouth Junction, such was the switch back nature of the line. Back at Exeter, it was time to return to the up platform again to await the arrival of the 14.15 from Plymouth, which I was taking through to Salisbury. The train engine was 'Merchant Navy' No. 35026 *Lamport and Holt Line* and it was another splendid run, cutting about fourteen minutes off the scheduled overall running time, which included stops at Axminster and Templecombe. The uphill climbing was particularly impressive, although I didn't note any maxima higher than 79 mph on the downgrades. Other travellers on previous occasions on this line were treated to speeds up to the middle 90s, in excess of the Southern's official speed limit for steam of 85 mph, but I was not to have that pleasure until over twenty years later, in the preservation era!

The following day, Saturday September 5th, saw plenty of steam activity, and I chose to enjoy it from the lineside with my camera. My vantage point was on the upgrade west of Templecombe station, where I planned to see the very last "ACEs", the 10.35 from Waterloo to Padstow and Bude, and in the traditional path, the 11.00 for Torrington and Ilfracombe. All went well at first, and while waiting I was able to photograph the unusual sight of a pair of unrebuilts, Nos. 34079 *141 Squadron* and 34106 *Lydford* on the 08.25 Plymouth to Waterloo, which was apparently a regular Saturday working. It was a hot late summer's day, so there was very little smoke or steam to make the photographs spectacular, although unrebuilt 'Battle of Britain' No. 34054 *Lord Beaverbrook* stormed up the gradient emitting volcanic quantities of black smoke, as it headed west with the 10.15 Waterloo to Ilfracombe and Torrington, which would divide at Barnstaple Junction. Then it was the turn of the 10.35 "ACE" running to Padstow, which passed me headed by a clean 'Battle of Britain' No. 34089 *602 Squadron*, but sadly it was not carrying the elusive headboard. Then, instead of waiting for the last true down "Atlantic Coast Express" I suffered one of those strange mental aberrations, and set off to walk back to Templecombe station. It was only when I was half-way back that my error dawned on me, but it was too late, and so I missed out again on photographing the "ACE", and yes, it was hauled by No. 35022 again, the same as the previous day!

I now decided to move on to the next station westwards at Milborne Port, catching, the 13.46 stopping train which was one of the regular Salisbury-Yeovil Town services. I stayed at Milborne Port long enough to photograph four more expresses

thundering by, and without realising it, I obtained a significant photograph to make up for the earlier failure. On Saturdays, the "Atlantic Coast Express' ran as three separate trains in the up direction, and the very last one to pass by was the 11.00 from Padstow, making its 384 minute journey to Waterloo. Unfortunately, again, it carried no headboard, and was hauled by nothing more powerful than a scruffy Standard class '5' 4-6-0, but at least I was there, camera at the ready! The engine assigned to this final working was No. 73085 *Melisande* and its running was certainly going out in style, because it covered the non-stop run from Exeter Central to Salisbury in 88 1/4 minutes. This cut nearly nine minutes off the schedule, to provide a fitting climax to a famous express train, if not a glamorous one!

The next day's 16.00 from Waterloo, on Sunday September 6th, was the last regular steam hauled express into Exeter down the SR line, and then the full impact of Westernisation and dieselisation took effect. However many failures of the new traction occurred during the next few weeks, bringing daily steam appearances to the West Country from London. There were also planned relief steam workings which penetrated to the Exeter area from time to time. But despite these incursions, it was clear that the LSWR's superb main line had been decimated by its old rival, and it would never be the same again.

For the time being, this was not the complete end of steam working from Exmouth Junction, although the other ex-SR sheds in Devon and Cornwall were officially closed with effect from September 7th. However, it did mean the immediate condemnation of eleven Bulleid pacifics, and eleven 'N'class 2-6-0s. A further eleven Bulleid pacifics were transferred from Exmouth Junction back into Southern Region hands. During October 1964, some 'N' class and Bulleid locomotives were still at work on the former LSWR routes across Devon and into Cornwall. As late as November 21st, 'West Country' No. 34101 *Hartland* was reported in action, when it had to rescue a failed dmmu at Crediton and haul it onwards to Okehampton and Plymouth. But by the end of the year, former Southern locomotives had faded from the scene at Exmouth Junction shed, which nevertheless still had a total steam allocation of thirty. However, the WR takeover meant that the shed's last months of steam were to be under Western auspices, with its WR depot code (83D) and a steam fleet in Western ownership, without a single SR survivor, all having been transferred back to their parent region or withdrawn.

Exmouth Junction's January 1965 allocation included five pannier tanks, nine 'Ivatts' and six Standard tender locomotives, as well as ten Standard tanks. The Bude and Okehampton-Padstow trains had retained steam operation since September, usually by BR 2-6-2T and 2-6-4Ts. However the WR turned these lines over to diesel railcar operation from January 4th 1965, and in the absence of any freight operation, that meant the abolition of steam workings. The Halwill Junction to Torrington line had been dieselised from September and was closed anyway from March 1st 1965, the last workings being with a three car dmmu on February 27th.

Another SR feature taken out of use was the famous concrete works at Exmouth Junction, which had been gradually run down over the previous two years and which succumbed at the end of January 1965. However in a strange twist of fate, two former LSWR branches saw a brief return to steam from February 15th due to a shortage of diesel units on the WR. Class '14xx' 0-4-2Ts Nos. 1442/1450 took up push-pull operation on the Seaton branch, and also to Lyme Regis! As

An overall view of the mixed ancestry shed at Yeovil on June 15th 1964, where a variety of Southern and Western locomotives are being serviced and WR pannier tank No. 6435 is operating the local passenger service.   *Peter Harrod*

trials on that severely curved line by the same class had failed back in November 1958, it wasn't surprising that a few days later 'Ivatt' No. 41291 had taken over and steam remained in control until at least March 6th. However a return to diesel unit operation soon ensued, using units released elsewhere, including by the closure of the Torrington-Halwill line. Services to Lyme Regis were in their last months by now and the branch closed completely on November 27th 1965.

Several local passenger services in the Exeter area, and some local freight workings, remained steam operated until the late Spring of 1965. The last regular steam passenger turn from Exmouth Junction was the 13.52 Axminster to Exeter Central, operated for the final time on May 22nd 1965, in the hands of Standard '3MT' No 82042. Exmouth Junction depot then closed to steam and the locomotives were transferred away, some to finish their days on the Somerset and Dorset at Bath Green Park mpd. Rather surprisingly, that was still not the end of steam working to the Exeter area, even apart from the occasional steam replacements for errant 'Warship' diesels. In the summer 1965 timetable there were three Saturday extra workings rostered between Waterloo and Sidmouth Junction, which turned out to be steam worked. On their last day, August 28th, the 08.00 Waterloo-Sidmouth, and return, was worked by Standard '5' No. 73089 *Maid of Astolat* which ran very well with a reported maximum speed of 83mph. After that, there were a few steam hauled railtours to Torrington and Ilfracombe before the end of the year, and a number of specials as far as Exeter during 1966, but as far as ordinary services were concerned, steam in the South West had truly disappeared from the scene.

Nearer to the new boundary of Southern control, at Yeovil, there was still a fair mix of SR and WR locomotives to be found in January 1965, including WR class '14xx' and

pannier tanks, although Yeovil shed no longer had any SR locomotives on its books. The WR's plans for the Yeovil area were to transform what had once been a fascinating spot, with three stations and two engine-sheds, and a host of local shuttle services, into nothing more than a stop on the much down-graded Westbury to Weymouth line, and a connecting bus service from a railhead at Sherborne. Such were the protests that Yeovil Junction was retained, but the old Southern station at Yeovil Town and its associated engine shed were to be closed and demolished. A few years earlier, 'M7's, 'U's, Bulleids and 'Standards' had pottered around the area, but all that would soon be forgotten.

The same weekend in 1964 that had seen the virtual end of SR through steam working to Exeter, also saw the closure of one of its other off-shoots, the Andover to Romsey line. This cessation was to all traffic, apart from a short siding linking Andover Town to Andover Junction for goods purposes. The passenger service comprised diesel electric units, as it had done since the late 1950s, as mentioned earlier, but on the last day, September 6th 1964, an LCGB special traversed the line, worked by Standard '3MT' 2-6-2T No. 82029. The tour started at Winchester's disused Chesil station, on the old D.N.&S. route, and reached that other truncated North-South route, the MSWJR, by travelling northwards from Andover to Ludgershall. There No. 82029 refreshed its tanks from a rather rusty looking water crane and was turned on the equally decrepit turntable, before its return down the Test Valley to Southampton.

This tour was probably the last passenger train to call at Winchester Chesil, although the northbound "Pines Express" had been diverted via the D.N.&S. on May 22nd 1964 following a derailment near Southcote Junction, outside Reading. It stopped specially at Chesil to pick up passengers ferried there by bus from Winchester's City station! At the beginning of the year, the D.N.&S. line still had a good number of freights, but the Fawley-Bromford Bridge oil tank trains were subsequently diverted away via the Basingstoke-Reading line. Most of the route was closed on August 10th 1964, apart from a section to Winnall sidings north of Winchester Chesil for daily freight trips, which continued for a couple of years more, before complete closure.

Despite the disappointing extinction of most steam activity on the West of England main line, there was still a fair amount left to savour elsewhere on the Southern in the autumn of 1964. Whereas normal services throughout most of Kent and Sussex were now worked by electric or diesel power, there were still some rather anachronistic survivals. Two corridors of steam power converged on Tonbridge. The first was the former South Eastern Railway cross-country route from Reading, via Guildford and Redhill. The second was the ex-LBSCR "Cuckoo Line" service from Eastbourne via Tunbridge Wells, still steam worked, mainly in the peak hours. In addition, the line from Three Bridges via Rowfant to Tunbridge Wells West was also partly steam worked.

The Reading-Redhill-Tonbridge line had been an enthusiasts delight right through from the beginning of the period covered by this book. It was last haunt of the elegant 'D' class 4-4-0s before their withdrawal in 1956, but the rebuilt versions, class 'D1', and the other 4-4-0s from the Eastern division, classes 'L', 'L1' and 'E1', all took their turn. This wheel arrangement seemed particularly popular on the line at the end of the 1950s, as LSWR 'T9s' were also to be seen in action and the Southern's 'Schools' class also started to appear on the line in November 1958. Class 'N15' 4-6-0s ('King Arthurs') also appeared towards the end of that year, but of

even greater interest were the regular visits by GWR 2-6-0s and 4-6-0s, one of which had a daily return passenger duty over the line. Members of the '43xx' classes and the 'Manor' class appeared, this practice continuing right through to the end of steam working.

There were one or two other fascinating workings, including the peak hour through trains between Reading and London Bridge via Redhill, which in 1962 were being worked by 'Schools' class locomotives until their demise at the end of the year. Class 'S15' 4-6-0s handled many of the freight workings (and also some passenger turns), together with the 'N' and 'U1' class 2-6-0s and 'Q1' 0-6-0s. There was also a duty for a Redhill class 'C2X' on the line, working freight trips to Betchworth from Redhill. With the demise of the Southern 4-4-0s, mentioned in Chapter 1, the various 'Mogul' types became dominant. Classes 'U' and 'N', and Standard class '4' 2-6-0s took the brunt of passenger working by 1964, with some appearances by Standard 2-6-4Ts. Guildford, Redhill, Tonbridge and Reading South sheds maintained a busy existence up to January 1965, by virtue of this almost entirely steam worked line. The end of steam was facilitated by the creation of six demus, known as "Tadpole" units. They were so-called because of the narrower width of two of the three carriages forming the units, hybrids formed of two ex-Hastings line diesel cars, coupled to a former emu driving trailer. As their planned introduction from January 4th 1965 approached, the line became a magnet for many enthusiasts wishing to travel behind pre-War Southern steam engines through the electrified zones around Reading, Guildford, Redhill and Tonbridge. Although the former SECR "Birdcage" three carriage sets which had been a feature of the line in the 1950s were no longer in use, there were a number of Maunsell and

The Redhill to Reading line had a daily return passenger duty for a WR locomotive and this practice continued until the end of steam working on the line. On November 23rd 1964 4-6-0 No. 7816 *Frilsham Manor* pauses at Guildford on its westbound journey.   *Peter Harrod*

Bulleid designed carriages, intermingled with BR Mark 1 stock, helping to give a true Southern flavour to these last weeks.

The weekend of January 2nd/3rd 1965 saw the end of full scale steam services on the line, with the Maunsell 2-6-0s playing a full part in the proceedings. A number of Standard 2-6-4Ts travelled light from Tonbridge shed to Redhill, as the decks there were cleared of surplus locomotives, and that was probably also the reason why the 10.45 passenger service to Redhill was double-headed by Nos. 80068/80089 on January 3rd. To mark the occasion, the LCGB's "Maunsell Commemorative" rail tour traversed the line, hauled from Reading to Redhill by class 'N' No. 31831, and thence via Tonbridge in the care of classmate No. 31411. However, from the following day the new diesel services proved to be less than fully reliable and steam appeared several times during the rest of the week. Also, a Guildford 'Mogul' continued to operate on the line after dieselisation, working the 12.45 Reading to Redhill parcels. The Redhill to Tonbridge section also saw daily steam hauled parcels trains, allowing changeover of the Standard 2-6-4 tanks between Redhill and Tunbridge Wells West for the Eastbourne services.

Those workings over the "Cuckoo" line were to continue into the summer of 1965, long after some of the other vestiges of steam working in the area had ceased. One of the first casualties had been the push and pull operations between Three Bridges and Tunbridge Wells West, which had attracted much attention, as the last preserve of the 'H' class 0-4-4Ts. The last three (Nos. 31263, 31518 and 31551) bowed out at the beginning of 1964 when services in the area were greatly revised. No. 31263 (later preserved on the Bluebell Railway) had the honour of the last working, the 09.00 East Grinstead-Three Bridges on January 4th. The operating revisions also effectively eliminated steam working on the Uckfield line but some activity still remained between Three Bridges-Tunbridge Wells West, but not with the use of motor trains. The last regular steam passenger working over the Uckfield line, also on January 4th 1964, was the 21.36 from Tunbridge Wells West to Brighton, with Standard '4' tank No. 80138. The remaining steam turns on the Three Bridges-Tunbridge Wells West and Tonbridge-Eastbourne lines were all scheduled for Standard 2-6-4T haulage, with one exception for an 'N' on the 07.27 Redhill-Eastbourne and return. However, as so often proved to be the case elsewhere, plans and realities turned out differently. The 17.20 London Bridge-Crowborough and early morning return, was formed of a strange hybrid mix of old emu stock, numbered set No. 900, electrically heated and therefore able to be operated by a 'Class 33' diesel electric locomotive. When this stock was unavailable, a set of SR steam carriages had to be substituted, as for example on January 23rd and 24th 1964, when 'West Country' No. 34006 *Bude* did an excellent job running down through Oxted on to the Uckfield line. There were to be other similar substitutions in the area from time to time. Nevertheless, by the time of the 1964 summer service, there were further reductions of scheduled steam working on the Three Bridges-East Grinstead line, requiring the services of only one 2-6-4T a day.

By that time, another surviving Sussex steam service had been brought to an end. The Brighton-Horsham line, running north via Steyning from the junction near Shoreham continued with steam haulage into 1964, although 'Ivatt' class '2MT' 2-6-2Ts had replaced the 'M7s' that used to predominate. Horsham (sub-shed of Brighton) had an allocation of four 'Ivatts', needed for the Brighton run, and also for use on the Cranleigh line to Guildford, to be mentioned

later. From the beginning of May 1964 five 'Hampshire' demus (Nos. 1114-1118) were transferred to take the Brighton-Horsham services, and also most of the rush hour steam trips from Three Bridges to East Grinstead. The last day of steam working on the Steyning line was May 3rd, when the duties were shared between 'Ivatt' tanks Nos. 41294 and 41313 and some of the newly arrived diesel units.

This helped to achieve the planned elimination of steam working in the Brighton area, and from June 15th 1964 all scheduled local steam working at Brighton ceased and the shed closed to steam traction. The "Lancing Belle", for so long a fascinating spectacle was handed over to diesel traction, although one of the 'USA' service locomotives at Lancing took it through the Works area to the platform. However the "Belle" was withdrawn on July 3rd 1964 and replaced by a conventional emu service. Nevertheless, steam activity continued at the Carriage Works at Lancing until its closure, when it had repaired its last coach (CK S5750S) on March 11th 1965. The Works sidings were then being lifted, but the 'USA' service shunters which had replaced the former 'A1x' class pilots remained until the bitter end. No. DS236 was reported to be still in use for about an hour each day in the spring of 1965, although No. DS235 was stored. The last employees were dismissed from Lancing on June 25th and the two 'USA' tanks departed for Eastleigh during the next week, where they were to be scrapped during August.

Despite the Southern's determination to abolish its own sources of steam activity, the sleeping car trains from Glasgow and Newcastle to Newhaven, which ran on several days of the week in the summer of 1964, remained steam worked, mainly by LMSR 'Black 5's. With the closure of Brighton shed after June 1964, any steam locomotives arriving in Sussex tended to go to Eastbourne for servicing, making it look quite busy on some evenings with a number of visiting 4-6-0s on shed. One or two members of the 'Jubilee' class sneaked down to Sussex, despite officially being banned, such as No. 45672 which was seen at Brighton on July 2nd 1964, having worked down on the Glasgow car-sleeper. A visit to Redhill for extra servicing seemed to be a necessity for a number of these infiltrators from the North, because there were still skilled fitters at that shed and the locomotives always seemed to need repairs on arrival!

One foreigner that made a protracted stay was "B1" class No. 61313 which arrived on a Edinburgh-Lewes van train, but was apparently not in the best of health. It was seen at Eastbourne depot on June 28th, but later arrived at Redhill depot on July 7th 1964 for repairs. After it had benefited from the attention of the local repairmen, it was reported in steam at Redhill on September 29th 1964 and even worked passenger trips to Reading on October 1st and 2nd! Running-in completed, it worked a special train of condemned wagons from Earlswood to Streatham Common on October 3rd, and then ran light engine to the London Midland region at Cricklewood and thence to its home depot at Canklow near Sheffield.

The story of the Brighton area in 1964 would be incomplete without reference to the "Regency Belle" which was an amazing ingredient of the night scene on some Saturdays in March and April 1964. Privately organised for an up-market night out in Brighton, its patrons normally were whisked down to the coast in a "Brighton Belle" emu. However, steam haulage sometimes intervened, such as 'Battle of Britain' No. 34088 *213 Squadron* and a formation of seven Pullmans and two vans, working from Victoria to Brighton and returning via Steyning in the early hours, due to engineering works on the main line.

Above: One of the many 'foreign' steam visitors to reach the Sussex coast, after the demise of local steam activity was LMR Class '5' 4-6-0 No. 45322, seen leaving Brighton with the 18.28 return excursion to Birmingham on July 17th 1964
Edwin Wilmshurst

Below: Eastern Region class 'B1' 4-6-0 No. 61313 makes a test run on the 12.05 Redhill to Reading train on October 2nd 1964, seen near Ash, before returning to its home depot of Canklow, following a month's sojourn on the Southern, under repair.
Peter Harrod

There were a number of other steam workings, some of a rather surprising nature during the winter of 1964 and early spring of 1965 in Sussex. From late September 1964 there was steam working through to Brighton again on the through train from Plymouth, as well as the appearance of members of the 'N' class and Standard '5s' on freights. The Christmas mail trains again brought quite a lot of steam to the Redhill-Brighton line, with 'Q1s', 'Ns', Standard '5s' and Bulleids in action, and they were also seen along the coast lines to the west of Brighton, and to the east as far as Bexhill and Hastings. 'Q1' No. 33006 was to be found working the Horsham to Petworth freight trip during January, and occasionally a freight from Three Bridges to Beeding Sidings, over the Steyning line. The following month the same engine was to be seen shunting at Littlehampton Wharf on most days. Other diesel substitutions occurred on the Oxted line, for example, on December 29th 1964 the 07.17 East Grinstead-London Bridge was steam worked by Standard '4MT' tank No. 80068 and made a good run in diesel timings with a top speed of 75 mph. This was due to a shortage of demus, as also no doubt was the use of Standard '4MT' No. 80034 on the 09.58 to Lewes on January 9th. Lewes was also seeing a daily steam worked empty stock turn from Eastbourne to Brighton during January 1965.

The Standard 2-6-4Ts had formed the normal motive power between Eastbourne and Tonbridge since the beginning of 1964, operating mainly on peak-hour services to supplement the demus, although there were also one or two short trips during the day. These workings allowed Tonbridge to continue as a pocket of steam in Kent, even after the dieselisation of the services from Reading. Alongside the 2-6-4Ts, a few of the Standard class '3MT' 2-6-2Ts were to be found for a while, from September 1964, including Nos. 82024/8, newcomers to the area. October 31st and November 28th 1964, were both very special days when Lingfield race traffic and other commitments led to extensive use of steam, using five or six diagrams based on Tunbridge Wells West, Eastbourne and Three Bridges.

With the New Year came the inevitable steps to steam elimination, and on February 27th 1965 came the virtual end of through working to Tonbridge by steam trains from Eastbourne. No. 80034 had charge of the 09.00 from Eastbourne and No. 80151 was on the 17.42 on the last day. From March 1st 1965, the 'Cuckoo Line' services were revised, with a diesel shuttle service introduced between Tonbridge and Tunbridge Wells West, so that nearly all steam services terminated at Tunbridge Wells West, leaving a solitary steam return working beyond to Tonbridge. This 09.56 service required the retention of some of the old narrower bodied "Restriction 1" coaches, although many others were now withdrawn. The 08.30 freight from Three Bridges to Eastbourne was still steam worked in early 1965, occasionally bringing 'N' class locomotives, such as Nos. 31405 and 31411 down to the Sussex coast. The diagram included a visit to Hastings with the 15.44 freight from Eastbourne, and returning to Lewes, extending steam operation into otherwise all-electric territory. Towards its final days, the train was still noted being worked by members of the 'N' class from time to time, such as No. 31811 on June 1st 1965.

However it was Standard '4MTs', drawn from Redhill's remaining steam fleet of seventeen such 2-6-4Ts, that performed the final rites on passenger services up through those evocative sounding consecutive stations of Hailsham, Hellingly, Horam, and Heathfield and thence via Rotherfield and Eridge to Tunbridge Wells West. No. 80141 hauled the last regular steam train, the 09.00 from Eastbourne on June 12th.

The last regular steam hauled train over the 'Cuckoo' line was the 09.00 from Eastbourne to Tunbridge Wells West on June 12th 1965. The locomotive, suitably adorned with chalked slogans, was class '4' tank engine No. 80141, photographed climbing away from Mayfield.

Edwin Wilmshurst

Above: Class 'N' 2-6-0s were still occasional visitors to the Sussex coast through to the summer of 1965 on the 08.30 Three Bridges to Eastbourne freight. No. 31405 was seen passing Hampden Park on April 15th 1965.

S. C. Nash

Below: Southern Region freight 0-6-0s from Guildford shed sometimes put in appearances on the branch line to Horsham. Here 'Q1' No. 33001 is seen departing from Bramley and Wonersh station with a train for Cranleigh.

Mike Esau

Later in the day, No. 80144 was in charge of a six coach BR sponsored return special, suitably attired with wreaths to mark the occasion. The last steam working of all was on the Sunday, when SR 'Moguls' Nos. 31803 and 31411 had charge of a ten coach LCGB special. It fell to the regular 'Oxted' demus to work the last services of all over the whole of the "Cuckoo Line", and passenger services were withdrawn north of Hailsham, with effect from 14th June 1965. The southern section to Eastbourne was subsequently in the hands of total demu operation, bringing to an end all scheduled steam services on the Central Division and the official closure of the remaining depots at Redhill, Eastbourne, Tunbridge Wells West and Redhill. The redundant locomotives congregated at Redhill before being dispersed to Guildford and points west.

Also closed at this time, on June 12th 1965, was the Guildford-Horsham service, totally steam worked until the end. Its sparse service was provided in latter days almost exclusively by 'Ivatt' tanks, just like the Steyning line, although the occasional appearance of a 'Q' or 'Q1' 0-6-0 provided some variety. Horsham shed had closed on June 15th 1964, so since then, locomotives had used Three Bridges for servicing, although that shed was also officially closed from the beginning of 1965. No. 41287 worked a six coach last ordinary train over the line on June 12th, the 19.34 to Horsham; No. 41299 was the other branch locomotive on that day. The Railway Enthusiasts Club organised a 'Q1' hauled trip over the line in the evening and two members of the class, Nos. 33006 and 33027, hauled the final working of all on Sunday June 13th, an LCGB railtour.

Now that the Central Division had finally rid itself of steam power, it seemed ironic that "foreign" steam engines continued to turn up much as in the previous summer. These workings were again on long distance scheduled summer Saturday passenger trains, and also on a variety of special workings. Bletchley's '8F' No. 48544 headed down the Brighton main line to Hove with a pigeon special from Newcastle on June 4th 1965, and a month later, on July 9th, a 'Black 5' made it through to Crawley on a similar working. Generally though, the Southern had apparently achieved its intention of making the Central Division as steam free as the Eastern Division by the autumn of 1965, although that goal was soon thwarted by the welcome return of steam power to the Brighton-Plymouth train, as explained in Chapter Four. The Christmas parcels season also undermined the steam "ban" and a 'Black 5', No. 45038, showed up at Redhill several times with vans from the Oxford area, while Guildford's 2-6-0s made a a number of trips along to Redhill as well, during the Christmas 1965 season.

Away from the ever-declining steam activities on the Central section of the Southern Region, there was much of interest taking place in the Hampshire and Dorset regions during the two years spanned by this chapter, particularly with regard to locomotive variety. Eastleigh Works continued to repair Southern Region based locomotives, and also those of other Regions, as well as scrapping steam locomotives, so it was still a good place to witness both predictable and unexpected arrivals. On New Year's day 1964, one of the last LSWR class '700' 0-6-0s No. 30700, officially withdrawn way back in November 1962, turned up hauling 'S15' class No. 30832 from Exmouth Junction shed. The following day another '700' appeared. this time itself being towed, by one of the former Exeter 'bankers', class 'Z' No. 30951. The 0-6-0s had been held in store for possible snow-plough duty, but now only the cutter's torch awaited them, as well as the 'S15' and the 'Z'.

More fortunate were the two withdrawn 'A1x' tank engines that appeared two days later, whose destiny was to be preservation not destruction. No. 32662 was seen towing No. 32636 up from Fratton shed, where they had both lain since the closure of the Hayling Island branch in November. Visitors included Standard BR engines which were being repaired at Eastleigh and run-in before returning north, such as No. 73014 from Bletchley, working on Waterloo-Basingstoke turns in April 1964. 'Britannia' No. 70017 *Arrow* was being retubed at Eastleigh Works during June 1964, after it was reported to have worked down on a special empty fruit train from Crewe on June 2nd. Other LMR and Standard class locomotives of various types continued to appear at Eastleigh during the next year.

Further variety was obtained during 1964 and into 1965, through the continued rostering of an ex-GWR 'Hall' class 4-6-0 on the York to Bournemouth West (and later Poole) through train and its return working. Many of these 4-6-0s looked in terrible condition by this time, usually bereft of nameplates, and often the smokebox and cabside number plates as well, indeed even the brass safety valve bonnets could not be relied upon to still be in place as the year progressed! Nevertheless they provided some welcome variety on the route westwards from Basingstoke. They were not always in good internal condition either, and on one notable occasion, New Year's day 1965, No. 6996 *Blackwell Hall* was reported as arriving at Bournemouth with the assistance of no less than two other locomotives! Following its failure at Christchurch, No. 76012 was attached at the front, and 'Merchant Navy' No. 35029 had to be added at the rear before the ensemble could move any further. The 'Halls' worked until the beginning of November 1965, when GWR locomotives were approaching their final hour, and they were superseded by Banbury's 'Black 5s', which then produced a new point of interest on the Southern, as explained later in the book.

Elsewhere in the Southern counties, it was now a time of steam decline, partly occasioned by line closures. The original main line from Southampton to the West, the route from Brockenhurst through Ringwood to Hamworthy and Poole was put up for closure, helping to speed the demise of the ailing 'M7' class 0-4-4Ts, which worked some of its services on a push-pull basis. By the time closure came in early May, the 'M7s' had been virtually excluded due to their unreliability, but they did continue to work the line, and also the picturesque Lymington and Swanage branches during the spring of 1964. The end came for these once numerous LSWR survivors at the same time as the Ringwood line, among the last 'M7s' active being No. 30052 at Brockenhurst on May 2nd, while No. 30254 was still in use at Salisbury as station pilot at about the same time. The old stagers had virtually disappeared from use by then and none was working after May 16th according to a report in the *Railway Observer*. The last nine 'M7s' were officially withdrawn in the period ending May 25th 1964, although No. 30053 worked a railtour on July 5th 1964, some 7 weeks after the class was officially extinct, and by all accounts did very well! The other locomotives were hauled away to Briton Ferry for scrapping in September 1964, but No. 30053 survived to be preserved, initially in the USA, and then by repatriation to a home on the Swanage Railway thirty years later.

As far as the Ringwood line was concerned, it was mainly left to the 'M7' replacements to take the final honours, although No. 30480 was reported to be at work on the last day on a two coach set. Standard '4' 2-6-0 No. 76027 worked several return trips, while the final turns were left to Standard '3MT' No. 82028. It worked the 16.07 from Brockenhurst to

WR 'Hall' class 4-6-0 No. 6923 *Croxteth Hall* departs from Eastleigh on September 1st 1965 with the Newcastle to Bournemouth train. Although it has lost its nameplates and safety valve bonnet, someone has obviously made an effort to smarten up its front end.   *Author*

Bournemouth, on what had proved to be a dull and dreary last day, and then took the final through trains, the 19.08 from Bournemouth West and the 20.56 Brockenhurst-Bournemouth West return. The stock comprised push-pull sets Nos. 608/614 and a van, and thus the little 2-6-2T gave the sizeable market towns of Ringwood and Wimborne their last normal passenger service. From the following Monday, May 4th, the line was closed to all passenger traffic between Broadstone and Lymington Junction, and to freight services over the eastern-most section from Ringwood.

Another Hampshire town to lose its train services that day was nearby Fordingbridge, which lay on another route closing from that weekend, the single track Salisbury to West Moors line. This endearing cross-country byway had a fairly sparse service, once the preserve of ex-LSWR 'T9s' with '700s' on its freight workings. However, it did come to life on summer Saturdays with a couple of through workings from South Wales to the South Coast, for which it proved a useful relief to the busy main routes. By 1964 'Moguls' of SR and BR origin were the normal motive power, and it was one of these, Standard class '4' No. 76066 which played a prominent part in the finale. Rather surprising however, was the rostering of a pacific to alternate with it. The Standard 2-6-0 worked north with five corridors on the 16.50 Bournemouth West-Salisbury and the unrebuilt 'West Country' No. 34091 *Weymouth* hauled eight coaches on the 17.20 Salisbury-Bournemouth West which attracted much local interest. I risked my parents wrath by staying on late at Bournemouth West to travel on the last up service to Salisbury, which was worked by No. 34091, the 19.50 to Salisbury. The journey through the little village stations at Verwood and Daggons Road was in the dusk, but I remember the platforms at Fordingbridge were crowded with sightseers and passengers.

Near Breamore we passed the last down service, the 20.30 from Salisbury, hauled by No. 76066, which was carrying a wreath and plaque. Streamers were hanging from the windows of our train, and there was an exchange of good-natured greetings between the passengers of the two slowly moving corteges. We arrived at Salisbury at around 22.00, but my attempts to get a flash photograph of the 'West County' and its train were thwarted by some sort of electrical problem on my little flash bulb gun, much to my frustration. Then I had to travel home, arriving near midnight, much to the concern of my mother who felt that a thirteen year-old should have been in bed long before!

While May 1964 marked the end of the 'M7' class, several other former Southern Railway locomotives were also now approaching final redundancy. One type was the Maunsell designed 'W' class, of which only five survived at the beginning of 1964, having lost their banking role at Exeter. Feltham shed had a couple of diagrams designated for the 2-6-4Ts, involving tasks such as freights from Wimbledon West Yard over the Wimbledon Chase line, which kept them active for a few more months. The last two survived into the summer, No. 31912 being seen on a coal train at Raynes Park on July 25th, however, it was withdrawn together with No. 31914, in August 1964, and towed away from Feltham to Cohens scrapyard in Kettering the following November.

Another Maunsell class to disappear at this time was the 'Q' class 0-6-0, a humble but effective goods engine of only twenty members at its peak, but which had been a familiar sight in Dorset, Hampshire and Sussex for thirty years. The first three withdrawals occurred at the end of 1962, but the remainder kept busy for the next eighteen months, being depleted by further condemnations on a sporadic basis. By the beginning of 1964, the 'Qs' seem to have been removed from

Above: On the last day of passenger services on the Ringwood line, May 2nd 1964, class '3MT' No. 82028 waits at Brockenhurst with a train of mainly Maunsell stock, forming the 16.07 to Bournemouth West. *Carl Symes*

Right: The last trains on the Fordingbridge line pass near Breamore on the night of Saturday, May 2nd 1964. Standard '4' No. 76066, carrying a wreath and plaque, heads southwards with the 20.30 from Salisbury and is photographed from the the 19.50 ex-Bournemouth West, which was hauled by 'West Country' No. 34091 *Weymouth*. Note the "streamers" (toilet rolls!) hanging from the windows of each train. *Author*

Below: An interesting view of 'Q' class 0-6-0 No. 30542 shunting freight wagons in the Longmoor Military Railway yard at Bordon on August 31st 1964. These Maunsell designed goods engines were fading from the scene by this time, but were still employed on some local workings of this nature. *Peter Harrod*

front line duty, but were on standby all over the place. For example, No. 30542 was fitted with a large snowplough and located at Basingtoke for the early part of the year and No. 30531 was in a similar role at Brighton. No. 30530 spent the latter part of the winter at Ashford, as a snowplough engine, and its journey to and from there brought a rare steam incursion to that part of Kent.

During the rest of the year, the remaining 'Qs' had little regular work, but filled in their time on shed pilot duties, yard shunting and the odd freight, and even passenger turn! Such an instance, was that of No. 30543 which worked the 07.27 Redhill-Eastbourne and return, several times in August and early September 1964, but then suffered a hot box and was put aside together with Nos. 30531 and 30542 at Redhill shed. Evidently it was considered worth repairing and it was seen shunting in the yards at Redhill in the week before Christmas 1964, just days before withdrawal. Final condemnation of class members occurred in the spring of 1965, and the last reported in steam was No. 30535 which steamed up to Eastleigh, still clad in snowplough, on July 11th 1965, three months after its withdrawal.

The other Maunsell designed locomotives to be eagerly sought out by enthusiasts in 1964 and the following year, were the handsome 'S15' class 4-6-0s, which continued on freight and passenger duties until the autumn of 1965, although in rapidly declining numbers. Once the mainstay of freight workings on the Exeter line, and a good number of passenger turns too, they spent the last two years of their lives mainly shedded at Feltham, working freight turns, usually between their home base and Southampton Docks, but also on the Salisbury-Chichester route. In 1964 'S15s' were also seen regularly on the 12.50 Reading General-Southampton Terminus vans which they took over at Eastleigh, as part of Feltham's 112 duty. This roster started with the 07.38 Clapham Junction-Southampton New Docks vans, continued with the 17.10 Southampton Terminus to Bournemouth stopping train and ended with the 21.25 Poole-Eastleigh freight and 04.30 Eastleigh-Feltham freights. Many of the remaining members of the class performed on this duty, and the passenger working, was very popular with enthusiasts, not least because it was often formed of unusual ex-LMSR stock including an articulated pair of carriages. The 'Sl5s' held sway on this duty until the end of the year. In October 1964 No. 30839 was in action from Redhill shed and worked freights to Brighton and Norwood Junction. Even in 1965, they still found the odd passenger duty turning up. For example, No. 30838 was seen substituting for a WR locomotive on the 10.50 Bournemouth West-York on May 26th. The locomotives continued to find intermittent employment until the end of the summer timetable, No. 30839 doing a Basingstoke-Salisbury and return passenger working as late as September 16th, but within a few days the last survivors were all condemned. The only exception was No. 30837, which as mentioned later in the book, was specially retained at Feltham to work two rail tours in January 1966. Also destined to survive into that year, but only just, were the 'Q1' class 0-6-0s. Although withdrawals of this class had only commenced in 1963, no more than twenty seven of the original forty were left at the beginning of 1964. The need for steam freight locomotives was increasingly limited, due to dieselisation and a further twenty of these 0-6-0s were eliminated during 1964, a very dramatic slaughtering of locomotives less than 25 years old. In summer 1964 the survivors found employment on duties such as the daily coal train from Wimbledon West Yard to Tolworth, which was part of a Feltham diagram. This certainly continued

at least until September 5th when No. 33006 was on the duty, and indeed 'Q1s' were still being seen on coal trains in the Wimbledon and Chessington areas in July 1965. An example was the twice-weekly freight from Raynes Park goods yard to Wimbledon West Yard, powered by No. 33026 on the 8th of that month.

However, the rugged-looking 0-6-0s did venture further afield, such as No. 33026 which was seen hauling a Basingstoke-Salisbury freight on October 16th 1964. At a personal level, the most interesting innovation was the sudden appearance of these 'Q1s' through Netley from the late autumn of 1964. They had been occasional performers on the line when they had been more numerous a few years previously, but their reappearance now, even though only two or three times a week, was very exciting. The reason behind this development was a new freight working, the 15.28 Fareham-Guildford, which continued into the late Spring of 1965. It involved stopping off at the exchange siding beside Hamble Halt to collect oil tank wagons which were to be delivered to North Camp on the Reading-Guildford line. If I was lucky I used to catch a glimpse of the 'Q1' labouring along with its tank train, somewhere between Bitterne and Netley, on my way home by train from school. Therefore, alongside my exercise and textbooks, I regularly carried my camera in my satchel, in the usually forlorn hopes of getting a photograph. The timing and days of the week on which the train operated were rather erratic, so I only succeeded on a few occasions, and the 'Q1' was invariably tender-first when I did!

Apart from their obvious work on freight, which included such interesting destinations as Farringdon on the remaining northern section of the Meon Valley line, the 'Q1s' also ventured onto passenger duty occasionally. No. 33006 was seen on the afternoon Southampton-Bournemouth 'S15' turn on a summer's day in 1964, but it was more common for them to take occasional strolls on the Horsham line, even during its last months in the spring of 1965. No. 33009 was used on the 08.04 from Guildford and 12.09 return from Horsham on March 6th 1965, while No. 33006, working tender-first, was seen with the 07.55 Horsham-Guildford on May 22nd. Towards the end of 1965, numbers had further dwindled, but on October 9th all three survivors were at Feltham, with No. 33006 arriving on a freight from Nine Elms Yard, while Nos. 33020 and 33027 stood facing each other in the shed yard. As mentioned in Chapter Three, much of the use of 'Q1s' in their last months was on nocturnal and weekend engineering trains in connection with the Bournemouth electrification.

No survey of Southern steam in 1965 would be complete without paying tribute to an extraordinary working which befitted the occasion it served. Sir Winston Churchill's death, on January 24th 1965, naturally demanded a full state funeral, and in the traditional manner accorded to several previous monarchs and leaders, his body was conveyed to its last resting place by train. Fortunately his namesake locomotive, unmodified 'Battle of Britain' No. 34051 still survived at Salisbury shed. It was brought up to a superb standard of cleanliness, and turned out on January 30th to work the funeral train, which comprised five pullman cars and a matching liveried bogie van, PMV No. S2464, in which the ex-Prime Minister's remains were conveyed. The stock was brought up from Clapham Junction to Waterloo by two spotless '4MT' tanks, Nos. 80143 and 80137. The driver of No. 34051 was A.W. Hurley, and his locomotive carried a distinctive disc pattern arranged appropriately in a 'V for Victory' formation. Like many others, young and old alike, I stood at the lineside on a cold, dull winter's day to watch the

Above: During 1964 class 'S15' 4-6-0s had a regular passenger turn on the Southern, working the 17.10 Southampton Terminus to Bournemouth stopping train. Here No. 30833 is seen setting out towards Northam with a six-coach haul of ex-LMSR carriages on a late summer afternoon. *Author*

Below:'Battle of Britain' 4-6-2 No. 34051 *Winston Churchill* conveying the body of the late Sir Winston Churchill, climbs upgrade from Virginia Water en route from Waterloo to Handborough on January 30th 1965. *Author*

Unrebuilt 'West Country' 4-6-2 No. 34102 *Lapford* draws to a halt at Netley station with the 09.30 semi-fast from Portsmouth to Cardiff on Saturday June 12th 1965, the last weekend of steam operation of these services.   *Author*

passage of Winston Churchill, the man and the machine. The route was from Waterloo to Twickenham, Virginia Water, Wokingham, Reading, Didcot North curve, Oxford to the little wayside station of Handborough, which was the nearest to Blenheim Palace. Soon after arrival, its place in history assured, the 'Battle of Britain' ran light back to Nine Elms depot. Another of the class, No. 34064 *Fighter Command* had been on standby at Staines in case of any mishap to the rostered locomotive.

After its day of greatness, No. 34051 returned to normal duties from Salisbury, which included participation in the semi-fast services to Portsmouth, which operated at roughly two-hourly intervals, comprised of either SR or WR stock, and originating at either Bristol or Cardiff. These lasted until the commencement of the summer timetable, when WR 'Inter-City' and 'Cross Country' dmmus took over. Needless to say, I photographed and travelled on these workings whenever possible in the last months, as they constituted the only regular steam passenger workings through my local station at Netley. Although most were non-stop, there were two services which did deign to call at my village, the morning 10.05 to Cardiff and the evening 18.22 to the same destination. Although modified and unmodified Bulleid 4-6-2s worked many of these turns, Standard class '4' 2-6-0s and 4-6-0s were probably more common by 1965. It was quite a difficult route and although trains tended to be quite short, just four coaches on some Sunday workings, the steep gradients and tight curves between Fareham and St. Denys demanded some skilled enginemanship.

I enjoyed just such a run in June 1965, when the 09.30 Portsmouth and Southsea to Cardiff General was worked as far as Salisbury by 'West Country' No. 34005 *Barnstaple* in excellent external condition. There were eight booked stops during the fifty mile journey for which an allowance of 95 minutes would have seemed generous, but for the nature of the line. The pacific was hauling seven carriages, including a buffet car, plus a parcels van. All the station arrivals and departures were made within a minute of those in the public timetable, and arrival at Salisbury was two minutes early. I thought that was a real tribute to Southern steam's efficiency in its latter days. The running was characterised by

acceleration to speeds in the high 50s or low 60s whenever possible, in view of the closeness of the stops. By way of comparison I retraced my steps as far as Southampton later on the same day, aboard the 17.45 from Portsmouth, but this time with the much smaller Standard '4' 2-6-0 No. 76065 in charge, Furthermore, the train was now a heavier proposition with three vans attached. To my surprise the Mogul also adhered to schedule very well, so much so that it was twice slowed down by signals due to the diesel stopping train ahead of it, and it was those delays which eventually caused a two minute late arrival at Southampton Central. The Standard '4s' were certainly capable of good acceleration, and also a fair turn of speed, as I recorded other members of the class travelling at speeds in the mid-70s on eastbound Cardiff-Portsmouth workings on other occasions in the spring of 1965.

The last weekend of steam operation was June 12th/13th 1965, after which the Western's diesel units took over all turns, apart from one or two Saturday extras. On the final Saturday, I was able to watch 'West Country' No. 34102 *Lapford* ease its train into Netley station, as it worked the final 09.30 Portsmouth and Southsea to Cardiff, passing beside the old LSWR signal box and under the watchful eye of signalman Harry Dudman. For me it was the end of an era, spanning back to my earliest memories of *Beachy Head* stopping at Netley on its journey in the opposite direction. My consolation, over thirty years later, is that Netley station still stands virtually unaltered, thanks to Listed Building status, the signal box is now preserved a few miles from my home at Ropley on the 'Watercress Line' and a similarly numbered 'West Country', No. 34105, still draws to a halt beside it, in much the same way, from time to time...

With the end of steam on passenger turns from Portsmouth to Salisbury, the closures elsewhere already mentioned, and the elimination of steam on the Central division, it was clear by the end of 1965, that the last months of Southern steam would be played out almost entirely on the Waterloo-Weymouth and Waterloo-Salisbury routes, and with a motive power fleet that had dwindled to a relatively small variety of classes. Despite those limitations it was to be a time of enormous interest and excitement for all involved, as the following chapters will show.

1965 was the last full year of steam on the two surviving Isle of Wight routes. Shown here are workings on the Ryde St. Johns Road to Cowes line, which closed completely in February 1966. *Left:* Class 'O2' 0-4-4Ts Nos. 28 *Ashey* and 24 *Calbourne* bring a bustle of activity to the once important junction station at Newport on Ryde and Cowes bound trains during September 1965; *Below:* A time-honoured ritual recorded as class 'O2' No. 20 *Shanklin* runs round its train at the terminus station at Cowes on September 18th 1965, the coaches having been propelled back up the curved approach tracks. The commodious footbridge has since been erected at Medstead and Four Marks station on the Mid-Hants Railway; *Bottom:* 'O2' No. 22 *Brading* shunts locomotive coal wagons for the engine shed at Ryde St. Johns Road during 1965. *Author*

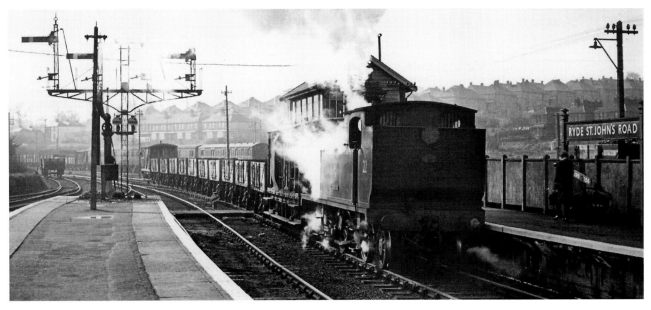

Table 1
Official Locomotive List for January 1966

BRITISH RAILWAYS

SOUTHERN REGION

NUMBERS & CLASSES OF STEAM LOCOMOTIVES 1ˢᵗ JAN. 1966

CLASS	TYPE & WHEEL DIAS.	SIZE OF CYLS.IN!	BOILD PRESS LB/IN!	BRAKE	TANK CAP. GALLS	MAKERS	ENGINE NUMBERS	QUANTITY
MERCHANT NAVY	4-6-2 TENDER 3'-1", 6'-2", 3'-7"	THREE 18" X 24"	280	S.E.	5000 5100 5250 6000	S.R. EASTLEIGH	35007 35010 35011 35012 35013 35014 35017 35026 35029 35009 35008 35022 35023 35027 35028 35030	16
WEST COUNTRY & BATTLE OF BRITAIN	4-6-2 TENDER 3'-1", 6'-2", 3'-1"	THREE 16¾" X 24"	280	S.E.	4500 5500	S.R. BRIGHTON EXCEPT E-EASTLEIGH	34002 34006 34015 34019 34023 34038 34041 34057 34064 34066 34076 34079 34086 34102	14
W.C./X. WEST COUNTRY MODIFIED	4-6-2 TENDER 3'-1", 6'-2", 3'-1"	THREE 16⅜" X 24"	250	S.E.	4500 5250 5500	MODIFIED BY S.R. EASTLEIGH ORIGINALLY BUILT BRIGHTON EXCEPT WHERE MARKED 'E'	34008 34009 34024 34034 34040 34056 34060 34077 34088 34089 34090 34093 34098 34100 34104 34035 34036 34108 34053 34001 34004 34006 34012 34013 34017 34018 34021 34026 34028 34037 34044 34047 34048 34052 34071 34082 34087 34096 34097 34101	40
N	2-6-0 TENDER 3'-1 & 5'-6" SUPERHEATED	19" X 28"	200	S.E. ENG. & V.C. TEN.	3500 4000	S.E.& C.R. ROYAL ARSENAL WOOLWICH S.R. ASHFORD	31816 31866 31873 31405 31408 31411	6
Q 1	0-6-0 TENDER 5'-1"	19" X 26"	220	V.C.	3700	S.R. A=ASHFORD B=BRIGHTON	33006 33020 33027	3
U	2-6-0 TENDER 3'-1" & 6'-0" SUPERHEATED	19" X 28"	200	S.E. ENG. & V.C. TEN.	4000 3500 4000	S.R. BRIGHTON S.R. ASHFORD	31803 31809 31791 31639	4
U.S.A.	0-6-0 TANK 4'-6"	16½" X 24"	210	S.E.	1000	VULCAN IRON WORKS U.S.A.	30064 30067 30069 30071 30072 30073	6
L.M.2	2-6-2 TANK 3'-0", 5'-0", 3'-0"	16" X 24" 16½" X 24"	200	S.E.	1350	L.M.R. CREWE	41224 41230 41284 41287 41294 41295 41298 41299 41301 41312 41316 41319 41320	13
B.R.3	2-6-2 TANK 3'-0", 5'-3", 3'-0"	17½" X 26"	200	S.E.	1500	W.R. SWINDON	82006 82018 82019 82023 82024 82026 82027 82028 82029	9
B.R.4	2-6-0 TENDER 3'-0" & 5'-3"	17½" X 26"	225	S.E.	3500	L.M.R. HORWICH	76005 76006 76007 76008 76009 76010 76011 76012 76013 76014 76016 76018 76019	26
	2-6-0 TENDER 3'-0" & 5'-3"	17½" X 26"	225	S.E.	3500 4725	E.R. DONCASTER	76028 76031 76033 76053 76057 76058 76059 76061 76063 76064 76066 76067 76069	
	2-6-4 TANK 3'-0", 5'-8", 3'-0"	18" X 28"	225	S.E.	2000	S.R. BRIGHTON	80011 80012 80013 80015 80016 80019 80032 80033 80034 80065 80068 80063 80082 80083 80085 80089 80094 80095 80132 80133 80134 80138 80139 80140 80141 80142 80143 80144 80145 80146 80151 80152 80154	33
	4-6-0 TENDER 3'-0" & 5'-8"	18" X 28"	225	S.E.	4725	W.R. SWINDON	75065 75066 75068 75069 75070 75074 75075 75076 75077 75078 75079	11
B.R.5	4-6-0 TENDER 3'-0" & 6'-2"	19" X 28"	225	S.E.	4250 4725	L.M.R. DERBY	73002 73016 73018 73020 73022 73029 73043 73037 73065 73080 73081 73082 73083 73085 73086 73087 73088 73089 73092 73093	31
	4-6-0 TENDER 3'-0" & 6'-2"	19" X 28"	225	S.E.	4725 5625	E.R. DONCASTER	73155 73169 73170 73171 73110 73113 73114 73115 73117 73118 73119	
							TOTAL	212

V.C. = VACUUM BRAKE COMPLETE
S.E. = STEAM BRAKE COMPLETE & VACUUM EJECTOR
R = CLASS N & U REBUILT FRONT ENDS
[ ] = FITTED WITH BRIQUETTE CONTAINER

W.14251

Chapter Three

Surviving Southern Steam Locomotives 1966-1967

At the beginning of 1966, the Southern Region had some 212 steam locomotives in capital stock, and a further 6 departmental locomotives, used for shunting at some of the Region's depots and Works. Compared to the figure of nearly 1,500 at the beginning of 1957, this was indeed evidence of a drastic decline.

As the official lists for January 1966 show, less than half of the surviving steam fleet was of truly Southern origin, as indicated by being numbered in the 3xxxx series. The bulk of these were Bulleid pacifics, mostly modified 'West Country' and 'Battle of Britain' 4-6-2s. There were also sixteen of the 'Merchant Navy' class surviving. The unrebuilt Bulleid pacifics were now down to just fourteen, the others having been withdrawn as they became due for overhaul, starting with No. 34055 *Fighter Pilot*, back in April 1963.

Not only had the Bulleid fleet been halved by the beginning of 1966, but all the other Southern steam classes had been eliminated or drastically reduced, as described in Chapters One and Two. The only pre-war Southern survivors left on the mainland which were to last well into 1966, were a handful of 'Moguls' (2-6-0s) based at Guildford of classes 'U' and 'N'. At that depot they were still accompanied by three of Bulleid's distinctive Wartime 'Q1' class 0-6-0s, the last

Table 2.

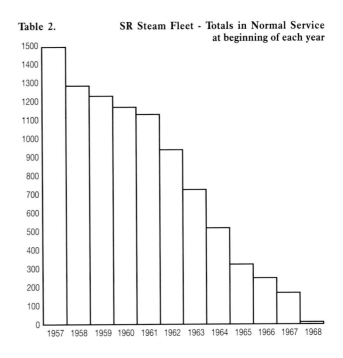

SR Steam Fleet - Totals in Normal Service at beginning of each year

'West Country' class 4-6-2 No. 34023 *Blackmore Vale* was one of the handful of original Bulleid pacifics which survived until the end of Southern steam, and happily into preservation also. It is seen in this splendid nocturnal view at Waterloo on September 13th 1966 with the 21.25 to Bournemouth.

Dr L.A. Nixon

51

Rebuilt 'Merchant Navy' class No. 35030 *Elder-Dempster Lines* hurries downhill towards Popham Tunnel, Micheldever on March 20th 1967 with the 11.30 Waterloo-Bournemouth.   *Author*

remnants of a class of forty, which ranked as the most powerful engines of their type in Britain. These were excellent machines, displaying in their gaunt rugged appearance all of Bulleid's aptitude for producing unusual and unconventional designs. Much of their strange appearance was due to wartime austerity and the need to keep fittings and decoration to a minimum, so that the locomotives would be able to travel over as many routes as possible, without being barred on weight grounds. They had a splendid record of service over most parts of the Southern during the 1950s and early 1960s, although they were rarely seen west of Salisbury. However, with the electrification projects, and the dieselisation of most freight workings from 1963, the need for the 'Q1s' had rapidly declined.

With the exception of the veteran '02' class tanks left on the Isle of Wight, to be mentioned later, the 1965 withdrawals had left only one other class with pre-Nationalisation connections. These were the American 'USA' class tanks, purchased by the Southern Railway in 1946 from the dump of American WD engines at Newbury race-course sidings. Fourteen were eventually taken into stock, having been 'Southernised' at Eastleigh Works by minor alterations and replacement of components. They had

been officially based at Eastleigh since the diesel shunters took over from them in Southampton Docks in 1962, as explained in Chapter One, whilst four had been transferred to departmental service. Thus ten members of the class still survived in one capacity or another on 1st January 1966.

In the course of 1966 withdrawals continued relentlessly. The three 'Q1s' were condemned in the very first week of the year, but in reality they soldiered on working engineers' trains, for a further month or two. No. 33006 was the last survivor, and its final working, was on the LCGB railtour on April 3rd. It shared haulage with 'U' class 2-6-0 No. 31639 on the return trip from Salisbury to Waterloo. The last 'U's and 'N's were also facing extinction in the spring of 1966. Although still hard at work from their Guildford base until May, the last survivors, Nos. 31405, 31408, 31639 and 31791, were taken out of use by June 5th. On July 1st, Standard '5' 4-6-0 No. 73082 hauled Nos. 31408 and 31639 to Eastleigh, ending Guildford's lengthy association with the Southern 'Moguls'. By mid-August the last 'Us' and 'Ns' were on their way to South Wales scrapyards.

The oldest engines surviving on the Southern by now were those in service on the Isle of Wight. The Island railway system had shrunk in the 1950s, leaving the Ryde Pier Head

Above: The 10.43 Southampton Central - Bournemouth strides out from beneath the famous signal gantry behind 'U' class No. 31639 on January 1st 1966. Use of the ex-SR 'Moguls' on passenger duty was rare by that time.   *Author*

Left: The end of the line for the 'N' and 'U' classes. Nos. 31405, 31791 and 31639 (inside shed) await removal to the scrapyards at Guildford on June 16th 1966.   *Ray Ruffell*

to Ventnor and Ryde Pier Head to Cowes lines alone surviving. Sadly the system was to be further pruned by the end of 1966, and steam operation was to be eliminated at the same time. At the beginning of the year, the Island steam fleet comprised fourteen Victorian built '02' class 0-4-4Ts. The 'E1' 0-6-0Ts, mentioned earlier, had long since been withdrawn. The '02' class, designed by William Adams, dated back to the period 1889-1891, and operated on the Island in conjunction with coaching stock from the early decades of the twentieth century. The result was a living museum, always operated most efficiently with the pride and professionalism that was a feature of Isle of Wight railwaymen.

Locomotive No. 14 *Fishbourne* was the oldest locomotive in regular service on the entire British Rail system by 1966. Appropriately it found itself playing a major role in the various 'lasts' during the year. On February 20th it was in charge of the final train from Cowes, on the night when passenger services between there and Smallbrook Junction were withdrawn. It was active again at Ventnor on April 17th when services between there and Shanklin came to an end. Most notably, it had charge of the very last steam passenger train of all, the 22.12 from Shanklin to Ryde on December 31st.

The Island engines retained their smart black lined-out livery until the end, although the now preserved No. 24 *Calbourne* had been outshopped in plain black and without nameplates, following overhaul in 1965. Nevertheless it still looked very smart, if a little naked, without its previous decoration. Following that precedent, the beautiful brass nameplates, each bearing the name of an Island location, were removed form the the '02s' by the Spring of 1966. They might have proved too tempting to amateur 'collectors' but in the true spirit of Wight enterprise, new tinplate names, each a little smaller than the originals, were manufactured and fitted at Ryde Works.

During the final year, four locomotives (Nos. 21, 26, 29 and 35) were withdrawn. Of the quartet, all except No. 35 were scrapped at Ryde Works, useful parts being removed to keep the other survivors going. The rest of the class were retired on the cessation of steam services on December 31st, when all services were suspended while electrification of the one surviving route, from Ryde Pier Head to Shanklin, was carried out. However, Nos. 24 and 31 were retained in service to work the associated engineers' trains as necessary, and to shunt the 'new' electric stock as it arrived on the Island. These too were withdrawn, in March 1967, No. 24 to survive in preservation and No. 31 to be cut up at the back of Ryde shed by A. King & Co. in September 1967. The other nine surviving '02s' and other items of vintage rolling stock that did not survive into preservation had been moved to the closed Newport station in the early part of 1967, where they made a sad but dignified sight, neatly lined up awaiting their fate.

Their end approached on April 18th, when the fire brigade provided water for the tanks of No. 27 *Merstone*, and driven by Driver John Townson, it was used to shunt the other engines into the Freshwater yard to suit the scrapmen's needs. Enthusiasts marked the event with chalk inscriptions on No. 27's smokebox, reading 'WIGHT LOCOMOTIVE SOCIETY PAYS ITS LAST RESPECTS. LAST 02 STEAMED ON BR.' The lamp brackets were painted white and the engine cleaned up for its last sad mission. Over the next three months these fine Victorian machines were reduced to heaps of metal pieces by local workers of Messrs. Joliffe's, treatment which the little tank engines surely did not deserve. This was especially true of No. 27 which had been overhauled at Ryde Works as recently as the previous July, the

The Isle of Wight steam abbatoir: the last '02' to be steamed, No. 27 *Merston* is the first to be dismembered in the yard at Newport.
Dr. J. Mackett

last major steam repair to take place there. After less than six months work it was certainly fit for several more years in harness.

Apart from the Isle of Wight there were two far more unlikely pockets of steam operation, isolated from the main concentration of steam on the Southern. At the geographical extremes of the former Southern Railway, in East Kent and Devon, survived a handful of departmental engines.

In the former location, at Ashford Works, there was a need for shunting engines to marshall wagons for repair in the yard. There were four sections known as the store road, broken road, 47 yard and Kimberley. Somehow two ex-SECR class 'C' 0-6-0s lingered on to perform some of these duties, mainly operating in the Kimberley sidings. They were originally numbered No. 31271 and No. 31592 in BR service, but when transferred to departmental work, they became Nos. DS240 and DS239. The reason the steam locomotives were able to survive so long in an otherwise steamless Kent, was that Ashford still had steam fitters and facilities for repairs, as well as a plentiful supply of spare parts in the Works.

The engines were watered by large hose pipes from hydrants, and coaled from special hoppers on a gantry in the Works. No doubt the works management also retained a particular affection for steam, which helps to explain these engines' longevity.

Although No. DS239 continued at work well into 1966, the role of the 'Cs' had diminished with the arrival of two 'USAs' in 1963. In a display of considerable initiative, the pair, ex-Nos. 30065 and 30070, were repainted in old Southern malachite green colours, and given names! The former became No. DS237 *Maunsell* and the latter No. DS238 *Wainwright*. These names were a tribute to two former SECR engineers whose careers were based on Ashford.

Class 'C' No. DS240 was eventually taken out of service on the advice of the drivers, because after the regulator was closed it would keep on taking steam and was therefore unsafe to work with. However, its life did not end completely because it was put to work as a stationary boiler to provide steam for axlebox cleaning. Although it could not have moved under its own power, it remained in use until late 1967 and was therefore, rather remarkably, the last steam engine to remain in use on the Southern! By then its appearance was rather bizarre, with the reported installation of a night watchman's hut on its footplate to provide weather protection for the crew. The drivers of these shunters were failed main line drivers, who had been forced to give up through poor health or eye-sight problems. The firemen were passed cleaners or main line firemen. Such a man was Keith Taylor, one of the regular firemen on No. DS239. He started work at Ashford shed in 1961 as an engine cleaner and was one of the last to pass out as fireman on steam locomotives. He says now that he thoroughly enjoyed his time working on the shunters and it was a complete contrast to his current work as a main line electric driver!

The other surviving 'C' 0-6-0 continued in use during 1966, before being purchased for restoration. It was specially steamed on October 8th, complete with a wreath on its front, and then No. DS239 retired, for transformation into its original condition, in which it now graces the Bluebell Railway.

The two 'USAs' continued hard at work in to 1967, working a 5½ day week at the wagon works. No. DS237 was reported to have been taken out of use in April, while No. DS238 seems to have survived in use until June 1967, although neither was officially condemned until September. They were eventually sold for scrap and destined for South Wales, but they showed no wish to head for the breakers and gave up at Tonbridge due to 'hot boxes'. It was there that preservationists stepped in to ensure

'C' class 0-6-0 No. DS239 shunting brake vans at Ashford wagon works on August 26th 1966.   *Derek Buckett*

that they did not leave the county, and they now enjoy the sanctuary of the Kent and East Sussex railway at Tenterden.

The other departmental 'USAs' were situated further westwards. Just outside Southampton was the Redbridge sleeper depot which was once a wagon works in the days of the LSWR. The depot was involved in the assembly of many of the track sections for the renewal of the Bournemouth line permanent way, as well as supplying conductor rails for the Isle of Wight electrification. Naturally such work needed the occasional services of a shunting locomotive, moving loaded wagons and marshalling engineer's trains. In 1962 the elderly 'O2' tank engine that performed the duty was up for retirement, and 'USA' No. 30061 was selected as a replacement, having just been made redundant in Southampton Docks and narrowly escaping scrapping. It was renumbered as No. DS233 in service stock, with its ownership and location indicated by italic writing on the side tanks. Otherwise it retained its black livery, unlike the Ashford shunters. It was moved to Redbridge in October 1962 and led a varied existence there until 1967. Its usage seemed to have declined by then, spending long periods 'dead', protruding from the small single road stone-built engine shed. In fact there wasn't

Above: 'USAs' Nos. DS237 *Maunsell* and DS238 *Wainwright* parked at Tonbridge following hot boxes sustained while being towed from Kent to the breakers' yards. September 4th 1968.   *John Scrace*

No. DS233 outside its damaged engine shed at Redbridge as a Standard class '5' passes on an 'up' passenger train in May 1966.   *Author*

much left of the shed to shelter within, as DS233 had managed to demolish the far end by failing to stop promptly on one occasion! In March its days came to an end when it was replaced by one of the 204hp Drewry diesel shunters, later known as class '03'.

No. DS233's move to Redbridge was paralleled by that of sister engine, No. DS234, to Meldon Quarry near Okehampton. It too replaced an old Southern 0-6-0T, this time a class 'G6', No. DS682. The takeover occurred on a snowladen December day in 1962, and the ex-No. 30062 remained exiled in Devon for the next four years. Its duties resembled those at Redbridge, marshalling trains of stone ballast for engineering department requirements. Its activities were confined to the Quarry precincts, never even wandering down to Okehampton itself. Any major repairs would have been carried out at Exmouth Junction shed, until steam was eliminated from there on May 24th 1965.

Right: The Meldon Quarry shunter No. DS234 was rarely captured on film. It is seen here in its normal surroundings with a train of ballast wagons.   *R.J. Sweet*

Of the Standard designs that operated on the Southern, the class '5' 4-6-0s would be judged among the most successful. Here No. 73022 is recorded on a secondary duty, the 17.02 local to Dorchester South, waiting departure at Bournemouth Central on December 30th 1966.   *Author*

The less powerful class '4' 4-6-0s remained in use until the very end of Southern steam. No. 75075 slows to a halt at Porton in bright early morning sunshine with the 07.18 Waterloo-Salisbury on March 21st 1967.   *Author*

Otherwise the engine was under the care of its regular driver, W. Blackmore, and his brief included routine servicing such as boiler washouts, checking and adjusting brakes and renewing firebars.

As Southern Region control in the south west withered away, the survival of Meldon Quarry as a BR owned enterprise was in doubt. The existence of a steam locomotive deep in what was now Western Region territory was very remarkable, especially after that region officially finished with steam at the end of 1965. However No. DS234 soldiered on, well after the last steam hauled ballast train had left the quarry. (That had almost certainly been on August 11th 1965, when 'West Country' No. 34057 *Biggin Hill* worked the 10.30 'up' ballast.) Eventually its charmed life came to an end when heavy repairs became due in August. However, even that was not quite the end of the story; on the SR and WR stock change sheets, the famous green 'USA', No. 30064, was shown as being transferred to the Western in mid-August as a steam replacement. There is no clear evidence that the engine ever made the move, although it was on exhibition at Bristol (Bath Road) diesel depot open day on October 22nd, and returned to Eastleigh three days later. Thoughts that it may have passed through Bristol while returning from Devon are dispelled by photographic evidence that it had been shunting at Salisbury shed a month earlier on September 24th! In any event it was transferred back 'on paper', from the WR to Eastleigh shed during the week ending October 9th. At Eastleigh, No. 30064 shared with a few of its brethren, the task of shunting the wagons of locomotive coal at the shed, and other shunting and marshalling duties in the Works yard. This included the haulage of the afternoon stores freight wagons out to the marshalling yard. Eastleigh Works was still repairing Southern locomotives during most of 1966, and so its facilities were also made use of for the overhaul of various engines from the London Midland Region.

'Black 5s', 2-6-0s and 2-8-0s of LMSR origin, as well as various Standards appeared for attention. A number of these were pressed into SR service, sometimes for longer than was strictly required for running-in purposes! The York to Poole inter-regional train also brought LMS 'Black 5' 4-6-0s to the region, working through from Banbury. On one occasion at least, a Standard '9F' 2-10-0 found itself on this duty.

British Railways' post-nationalisation standard designs generally played a prominent part in the last years of Southern steam activity. The Region had an allocation of BR class '5' 4-6-0s, mainly intended for fast passenger work, and also the smaller '4' 4-6-0s, which were suited to lighter passenger and freight duties. The Standard class '4' Moguls in the 76XXX series also found widespread employment on passenger and goods turns. Since the once extensive heritage of ex-Southern railway tank engines had been destroyed, apart from the 'USAs', the Standard equivalents were now the only non-tender representatives to be found. The large class '4' 2-6-4Ts could be used on almost any duty from branch passenger to main-line freight, while the smaller '3' 2-6-2Ts (82XXX range) were more typical of the traditions of small tank engines. These were matched by the very similar Ivatt designed '2' tanks of LMSR origin, which were well used by the Southern, particularly on the Lymington and Swanage branches.

The domination by standard British Railways-built designs detracted somewhat from the Southern flavour of the last two years, compared to the Western or North Eastern Regions, where many elderly locomotives survived to the end.

However, there were many compensations which must be remembered. The last active Maunsell-designed 'S15', No. 30837, was specially retained at Feltham after withdrawal to work two enthusiast's specials in January 1966. Beautifully cleaned, with exposed metal burnished like a Royal Train

A last chance to show its paces on a main line passenger turn for a Standard class '4' 2-6-0: No. 76066 attacks the climb to Beaulieu Road with an 8-coach load of mainly Bulleid carriages on June 10th 1967. The working was the 11.24 Waterloo-Bournemouth, running about 25 minutes late through the New Forest area.

Author

The Ivatt designed class '2' 2-6-2Ts took over the tank engine role previously performed on the Southern by types such as the 'M7' class 0-4-4Ts. Pilot and empty coaching stock duties from Waterloo were typical assignments, as with No. 41298 taking water at the terminus on October 14th 1966.

Ray Ruffell

locomotive, the 4-6-0 was a fitting tribute to the long association of such mixed-traffic engines with the then declining Feltham shed. The engine returned to store at Feltham afterwards and was not despatched to the scrapyards until July, dashing hopes that such a fine locomotive might be preserved.

Other enthusiast events brought a number of 'foreign' engines to SR tracks. These included ex-LNER classes 'A2', 'A3', 'A4', 'K4' and 'V2', BR 'Britannias', and 'WD' 2-10-0 No. 600 *Gordon*. The rumours of LMR 'Duchesses' being drafted on to the Southern were not enacted of course, fortunately for supporters of the SR's own motive power. However, there were a few small scale transfers of locomotives, most surprisingly that of standard class '3' 2-6-0 No. 77014. This unlikely arrival, the first and only of its type ever to appear in the south, occurred on March 17th 1966, when it reached Basingstoke from Northwich, Cheshire. Replaced at its former depot by LMR 2-6-0s

Nos. 46405/14, the exile was used to take over from some of Guildford depot's ex-SR Moguls. It played a prominent part in the last months of steam, becoming the last steam engine to arrive at Weymouth on July 9th 1967.

Another strange arrival in the South was also a standard, class '2' 2-6-2T No. 84014. Engines of that type had worked on the region in the 1950s, but not since. In October 1965, the tank was hauled onto the Southern, but stopped at Basingstoke shed with a 'hot box'. After repair it was seen heading for Eastleigh with a van train some weeks later. The reason for its transfer was a plan to use locomotives of this type on the Isle of Wight to replace the old LSWR class 'O2' tank engines. On paper, ten of the class were passed over to the Southern, with the movement of four to Fratton on November 10th reported. However, before the programme of alterations and modifications could be carried out to the 2-6-2Ts, policy was changed. The Isle of Wight was to be

One of the 'foreign' visitors to the Southern in 1966 was the magnificent ex-LNER 'A4' No. 60024 *Kingfisher* seen at Eastleigh shed on March 26th 1966. It was being serviced while working a rail tour from Waterloo to Weymouth, Yeovil and Salisbury.

Author

Reinstated for the Christmas period, 'West Country' class No. 34005 *Barnstaple* awaits departure from Bournemouth Central on December 30th 1966 with the 17.09 to Waterloo.   *Author*

electrified instead, and the movement of the 84XXXs was cancelled. No. 84014 remained dead on Eastleigh shed for several months until it was sent for scrap to Cashmore's of Newport.

On average, about eight locomotives a month were withdrawn during 1966. The bulk of the withdrawals took place in September and October however, with forty-two being taken out of service in those two months. This large scale slaughter of the steam flock was, perhaps, too drastic. There was a long tradition of bringing stored locomotives back into service for Christmas parcels activity, and 1966 saw the last ever resuscitation efforts on moribund locomotives.

On December 10th, Nos. 34005, 73169 and 75069 were fired at Eastleigh, although they had been officially withdrawn at the end of September. Other engines brought back into service at Eastleigh and Bournemouth included Nos. 34026, 34032 and Standards Nos. 73087, 73088, 73089 and 76016 and 76057. They were officially reinstated from December 12th, with the intention of being retired again in the New Year. For that reason it was decided not to restore their AWS equipment. It is not clear when they were all withdrawn again, but Nos. 34005, 73088, 73089, 73169, 75069 and 76057 were all observed at Eastleigh shed, out of use, on April 15th 1967. However, only Nos. 73169 and 76057 had been stripped of their motion parts at that stage, the ultimate sign of condemnation. In fact each of these ten engines was sold for scrap between April and June 1967, and were subsequently reduced to pieces of metal at Newport in South Wales. The only exception was No. 75069 which managed to get itself sold to Woodhams of Barry, and thus was eventually saved for preservation, on the Severn Valley Railway.

It should be mentioned that one of the author's photographs, of 'Battle of Britain' class No. 34087, was published in the 'Railway Magazine' during 1967, purporting to show the 'previously withdrawn' locomotive working the 'Bournemouth Belle'. In fact, this was the result of a mistake in the official lists which had reported No. 34087's withdrawal the previous April, when the engine concerned was really No. 34097. So although there were some genuine reinstatements, No. 34087's existence was never questioned at that time, and it survived until the very end of Southern steam.

During 1966 the external appearance of most of the locomotive fleet was generally appalling. Grimy Bulleid pacifics and standards, covered in thick coats of oily dirt, were the order of the day. Nameplates had already begun to disappear during 1965, and there was a systematic removal from most engines subsequently. Their value to enthusiasts and dealers made them targets for theft, and they were removed by shed staff and put into store. A box van full of nameplates turned up at Salisbury shed, and its highly prized contents were locked away.

It wasn't only nameplates that became collectors' items: numberplates and shed allocation plates began to disappear too. Unlike nameplates they were easily removed with a spanner, and a few minutes purposeful activity could no doubt 'liberate' a piece of cast iron for a personal collection. The ugly result of all this official and unofficial activity was increasingly anonymous looking locomotives. In some cases identification became virtually impossible, as a filthy, travel stained Bulleid sped past, with even the cabside painted numerals obscured.

The Eastleigh Sunday cleaning ritual as men earn overtime pay to put some glory back into the dying days of steam. 'West Country' class No. 34024 *Tamar Valley* is receiving the treatment on June 4th 1967. *E.H. Sawford*

Fortunately the problems of cleanliness and identity were partially dealt with through some private enterprise. Salisbury shed had a long-standing reputation for keeping engines clean, and it was obvious that its Bulleid pacifics and Standards were the cleanest engines on the Southern during 1966. Most of them appeared to be awaiting Royal Train duty, such was the effort lavished upon their appearance! Salisbury shed did not have the same shortages of men that were experienced nearer London, and could still enlist cleaners to continue the traditions of former days. Shedmaster Claud Dare was very willing to detail men to keep up the external appearance of his machines.

When Mr. Dare was transferred to Eastleigh, it provided the opportunity for cleanliness to appear there as well. Engine cleaning was a potential source of overtime for firemen and drivers who didn't mind putting in some hard graft on Sundays. Much of the inspiration for this came from diesel depot fitter, Ron Cover, who described in an article in 'Steam Railway', how he was instrumental in starting cleaning operations. A number of other Eastleigh men volunteered for the twelve hour Sunday shifts, including Ray Glassey who had been one of the regular Lymington branch firemen until it was dieselised in April 1967. Ray recalls using shovels to scrape the dirt off the tenders, before real cleaning could commence! Over forty engines were cleaned by the two Sunday gangs during the last months of Southern steam.

Ron Cover's most obvious contribution to locomotive appearance was his manufacture of 'Soup Tin Specials'. The famous painting by David Shepherd of 'Nine Elms – the last hours', features Standard '5' No. 73155 bearing a red number-plate. This was just one of at least fourteen replacement

An example of the famous Cover 'Soup-Tin specials', carried as a replacement numberplate on a Standard class '4' tank. *Ron Cover*

smokebox plates manufactured by Mr Cover, using soup tins and redundant destination boards from Hampshire diesel units. The numerals were cut out from the tins and stuck to the destination boards which were virtually the right size to replace the original numberplates. Although a few were painted in black with silver numbers, the majority were really eye-catching due to their background hues. For example 'Battle of Britain' No. 34077 acquired a light blue numberplate with silver numerals, while others like that for No. 73155 were red. Two Standards ended up with gold or yellow numbers on a black base, being Nos. 73029 and 80133. Nameplates were almost impossible to make or to affix, but 'West Country' class No. 34037 kept its backing bracket when the nameplate was removed, and so the intrepid Mr Cover was able to paint its *Clovelly* designation on to a smart red background.

Other sheds also had examples of unofficial numbering practices. Usually these were crudely drawn in chalk, and soon wiped off by the elements. Some of Guildford's 'Q1s' had sported their old Southern numbering before withdrawal, as it was quite easy to turn '33020' into 'C20' by careful blacking out of parts of the number. Likewise 'Merchant Navy' class No. 35010 was photographed by G. Marks at Basingstoke on April 9th 1967, with '21C10' chalked on its smokebox, yet later on May 28th,

Ron's one successful attempt to restore a Bulleid pacific's nameplates: the hand-painted inscription in gold paint on 'West Country' class No. 34037.   *Ron Cover*

when he saw it at the same place, it had gained a home-made No. 35010 plate instead.

When the New Year arrived, it was clear to many that it would be a struggle to keep the steam fleet going until full electrification. The new electric trains and electro-diesel locomotives were behind schedule and the decision had been taken to delay the inauguration of the new services by one month from June to July. As Eastleigh Works was no longer carrying out overhauls, it was a case of shed fitting staff doing their best to keep engines running. It is probably true to say that no locomotive was allowed to run in a dangerous condition, but many were very run down indeed.

In the circumstances it was fortunate that the Southern had received an allocation of Brush Type '4' diesel electric locomotives, more recently known as Class 47s. The first to be transferred from the Western was D1923 which arrived in September 1966, followed by five others in the next two months. They were rostered to many of the main passenger duties taking the burden off the steam fleet, although they soon showed that they were not infallible either, and had to be substituted by steam engines from time to time.

On January 1st 1967, the Southern had a total allocation on its books of 130 locomotives, although this figure needs some clarification. It includes eight 'O2's which were actually withdrawn on that day, although in reality they had been taken out of service on the previous day when Isle of Wight steam services ended. Thus 122 is a more accurate total, but then that also needs amending to take into account the ten engines put back into service over the Christmas period after previous withdrawal. Mention should also be made of departmental 'USA's DS233, 234, 237 and 238 still on the books, and class 'C' No. DS240 in its steam raising role at Ashford Works.

Table 3 shows the surviving engines which were available for use at the start of the year, excluding the condemned Isle of Wight tanks, the departmentals and the short-term reinstatements. It can be seen that Bulleid light pacifics remained the dominant type, with twenty-nine rebuilt and seven unmodified surviving. Together with ten 'Merchant Navies' and the six 'USA' tanks, they comprised the only remaining engines with '3' prefixed numbers, the one-time hallmark of Southern steam in the British Railways era. With the exception of eight Ivatt '2' 2-6-2Ts, the remaining steam fleet was now composed entirely of Standard types of post-nationalisation build.

Unofficial engine cleaning also took place and in this picture a pair of youthful enthusiasts are excavating the nameplates of 'Battle of Britain' class No. 34060 from beneath the usual layers of filth. The scene occurred on December 5th 1966, by which time many of the pacifics had already lost their nameplates.   *John Fairman*

Another SR steam locomotive surrenders to electric traction! Standard class '3' 2-6-2T No. 82023 came off the worst in this collision at Vauxhall and was promptly withdrawn. September 28th 1966.   *Ray Ruffell*

The sixty standards were, in the main, class '5' 4-6-0s of which there were now eighteen left, and the class '4' 2-6-0s and 2-6-4Ts, with seventeen representatives each. The rest consisted of five class '4' 4-6-0s, the solitary class '3' No. 77014, and two 2-6-2Ts Nos. 82019 and 82029. As already mentioned, two class 'O2' tanks remained on the Isle of Wight for shunting duties while the electrification work was in progress.

Table 3
SR Locomotives at January 1st 1967
and Shed Allocations

70A Nine Elms
Rblt 'WC'	34001, 34008, 34018, 34021, 34034, 34036, 34037,
Unrblt 'WC'	34002, 34019
'2'	41284, 41298
'5'	73022, 73029, 73037, 73043, 73065, 73085
'4'	80012, 80015, 80085, 80133, 80140, 80143, 80145, 80154
'3'	82019, 82029

70C Guildford
'USA'	30072
'5'	73092, 73093, 73110, 73115, 73117, 73118
'4'	76031, 76033, 76053, 76058, 76069
'3'	77014

70D Eastleigh
'USA'	30064, 30067, 30069, 30071, 30073
Rblt 'WC'	34093, 34095, 34098, 34104
Unrblt 'WC'	34023, 34102
'BB'	34060, 34071, 34077, 34087, 34088, 34090
'2'	41319
'5'	73119, 73155
'4'	75068, 75074, 75075, 75076, 75077
'4'	76061, 76063, 76064, 76066
'4'	80016, 80139, 80151, 80152

70E Salisbury
Rblt 'WC'	34013, 34100, 34108
Unrblt 'WC'	34006, 34015
Rblt 'BB'	34052, 34056, 34089
Unrblt 'BB'	34057
'4'	76007, 76008, 76067

70F Bournemouth
Rblt 'WC'	34004, 34024, 34025, 34040, 34044, 34047
'2'	41224, 41230, 41295, 41312, 41320
'4'	76005, 76006, 76009, 76011, 76026
'4'	80011, 80019, 80032, 80134, 80146

70G Weymouth
'MN'	35003, 35007. 35008, 35012, 35013, 35014, 35023, 35026, 35028, 35030
'5'	73002, 73018, 73020, 73113

70H Ryde
'O2'	W24, W31

The story thence forward was a melancholy one as the above engines were progressively withdrawn as they failed and became incapable of being repaired economically. The introduction of electric trains onto some workings between Waterloo and Bournemouth from the beginning of April also reduced the need for steam, together with the end of the steam heating season at the beginning of May. That enabled Crompton Type '3' diesels to be used on passenger services at weekends, to join with the Brush Type '4s' already mentioned. The number of electro-diesel locomotives increased until the last of the smaller engines (now Class '73') was delivered in January making a total of forty-nine available for service. They played their part on passenger services too working 'TC' stock on scheduled services, and ordinary carriages, once heating was not required.

By July 9th, when steam was eliminated from the Southern, just seventy-three locomotives remained to be officially condemned. The withdrawals in the preceding six months had fallen evenly among the majority of engine types, with the notable exception of the unrebuilt Bulleid pacifics. The seven that started the year were whittled down to two, Nos. 34023 *Blackmore Vale* and 34102 *Lapford* both of the 'West Country' class. The last unrebuilt 'Battle of Britain' No. 34057 *Biggin Hill*, managed to survive until the first week of May before succumbing. Indeed, it actually found itself working the down 'Bournemouth Belle' on May 4th, in its very last days in service. The 'Battle of Britain' class was reduced to a handful of rebuilt engines therefore by the end of steam, just five surviving as against eleven 'West Country' rebuilds. Three Standard classes dominated the final stock count, namely ten class '5' 4-6-0s, ten class '4' 2-6-0s and ten class '4' 2-6-4Ts. Only two classes survived intact without further withdrawals during 1967, these were the five Standard class '4' 4-6-0s at Eastleigh and the two Standard '3' 2-6-2Ts, based at Nine Elms.

Withdrawals and transfers during the year reduced Salisbury's locomotive fleet to just three Bulleid pacifics for the last week while, on paper at least, Weymouth shed had no steam allocation at all after April when its 'Merchant Navies' were transferred to Nine Elms and its Standards to Guildford. The final allocations of the last seventy three Southern steam engines is shown in Table 4.

Table 4
Final Steam Allocations – July 1967

70A Nine Elms
34001, 34018, 34021, 34023, 34036, 35003, 35007, 35008, 35013, 35023, 35028, 35030, 41298, 41312, 41319, 73029, 73037, 73043, 73065, 80015, 80133, 80140, 80143, 82019, 82029	(Total 25)

70C Guildford
30072, 73018, 73020, 73092, 73093, 73118, 73155, 76031, 77014	(Total 9)

70D Eastleigh
30064, 30067, 30069, 30071, 34037, 34060, 34087, 34090, 34093, 34095, 34102, 75068, 75074, 75075, 75076, 75077, 76064, 76066, 80016, 80139, 80152	(Total 21)

70E Salisbury
34013, 34052, 34089	(Total 3)

70F Bournemouth
34004, 34024, 34025, 41224, 41320, 76005, 76006, 76007, 76009, 76011, 76026, 76067, 80011, 80134, 80146	(Total 15)

With these three score and thirteen locomotives, the era of steam on the railways of Southern England came to an end in July 1967. The last survivors had battled to the last, but had now succumbed to the electric victors, bringing steam operations to a close.

Table 5
Declining SR Fleet January – July 1967
(showing locomotives in service
at the beginning of each month)

In Service On:

1.1.67	1.2.67	1.3.67	1.4.67	1.5.67	1.6.67	1.7.67	9.1.67	Allocation on and changes after 1.1.67
24	24	24						70H
31	31	31						70H
30064	30064	30064	30064	30064	30064	30064	30064	70D
30067	30067	30067	30067	30067	30067	30067	30067	70D
30069	30069	30069	30069	30069	30069	30069	30069	70D
30071	30071	30071	30071	30071	30071	30071	30071	70D
30072	30072	30072	30072	30072	30072	30072	30072	70C
30073								70D
34001	34001	34001	34001	34001	34001	34001	34001	70A
34002	34002	34002	34002					70A
34004	34004	34004	34004	34004	34004	34004		70F
34006	34006	34006						70E
34008	34008	34008	34008	34008	34008			70A
34013	34013	34013	34013	34013	34013	34013		70E
34015	34015	34015	34015					70E
34018	34018	34018	34018	34018	34018	34018		70A
34019	34019	34019						70A
34021	34021	34021	34021	34021	34021	34021	34021	70A
34023	34023	34023	34023	34023	34023	34023	34023	70D 70A
34024	34024	34024	34024	34024	34024	34024	34024	70F
34025	34025	34025	34025	34025	34025	34025	34025	70F
34034	34034	34034	34034	34034	34034	34034		70A
34036	34036	34036	34036	34036	34036	34036	34036	70A
34037	34037	34037	34037	34037	34037	34037	34037	70A 70D
34040	34040	34040	34040	34040	34040	34040		70F
34044	34044	34044	34044	34044				70F
34047	34047	34047	34047	34047	34047			70F
34052	34052	34052	34052	34052	34052	34052	34052	70E
34056	34056	34056	34056	34056				70E
34057	34057	34057	34057	34057				70E
34060	34060	34060	34060	34060	34060	34060	34060	70D
34071	34071	34071	34071					70D
34077	34077	34077						70D
34087	34087	34087	34087	34087	34087	34087	34087	70D
34088	34088							70D
34089	34089	34089	34089	34089	34089	34089	34089	70E
34090	34090	34090	34090	34090	34090	34090	34090	70D
34093	34093	34093	34093	34093	34093	34093	34093	70D
34095	34095	34095	34095	34095	34095	34095		70D
34098	34098	34098	34098	34098	34098			70D
34100	34100	34100	34100	34100	34100	34100		70E
34102	34102	34102	34102	34102	34102	34102	34102	70D
34104	34104	34104	34104	34104	34104			70D
34108	34108	34108	34108	34108	34108			70E
35003	35003	35003	35003	35003	35003	35003	35003	70G 70A
35007	35007	35007	35007	35007	35007	35007	35007	70G 70A
35008	35008	35008	35008	35008	35008	35008		70G 70A
35012	35012	35012	35012					70G 70A
35013	35013	35013	35013	35013	35013	35013	35013	70G 70A
35014	35014	35014						70G
35023	35023	35023	35023	35023	35023	35023	35023	70G 70A
35026	35026	35026						70G
35028	35028	35028	35028	35028	35028	35028	35028	70G 70A
35030	35030	35030	35030	35030	35030	35030	35030	70G 70A
41224	41224	41224	41224	41224	41224	41224	41224	70F
41230	41230	41230						70F
41284	41284	41284						70A
41295	41295	41295	41295					70F
41298	41298	41298	41298	41298	41298	41298	41298	70A
41312	41312	41312	41312	41312	41312	41312	41312	70F 70A
41319	41319	41319	41319	41319	41319	41319	41319	70D 70A

In Service On:

1.1.67	1.2.67	1.3.67	1.4.67	1.5.67	1.6.67	1.7.67	9.1.67	Allocation on and changes after 1.1.67
41320	41320	41320	41320	41320	41320	41320	41320	70F 70A 70F
73002	73002	73002						70G
73018	73018	73018	73018	73018	73018	73018	73018	70G 70C
73020	73020	73020	73020	73020	73020	73020	73020	70G 70C
73022	73022	73022	73022					70A
	73029	73029	73029	73029	73029	73029	73029	70A
73037	73037	73037	73037	73037	73037	73037	73037	70A
73043	73043	73043	73043	73043	73043	73043	73043	70A
73065	73065	73065	73065	73065	73065	73065	73065	70A
73085	73085	73085	73085	73085	73085	73085		70A
73092	73092	73092	73092	73092	73092	73092	73092	70C
73093	73093	73093	73093	73093	73093	73093	73093	70C
73110								70C
73113								70G
73115	73115	73115						70C
73117	73117	73117						70C
73118	73118	73118	73118	73118	73118	73118	73118	70D
73119	73119	73119						70D
73155	73155	73155	73155	73155	73155	73155		70D 70C
75068	75068	75068	75068	75068	75068	75068	75068	70D
75074	75074	75074	75074	75074	75074	75074	75074	70D
75075	75075	75075	75075	75075	75075	75075	75075	70D
75076	75076	75076	75076	75076	75076	75076	75076	70D
75077	75077	75077	75077	75077	75077	75077	75077	70D
76005	76005	76005	76005	76005	76005	76005	76005	70F
76006	76006	76006	76006	76006	76006	76006	76006	70F
76007	76007	76007	76007	76007	76007	76007		70E 70F
76008	76008	76008	76008	76008				70E 70F
76009	76009	76009	76009	76009	76009	76009	76009	70F
76011	76011	76011	76011	76011	76011	76011	76011	70F
76026	76026	76026	76026	76026	76026	76026	76026	70F
	76031	76031	76031	76031	76031	76031	76031	70C
76033	76033							70C
76053								70C
76058	76058	76058						70C
76061								70D
76063	76063	76063	76063					70D
76064	76064	76064	76064	76064	76064	76064	76064	70D
76066	76066	76066	76066	76066	76066	76066	76066	70D
76067	76067	76067	76067	76067	76067	76067		70E 70F
76069	76069	76069	76069	76069	76069			70C
77014	77014	77014	77014	77014	77014	77014	77014	70C
80011	80011	80011	80011	80011	80011	80011	80011	70F
80012	80012	80012						70A
80015	80015	80015	80015	80015	80015	80015	80015	70A
80016	80016	80016	80016	80016	80016	80016	80016	70D
80019	80019	80019						70F
80032								70F
80085	80085	80085	80085	80085	80085	80085		70A
80133	80133	80133	80133	80133	80133	80133	80133	70A
80134	80134	80134	80134	80134	80134	80134	80134	70F
80139	80139	80139	80139	80139	80139	80139	80139	70D
80140	80140	80140	80140	80140	80140	80140	80140	70A
80143	80143	80143	80143	80143	80143	80143	80143	70A
80145	80145	80145	80145	80145	80145			70A
80146	80146	80146	80146	80146	80146	80146	80146	70D
80151	80151	80151	80151	80151				70D
80152	80152	80152	80152	80152	80152	80152	80152	70D
80154	80154	80154	80154					70A
82019	82019	82019	82019	82019	82019	82019	82019	70A
82029	82029	82029	82029	82029	82029	82029	82029	70A

Chapter Four

Steam Operation, 1966-1967

On New Year's day 1966, I stood at one of my favourite vantage points, the cinder track that ran beside the lines west of Southampton Central station. It was a beautiful bright winter morning and I watched a festival of steam parading beneath the sun's golden spotlight. In the bay platform, No. 5, an immaculate Mogul, 'U' class No. 31639, simmered quietly at the head of a short stopping train to Bournemouth. Alongside, passengers waited for the semi-fast from Waterloo to arrive. In due course it crept in, stopping with its tender beside the water column. The crew dismounted from the cab of the grimy but powerful looking Bulleid pacific and set about dropping the bag into the filler hole and taking on several thousand gallons of water. The locomotive, No. 34021 *Dartmoor*, sat beneath the majestic Southampton signal gantry, steam rising idly from its safety valves, awaiting the driver's call to action once again. Its concealed impatience

diminish, both on passenger and freight services, leading up to its disappearance during 1967. From being a predominantly steam-worked main line in these early months of 1966, the Waterloo to Bournemouth and Weymouth artery was to become a veritable hotch-potch of traction types by April 1967. Between then and July, a passenger might find a train composed of traditional green Southern carriages hauled by a 'Merchant Navy' steam locomotive, or a similar train hauled by a 'Brush' diesel on loan from the Western Region. Alternatively the journey might be undertaken in a set of blue carriages (TC sets), driven from a driving cab at the front, yet propelled in the rear by a Southern Type '3' diesel-electric. For further variety you could replace the diesel with one of the new electro-diesels, or maybe two. Then there were also the new electric units of course, the '4-REPs', which might be hauling or propelling TC sets.

New Year's Day 1966 and Southampton Central greets No. 34018 *Axminster* arriving with the last steam hauled 'Pines Express', No. 34021 *Dartmoor* taking water on the 08.35 Waterloo-Bournemouth and 'U' No. 31639 with the 10.43 to Bournemouth.   *Author*

was soon displayed as a loud explosion of steam broke skywards from the safety valves, showing a boiler in excellent fettle. Meanwhile the steam vista was completed by the clanking of wheels and coupling rods, as another Bulleid, sister engine No. 34018, rolled into the upside platform. It was hauling a string of maroon carriages, indicating an inter-regional working off the Southern. In fact it was the famous 'Pines Express' once routed over the much lamented Somerset and Dorset line on its journey from Bournemouth to the North West. This was an historic trip indeed for the 'Pines', as it was the last scheduled steam working of the train. From the following Monday it would succumb to diesel haulage by a Brush Type '4' locomotive.

There lay the portent in a scene otherwise reassuring to a steam enthusiast. . . the writing was on the wall for steam. Although it was hard to accept at the time, this was the start of the last full year of steam working on the Southern's south-western division. As the year progressed, steam working was to

While the variety was to prove of great interest to students of railway operation, thought must be spared for the crews who had to be trained intensively to operate the new rolling stock alongside the old. They faced the likelihood of turns of duty toiling amongst the heat and dirt of a locomotive footplate, interspersed with effortless operation of the new, clean and comfortable electrics. This could be very unsettling, especially for men with a lifetime of footplate work behind them. (Their feelings and reactions are discussed in later chapters.) In this chapter the purpose is to describe the type and level of steam activity on the Southern during 1966 and 1967 as was intended by the working timetables of the period, and the reality as determined by locomotive availability and the intervention of people 'behind the scenes'.

At the beginning of 1966, Southern steam operation was focussed on the main line from Waterloo to Southampton, Bournemouth and Weymouth. Nearly all the express and semi-

65

fast passenger trains were scheduled for steam haulage, as well as many of the local stopping trains. The exceptions here were the Woking - Basingstoke locals which were mainly operated by Western diesel mechanical multiple units (dmmus) and, of course, the electrified services in the London suburban area. Some of the Waterloo - Salisbury workings were also steam worked, over this remaining Southern controlled part of the former LSWR main line to Exeter and the West Country. By 1966 all through workings to Exeter were in the hands of 'Warship' diesel hydraulics of the Western Region, operating a two-hourly semi-fast service, serving the stations west of Salisbury that had not been closed since the WR takeover. This was a poor substitute for the SR steam expresses of the period before 1964, but at least there were still some steam departures from Waterloo carrying the traditional West of England headcode of two white discs, one just below the chimney, and one above the centre of the buffer beam. These were the services which operated between London and Salisbury only, particularly during the morning and evening peaks, some of which remained steam worked until July 1967. Indeed there was still a single booked steam turn on to the Western, the 18.10 Salisbury to Yeovil passenger, the engine of which worked back on the 20.23 Yeovil Junction - Waterloo vans. That lasted until March 4th, when Salisbury shed's 'West Country' class No. 34108 *Wincanton* performed the final rites.

Apart from these two main lines, there were other examples of steam passenger operation. The branch lines from Wareham to Swanage and from Brockenhurst to Lymington were still exclusively steam worked, by Standard or ex-LMSR Ivatt tank engines. The line from Clapham junction to Kensington Olympia also saw steam in a small way. In the morning and evening peaks two steam trains operated, providing a service for Post Office employees, which was not advertised in the public timetables. There were also a few steam turns on the line from Portsmouth to Eastleigh, mainly for the benefit of workers from the SR's Eastleigh plant. Lastly, despite the dieselisation of the 'Pines Express', the cross-country route from Reading to Basingstoke still saw regular steam operation of the York - Poole through train and its return. Rather strangely this remained steam powered until September 1966 and brought the daily spectacle of a Banbury 'Black 5' from the London Midland Region to the south coast.

The only part of the Southern Region where steam reigned supreme was the Isle of Wight. The once extensive network of Island railways was already much reduced by the mid-sixties, but the lines from Ryde to Cowes and Ventnor still survived for passenger and freight traffic. Isolated from the mainland's mania for modernisation, the elderly class '02' tank engines and equally venerable rolling stock plied on with no apparent intention of surrendering. Sadly, the Island branches were continuing to wither and steam, too, would shortly perish. The Cowes line was closed to passenger traffic on February 20th 1966 and April 17th was the last day for the furthest section of the other line, involving the closure of Wroxall and Ventnor stations. The remaining stretch from Ryde Pier Head to Shanklin remained under steam operation until the end of 1966, when it was closed for three months to enable it to be electrified. Thus the Island's railways paralleled those of the mainland in motive power transition.

Apart from the areas mentioned where steam provided a regular or occasional passenger service, there were also one or two areas of the Southern which saw steam passenger trains intermittently. A good example was the coastal line from Cosham to Havant and thence via Barnham to Brighton. Just before Christmas 1965, the daily through trains between Brighton and Plymouth reverted from diesel to steam haulage.

The reason for this was a problem with heating the train during the winter months. The Southern Region had very few sets of electrically heated carriages, but its fleet of Type '3' diesel locomotives were only equipped with electric rather than steam heating. On the line from Victoria to Oxted the problem had been overcome by borrowing two special boiler vans from the LMR to be used with the Type '3' diesels and steam heated carriages. But the vans proved unreliable and so it was decided to transfer the electrically heated carriages from the Plymouth train to the Oxted line. This ruled out diesel haulage of the Plymouth train, although the operating authorities did not want to run steam over the electrified Central Division. Attempts to use the former SR electric locomotives, which did have steam heating, between Brighton and Havant proved unsuccessful, and so steam recaptured some lost ground. At first an electric locomotive was diagrammed to work the 10.25 from Brighton as far as Chichester, where steam would take over for the run via Havant, Fareham and Netley to Salisbury. On the return working, the 10.55 from Plymouth, steam was booked from Salisbury right through to Brighton, the engine to return light to Fratton for overnight stabling. By the first week in January 1966, this arrangement had been abandoned, and the steam locomotive was running down from Fratton at 06.00 to Brighton to work the 10.25 to Salisbury, and then returning as described above, head-ing back to Fratton which was reached at 20.12. A variety of Bulleid light pacifics and Standards were used, such as No. 34014 *Budleigh Salterton* on January 22nd and No. 73118 two days earlier. This arrangement involved four hours of light engine running daily, the price to pay for working steam into an area where it was no longer catered for. It continued until the end of the 'winter', as far as train heating was concerned, and diesel operation resumed on May 2nd. Sadly the following winter did not see a resumption of steam working!

In the course of its journey from Brighton to Salisbury, that working also brought steam hauled passengers over the otherwise completely dieselised Fareham to St. Denys link and likewise between Redbridge and Tunnel Junction on the outskirts of Salisbury. Lines such as these did tend to receive steam passenger trains at weekends though, due to rerouting of the main line services arising from engineering works. The line from Woking to Winchester via Alton and Alresford (now operated in part by the Mid-Hants Railway), was a favourite diversionary route. The spectacle of steam hauled expresses on the single track, provided a dramatic contrast with the usual two-car Hampshire demus. The other main diversionary route from Woking was down the Portsmouth main line via Guildford to Havant and then across the northside of the Cosham triangle to Fareham and thence by way of Eastleigh or Netley, to regain the main line. Both diversionary routes involved demanding work for the engines and crews, with Guildford shed being called upon to provide pilot engines and relief men. The climb from Alton to Medstead was a particularly tough proposition, and several times proved the undoing of steam workings. On October 2nd 1966 for example, 'West Country' No. 34025 *Whimple* stalled while working the 10.30 Waterloo - Weymouth. There was a two hour delay before Type '3' diesel D6539 arrived from Guildford to provide assistance. On another occasion the same Bulleid pacific slithered to a halt in the middle of the night at much the same place with the 02.25 Waterloo - Poole newspaper train. It had to wait until the following train, hauled by a 'Warship' diesel, was able to buffer up to the rear and get the steam train moving. Delays such as these meant late newspaper deliveries in the Southampton and Bournemouth areas and caused much bad publicity in the local newspapers.

The 'down' 'Bournemouth Belle' takes one of its occasional Sunday detours down the Portsmouth line and heads south from Guildford on March 13th 1966 with 'West Country' class No. 34017 *Ilfracombe* in charge.   *Roy Bicknell*

'West Country' class No. 34102 *Lapford* restarts from a water stop at Guildford on June 11th 1967 with the diverted 06.00 Weymouth Quay-Waterloo boat train.   *Roy Bicknell*

These maps are taken from the 1966 edition of the Southern Region's working timetables and show the majority of the lines mentioned in the text which saw steam working in the final months.

MAP OF LINES
INCLUDED IN
WORKING TIMETABLE
SECTION D

- - - - SINGLE LINES

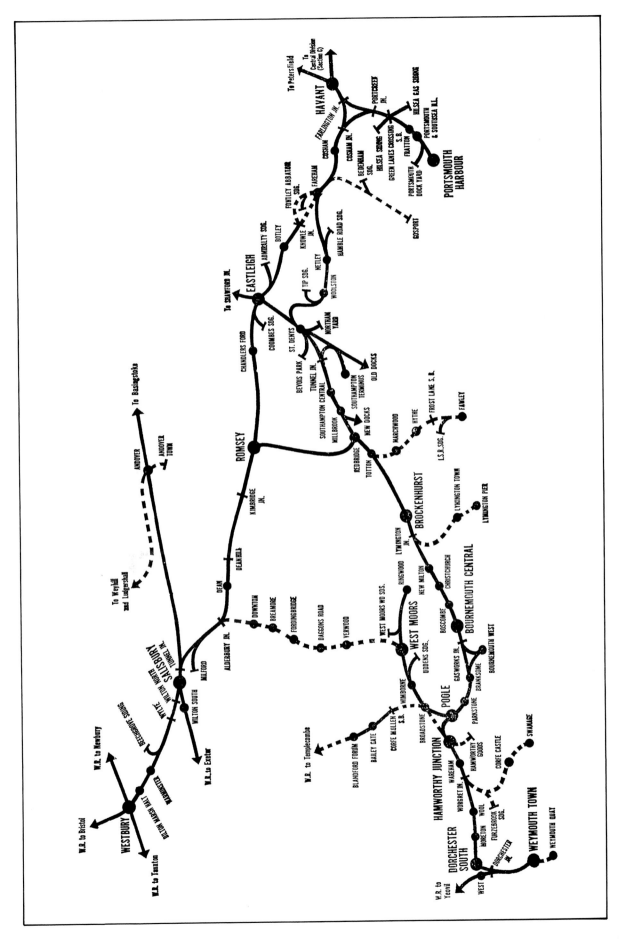

However, for the enthusiast, such meanderings off the main line were a special delight. Armies of cameramen and tape-recordists would line the track from Alton to Itchen Abbas on weekends when steam was due to run. During 1966 two days stood out as being of particular interest. The sunlit Mayday was notable for the routing of all 'down' trains up to and including the 20.30 ex-Waterloo over the Alton line. Under ideal conditions for photography, the 09.33 from London hammered its way up Medstead bank emitting columns of black smoke from its double-headed team of standard '5' No. 73169 and 'Battle of Britain' No. 34077 *603 Squadron*. The 10.30 made a similarly impressive departure from Alton under the charge of 'Merchant Navy' No. 35008 *Orient Line*, while a welcome sight was unrebuilt 'West Country' No. 34002 *Salisbury* on the 11.30 from Waterloo. The only major disappointment was that the 'Bournemouth Belle', which had been steam hauled the previous Sunday, turned up behind the Brush diesel normally allocated to the 13.30 working. No doubt this was the work of one of the more diesel-minded clerks in the diagram office at Wimbledon, who was anxious to avoid the need for double-heading with steam on such a heavy train.

However, it was victory for the "puffer-nutters" on another Sunday, September 18th. On that occasion, not only was the 'Belle' rostered for steam over the Mid-Hants, but it was provided in the shape of unrebuilt 'West Country', No. 34102 *Lapford*, a type rarely seen on the Pullmans. If that wasn't enough, Guildford shed had been primed to provide a pilot steam engine, none other than the little No. 77014, unique on the Southern Region. As it did not have a bracket on its smokebox in the right position to carry a headcode disc, the white circle was painted on in the appropriate position! Many photographers turned out to record this spectacle, some forewarned by the enterprising man who had diagrammed the whole operation from the control office at Wimbledon.

The 'Belle' undoubtedly brought a touch of class to the Bournemouth line. Its opulence may well have been faded, but the assemblage of Pullman cars in their distinctive brown and cream livery, had a dignity and charm all of their own. Sadly, the brake Pullmans with guard's accommodation disappeared from the scene during 1966, necessitating ordinary luggage vans to be marshalled at each end of the train. They were painted in the then new blue British Rail colours, which clashed unaesthetically with the Pullmans. That apart, the nightly routine of the up 'Belle' running into Southampton Central, brightened the home-going of local commuters as it rolled into platform 1 at about 17.10. Many an envious inspection of the carriage interiors evoked desires of a leisurely evening meal up to town in the comfort of an armchair, instead of the spartan provision of, say, the 17.20 demu to Portsmouth. As the train stopped the smartly uniformed attendants would stand on the running steps of each carriage, to assist passengers on or off the train. The cars also displayed metal squares, bearing letters of the alphabet, on brackets beside the doors, so holders of reserved seats could find their place quickly. To travel on the train it was necessary to purchase a supplementary ticket, which indicated the coach letter and seat. For the short run up from Bournemouth only an extra 2 shillings (10p) was charged, which gave the opportunity for an afternoon tea, Pullman style, for just 3/6d. However, it had to be consumed in about 25-30 minutes as the 'Belle' sprinted up through the New Forest, black smoke rolling back from the Bulleid's chimney, as it recovered after the difficult climb up to New Milton. At this late stage, the 450 tons of train was a demanding proposition, with locomotives no longer at their best.

It came as little surprise that the train was handed over to diesel haulage from the beginning of 1967, proving little problem for a Brush type '4' diesel, although once or twice steam returned to the duty, due to non-availability of the diesel, even in the very last week of steam on the Southern.

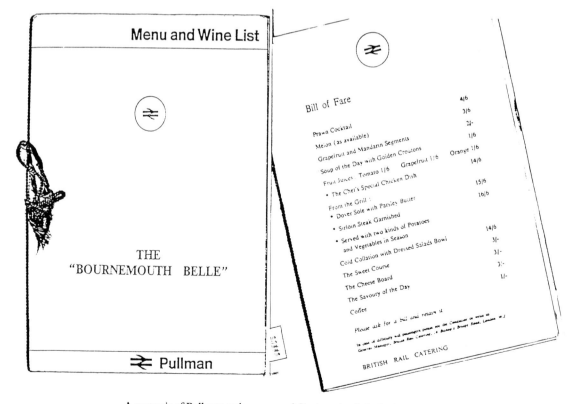

A souvenir of Pullman style . . . . . and Sixties prices! *Author's collection*

Strange companions at Waterloo in the shape of 'Black 5' No. 45349 and 2-BIL emu No. 2058 at the rear of an earlier arrival. The ex-LMSR locomotive was working the 09.30 to Bournemouth on June 22nd 1966.   *Ray Ruffell*

The 08.30 Newcastle-Poole rattles through St. Denys behind regular performer No. 45493 on July 2nd 1966. Note the gas lamps and SR style signs which were replaced soon after by electric lamps and standard BR 'station furniture'.   *Author*

The yielding by steam to diesel on the 'Bournemouth Belle' was symptomatic of the gradual but persistent decline of steam operation during the final eighteen months. Whereas steam had predominated in the early part of 1966, as already described, it was not long before changes began. The Brush Type '4' which reached the Southern daily on the 'Pines Express' was put to good use overnight from February 7th. It was given a diagram which took it up to Eastleigh for refuelling and then it took over the 20.30 from Bournemouth up to Waterloo, returning on the 02.15 Weymouth newspaper train as far as Bournemouth, ready for the 'Pines'. On Sundays when the inter-regional train did not operate, the Brush saw daylight operation from Waterloo with the 13.30 to Weymouth, the first major steam express to succumb.

A less dramatic diesel takeover came about on May 16th when the 07.30 Woking – Basingstoke stopper was taken over by a Western dmmu. The real significance of this change was that it ended the last booked passenger working by an ex-Southern Mogul, as it had been rostered for one of Guildford's dwindling 'N' class 2-6-0s. In fact, the appearance of an 'N' had been infrequent latterly, with their complete withdrawal only a month away. However, 'U' class No. 31791 was reported as working the 07.20 Waterloo – Salisbury as late as April 22nd, possibly the last ordinary passenger working by a Mogul out of London.

An interesting working which had appeared by now, was the use made on Sundays of the ex-LMSR 'Black 5' off the York – Poole train. Instead of laying over at Bournemouth shed, it was utilised on the 08.55 up to London, returning on the 20.30 from Waterloo. Whether the LMR knew of the extra mileage being extracted from its locomotive is unknown, but it added to the diversity of operation that characterised the Southern in its last year. Amazingly enough this rostering continued when the summer timetable became operational, even though virtually all the other Sunday main line trains were dieselised with Type '3s'. The 'Belle' was entrusted to a pair of diesels, which put in some spritely performances with almost as much power as a 'Deltic' available.

Saturdays were not so easy to dieselise as Sundays. In the summer there were far more trains to operate, including through trains to Lymington and Swanage, as well as extra cross-country workings through Southampton. It seemed to prove necessary to run a number of special freights as well, and any steam lover worth his salt in the diagramming office would ensure that these were assigned to diesels! This left more passenger work to be covered by steam. It soon showed if a particular clerk was on holiday, for if one of his less steam orientated colleagues took over, the change to diesel on the motive power front was quickly noticed. On a typical summer Saturday about half the main-line passenger movements to and from Waterloo were likely to be steam at this stage. An observer at Worting Junction, west of Basingstoke, noted thirty-seven steam engine movements during a ten hour period on July 2nd. These comprised fourteen 'West Country' and 'Battle of Britain' class 4-6-2s, nine 'Merchant Navies', twelve Standards and two 'Black 5s'.

During the summer months there were occasional shortages of Bulleid pacifics, when Standard class '5s' had to step in. At times it seemed to fans of the pacifics that someone was deliberately putting the smaller BR engines on to important expresses in an act of petty vindictiveness. But the reality was that the Bulleids were not standing up as well to the Standards to the decline in maintenance and overhauls. On July 21st even the 09.30 Waterloo – Bournemouth found itself underpowered, worked by a 'Black 5', No. 44710, which was extremely unusual on a weekday.

Probably the best time to see a lot of steam passenger trains at Waterloo was now the evening peak period. Especially on a

Friday evening when there were several extras, it was possible to see no less than ten steam departures between 17.30 and 19.30, plus the added bonus of the arrival of the 'Belle'. These comprised three trains to Salisbury, usually worked by the superbly clean locomotives returning to their home depot. There were four Bournemouth fasts, one to Weymouth and a relief boat train to Weymouth Quay, as well as a stopper to Basingstoke. Not surprisingly many photographers turned out after work on pleasant summer evenings to record this feast of steam activity.

The end of the 1966 summer timetable saw a number of significant changes in the pattern of steam operation. The Newcastle - Poole cross-country service which had brought LMR 'Black 5s' to the Southern was diverted away from the former Great Central route in the Midlands, with the closure of much of that main line from the first weekend in September. A wide assortment of 4-6-0s had worked the turn during the previous twelve months, starting with WR 'Hall' class, and then Stanier 'Black 5s'. Two frequent performers were Nos. 44942 and 45493, both of which were usually very clean and tidy compared to many of the other scruffy examples which appeared. Detailed records kept by Mr. C. Stone and Dr. Jim Boudreau suggest that at least thirty-five different members of the class were involved in the working during 1966. The last to be seen was No. 45132 on September 2nd. One of the more interesting variations was the employment of Stanier '8F' 2-8-0 No. 48276 which worked south on February 22nd 1966, the use of a heavy freight locomotive on passenger duty being very unusual. Equally surprising was the use of Standard '9F' No. 92002 which appeared on the northbound train on August 20th, and reportedly kept very good time all the way to Banbury. Photographers turning out to record what was expected to be the last LMR powered turns on September 3rd were faced with disappointment however; Bulleid pacifics Nos. 34005 and 34034 shared the honours.

The same day also marked the end of another chapter of railway history. The original country terminus of the London and Southampton Railway closed after 127 years, together with

The last steam departure from Southampton Terminus on the day of its closure (September 3rd 1966) was the 16.02 stopper to Bournemouth, hauled by No.76061.   *Author*

the adjacent station at Northam. Although the Terminus, with its classically styled building, was much less used than the Central station, by virtue of being off the main line and its express services, it retained some local demu services and was the starting point for many of the stopping services to Bournemouth. Indeed, its last steam working was one such, the 16.02 to Bournemouth Central, which was powered by No. 76061. It carried a small black and white plaque on the front buffer beam, commemorating the significance of the event. Although Southampton Terminus station closed that night, the track thence to Northam Junction remained open for traffic to Southampton Eastern Docks (see later in the chapter) and the station was itself specially reopened at Christmas to handle the glut of seasonal mail traffic.

The weekend also meant the end of one of the last steam branch services in the country. The picturesque 11¼ mile line from Wareham to Swanage through the Isle of Purbeck retained a traditional byway atmosphere. It was usually worked by Standard '4' and Ivatt '2' tanks from Bournemouth which used the small stone engine shed at Swanage for servicing and overnight stabling. On summer Saturdays there was sufficient patronage for two through workings from Waterloo in the 1966 season. These were mainly Type '3' diesel hauled, but Bulleid pacifics also took a share of the work.

The branch service was scheduled for dieselisation from Monday September 5th, and so its summer only Sunday services on the previous day were the last normal steam passenger working on the branch. Standard class '4' No. 76010 with two Bulleid

Above: Memories of the Swanage branch are roused by the sight of class '4' tank No. 80134 running round its two Bulleid coaches at Wareham on August 31st 1966, a couple of days before the service was dieselised. *Author*

Left: There were occasional steam visits to the Swanage branch right up to the end of Southern steam with the morning freight working to Furzebrook sidings. Seen here is 'West Country' class No. 34025 *Whimple* at Furzebrook on June 30th 1967. *G.M. Moon*

carriages was in action that day, while the 18.12 Swanage - Eastleigh stopper, rostered for a Brush '4' diesel, was taken through by Standard tank No. 80140. There was a fair turn out by enthusiasts for the final day (see chapter five), and the last trip of the evening, the 20.14 from Swanage, was crowded, with No. 76010 marking the end of steam services. Nevertheless steam did manage to penetrate the branch until the following summer on freight trips and on several rail tours. It has been generally argued that the last steam working on the line was a freight from Furzebrook sidings on June 30th 1967. However, Michael Hardy claims to have seen 'West Country' No. 34021 on the same duty, hauling clay wagons, on Friday July 7th, the last weekday of Southern steam operation. His recollection is supported in two ways. Firstly, another enthusiast saw the same locomotive leaving Poole for Wareham early that morning with freight wagons. Secondly, Mr. Hardy spent the following Sunday in Boscombe Hospital receiving treatment for damage to his ankle, sustained when he fell from his photographic position at the top of an embankment at Furzebrook! It is heartening, three decades later, to be able to travel once again from Swanage to Corfe Castle and beyond, by courtesy of the supreme efforts of the preservationists.

The autumn of 1966 saw further decline on the steam front as full electrification loomed only nine months away, yet the English climate and technology limitations would once again revive some steam influence. The winter service brought again the need for train heating but the Type '3' diesels could only operate with electrically heated stock. The newly delivered 'TC' coaching sets were suitable but insufficient in number, although since August 15th a Type '3' and 'TC' set combination had been working a diagram which included the 09.30 Waterloo - Bournemouth. This situation would have guaranteed extensive employment for steam had the operating authorities not intervened. They were not happy with entrusting the winter service to the ailing Bulleids and Standards, and as explained in chapter eight the decision was taken to bring some WR Brush type '4'

diesel electric locomotives to help out. As they were equipped with steam heating boilers, they were not ruled out like the Type '3s'. Fortunately they were not totally reliable and this allowed steam to continue, albeit in an unpredictable pattern.

No. D1921 was noted at Pirbright junction on September 19th on one of a series of crew-training trips. It was soon joined by Nos. D1922-6 and D1928 over the next three months. As a result steam working took a heavy hammering from October 3rd. On weekdays the 08.30, 16.35 ('Royal Wessex') and 17.30 departures from Waterloo were assigned to Brush diesels together with balancing up duties, with similar rosters at weekends. However, the availability of the diesels was not good initially and there were many steam substitutions. Even Standard class '4' 4-6-0s found themselves on regular mainline work, such as No. 75074 on the 19.30 Waterloo - Weymouth on October 30th, and the same engine on the 15.23 Bournemouth - Waterloo on November 19th. With a number of 'Merchant Navies' out of use, including No. 35026 *Lamport & Holt Line* which spent nearly a week away on northern rail tour duty, it was a dire time on the motive power scene.

However, the problems with the diesels were gradually resolved as the full batch of six became available, and this allowed the authorities to plan for a further reduction of steam activity from the beginning of the New Year. Yet, as described in the previous chapter, it was also necessary to reinstate ten steam locomotives to cope with the extra demands of the Christmas period! The new rosters from January 2nd saw the end of planned steam haulage of the 'Bournemouth Belle', a particularly sad decision, although an understandable one in view of the motive power situation. That had been highlighted on December 29th, when the 'down' 'Belle' had made a disastrous journey under steam. At its head at Waterloo was an indescribably filthy and virtually unidentifiable 'Battle of Britain', No. 34077. The task of hauling the Pullmans was clearly beyond it on that day, and after a normal start as far as Esher, where 59 mph was attained, speed began to decline down to 42 mph at Woking, with the climb to

Diesel to the rescue of steam on December 29th 1966. The ailing 'Battle of Britain' class No. 34077 *603 Squadron* at Southampton Central on the 'down' 'Bournemouth Belle' has been hauled from Farnborough by Type '3' No. D6549.   *Author*

Approach to Waterloo by steam . . . . 'Battle of Britain' class No. 34060 *25 Squadron* rounds the curves near the terminus with the 11.18 Weymouth-Waterloo on June 29th 1967. Note the variety of coaching stock, with a blue and grey liveried example between the SR and BR designs in green.
Author

Hustle and bustle in the sidings down the line at Clapham Junction attract the interest of the spectators. A variety of coaching stock and pilot duties occupy the attentions of four Standard tank engines.
Mike Esau

Above: Isle of Wight steam memories . . . . the smallness of Smallbrook Junction signalbox is apparent as 'O2' No. 31 *Chale* passes with a Ryde-Shanklin service during 1966.

Dr. L.A. Nixon

Left: Nestling beneath the Downs, Ventnor station seems to have been untouched by the years of nationalisation judging by this view on April 9th 1966. No. 29 *Alverstone* has recently arrived from Ryde and is about to run-round its train.

P.J. Lynch

milepost 31 looming ahead. A few miles beyond Brookwood the 'Belle' ground to a halt in disgrace, while the crew of the Bulleid tried to raise some steam. A twenty minute 'blow-up' got the Pullmans moving again but only at about 30 mph and after another stop, Farnborough was reached where fortunately assistance was waiting. The pilot turned out to be Type '3' diesel No. D6549, but the steam locomotive was retained through to Bournemouth, presumably to provide steam heating for the unfortunate samplers of the luxuries of Pullman travel!

Arrival at Southampton was 45 minutes late, where the unusual motive power caused much interest. Although a steam pilot would have been more photogenic, the combination of the diesel and steam locomotives at the front end provided a poignant image of the surrender of steam to diesel on the 'Belle' which was to follow just three days later. Under the new diagrams, apart from the loss of the 'Belle' to steam, other changes meant that only seven 'down' Bournemouth line departures from Waterloo would now be steam booked, as against nine for diesel power. At the same time electric working of some services between Basingstoke – Woking – Waterloo was introduced, emphasising that the final death throes of Southern steam were not far away in the coming months of 1967.

Steam had actually succumbed on the Isle of Wight, during the last weekend of 1966. Since the withdrawal of passenger trains to Cowes and the closure of Ventnor and Wroxall stations, earlier in the year, the truncated 8½ miles between Ryde Pier Head and Shanklin were all that remained. Steam services continued with vigour in their final 'Indian summer' and on high season Saturdays there were an incredible 87 advertised passenger runs along the mainly single-track line. This represented eight trains an hour calling at an intermediate station such as Brading for much of a summer Saturday. The workings required ten class 'O2' in action, which with only eleven left was stretching availability to its uttermost limits. That these workings were largely adhered to is another tribute to the outstanding railwaymen of the Isle of Wight already effectively recorded in other books.

Mention must be made of the famous, but minute, signalbox at Smallbrook Junction, which was needed to control the intersection of the Cowes line with the Shanklin line. The signalmen must have been relieved that 1966 was their quietest year ever, as they did not have the Cowes passenger service to worry about as well! The 'box was closed down for the last time at the end of the summer season, signal arms being removed and the Newport and Cowes line being designated as a siding. However,

the Newport line had seen *some* use during the summer of 1966. Freight was still handled at Newport and Medina Wharf, where locomotive coal was landed. Also the impending electrification required the movement of equipment such as conductor rails from the mainland, and this was brought over from Redbridge to the Wharf and then worked up to Ryde.

From September onwards a much reduced service was operated. It was basically hourly and trains crossed at each end of the line only. Just three engines were needed to maintain this pattern. From October the Pier tracks were taken out of use at Ryde to allow reconstruction prior to electrification. This meant a new form of working as services now began from Ryde Esplanade where there were no run-round facilities. The procedure was for trains up from Shanklin to attach an engine at the rear at Ryde St. Johns Road, to enable it to lead for the return journey. The original train engine would then drop off at St. Johns, to be serviced, before buffering up to the rear of the next up service. This required three engines minimum, with trains now passing at Sandown. However, there was usually a fourth in steam for shunting or works trains, and as a standby. On October 8th, for example, Nos. 24, 27 and 33 were in charge of the passenger services with No. 20 in reserve.

The steam-free future of the Isle of Wight was portended on October 7th when a diesel shunter, No. D2554, arrived on the back of a Pickfords' trailer having travelled on the Fishbourne car ferry. This was followed in the ensuing months by the shipment of the 'new' ex-Tube trains which as relative veterans themselves, were destined to replace the vintage steam stock. The final day for steam services was set for the last day of the year, leaving an interval of about 10 weeks with no trains at all, while electrification was carried out.

For the last day, six 'O2s' were steamed, being Nos. 14, 17, 24, 27, 28 and 31. A wreath and suitable notices were carried on the front of No. 17 which worked the 10.30 Ryde Esplanade – Shanklin and the subsequent 14.30 as well. The LCGB farewell special had to be fitted in to the hourly interval service, and this was accomplished by using the stock of the 11.45 ex-Shanklin hauled by No. 17. At St. Johns Road the tour engines, Nos. 24 and 31, were attached to the rear, ready for subsequent departure from Ryde Esplanade at 12.16, making the unusual spectacle of three engines working five carriages! After the special had departed, in very dull and wet weather, there had to be a special working of empty stock up to Esplanade in time for the 12.30 departure to Shanklin, another example of smart operating on the Island.

There were many enthusiasts out for the last day, as well as Islanders, of course, for whom the steam railways always held a special affection. The sight of the immaculate shiny, black Nos. 31/24 returning from Brading with the railtour was unforgettable. By then the weather had been transformed, providing a beautiful crisp sunny day, for the Wight steam finale. That was not quite the end, for these same two 'O2s' were retained in service for the benefit of the engineers working on the electrification. However, one of their most sombre duties was to haul their erstwhile tank engine compatriots up to Newport for storage and eventual scrapping, as well as most of the carriages and some wagons. The last two 'O2s', their work completed, were withdrawn from March 19th, 1967.

Wroxall station closed on April 17th 1966 when services were withdrawn between Shanklin and Ventnor. Its days were numbered when No. 35 *Freshwater* departed with a train from Ryde on April 9th. *P.J. Lynch*

77

By spring time on the mainland, another and momentous stage in the disappearance of steam working was about to unfold. As described in chapter eight, the conductor rails to Bournemouth were energised during March, and test running soon started. From April 3rd, new rosters were introduced with electric services to Bournemouth from Waterloo for the first time. Of course, had there been sufficient electric stock, it would have been possible to eliminate virtually all steam working but as yet only a few electric trains had been delivered. The steam booked weekday passenger turns in the 'down' direction were now reduced to those shown in Table 6.

It will be noted that of the forty-one rostered workings, nineteen were west of Eastleigh, and only eleven ran east of Basingstoke, apart from the three Fridays only extras. Similar patterns would emerge from a study of the 'up' direction steam workings. Undoubtedly the focus of interest for steam working for the last three months would be on the Eastleigh – Southampton – Bournemouth – Weymouth corridor, at least, if the diagrammers hopes were fulfilled! On paper the 05.30, 08.30, 09.30, 10.30, 11.30, 12.30, 13.30, 15.30, 15.35, 16.35, 17.30, 18.30, 19.30 and 21.20 mainline departures from Waterloo were all allocated to either electric multiple unit, electro-diesel locomotive or Type '4'

Table 6
Rostered Down Weekday Steam Turns
from April 3rd 1967

01.57	Eastleigh – Portsmouth Harbour	70D	Std. '4' 2-6-4T		13.08	Bournemouth – Weymouth	70C	Std. '4' 2-6-0
02.30	Waterloo – Portsmouth Harbour	70A	'WC'		15.01	Bournemouth – Weymouth	70F	'WC'
02.45	Waterloo – Bournemouth	70F	'WC'		14.02	Eastleigh – Bournemouth	70F	Std. '4' 2-6-4T
03.40	Waterloo – Basingstoke (from Woking)	70C	Std. '5'		16.03	Brockenhurst – Christchurch	70F	'WC'
04.40	Waterloo – Woking	70A	Std. '5'		17.02	Bournemouth – Dorchester S'th	70F	Std. '4' 2-6-4T
		70F	'WC' (Mons)		16.20	Southampton – Bournemouth	70D	Std. '4' 4-6-0
07.08	Bournemouth – Weymouth				16.22	Eastleigh – Bournemouth	70D	Std. '4' 2-6-4T
05.49	Eastleigh – Weymouth (from B'mouth)	70F	Std. '4' 2-6-4T		17.16	Southampton – Bournemouth	70D	Std. '4' 2-6-4T
05.30	Waterloo – Weymouth (from B'mouth)	70F	Std. '4' 2-6-4T		17.20	Eastleigh – Fratton	70D	Std. '4' 2-6-4T
06.30	Woking – Salisbury	70A	Std. '5'		16.51	Basingstoke – Salisbury	70C	Std. '4' 2-6-0
		70F	'WC' (Mons)		18.30	Southampton – Bournemouth	70F	Std. '4' 2-6-4T
07.56	Brockenhurst – Bournemouth	70F	Std. '4' 2-6-4T		17.09	Waterloo – Basingstoke	70E	'WC'
08.29	Eastleigh – Bournemouth	70F	Std. '4' 2-6-0		17.23	Waterloo – Bournemouth (FO)	70A	'WC'
07.18	Waterloo – Salisbury	70D	Std. '4' 4-6-0		19.06	Basingstoke – Southampton	70A	'MN'
08.10	Waterloo – Weymouth Quay	70A	'WC'		19.11	Basingstoke – Salisbury	70F	'WC'
08.16	Clapham Jct. – Kensington Olymp.	70A	Std. '4' 2-6-4T		18.22	Waterloo – Bournemouth (FO)	70D	'WC'
08.30	Waterloo – Weymouth (from B'mouth)	70F	Std. '4' 2-6-0		18.30	Waterloo – Weymouth (from B'mouth)	70A	'MN'
08.35	Waterloo – Weymouth	70A	'MN'		18.54	Waterloo – Basingstoke	70A	'MN'
08.46	Clapham Jct. – Kensington Olymp.	70A	Std. '4' 2-6-4T		19.50	Eastleigh – Bournemouth	70A	'WC'
09.20	Waterloo – Soton W. Docks (FO)	70D	'WC'		22.35	Waterloo – Weymouth (from E'leigh)	70A	'WC'
10.43	Southampton – Bournemouth	70C	Std. '4' 2-6-0					

One of the commuter trains which remained steam worked in 1967 was the 07.05 Basingstoke-Waterloo. On May 10th 'West Country' class No. 34025 *Whimple* was greeted by briefcases and business suits on arrival at Farnborough. *Ray Ruffell*

High noon at Bournemouth Central: the clock up in the remains of the overall roof greets the arrival of the 10.43 stopping train from Southampton on April 4th 1967, over which class '5' No. 73065 had charge. Unusually it is carrying a lamp rather than disc headcode, despite this being a daylight hours working. *Author*

'Merchant Navy' class No. 35008 *Orient Line*, nameplateless but clean, crosses the river Test and nears Redbridge with the 17.30 Weymouth-Waterloo on May 27th 1967. *Author*

Further west, in ex-GWR territory, Standard class '4' No. 76031 slows for Upwey and Broadway station with the 16.47 Weymouth-Bournemouth on July 7th 1966.   *John Scrace*

On the SR's only other steam worked main line (and only on some services), double-chimneyed class '4' 4-6-0 No. 75068 passes Tunnel Junction, Salisbury with the 16.51 from Basingstoke on March 21st 1967.   *David M. Smith*

The headcode carried by Standard class '4' tank No. 80151 indicates a train terminating at Portsmouth and Southsea. In fact this particular working only carried passengers as far as Fratton, being the 17.20 from Eastleigh seen departing from Fareham on March 21st 1967. This service was mainly provided for homegoing employees from Eastleigh Works, and brought a rare whiff of steam to the Botley line to relieve the normal diet of diesel units.

Author

diesel operation. Steam's surrender appeared to be nearly at hand.

However, steam did not disappear from the weekday express scene as easily as intended. During April there were numerous examples of the booked Type '4' diesels not appearing, to be replaced by pacifics or standards. There were only three 'Merchant Navy' diagrams now, and these comprised secondary passenger and parcels turns. As a result the 'Merchant Navies' could assume a standby role at Nine Elms, where they had just been transferred from Weymouth. On April 21st, for example, No. 35028 filled in on the 05.30 from Waterloo to Bournemouth, and then returned on the 11.07 back to London. On the same day, even more remarkably, No. 35030 managed two return trips to Bournemouth, its departures from the Capital being on the 08.30 and the 18.30 services. Also, the 'Royal Wessex' (16.35 from Waterloo), rostered as an electro-diesel locomotive and 'TC' sets, was returned to ordinary stock and steam haulage several times, No. 35007 being in charge on three consecutive days in mid-April.

Even the 'Bournemouth Belle' managed to retain occasional steam haulage throughout the period from January to July. Notable occasions were on February 24th, when a spotless unrebuilt 'West Country' No. 34006 took the 'down' working, and May 4th when unrebuilts Nos. 34023 and 34057 shared the 'up' and 'down' runs. There were sporadic episodes of steam haulage of the 'Belle' right through to the last week of its existence.

There were also a few instances of steam substitutions on the inter-regional trains during April and May. Ever since the demise of the LMR 'Black 5s' on the Poole – York (Newcastle in the summer months), the train had been rostered for a Bournemouth 'West Country' between Poole and Basingstoke. From March 6th however, the services were recast with extra services between the south coast and Birmingham. On March 4th, 'WC' No. 34004 was turned out for the last official steam run of the York train, henceforward it should have been diesel worked throughout and running at new times. As might be expected this did not always happen, and steam not only filled in but even worked right through to Reading from time to time. Given that steam had been banned on the Western since December 31st 1965, these occurrences were really rather extraordinary. The late John Fairman, a meticulous recorder of the Southern steam scene, who was working at Reading at the time, noted several appearances by steam during the spring of 1967. The last steam visit *he* noted was on May 19th, when he recorded 'Merchant Navy' No. 35030 arriving at Reading General on the northbound train.

Reading was also reached from the Southern via the cross-country route from Guildford and Redhill. There was a little steam penetration during 1966/67, usually following diesel failures, but rarely involving passenger duties. For example, on November 16th 1966, Standard '4' No.76031 was sent up from Guildford in

81

place of a Type '3' diesel to take the through parcels vans from Blisworth. It worked through to Redhill and then travelled light engine to Norwood to turn on the Selhurst triangle. This meant a rare visit by steam to the Central Division of the Southern.

Two weeks later another Standard appeared at Reading, but this time on passenger duty! It was the turn of No. 76033 which was turned out for the 17.09 service to Redhill, again in the place of a failed diesel. There were very few instances of steam passenger operation in 1967, until the very last weeks of steam. Then on June 16th, the 16.34 Redhill – Reading train was assigned to Standard '5' No. 73018, which had arrived on parcels duty. This was almost certainly the last steam passenger working over the route. It should be recorded that there were also occasional steam freight workings into Reading, both from Basingstoke and from Guildford, and always due to unavailability of diesel power. Thus, there was an afternoon BP oil tank train, which sometimes produced steam haulage, as with No. 76067 on May 1st 1967, and unrebuilt 'WC' No. 34102 on May 19th.

Probably the saddest event in the motive power reorganisation of April 1967 was the end of steam on the Lymington branch. With electric services commencing on the main line it was not surprising that a steam connection at Brockenhurst was thought anachronistic. Yet the line was not yet ready for electric services,

so a 'Hampshire' diesel unit was drafted in on a temporary basis, electric services not beginning for another month. The last day of steam working was Sunday, April 2nd, with Ivatt '2' 2-6-2T No. 41312 working the final services.

The accolade 'Britain's last steam branch' was surely correct for this single-track meander through the New Forest. It had a special charm all of its own, a family feeling brought about by its regular team of footplate men and guards. The last train was driven by Bert Farley, with Ray Glassey doing the firing. The pair of them had been regular mates on the branch for seven years, although Driver Farley had been working it since 1947! It was a miserable wet day for the finale, but the rest of the last week had been more spring-like. The branch engines had been carrying a Ron Cover manufactured headboard proclaiming 'The Last Steam Branch'. Ron had earlier painted one in red, but this caused official complaints, so a driver repainted it in light blue and it stayed on thereafter!

The Lymington branch had been operated by two sets of men latterly, with two engines involved daily. The Ivatt normally spent most of the day on carriage shunting at Branksome, setting up formations for London bound trains. Then it ran light up to Brockenhurst for the two evening trips down the branch, ending up at Lymington Town station at 21.02. After stabling the usual two carriages, it retired to the little engine shed for the night. This was the responsibility of one of the two sets of Lymington men, whose job it was to perform minor servicing on the engine as well.

The other set of enginemen were booked on from 05.00 to light up and have the engine ready to work the 06.02 to Brockenhurst. To raise sufficient steam in under two hours was very ambitious from what was supposed to be a dead engine! It would be surprising if the tank didn't sometimes stay in light steam overnight, to ensure the first train of the morning got away on time! Overall it was very demanding work for the enginemen, for the morning set had to work through until 13.17 when they were relieved at Lymington Town. Bert Farley lived locally, but Ray Glassey had to drive in from the Southampton area which meant a very early start when he was on the morning shift. After working the first two morning trips up from Lymington, the Ivatt returned to Bournemouth to resume the daily carriage shunting duties. It changed over at Brockenhurst with a Standard '4' 2-6-4T which had come up from Bournemouth with the 06.35 local passenger. Since goods services to Lymington had ceased, coaling was no longer carried out there and so the Standard tank was required to be fully coaled at Bournemouth to last until the evening. It was a constant worry for the footplate crew whether their bunker-full of coal would last the whole day.

During the final week, there were plenty of enthusiasts about to pay their tribute to the end of branch line steam operation. For the final Sunday, special commemorative boards had been made for the buffer beam brackets of No. 41312 by members of the Portsmouth Railway Society. Ray Glassey recalls: 'We had

Right: 'The Last Steam Branch' proclaims the home-made headboard, as No. 80146 pauses in the spring sunshine at the Town station on March 29th 1967. The train is the 15.25 Lymington Pier-Brockenhurst: four days later steam working on the branch came to an end.
Author

Carrying the single disc above the centre of the buffer beam which was the headcode for the branch, No. 80032 is about to traverse the level crossing at Lymington Town on December 3rd 1966.
Author

a load of fanatics. I think they had been there all night long, sleeping in the carriages. There were about a dozen of them and they cleaned the engine and set to work with whitewash and paint!' The last runs were well covered by the media, and Bert Farley recalls having a crowded cab, with members of his family and two gentlemen of the press taking the final ride. Then that was the end of Lymington steam. A well-known driver 'The Mad Monk' arrived to work the Ivatt up to Nine Elms, its new depot, and the carriages went up to Eastleigh. For Bert it was a bottle of Scotch in the local pub and the thought of redundancy, and for Ray a transfer to Eastleigh for the death rites of Southern steam.

At Nine Elms, No. 41312 was able to take turns on what some diehards also liked to call England's last steam branch. That might not be quite true, but certainly the route from Clapham Junction to Kensington Olympia did have something of the flavour of branch working. The twice daily passenger workings over what was basically an inter-regional connecting route were not advertised in the public timetable. They were provided in the morning and evening peaks purely for the convenience of office workers and were diagrammed for Nine Elms steam power until the very end of steam working. The two evening workings from Kensington, timed variously at 16.36, 17.06 or 17.36 depending upon the day of the week, were planned for an Ivatt tank. The two morning trips from Clapham Junction at 08.16 and 08.46 were booked Standard '4' 2-6-4T turns. Thus it was a motive power recreation of the Lymington and Swanage branches, although usually with a four coach set of stock.

In fact, towards the end, Standard '3' 2-6-2Ts Nos. 82019 and 82029 frequently appeared, giving them a rare opportunity to haul carriages actually containing passengers, instead of the empties they usually plied to and from Waterloo with! Empty coaching stock (ecs) and pilot duties at Waterloo were in the hands of these three classes of Nine Elms tank engines, continuing a tradition once carried by 'M7' and WR pannier tanks in the early 1960s. After April, with the increased use of electric multiple unit stock on the Bournemouth line, the ecs needs were greatly reduced, but there were still six tank engine duties each weekday. There was also a turn for an Ivatt 2-6-2T at the depot shunting wagons of locomotive coal and stores, a duty performed at Eastleigh and Guildford sheds by 'USAs' and at Bournemouth

by one of the several tank engines otherwise occupied at the Branksome carriage sidings.

Unlike the North Eastern and London Midland regions where steam ended its days confined mainly to freight working, the Southern had already entrusted most of its non-passenger turns to diesel haulage. The steam goods duties that remained at the beginning of 1966 were mainly a few long distance freights between Feltham and Southampton Docks, and local trip working in the London suburbs, around Guildford, and on some of the secondary lines in Hampshire and Dorset. A number of parcels turns were also steam worked into 1966, but the picture was to change steadily. The main reason for this was the progressive delivery of the new electro-diesel locomotives during the year. These eliminated most of the Feltham area steam workings, and most of those previously worked from Guildford shed, including such interesting destinations as the occasional freight trips down the remains of the Meon Valley line from Alton to Farringdon.

In the working timetable for freight trains dated April 18th 1966, there were no freights designated for steam haulage at all! However, closer scrutiny shows that a number were not actually diesel rostered either: their fate being decided by what was available, and that generally meant steam. Any extra special freight or parcels workings were likely to be steam rostered too, and much of the extra weekend haulage of special traffic for engineers trains was also steam powered.

The sort of turns which appear for steam in the 1966 timetable included the 02.46 Southampton West Docks – Nine Elms and the 13.16 from the Docks to Feltham. Both were 'Q' trains, meaning that they only ran when required. The Feltham train was an express class '4' freight, therefore it was required to have at least 90% of the vehicles fitted with the automatic brake controlled by the engine, and was authorised to run at up to 50 mph. Most of the remaining steam freights were unfitted class '8s' limited to 35 mph, and comprised almost entirely of wagons fitted with handbrakes only. The sight and sound of those slow-moving goods trains has all but disappeared now from British railways. Few will forget the noise of buffers clanking against each other consecutively as the driver eased away and the force was transmitted down the line of vehicles through their slack coupling chains.

In the surroundings of Kensington Olympia, class '3' 2-6-2T No. 82019 waits to return to Clapham Junction with the 16.36 service on June 29th 1967. This peak-hour was steam worked until July 7th by locomotives of this type, the larger Standard class '4' tanks or Ivatt class '2' 2-6-2Ts. *Author*

Above: Westbound freight trains from Feltham joined the main line at Byfleet Junction, just a few hundred yards before Byfleet and New Haw station. About to pound its way under the signal gantry as it drags its load up the steep connecting single line is class '5' No. 73115, on February 13th 1967. *Author*

Right: Another of the same class, No. 73043 leaves an impressive smoke trail as it canters along the 'down' slow line near Fleet with a train load of cement wagons. The 'SPL 33' pasted on the upper disc suggests that this was a special steam working, probably substituting for a rostered diesel. *Author*

The daily freight trips from Eastleigh to destinations such as Fareham and Cosham, Northam, Redbridge Engineers' Yard, Millbrook and Brockenhurst presented such scenes in 1966. There was also the regular ritual of bringing wagons of stores and repaired vehicles out of Eastleigh Works and into the marshalling yard, returning with the next load for attention. This was usually a task for the 'USA' shunter assigned to Works' pilot duties and it used to appear through the Works exit siding just before 16.00 each day.

Eastleigh shed was responsible for providing the standard 2-6-4T which had a daily sortie up the Ludgershall branch, part of the old M&SWJR route to Swindon. It also did an occasional

shunt at Andover Town station, on the 'Sprat and Winkle' line that ran on to Romsey. The tank was outshedded at Basingstoke for a whole week at a time; in the spring of 1967 this duty (313), had become the regular preserve of No. 80151. This looked particularly smart, having been 'bulled up' for railtour working. Unfortunately, its career came to an abrupt end on April 28th when it failed at Overton, while returning with the 15.05 freight from Andover. It was rescued by unrebuilt 'West Country' No. 34102 *Lapford*, which must have made an interesting sight. The Standard was damaged beyond economic repair and it was condemned a few days later, fortunately to survive in preservation. Its place on duty 313 was soon taken over by class partner No. 80152.

The disused 'Sprat and Winkle' line was still in situ between Andover Town and Romsey in 1967. Its retention had been one of the conditions on which closure had been granted, in case there was ever a pressing need to re-open the route. As such it made an ideal location for a 'secret' overnight berth for the Royal Train. It is reported that on July 14th 1966, under cover of darkness, a steam locomotive was attached to the rear of the train at Kimbridge Junction and worked it to the vicinity of the former Mottisfont station. The Royal engine, a 'Warship' class diesel, remained on the rear of the train, and hauled it away next morning to continue the royal journey from Truro to

Left: Photographs of the latter days steam goods workings on the Ludgershall branch are rare. This view shows class '4' tank No. 80065 pausing at Weyhill, the intermediate station, with the 10.05 freight from Andover. Messrs. Wilton, James, Stole, Ilsley, Patman and Wade pose for the photographer. *Ray Ruffell*

Freight train in Hardy country: a Standard class '4' 4-6-0 heads an assortment of wagons past a scene of bovine indifference in the Dorchester area.
Mike Esau

Bournemouth. Another steam working on the line occurred in August when 'West Country' class No. 34004 *Yeovil* was noted waiting to join the main line at Kimbridge with an engineers train.

In the Bournemouth area there were further lines closed to passengers, which saw steam working. The 'Old Road' to Brockenhurst via Wimborne had been closed in 1964, leaving freight operation only from Ringwood westwards. In the 1966 freight timetable its daily goods working was allotted to a diesel, but from January 1967 Bournemouth duty 407 (404 from April) involved a Standard '4' tank working round to Ringwood. The siding status of the eleven miles from Broadstone was confirmed by the decision to lift the former 'down' track. In February 1967 there was a regular engineers train along the line to recover materials. Standard '4' 4-6-0 No. 75077 was noted making sedate progress along the line on the 11th of the month, stopping many times to allow level crossing gates to be opened and closed.

The above route shared a trackbed with the remains of the famous Somerset and Dorset railway, from Broadstone south to Poole. Since the closure of the S&D on March 6th 1966 only the stub from Poole to Blandford Forum survived from former glories, and that for freight only. Blandford produced some general goods traffic, and also a quantity of army traffic which helped to justify its retention. The dairy and sidings at Bailey Gate generated some further traffic, such that there was a daily 'Q' timing for a steam trip from Poole with vans. The Blandford freight was supposed to be diesel worked in 1967 but steam appeared from time to time. There were even a few charter passenger trips from the station, including a famous excursion to

Brighton on June 11th 1966, which was hauled throughout by a filthy 'West Country' class No. 34012.

That was a token of the great days of the 'Slow and Dirty' when passenger trains such as the 'Pines Express' and locomotives such as *Evening Star* had fought their way from the Hampshire coast over the Mendips to Bath and the Midlands. The closure of the line was originally intended on January 1st 1966, but problems with alternative bus services gained a two-month reprieve. The railway was predominantly Western controlled, and the postponement of the closure foiled that region's plans to get rid of all its steam engines by the end of 1965. It was forced to retain a handful at Bath and Templecombe sheds to operate the 'emergency service' which was introduced from January 3rd.

The surviving passenger trains seemed to be timed to deter travel as much as possible, with the line north and south of Templecombe being treated as if two separate sections. However, Bournemouth shed still had to provide power for the southern section services, with Standards in charge of the sparse workings. The ghost of the old S&D was finally laid to rest on March 5th, when the last ordinary trains ran, amid much local mourning. Noted on the last day were No. 76026 on 09.05 Templecombe – Branksome and Nos. 41307 and 80138 double-heading the 14.00 Templecombe – Bournemouth.

Happily, one of the other cross-country routes shared by the Southern and Western has enjoyed a far more stable existence. The Portsmouth to Bristol and South Wales service was handed over to diesel working in 1965. On the Southern section that meant the end of steam passenger trains between

Standard class '4' No. 75077 restarts its very short engineers' train over the level crossing at the former Ashley Heath Halt, the gates having been opened manually. The train was returning from Ringwood to Bournemouth in connection with the singling of this route, the 'down' track having already been removed in the vicinity.

Author

Fareham and St. Denys and Redbridge and Salisbury. Freight trains brought a few steam workings to the former section though. In 1966 there were also regular trips from Bevois Park sidings, Southampton to the engineers' disposal tip at Woolston. There were also a few parcels turns over the line.

From August 1st 1966 nearly all these trains were dieselised and the only regular steam turn left was the evening parcels from Portsmouth to the Midlands, worked by a Salisbury locomotive to its home town. The regular choice for this duty was Standard '4' No. 76067, regularly cleaned like all that Wiltshire depot's engines. Its appearances declined after its transfer to Bournemouth in March 1967 and thereafter the Netley line was host each evening to an immaculate Salisbury pacific, drawn from Nos. 34052, 34089 or 34108. This working continued until July 6th (see chapter nine).

The other link between the Southern and the Western in Wiltshire was the route from Weymouth to Westbury via Yeovil. Normally it was operated by Western dmmus, but any special freight workings were usually steam, covered. The Channel Island boat services brought seasonal cargoes for distribution all over the country, and so steam hauled trains of tomatoes and flowers were not unusual. The line through Yeovil is picturesque and has some sharp gradients, as well as being single-track. Had there still been steam passenger services in the mid-1960s, it would have been very popular with enthusiasts. No doubt foot-platemen were glad that steam working was irregular, for the upgrades put heavy demands on firemen and the downgrades needed careful use of the brake by the driver.

Nevertheless, there was a fair amount of steam activity on the line, providing Westbury with at least one daily visit by a Southern steam engine. There were even some steam worked passenger services, due to diesel failures, the 07.41 up from Weymouth being a frequent example in the winter months of 1966-7. Motive power was usually a Standard '5' or a Bulleid pacific. On April 13th 1967 though, No. 76006 was provided. This may well have been the last steam hauled passenger train over the line. The same engine had double-headed a coal train over the line with No. 73155 four months earlier. There was also a fairly regular 11.35 freight up from Weymouth in early 1967, bound for Worcester, and that yielded a variety of steam power. To illustrate the diversity, engines utilised included unrebuilt 'West Country' No. 34019 on February 9th, rebuilt 'Battle of Britain' No. 34052 on March 7th, and the following Standards,

No. 73018 on March 8th, No. 75075 on March 9th and No. 76007 on February 28th. As mentioned later in the book, workings such as these continued until the very last day of steam on the Southern Region.

The Southern line from Salisbury passed into Western ownership east of Westbury, and it too brought occasional steam activity to the Western junction station. All regular passenger and freight working on the line was diesel, but special workings would throw up steam from time to time. Thus on May 27th 1967, a senior citizens excursion to Waterloo via Warminster and Salisbury was worked by No. 34036. A week earlier Salisbury's No. 34089 turned up at Westbury while working one stage of a Dover to Churston special. More frequent were special freights from Southampton Docks, especially for seasonal goods such as bananas. In May and June 1967 these were turning up every few days, particularly at 16.50 timing from Southampton, which brought unrebuilt pacific No. 34057 on April 27th, No. 75077 on May 1st and No. 76066 on June 14th, as well as a number of others. The other main cause of steam useage was a melancholy one however; the use of an engine to haul its dead compatriots from Eastleigh or Nine Elms en route to South Wales scrapyards.

Apart from the Western region, Southern steam could also stray onto the London Midland and Eastern, in the London area. Such events were unusual, but arose when through passenger trains had to be handed over at the regional boundary, and also, more rarely with cross-London freights. There were also instances of 'foreign' steam engines transgressing onto the Southern, apart from those brought down specially for enthusiasts' tours. A good example of this was the surprise appearance of 'Britannia' class 4-6-2 No. 70002 which worked a troop train originating from Elgin in Scotland to Portsmouth Harbour on May 11th 1966. The 4-6-2 took over at Crewe and stayed with its train while travelling over the Western Region from Banbury to Reading, and over the Southern too! The train was so long it had to be divided at Fareham so that it could be accommodated at Portsmouth. The stranger was sent back promptly to Willesden, but was apparently not welcome to the London Midland authorities there and returned to Nine Elms. The Southern did not waste the presence of an extra pacific and it was used on the 09.20 boat train to Southampton Docks on May 12th. It then languished at Nine Elms before returning light to the north a week later.

Standard 'Britannias' made no more than a couple of appearances at Waterloo in the 1960s. One occasion was on May 12th 1966, when No. 70002 *Geoffrey Chaucer* was turned out for the 09.20 boat train to Southampton Docks. The boat train headcode required a disc to be placed at the top of the smokebox door, but in the absence of a bracket, the white circle has been chalked on!
Ray Ruffell

Diverted over the Portsmouth Direct Line, 'West Country' class No. 34098 *Templecombe* passes Witley on March 20th 1966 with a Bournemouth –
Waterloo train.
Roy Bicknell

One of Salisbury's unrebuilt Bulleid pacifics, 'Battle of Britain' class No. 34066 *Spitfire* steps gingerly away from Bournemouth Central on
August 18th 1966 with the 12.59 to Waterloo.
Author

Standard class '4' No. 80133 canters under the attractive signal gantry and past Walton-on-Thames signalbox with the 11.05 Waterloo – Basingstoke parcels on May 6th 1967.
K.P. Lawrence

Another Standard class '4', No. 80139, rounds the now lifted west curve of the Northam triangle on March 23rd 1967 with a boat train portion from Southampton Central to the Eastern Docks. The carriages and luggage van would have been detached from the 13.20 boat train from Waterloo to the Western Docks.
Author

The following month the Southern responded by sending out a standard class '5' on an excursion to the Midlands, which managed to stay with its train right through to Coventry! There was still further reciprocation on August 13th, when 'Black 5' No. 44710 turned up on the non-steam Central division at Emsworth with a special working from Manchester. It then proceeded still further into alien territory by taking the empty stock on to Hove. Although at that time, some Southern steam did occasionally penetrate the Central section as far as Chichester with a couple of nocturnal freights, the appearance of a London Midland engine was exceptional. (Under cover of darkness, engineering works sometimes took the 03.30 Waterloo – Portsmouth newspaper train down the Horsham line, but that was about the limit of steam working through Sussex).

In the London area, Southern steam engines worked as far as Brent on September 24th 1966 with party specials. On November 24th it was the turn of Stratford to host two Bulleids, allegedly the first steam engines seen on the ex-Great Eastern since 1964. The locomotives involved were 'West Country' Nos. 34013 and 34023 working specials from Southampton Docks to East Anglia. Their rostering can best be understood in terms of the enthusiasm of a clerk in the diagram office at Wimbledon! Infrequent, but fascinating incursions such as these continued, even in the very last weekend before steam ended on the Southern.

Normally, all internal boat train workings on the south western division of the Southern were steam hauled, whether making for Southampton or Weymouth. The 'Channel Islands Boat Express' to Weymouth Quay was a daily occurrence, steam hauled to the very last Saturday, July 8th. It had formerly been steam tank hauled from Weymouth junction through the streets

Above: The 'Channel Island Boat Express' is not far from journey's end at Weymouth Quay as it passes Moreton on May 6th 1967 behind 'West Country' class No. 34021 *Dartmoor.* The three discs headcode was uniquely carried on this working. *C.L. Caddy*

to the Quayside, but diesel shunters had taken over by 1966. However, at Southampton it was still possible to see a steam train running across a public road! The crossing into the Eastern (Old) Docks involved crossing Canute Road, and was accompanied with some ceremony, including the services of a flagman and the ringing of a brass hand bell. The Docks were still handling the

Below: Little more than an hour earlier I had also photographed the boat train threading the attractive countryside west of Sway. The covered van behind the engine was a normal part of the working, to convey passengers' baggage. *Author*

'Trains Cross Here' proclaims the road sign and No. 76064 provides the evidence as it spans Canute Road, Southampton. Protected by a flagman it is drawing a boat train out of the Eastern Docks on June 9th 1967. To the left is the opulent South Western House, which contrasts interestingly with the post-War architecture of Dock House across the road.

Author

Many boat trains carried their headboards until the very end of steam. The cleanliness of No. 34021 was more unusual however, as it stands flanked by two generations of emus at Waterloo, waiting to whisk passengers for one westwards on the first stage of the journey to South Africa on one of the 'Union Castle' vessels.

John Scrace

great Cunard 'Queen' liners operating trans-Atlantic passenger services and their arrival and departure required numerous boat trains. These ran direct from Waterloo to the splendid Ocean Terminal, alongside which the liners docked. Sadly the Terminal and the original 'Queens' have long since disappeared, yet remarkably, steam-hauled boat trains into the Docks were revived in the mid-1990s through the auspices of the VSOE Organisation, linking with sailings of the 'Queen Elizabeth II'.

There were many other sailings from the Eastern Docks, particularly on the South Aftican run, which required boat train facilities. In the Western Docks there was also much activity, including P&O liners such as the *Canberra* which plied to Australia. Boat trains were run for them as well, entering the dock by way of the connection to the main line just west of Millbrook station.

There was a certain amount of glamour still associated with these trains, as they occasionally carried celebrities, or were the starting point for emigration and a 'new life'. At that time, in the pre-'Concorde' and 'Jumbo Jet' era of air travel, the trans-Atlantic liners still performed an important travel function. Some of the glory rubbed off on the Southern Region's connecting train services. Many of the boat trains carried headboards, indicating the shipping company involved. This practice continued right up to the end of steam, rather surprising when trains such as the 'Bournemouth Belle' and 'Royal Wessex' never carried their designations up front. The cast iron headboards were kept securely at Nine Elms shed; they were very heavy and required the services of at least two men when they were fitted on to metal brackets on a locomotive smokebox. Towards the end, their appearance on otherwise totally anonymous and dirt encrusted engines seemed a little anachronistic to say the least.

While passenger and freight trains brought tender engines into both the Eastern and Western docks, there was also some shunting and trip working between the two Dock systems themselves. This was in the hands of the Ruston and Hornsby diesel

Above: An 'up' boat train bursts through Byfleet and New Haw behind a well turned out 'West Country' class No. 34093 *Saunton*; on its way from Southampton Docks to Waterloo. *Author. Below:* A unique record of a little known working: this is the *last* steam hauled bullion special from Southampton Western Docks to Waterloo, seen near Millbrook on July 3rd 1967. The locomotive is 'West Country' class No. 34036 *Westward Ho*. These top security trains were not widely publicised even among railwaymen; apparently the rear carriage conveyed a police escort to ensure the security of the cargo. *Ray Ruffell.*

The work of the SR's engineers' department is depicted in these three illustrations. Standard class '4' No. 76069 (banked in the rear by a diesel shunter) slogs upgrade between Hinton Admiral and New Milton (the 'up' line being under engineers' possession) during April 1966. Single line working was in operation by all other trains over the 'down' line while relaying was in operation.
Author

Right: No. 76008 attends trackwork operations during relaying and reballasting activities near Wimbledon on March 19th 1967.   *Ray Ruffell*

Below: Class '3' No. 77014 was rostered to work the daily Woking-Farnham waste ballast train. On January 10th 1967 it accelerates through Aldershot, a few miles from its destination at the engineers' rubbish tip.   *Ray Ruffell*

The larger and smaller versions of Standard class '4' tender locomotives, represented by Nos. 75077 and 76007, pass St. Denys with the 09.15 Redbridge Sleeper depot-Winchester. The load comprises 600 feet sections of continuously welded rail, which was carried along the lengths of several wagons, being sufficiently flexible to bend with curves on the railway. *Author*

shunters which were the mainstay of Dock shunting and trip work. They would be seen travelling along the link lines which passed in front of the Town Quay, but which no longer exist. It was not unknown to find a 'USA' tank doing such work, even in 1967. The ex-American shunters had been largely eliminated from the Docks in 1962 by dieselisation, as described in chapter three. They were not displaced completely though, as they were called in to help from Eastleigh whenever traffic exceeded the diesels' capacities. Such a time was when the banana season was at its height, and Nos. 30067 and 30069 could be found at work in the Docks even in the summer of 1967.

A survey of operations during the last months of Southern steam would be incomplete without reference to the unglamorous but essential work of the civil engineering (CCE) section. Providing and maintaining the railway infrastructure is a major and continuing task, and like all regions the Southern had an extensive department. With its own fleet of special purpose wagons, all endowed with marine names, like 'Walrus' and 'Dogfish', it had a mystique of its own. The fact that much of its operation took place nocturnally added to the air of mystery. With the enormous extra burden imposed by the Bournemouth electrification scheme, the Region's steam engines were kept busy providing some of the motive power for all manner of engineers' trains.

There were regular workings of stone ballast from the Region's Quarry at Meldon to Salisbury and Woking. These were diesel

hauled, but the subsequent distribution of ballast was often steam worked. In the early months of 1966, for example, steam was occasionally working through to New Cross Gate on an 11.24 stone train from Woking via Redhill. Such interesting motive power as class 'N' No. 31803 was noted on February 10th and class 'U' No. 31639 on April 21st. However, by June 2nd, when class '5' No. 73082 was in charge, such workings with steam had become very rare. On the South Western division, steam-worked ballast trains continued to predominate. Guildford depot played a major role in providing motive power for such trains, and many other permanent way specials too, conveying items such as cranes, track relayers and rails and sleepers.

The weekly special traffic notices, issued to all railway staff, confirm Guildford's heavy involvement. On the night of November 12th 1966, there were no less than twelve workings booked off 70C, three of which were for pairs of engines, between the hours of 19.25 and midnight. While some of these may have been diesels, the bulk would have been steam drawn from Guildford's repertoire of 'Standards'. Incidentally, not all engineering work was constructive: Guildford also had to provide an engine each day in November 1966 to work a demolition train from Bentley. Its purpose was to remove all traces of the closed branch line to Bordon and recover all useful materials.

In the early part of 1966, the officially withdrawn 'Q1s' and the surviving 'Us' and 'Ns' were prominent in working engineers

The 'V' formation of the head-code discs denotes the breakdown train; this is the Nine Elms 'heavy lifter' attending the derailment of a van train at Waterloo on May 27th 1967. 'West Country' class No. 34025 *Whimple* provides the motive power.

Ray Ruffell

trains. When Standard '3' No. 77014 arrived, it quickly slotted in too. As the sole representative of the class, it had its own regular working, duty 170, right through to the end of steam. It was supposed to work the daily trip freight from Woking, conveying redundant ballast and other materials for tipping at Farnham. It often strayed on to other duties though, including an interesting interlude with the weed-killing train on July 28th 1966. It was rostered to pull that train, composed of mess and control coaches, and a string of redundant tenders containing the weed-killer

down the Meon Valley line's remains to Farringdon, and then 'Over the Alps' to Winchester and Eastleigh. The next day it made its way back home, by way of the 07.10 Southampton Terminus – Fareham parcels train, thus making its debut on the Netley line as well. Twelve months later, the weed-killer was again in operation, and was seen on the Netley line hauled by spotless 'Battle of Britain' No. 34090. The old tenders had by then been replaced by tank wagons. Another year later and the steam engine would have been replaced by a diesel, forever!

The 1967 weed-killing train, comprising adapted utility vans equipped to control spraying, and old tenders and tanks to convey the chemicals, is propelled past Northam on June 11th 1967 by 'Battle of Britain' class No. 34090 *Sir Eustace Missenden, Southern Railway*. The train is spraying the section as far as the Docks entrance at Canute Road.

Author

Chapter Five

Men and Machines

There is no doubt that some of the finest steam running ever seen on the Southern took place during the final eighteen months – and also some of the worst! It is probable that main line passenger running has never been subjected to so much assessment by hundreds of students of locomotive performance. Nearly every working, no matter how humble, had its stop-watch clasping traveller, determined to record the time taken between stations and the speeds attained. In the case of certain steam worked trains, the number of 'timers' may well have reached a hundred or more. Fortunately many drivers and firemen responded to this intense interst in their work, and got the very best in performance out of their charges. This chapter is a description of the varied feats achieved during 1966 and 1967, as seen by some of the drivers and firemen responsible, and also by some of the army of youths and men who dedicated so much of their time to experiencing them.

For those drivers to whom high speed running and record breaking was an exciting challenge, this was an unforgettable time. Their ardour was kindled by a love of steam, and in some cases it was further fanned by financial incentives; ten shilling notes were the going rate for footplate fireworks! For men like

Bert Hooker, who had taken part in the Locomotive Exchanges in 1948, engine driving was an art and a science to be perfected. Others just gloried in the sensations of power that arose from pushing a Bulleid pacific up to 100 mph.

Jim Evans, based at Nine Elms in the last years of steam, describes the magic of the footplate most eloquently:

'I still remember the thrill I used to get as I walked into Nine Elms, with my lunch bag over my shoulder . . . There is my engine, a 'Merchant Navy' with smoke tumbling lazily out of the short, squat chimney, and a dull glow lighting up the dark interior of the enclosed footplate. I go to sign on, and then climb on board, followed by my fireman, Brian, with the smell of freshly made tea coming from the can he carries. He puts the tea on the tray over the fire door, while my experienced eye checks round to see that everything is ready for departure. Of course it is: the enthusiasm of this young fireman who has prepared the engine, far outweighing his lack of years. I open the small jet and create the vacuum brake, destroy it again as my fireman takes off the handbrake. Fore gear, brakes off, this is it! "Ready mate?". "Yeah, OK". I give a blast on the whistle to let the points man know I am ready, then I get that feeling of excitement as I ease open the regulator and watch the steam chest gauge start to register. Slowly the pistons

A powerful image from a creative photographer: Bulleid pacific and engineman at Eastleigh shed on June 30th 1967.   *Rod Hoyle*

take steam and the great lumbering giant becomes *mine* for eight hours. A green light from the points man, more regulator as she digs her smokebox into the climb up the bank out of the Elms. Then onto the loco reception road to await the signal to proceed up to Waterloo. The fire has livened up and the blower is eased on to hold back the smoke that is foaming out of the firedoor. "Stick the milk in mate, let's have a cup of tea while it's quiet", I call across to my fireman. Presently all hell will be let loose as we hit the rails out of Waterloo, a thrill that will soon never be recreated.

Fifteen minutes later at Waterloo, the guard shouts up to me, "Fourteen on driver, 462 tons". "OK, Bruv", I reply. The engine's fire is now burning hotter, the boiler pressure creeping up to bursting point, and the water in the gauge glass is playing hide and seek with the top nut. My fireman's skill shows as he manages to hold the engine just below maximum output with skillful use of the shovel and the injector. Now the signal shows green and the guard's whistle blows. The adrenalin really starts to flow through my veins, just as fast as the steam will rush through all those boiler tubes. But I dare not show it, I act as if it is nothing to me, an every day occurence.

I open the regulator and feel the loco take up the strain and heave like some great shire horse. The steam blasts full force from the cylinder cocks to clear out any water there. I close the cocks, give her more regulator and then watch as the smokebox snakes and jerks over the points out of the terminus. Soon I pull the lever up into 45 and settle down for a fast run to Southampton, signals permitting. The footplate is now alive with noise, as me and my fireman control our loco from our little isolated capsule, mounted up behind the boiler. I don't need to look at the steam pressure gauge to know how she's doing; the regular ring of the shovel on the edges of the firedoor, as my mate shifts coal, is my reassurance. As he feeds that great glowing mouth, and I hear the continuous drone from the injector, I know he has everything under control.

My excitement mounts as over five hundred tons of train hurls itself down through the Hampshire countryside, and the 'speedo' needle is not so far away from the magic 'ton', assisted by the long drop from Litchfield tunnel towards Winchester. I hang on to the side of the cab as the engine kicks hard to the right and then to the left, as we flash through Micheldever. Brian yells above all the noise, "OK Weston", as he catches a brief glimpse of the distant signal showing clear ahead. At Weston box, the straight four line section comes into view as we make for the next box at Wallers Ash. Now we are really hurtling downhill and the excitement is enormous. I glance up at the speedo hanging like some great moon up in the black heights of the cab. What shall I do? Ease up, or see what she can do? Just this once I am going to let her go and see what she can get up to. She's got plenty of steam, there's perfect visibility and the track is right for high speed.

We're up to 95 on the speedo, can we make it for the 100? Every single item and unit on the loco is trying to tear itself away from its fixings. The noise is fantastic! The fire starts to vibrate down to the front of the firebox and dust and cinders are shaking through the firebars and finding their way up on to the footplate. To add to the drama, the tender joins in the antics. Its oscillations start to shake the coal down, resulting in great clouds of coal dust billowing onto the footplate. The result is my eye-lids and nostrils are beginning to cement together with that grotesque mixture of sweat, coal dust and grey ash. And then the final blow . . . an extra big lurch of the engine and the teacan decides it has had enough and vacates the tray, spilling well stewed tea over the boiler and footplate, and adding a few more chips to the can's well worn enamel. Down through Wallers Ash tunnel now but we don't quite reach the 'ton'. I ease her back and sense a sigh of relief from my fireman as he surveys what is left of his furnace and well ordered footplate!

I ease a little brake into the train for the curve through Shawford Junction, and then I realise, as everything settles back to normality, that my heart is still pounding. Yes, I was excited, excited to the point of being terrified!

After that the rest of the journey to Southampton is quite routine. Arrival several minutes early and another good job done.'

Such was the intense and sustained drama of footplate life for some enginemen. In the last eighteen months, these men became known by name to the enthusiast fraternity, and they built up their own following. Men like Jim Evans and Gordon

A wintry morning at Woking and Driver Anderson of Nine Elms is topping up the tender of No. 34098 *Templecombe* before it sets off on a diverted journey to Bournemouth via Fareham and Netley. The working is the 09.33 excursion from Waterloo, a regular Sunday train which did not appear in the public timetable. January 15th 1967.

Ray Ruffell

Porter, were enthusiastically patronised whenever they were known to be rostered for steam passenger work. Some of the older and more experienced drivers were rather unimpressed by some of these exploits. Words like 'reckless' have been applied, but there is no doubt that their actions were greatly appreciated by the train-borne fanatics.

Bert Hooker also enjoyed fast running, which he always tackled in a professional manner, not surprising in view of his long and distinguished record on the footplate.

He drove 'Merchant Navy' class No. 35023 on its outstanding Waterloo – Salisbury run on October 15th 1966. That was the first leg of the privately sponsored excursion to Exeter, one of the last steam trips down the ex-LSWR main line to the West Country.

'I didn't have my usual mate, Alan Newman, instead I had old 'Rocker' Dedman. Inspector Jupp was on the footplate, and I said to him, "I'm going to let my hair down today!' I should have been working a Bournemouth turn, but the roster clerk made a three-way change and I gave away six hours pay to get the turn. I was certain it would be my last chance to drive a fast train to Salisbury.

When we got under the hopper at Nine Elms, I was preparing the engine, when they absolutely buried her in coal! They hadn't been able to shut the delivery chutes off and we weren't half in a state, with the engine blowing off madly. We had to ease her back onto the pit and them my mate went and got the blow-down man, to blow some water out of the boiler. Then we were able to get the injector on, and get some cold water into the boiler to stop her blowing-off. Then I got onto the firebox and cleaned all the coal and dust off. When we left the shed we only had about twelve minutes to get up to Waterloo before departure!

Fortunately the signalman was good to us and somehow we managed to leave Waterloo on time. It was a marvellous ride, we did the 'ton' at Andover, 82 over the top at Grately and got up to 99 again at Porton. We covered the thirty miles from milepost 51 in just over twenty minutes and it was the fastest ever recorded time between Woking and Salisbury. The faster the engine went, the better she rode. Arthur Jupp was a bit anxious that we were exceeding the 85 mph limit, so he said "I'll put this cloth over the speedometer dial!" Allowing for stoppages and so on, we did Waterloo – Salisbury in 70¼ minutes altogether.'

Those who had paid to travel on that special were entitled to expect a fast run; on ordinary passenger workings it was often

Three men on the footplate at Southampton Central as 'West Country' class No. 34015 *Exmouth* waits to restart a Waterloo-bound express on August 17th 1966.

Author

just luck or inside knowledge that yielded exciting displays of steam power. John Corkill and Ron Coffey came down from the North, like many others, to spend a fortnight travelling on the Southern in the autumn of 1966. It was to prove an eventful time for them in a number of ways:

'The weather that fortnight could not have been better. We booked our tickets, Southern Region railrovers, giving a week's unlimited travel on any train. We had arranged to stay at the London flat belonging to a friend of ours and his wife. We started in style, our first run being on the 'Bournemouth Belle' with an immaculate 'West Country' class at the head, No. 34013 *Okehampton*. The splendour of those Pullmans was a luxury in itself not to be missed, and a small sum paid to the attendant, was but little cost for the pleasure of riding in that magnificent train. We disembarked from our first expedition at Southampton and had a bite to eat and a couple of pints. We heard that the best train to ride back on was the 17.30 from Weymouth, which picked up at Southampton, leaving at 19.15. That was the story going round the pub outside the station, and in fact we found ourselves talking to the driver and fireman. They were Nine Elms men and they were working the job all week. They were not a great deal older than us, in their late twenties and were very enthusiastic about getting the best out of steam. Bearing in mind that the track had been thoroughly relaid, 100 mph running was reasonable.

The crew's technique was to take things fairly easy until past Eastleigh and then let the thrashing really begin. On that Tuesday night, there wasn't much sign of taking it easy. The engine was No. 35029 *Ellerman Lines* and we were already up to 68 mph at Eastleigh. We didn't keep a detailed record of the running, but the train was packed almost to bursting point with enthusiasts, so it was easy to get a note of the speeds attained from somebody else. We went up through Winchester at a steady 75 mph, with ten coaches on, but the incredible feat was to accelerate to an unbelievable 85 mph over the last couple of miles to the summit at Roundwood. Nothing like it had ever been known before. That was just the start! From Worting Junction it is a downhill sprint, and the young crew whipped the 'Merchant Navy' up to 96 mph through the station, with the whistle screaming, sending late returning commuters scurrying for cover. Near Hook we topped a hundred, and then we carried on accelerating to a maximum claimed speed of 104 mph.

Then suddenly it had to stop . . . the brakes came on sharply and we had to come down to about 30 mph for a speed restriction where trackwork was being done. But that wasn't really quite the end for the lively men on the footplate and that immensely powerful engine were at it again. The Farnborough curves were given scant respect, and another 'ton' was in sight at 96 mph, but then the engine wilted and died. Thick black smoke started rolling out from the chimney and speed dropped to a crawl, until we came to a stand at the Woking home signal. Our mutual looks of dismay confirmed that something had gone drastically wrong with our engine. The excesses of the crew had, perhaps, taken their toll, and that 'Merchant Navy' had seen its last trip. What a way to go! We heard that the trouble was a burst superheater element tube, but it was the end of the road for a fine machine. We had to put up with a replacement diesel into Waterloo.

On the Basingstoke to Woking racing stretch, an unrebuilt 'West Country' blows off as it heads for Waterloo through the cutting near Deepcut.
Mike Esau

As if that wasn't enough drama for one evening, more was to follow. After several pints and armed with some excellent fish and chips, we let ourselves into the flat and settled down to enjoy the memories of that fabulous run. All too soon we were disturbed by a violent banging on the door and a bellowing voice demanding that we open up or the police would be called. We naturally responded as requested and were confronted with a huge figure of a man, who claimed that we had broken in and he was going to call the police. Our explaining was futile, so clutching the remaining fish and chips and our bags we fled . . . for Waterloo, where else? But it was almost midnight by then!'

Ron and John found sanctuary on the newspaper train to Weymouth, which was powered by Standard No. 76069 from Eastleigh. Wisely, it would seem, they spent the rest of their Southern sojourn in a pub beside Eastleigh station. Needless to say they made sure of a trip up to Waterloo on the 19.15 from Southampton Central as often as they could. As John concludes:

'The main thing in our minds was to ride as much as possible behind steam. We came away from the Southern feeling well satisfied with our two weeks. It was really a memorable fortnight on the Southern!'

There was naturally a special excitement generated by travelling on a non-stop express, such as the 17.30 Weymouth, from Southampton to Waterloo. However some of the most dramatic acceleration and high speed feats were performed by the semi-fast services, particularly over the Woking to Basingstoke section. Admittedly many of the fast runs timed over that 23½ mile stretch were with very short, light-weight trains, but they still provide interesting evidence of steam capabilities. Despite the competition of electric and diesel traction alongside, steam did not suffer by comparison, when crews were enthusiastic and prepared to interpret speed regulations with some personal discretion.

One driver has described a run along from Basingstoke, which sums up the atmosphere and spirit of those occasions. Even now it is probably best that he remain anonymous:

'I must say we went a little bit mad towards the end. I had the urge to get the regulator up into the roof! On one occasion I had eleven blokes on the footplate, and we did the run in a very short time indeed! We were doing way past 90 through Farnborough, they were terrified and so was I! I didn't slow down until the last minute, but as we passed Woking signalbox, I dropped the brake handle and we *just* stopped at the end of the platform!'

The excesses being practised by some drivers did not escape the attention of the operating authorities, but there was little that they could do to stamp it out altogether. There were not sufficient inspectors to police every working and the best that could be done was to put them with drivers known to have some tendencies towards recklessness. In any case, as with any large organisation, there was a certain amount of tolerance exercised. It was a case of 'Nelson turning the blind eye', in the words of S.C. Townroe, for so long a major figure on the motive power front on the Southern.

Some critics have challenged the high speeds claimed for steam during 1966 and 1967. Their scepticism is based on the fact that some of the runs took place at night, when mileposts are virtually impossible to discern making accurate timing very difficult. This was compounded by the widespread application of continuous welded rail to the main line by them, so that there were no rail joints to provide 'clickety-clicks' every 60 feet, which was the other basis for calculating speeds. Nevertheless, Mr. D.W. Winkworth in his study 'Bulleid Pacifics' has put forward a number of logs of steam runs, which appear to be well authenticated. He has followed this up with further articles in other journals, which probably represent the last word on the highest steam speeds recorded on the Southern.

The highest speed of all is credited to 'Merchant Navy' class No. 35003 *Royal Mail* which on June 26th 1967, managed to run the 3.3 miles between Winchfield and Fleet in just 1 minute 56 seconds! That represents an average speed of some 102.4 mph, and the top speed achieved was recorded at 106 mph, which is well justified by the claimed speeds of 98 mph passing Winchfield and 100 mph through Fleet. The train was the 18.15 ex-Weymouth, which departed from Basingstoke at 21.52 during its semi-fast progress to Waterloo. It was a lightweight load for the 'Merchant Navy', just five vehicles totalling no more than 170 tons! Nevertheless it did demonstrate the acceleration potential of steam, with the first 5.6 miles out to Hook being reeled off in 'even time', 5 minutes 37 seconds. At that point the train was already travelling at 90 mph! Given that there was a slowing east of Farnborough for track work, and a signal delay outside Woking, the achieved time of 18 minutes 48 seconds for the 23½ miles was remarkable. Unchecked, who is to say that Driver Burridge might not have completed the run in 18 minutes or less, a pretty remarkable improvement on the 28 minutes allowed in the timetable!

Table 7
Basingstoke – Woking 26th June 1967
No. 35003 *Royal Mail* Load: 5/160/170

Miles		Mins.	Secs.	Speed
0.0	BASINGSTOKE	0	00	—
5.6	Hook	5	37	90
8.0	Winchfield	7	09	98/106
11.3	Fleet	9	05	100
14.6	Farnborough	11	07	71
	p.w.s.			
16.8	Milepost 31	13	03	74/95
19.8	Brookwood	15	06	91
	sigs.			
23.5	WOKING	18	48	—

Recorded by Mr. D.E.J. Benn

This was not the only high speed run with that particular working during the last few weeks of steam: for example 105 mph was achieved two nights later with the same train, same engine and same driver. The highest known speed for an unrebuilt light pacific was also notched up on this working. On June 14th No. 34102 *Lapford* with a slightly heavier load of 230 tons, comprising seven vehicles, was whipped up to just touch 100 mph at Bramshot. Not only were 'tons' being picked up with some regularity, but there was also first class uphill running on this same working and others. On March 9th Driver Anderson of Nine Elms accelerated up the long bank to Roundwood from the standing start at Winchester to clear the summit at 83 mph with 'Battle of Britain' class No. 34087 and six coaches. Probably of even greater merit was another 'Battle of Britain' class No. 34060 on June 23rd. In the hands of Driver Hendicott, despite being pulled back to 15 mph at Winchester Junction by a permanent way slack, 80 mph was reached at Roundwood, and this with one extra coach into the bargain.

Another man who had shown a liking for speed was Driver De'Ath of Basingstoke, who had a number of fine runs on the 18.35 Salisbury – Waterloo. This was another light train, and it was formed of six coaches on July 5th 1967 when No. 35008 *Orient Line* was whisked along at no less than 102 mph east of Grateley. The same driver had previously extracted 92 mph from No. 34001 *Exeter* at the same spot on the same train, but with nine coaches trailing.

It is interesting to compare steam performance with the standards subsequently set by the high powered electric multiple units on the Bournemouth run. With the benefit of colour light signalling and raised speed restrictions public schedules of

Top left: Salisbury driver Jack Terry in charge of No. 34015 *Exmouth* on the occasion of the first 'last' steam special to Exeter on January 8th 1966. Jack had served on the railways for nearly fifty years by then. *David M. Smith. Top right:* A younger footplate generation exemplified by Driver Walker of Nine Elms with his fireman at Kensington Olympia on board No. 41312 waiting to haul the 17.06 to Clapham Junction. *Ray Ruffell.*

The driver of class '5' No. 73065 waiting for the guard's signal to resume westwards from Eastleigh station. Note the grimy condition of the engine with just the cab number cleaned up, also the colour light signals waiting to be brought into use, and the large Southern Railway notice which banned the practice of walking along the tracks to the Works or engine sheds.

John Marshall

67 minutes between Waterloo and Southampton became the norm, and actual running showed the capability for a non-stop time of around the hour. Nothing achieved by steam could compare with that, partly because the circumstances were different. It is possible that a 'Merchant Navy' in peak condition could now cover the route in 67 minutes, but very difficult to visualise the 60 minute threshold being approached. Probably the best run ever took place, not in steam's final months, but back in 1959 when Driver Letchford of Nine Elms was in charge of the 10.30 from Waterloo with No. 35030 *Elder Dempster Lines*. Although his progress was delayed by two signal stops east of Micheldever, he reached Southampton in 85½ minutes, with a top speed of 92 mph at Shawford. Close examination of the time lost due to the hold-ups *en route* suggest that an unchecked run would have been completed in about 70½ minutes. (It is worth noting that he went on to make one of the fastest runs thence on to Bournemouth, covered in 29 minutes 53 seconds, which allowing for another signal stop could have been managed in 28 minutes! This may well have been the fastest steam run from London to Bournemouth of all time.)

During 1966/7 the inevitable delays caused by engineering works prevented full length runs to Southampton taking place without some slowings or stops due to track work or signals. Actual journey times were often in the 90 to 100 minute region, and sometimes even slower, by so-called 'expresses'. However, when the out of course problems are allowed for, we are left with some pretty outstanding efforts. Pride of place should probably go to 'West Country' class No. 34044 *Woolacombe* which was in the demanding care of Driver Hooper of Nine Elms, who usually could be relied upon for a lively journey. On this occasion, in February 1967, the 15.14 from Southampton, 400 tons worth, was brought up to the City in a shade over 86 minutes, with a top speed of 95 mph at Fleet. Allowing for two permanent way slowings and two signal checks, a net time of 72½ minutes may be computed. The following month, the same driver showed his prowess in the down direction, with the famous *Clan Line*. With a lighter load of ten coaches, No. 35028 managed a net time of about 74 minutes, although it suffered so many checks during the overall 89 minutes that the corrected time is somewhat speculative. Another Hooper run, also deserves mention, on the 08.30 from Waterloo, loaded up to 445 tons in thirteen coaches with No. 35008 *Orient Line*. This journey was typical of the driver in making light of a sequence of enforced stops and slowings, and doing his best to regain time in between. The total journey consumed an enormous 98¼ minutes, but the four impediments to progress, notably a signal stop outside Eastleigh which put an end to a burst of 90 mph+ running, accounted for some 23¾ minutes of that. Thus it can be argued that an unhindered run would have seen Southampton's Platform 4 gained in about 74½ minutes.

There was less scope for fast running west of Southampton; the best hope of a record time lay in ignoring the speed limits at places like Brockenhurst and Christchurch, and braking as late as possible when approaching stations. In the 'up' direction, a minute or two could also be saved by a determined attack on Hinton Admiral bank. It is pleasing to record that the now preserved No. 34023 *Blackmore Vale* can be credited with one of the best 'up' runs during our period of review. With the 18.33 from Bournemouth, and Driver Allen of Weymouth in control, an actual time of 30 minutes and 2 seconds was recorded, including a very slight speed reduction due to signals before Brockenhurst. No. 34023's running was also noticeable for the fact that no speed restrictions were broken, apart from a small transgression between Totton and Redbridge. In the opposite direction, Jim Evans had a fine run with No. 35007 *Aberdeen Commonwealth* towards the end of steam on the 08.30 from Waterloo. With a load

of eleven coaches, grossing 400 tons, he managed to clear Brockenhurst in just over 15 minutes, despite two slight signal checks, and then powered down the bank to Christchurch at 88 mph. Reaching Bournemouth in a net time of 28½ minutes was quite possible but for a cruel signal stop just outside the terminus, eventually leading to 32¾ minutes actual running time.

One can envy the many enthusiasts who crowded into the last 02.45 newspaper train from Waterloo on July 8th. With Driver Porter at the helm, there was no doubt that an eventful journey was in store. He had already turned in a phenomenal run four nights earlier with No. 34001 *Exeter* between the Woking and Basingstoke stops. He had accelerated the light 185 ton train up to 83 mph at the summit of the westward climb at milepost 31, and then with a maximum of 94 mph completed the 23.5 miles in 20 minutes 49 seconds start to stop, including a signal check approaching the station. On the last night the running was less dramatic from Woking, not exceeding 87 mph. Instead the fireworks came later; the 18.8 miles from Basingstoke to Winchester City were covered in 18 minutes 12 seconds with a top score of 94 mph and reports of broken carriage windows caused by coal falling off the tender at speed. The Southampton to Brockenhurst sprint needed just 13 minutes 58 seconds with 83 mph achieved, and with everyone on the train still hoping for a 100 mph, there remained the short downhill fling from New Milton to Christchurch.

It was a bit much to expect even Driver Porter to reach a 'ton' in a start to stop distance of only 5.8 miles! However, the train was now down to just five vehicles, and it was probably the driver's last chance to enter the history books. He certainly tried . . . No. 34095 *Brentor* was driven flat out and Hinton Admiral was passed at 81 mph with 3.3 miles left to break a record and stop at Christchurch . . . neither target was quite achieved! Top speed was 93 mph and Christchurch station was left some 250 yards behind before the humble newspaper train squealed to a halt! It was definitely a dramatic way to start the last weekend of Southern steam.

During the last eighteen months ever more men and youths had turned over their spare time to the pursuit of steam. It was essentially a masculine activity, the appearance of a young (or not so young) lady being extremely rare. Psychologists would probably view the activity as an extension of primitive hunting instincts, a desire to be in on the chase and in at the kill. As far as we know there have been no historical or sociological studies of the behaviour of railway enthusiasts during the final years of Southern steam, but there is plenty of evidence of the level of commitment practised by its devotees. For some it involved manipulation of work or education situations to achieve the desired goal. For example, David Druce was in the 5th year at Alleynes School at the time, which was conveniently near to Nine Elms depot. On games afternoons he would sidle off and 'bunk' the shed. He describes his technique:

'I used to get up to Nine Elms in the early afternoon and go up the steps to the main office. Then I would duck down below the windows and creep round the front. I would then make my way round the back of the turntable operator's hut, and then hug closely to the rear wall. There were often false starts if the foreman came out, and sometimes I got caught in the shed, and was thrown out, with a flea in my ear!'

But it wasn't only the pupils who had to use their wits: at least one teacher had to know how to exploit the system. Klaus Marx, now a headmaster, used to find himself umpiring cricket matches on Saturday mornings:

'We used to play a school called Coombe House, situated just between Raynes Park and New Malden, right beside the main

Eastleigh, a 'railway town' being largely created by the arrival of the LSWR, offered an ideal vantage point to rail enthusiasts in the shape of the Campbell Road bridge. This was also the only way of access to the Works and Eastleigh shed, attracting generations of trainspotters to view the assembled locomotives. In these 'before and after' pictures men, young and old, watch and photograph the passing of steam. The date is July 2nd 1967, the locomotive 'Merchant Navy' class No. 35008 *Orient Line* and the occasion is the Southern Region's own 'Farewell to Steam' special to Weymouth.

Both Rod Hoyle

Bournemouth line. I used to make sure that I always 'stood' at the right end so that I had a good view of the line beyond the wickets. With my camera in my pocket, I was always ready to 'snap' an interesting steam working. The trouble is, I really can't say just how many five or seven ball overs I allowed, if a 'Merchant Navy' happened to pass at an awkward time, as it often did!'

I was able to spend nearly every weekend during 1966 and 1967, either photographing steam trains or travelling on them. It was always a terrible choice to make, for timing was an exciting pastime, always hopeful of clocking up 10 seconds or less on my stop-watch for a ¼ mile section. That was the magic time which indicated 90 mph travelling speed, and like many others I compiled hundreds of 'logs' detailing the travelling times and speeds achieved on the way, with expresses and even local stopping trains. If it was steam, and I was on board, then I wanted to keep a record. But the dilemma was appalling: when I was in the train I looked out with envy at the cameramen at the lineside recording our progress. If I took my camera to some suitably photogenic spot and started 'banging away' at everything that steamed past, I would be wishing that I was on the train to enjoy the whole experience and not just the fleeting instant miniaturised in the viewfinder. The result was that I usually combined each activity, regretted that I couldn't cope with a tape-recorder as well, and marvelled at those who seemed to manage to handle all that technology, and were perhaps even festooned with a movie camera too!

As an example of one of my busiest days, I extract the following from my note-book:

'August 18th 1966. Left Netley 09.34 to Salisbury diesel unit. At Southampton Ctl. changed to 08.30 Waterloo to Weymouth, departing 10.12. Loco No. 35013 (load 11). Ran to Bournemouth Ctl. in 33 mins. 18 secs.: max. speed 80 mph. Thirteen minutes to board Poole – York train, departure 10.58. Load 11 also, engine No. 44942. Slow run, took 12 minutes from Christchurch to New Milton (start to stop). Top speed between Brockenhurst and Southampton only 57 mph. Arrived So'ton at 11.58, one hour journey time. Back to platform 4 again for 10.30 from Waterloo. Left 13 minutes late, with No. 35030 and 11 bogies. Excellent run, reached Bournemouth in 30m. 57s. Top speed, 77 mph. Rapid dash through Bournemouth subway to catch 14.34 to Waterloo, left 5 mins. late. No. 35008 with 10 coaches. Max speed 74 mph beyond Beaulieu Road. Net time, 31¾ minutes. Travelled on 15.49 diesel to Salisbury. Noted No. 34004 at Kimbridge Jct. on old Andover line with crane. Transferred to 14.10 from Exeter, waiting to depart, steam powered! No. 34006 with load 10. Took 22m. 09s. to Andover, top speed 80 mph. Returned west on 16.51 ex Basingstoke stopper, with No. 75076. Alighted at Idmiston Halt for photography. Recorded No. 34015 on 18.35 Sals. – W'loo, No. 34013 on 18.00 W'loo – Sals. Caught 17.41 W'loo – Sals. stopper with No. 34032. At Salisbury photographed No. 35029 with ecs of 20.35 to Basingstoke. Returned to Netley on 20.42 demu, arriving 21.37.'

The fascination of steam, even the humble branch train . . . . . Standard class '4' tank No. 80082 pauses at Lymington Town *en route* from Brockenhurst to the Pier station. The leading carriage is a Bulleid designed Corridor Brake Composite dating from September 1948. *Author*

Trainspotters at Bournemouth display a variety of 'uniforms' and strike contrasting poses: a Standard class '5' 4-6-0 'on shed' provides the backcloth.
Mike Esau

So that was how I filled one day of my long school summer holiday with twelve hours spent in the quest for steam. I had travelled behind seven different steam engines, and photographed four others in action, apart from those on shed at Bournemouth. I had also travelled about 200 miles in the process. However, my efforts pale into insignificance behind the real diehards of steam travel.

While the average enthusiast was content to turn out for an odd weekend or two, some devoted themselves totally to their addiction – steam. Paul Gibbons had just finished his A-levels in the summer of 1967, and had several free weeks before going to University, which he put to very good use:

'I bought a six guinea rail rover ticket, and spent almost the entire week on trains or stations. I didn't really bother to go home, it wasn't worth it! I was armed with my notebook and my wristwatch, which I used to record timings, but it wasn't a very good watch for working out speeds accurately. I used to exist out of my duffle bag, which I've still got somewhere! I had tried taking milk in a thermos the previous year, but it didn't work, so in '67 I bought food and drink when I could. I've still got a record in my notebook of my spending, mostly in station buffets and fish and chip shops! I remember that cups of tea were 6d and coffee 10d in the railway buffets. Mostly I lived on bars of chocolate, according to my notebook!

I met a lot of people who used to travel on the evening trains. Some of them used to work at the divisional HQ at Wimbledon and they seemed to know the drivers. They had targets that they used to set the crews; like the fastest start from Basingstoke out to one of the bridges towards Hook. I was lucky enough to be on the 18.15 up from Weymouth on my first day,

and we reckoned we'd reached 106 mph, with No. 35003. Then I travelled down to Weymouth on the 23.55 from Woking, which had standard No. 75075 from Eastleigh. I did Weymouth shed at 05.00; there were eighteen steamers present. I had steam trips up to Southampton and back and then went round Weymouth shed again at 15.00! I returned to London on the 17.30 with No. 35023. Then I caught an electric down to Portsmouth for my second night's 'sleep'! Actually it was a good way of getting some 'shut-eye' because you couldn't go any further than Portsmouth even if you did doze off. I'd get a couple of hours before the guard would wake me up with "Where's your ticket, son?".

I went straight back up to Waterloo in time to catch the 02.30 newspaper train to Eastleigh and, yes, back to Portsmouth again! That was with No. 34087 and it ran into the Harbour station and then reversed its train back out to Fratton for servicing and to turn the engine on the table. Then it pushed the stock back into Portsmouth and Southsea (Low Level) station to form the 07.30 to Eastleigh. I spent some time in the Southampton/Bournemouth area, then travelled up to Waterloo behind steam, and made one of my few visits to Nine Elms, having also done Bournemouth shed earlier in the day! I then tried my luck on the Clapham – Kensington service which had Ivatt No. 41312. I caught the Fridays only Bournemouth service from Waterloo at 18.22 back down to Bournemouth with No. 34093 and by midnight I had made my way to Portsmouth, and was riding in the late night stopper to Eastleigh. I remember it was hauled by Standard tank No. 80133, and I think it had a yellow painted back to its number plate. Then it was a Class '47' diesel up to Waterloo and the prospect of another night with no real sleep.

In fact I had to wait around the terminus until I could catch the 04.40 to Woking and thence Salisbury. I think it may have been that night or another that I was accosted by one of Waterloo's nocturnal 'down-and-outs'. To escape his attentions I had to catch an electric out to Clapham Junction and back . . . I didn't get much sleep that night!

Another night, to escape the tramps at Waterloo, I got on the 'Warship' diesel hauled Exeter train which left London at 01.10. I was terrified of falling asleep and ending up in the West Country so I had to hang out of the corridor window most of the way, so the rush of cold air would keep me awake. I remember getting into Salisbury at 03.07 only to find the waiting room locked and nowhere to rest. So I walked the streets of Salisbury for a couple of hours until I found a milkman and breakfasted on a bottle of milk and some Jaffa Cakes!'

Paul's rail-rovers took him on many other adventures during the last two weeks of Southern steam, and one can only marvel at his youthful resilience in maintaining a constant vigil at the trackside to watch and experience the passing of steam.

Another enthusiast who has pleasant memories of the latter months of Southern steam is Richard Adderson. In fact he was not fully conversant with Southern operations, being a resident of Norwich. So it was a complete surprise when he inadvertently stumbled on the last day of steam on the Swanage branch:

'I was staying in Bournemouth with a friend who was not very interested in railways. On the Sunday afternoon, September 4th 1966, we wanted to go somewhere, and purely by chance I suggested Swanage. Having no car it meant a train journey of course. To my disgust we had Type '3' diesel No. D6553 to Wareham, but things improved there as we found Standard No. 76010 waiting in the bay platform with the 15.34 to Swanage. There were a few photographers around but no more than I would have expected on a normal day. It wasn't until we got to Swanage that we found a notice displayed announcing that it was the very last day of steam. We hitched back to Corfe Castle and clambered up the ruins to watch the line. We saw No. 76010 return to Swanage with the next branch working, and then No. 80140 coming down 'light' from Wareham to work the 18.12 Swanage to Eastleigh. I decided there and then to travel on the last steam train on the branch.

To make it more interesting I caught the 17.57 ex-Swanage with No. 76010, with a view to transferring to the closely following 18.12 at Wareham. I would stay on that to Poole and then return on the 16.30 from Waterloo in time for the last return steam trip down the branch, at 19.44 from Wareham. All went well to Poole, although my friend announced he had no intention of going back to Swanage again, and went on to Bournemouth in disgust! So, alone now, I was standing on Poole station feeling rather pleased with the itinerary I had worked out. I even had time for a quick pint and still get back for the 19.26 departure.

Inevitably it was not to be! It was 20.15 before a filthy anonymous No. 34090 crept, almost shamefacedly, around the curve into the station. It just managed to get me back to Wareham in time to see No. 76010 getting *back* from Swanage on the 20.14 last run . . . As if that wasn't bad enough my attempts at night photography of this epic moment were also doomed to failure. I managed two nice time exposures of the train, but after it had gone I realised that I had forgotten to wind on the film between each picture!'

Richard Adderson's recollections are a timely reminder that things did not always go well during Southern Steam's dying days. It would be quite wrong if this chapter left the reader with the impression that nearly every steam train ran at speeds in the 90s, and every enthusiast had a continuous diet of superlative experiences. Nor was every driver and fireman committed to making the most of their increasingly run-down motive power; many couldn't wait to see the back of it and to gain the expected benefits of modern, clean comfortable traction.

At Nine Elms in particular, the shortage of men meant that promotion up the links could be very rapid. Older men who, in their day, had waited decades to be allowed to fire expresses, now saw other men *driving* who were many years their junior. In general the situation was accepted with good grace, but it did mean that some *very* young men found themselves out firing on demanding main line duties. Jim Robinson had the 'benefit' of just such a novice on one occasion:

'I booked on at Waterloo for the 10.30 to Weymouth: my regular mate was on holiday, and no replacement fireman had turned up. I got the foreman to call up Nine Elms and about 10.28 this young lad turned up. I said "Have you ever been on one of these before then?". He said what I feared, "No!". What was worse I had a gentleman with a pass riding on the footplate that day. Fortunately we had the best 'Packet', No. 35028. You only had to throw coal on and she would steam. We got away on time but by the time we'd reached Woking, the lad hadn't done a thing! Fortunately *Clan Line* had been well prepared with a good fire to start with. So now I had to leave the regulator and go across to put the injector on, as the glass was halfway down. Then once we were up at Brookwood, I went across and started putting some coal on. I almost felt like asking the gentleman to watch for the signals for me, but fortunately they were all greens.

When we got to Southampton I climbed up on the tender and pushed some coal forward and then put enough coal on the fire to get us to Bournemouth. I asked the gentleman to swing the water pipe round and give it to the fireman to fill her up. I was as black as a rook by the time we got to Bournemouth. I turned to the lad and said very firmly, "See that train over there, son. Get yourself in the guard's van and get back to London . . . now!" So he said, "Alright, driver." I don't know where that gentleman got to in the middle of all that, but when I handed over to Robbins who relieved me, he said "What's wrong with you, Robbo?" I said, "They gave me a cleaner laddy for the 10.30!". Then to finish matters, the guard came up and gave me a time ticket for being three minutes late into Bournemouth. So I wrote on it, I THINK YOU CAN FORGET ABOUT THIS ONE AS I HAVE DONE BOTH JOBS FROM WATERLOO.'

Problems were not confined simply to inexperienced men; there was a constant battle to be waged by crewmen to find a full set of locomotive tools. At least one fireman used to take his

There wasn't much to smile about when shovelling ash out of a smokebox, but Salisbury's Fireman Paddick does his best for the photographer!   *David M. Smith*

shovels, darts and prickers home after each shift and leave them parked in the hallway till his next duty! What his wife felt about the new domestic ornaments is not known. Generally though the role of wives and mothers in all this male domain must not be left unrecorded. Most wives of former steam men still throw up their hands in horror at the mention of the old days. The endless washing of filthy clothes, sinks and baths with grimy fingermarks and dirty rings, gave the lady of the house a never ending routine of cleaning tasks. Added to that were the difficulties of adapting to the shift work pattern of locomen. Eight hour shifts which could start in the middle of the night, or equally well end in the small hours too. The delays caused by late running or failure added to the difficulty in leading a predictable home life. Little wonder that most wives welcomed the changeover to the electrics with the clean uniforms and better punctuality. It took a very special kind of woman to share in the man's enjoyment of steam power and to put up cheerfully with the eccentricities of his working pattern.

While many recorders were privileged to take part in exciting steam runs, looking back I seem to have had more than my fair share of the mundane and the appalling. The old two-hour schedules between Waterloo and Bournemouth, including the Southampton stop, were inflated by 15 minutes or so for the duration of the electrification programme to allow for delays due to engineering works. Thus the best time from Waterloo to Southampton was now 93 minutes, achieved by both the 10.30 down and the 'Bournemouth Belle'. On occasions when there were relatively few speed restrictions or slow line diversions, the extra minutes available were no incentive to energetic running,

Above: Driver Jim Robinson, known generally as 'Robbo', had charge of LNER 'A4' class No. 4498 *Sir Nigel Gresley* on its run from Waterloo on June 4th 1967. He looks unimpressed by his famous mount, which nevertheless gave an excellent performance.
Ray Ruffell

Left: Blue skies above *Blue Funnel:* 'Merchant Navy' class No. 35013 betrays some faint evidence of its cabside lining beneath the travel stains, and the driver pauses for reflection, perhaps on the impending demise of his locomotive.
John Marshall

and it was quite common to experience speeds not greatly in excess of 60 mph. On the other hand if an engine was steaming badly or a rough rider, even the new decelerated times might not be adequate to enable a punctual arrival to be recorded.

I had a series of particularly disappointing runs with the down 'Royal Wessex' during the latter part of 1966. As one of the few named trains on the line (even though it never carried a headboard) it seemed reasonable to suppose it would merit better engines and some enthusiasm from drivers and firemen. Indeed it was one of the workings chosen by the authorities to give demonstration rides to commuters of the electrification works in progress, from the comfort of the inspection saloon attached to the rear of the train. Perhaps it was to give the invited guests as much time as possible to see what was being done for them, that each time I travelled the result was a pedestrian effort. The log (Table 8) details one of my runs and for comparison is presented with another over the same Waterloo – Winchester section, showing what steam could achieve in 1966/67.

In each case the trains were mid-afternoon workings: the first being 'The Royal Wessex' in September 1966, and the second the 15.30 from Waterloo in February the following year. Both trains were hauled by rebuilt 'West Country' class engines: it must be said that No. 34004 *Yeovil* looked very smart on the second occasion and still had its nameplates in place: the same could not be said of No. 34040. While it must be conceded that the latter had a heavier train to contend with, that does not seem sufficient explanation of the wide variation in performance. *Yeovil* generally ran at about 15 mph greater speed throughout the journey, and made light of the delays incurred *en route*. On the other hand, No. 34040 did not even manage to touch 60 mph during the first sixty miles of its journey out of London, and it was only on the downhill final section towards Winchester that it

peaked at 64 mph. Speed dropped as low as 44 mph on the moderate climb from Woking out to Milepost 31, at which point No. 34004 was accelerating up to 56 mph from the slowing at Woking to 39 mph caused by a signal check. Likewise, on the racing ground thence to Basingstoke, the 'Royal Wessex' plodded along at about 55 mph, where any self respecting express would be expected to attain 70 mph at least. The irony is that despite its pedestrian progress, the 'Wessex' was only just over three minutes late at Winchester. The expanded schedule allowed, or perhaps encouraged, some drivers to take it very easily indeed and still arrive near enough to time to earn no major reprimands.

After allowing for the few delays incurred on No. 34040's run, I would estimate that it would have reached Winchester in 83 minutes unchecked. By comparison No. 34004 on the February run, managed to complete the 66.60 miles in a shorter *actual* time of 81 minutes 31 seconds. Out of course delays for signals and permanent way slacks probably added about 15½ minutes to the running time. Thus No. 34004 is credited with a net time to Winchester of only 65¾ minutes, a very fine achievement, especially since it was achieved without exceeding about 76 mph at any point on the journey. The subsequent downhill sprints to Southampton allowed the 15.30 from Waterloo to achieve a right time arrival, while the 'Royal Wessex' paid the price for minutes squandered earlier and ran into signal checks near St. Denys, eventually drawing up at Southampton at 18.23, nearly five minutes late. No doubt some would say that was pretty satisfactory with 440 tons of train, an out of repair locomotive and various delays on the way. From what happened in the last few weeks of steam, and before, we can also say that it was pretty appalling with such a potentially excellent locomotive at the head of the train.

A splendid portrait of Firelighter Ben Nash going home after a shift at Basingstoke depot. 'Battle of Britain' class No. 34052 *Lord Dowding* simmers in the background.

Ray Ruffell

Table 8
Waterloo – Southampton Central

Date		September 1st 1966			February 13th 1967		
Train		16.35 Waterloo – Weymouth			15.30 Waterloo – Weymouth		
Locomotive No.		34040			34004		
Load		12/402/440			10/345/370 tons		
Miles		**Sched.**	**Actual**	**Speeds**	**Sched.**	**Actual**	**Speeds**
0.00	WATERLOO		0.00	—	0	0.00	—
1.30	Vauxhall		3.57	30		3.28	41/50
3.90	Clapham Junction	7	8.00	38	7	7.13	37
5.55	Earlsfield		10.27	44		9.45	47
7.20	Wimbledon		12.38	45		11.40	55
						p.w.s.	
8.60	Raynes Park		14.22	50		14.05	14
9.75	New Malden		15.40	51			
10.95	Berrylands		16.58	54		18.30	41
			p.w.s.				
12.05	Surbiton		18.20	36		20.02	50
13.35	Hampton Court Jct.	18	20.43	31	18	21.25	60
14.40	Esher		22.27	47		22.25	66
15.95	Hersham		24.27	50		23.51	68
17.10	Walton		25.47	50		24.51	68
19.10	Weybridge		28.14	53/56		26.36	69
20.40	Byfleet and New Haw		29.42	58		27.41	75
21.65	West Byfleet		31.00	56		28.43	72
						sigs.	
24.30	Woking	33*	33.58	53	34*	31.28	39
28.00	Brookwood		38.23	46		36.15	53
31.00	Milepost 31		42.23	44		39.29	56
33.25	Farnborough		45.00	55/58		41.33	69
36.50	Fleet		48.33	56/58		44.21	72/75
39.85	Winchfield		52.08	53/56		47.06	70
42.20	Hook		54.53	53/56		49.12	69
						sigs.	
47.80	Basingstoke		60.08	48		55.25	15
50.30	Worting Junction	62	64.05	38	60	61.12	43
52.55	Wooton		68.14	36		64.04	53/61
58.10	Micheldever		75.44	57		69.35	66/20
						p.w.s.	
61.80	Wallers Ash		79.13	64/46		75.54	50/72
			p.w.s.				
64.50	Winchester Junction	79	82.29	53	75½	78.30	69
66.60	WINCHESTER CITY	82	85.47	—	78½	81.13	—
3.10	Shawford		4.48	64/68		4.48	65/71/56
						sigs.	
6.95	Eastleigh	9½	8.17	60/66	10	8.25	60/64
8.30	Southampton Airport					8.46	64/66
9.20	Swaythling		10.27	65		10.34	59/62
			13.20				
	sig. stop		14.00				
10.65	St. Denys		14.27			11.57	63
11.60	Northam Junction	16½	17.30		15½	13.27	
12.65	SOUTHAMPTON CENTRAL	20	21.25		19	16.53	

Actual arrival times:	Winchester	3¼ late	2½ late	
	Southampton	4¾ late	Right time	
Estimated net times:	Waterloo – Winchester	83 mins.	65¾ mins.	
	Winchester – Southampton	17¼ mins.	16½ mins.	

*Schedule to Woking Junction

110

Chapter Six

Works and Sheds 1966-1967

In 1957, the Southern Region had control of thirty six engine sheds (see Appendix One), stretching geographically from Ramsgate in the far east of Kent, to the little depot at Wadebridge, between Bodmin and Padstow in Cornwall. The most northerly servicing outpost was at Reading, followed closely by Bath Green Park on the Somerset and Dorset Railway line to Bournemouth. The most southerly mainland shed was at Plymouth Friary, but there were also the two Isle of Wight sheds, at Ryde and Newport. There were also a further eighteen sub-sheds, typically small buildings tucked away at the ends of branch lines, to provide overnight accommodation for the branch locomotive. Examples of these were to be found at Lyme Regis and Torrington, although the sub-shed at Folkestone Junction was a rather grander affair, hosting the tank engines which worked as bankers up the steep incline from the Harbour station. Over the next ten years the number of engine sheds fluctuated, as the WR took control of some, while handing over others. The overall trend, naturally enough, was for the number of sheds to fall, as dieselisation and electrification removed the need for steam stabling.

The building and repair of steam locomotives in the 1950s was the responsibility of the three major locomotive works at Ashford, Brighton and Eastleigh. There was also a small, but highly effective, workshop at Ryde on the Isle of Wight. Carriage building and repair was undertaken at Lancing and Eastleigh, while the Pullman Car company had its own workshops at Brighton. By 1966, the contraction of the Southern's area of management, and the concurrent elimination of steam power left a mere seven main running sheds, with six other minor

depots, where engines could be serviced, and men sign on and off duty. There were also the departmental shunting engines which had bases at Meldon Quarry in Devon, Redbridge Sleeper depot near Southampton and Ashford Works in Kent. Locomotive repairs were by now concentrated at Eastleigh Works alone, and at the surviving establishment at Ryde. In this chapter, the seven sheds extant in 1966 with their own locomotive allocations, are described in some detail, as are most of the lesser sheds. Those at Lymington and Swanage were very simple, being only large enough to stable a single branch engine overnight, but they remained in use until the end of steam working on their respective branches. However, they are not given a separate mention in the following pages. The works at Eastleigh and Ryde do receive coverage, however, while the departmental locomotives have been referred to already.

In common with all British Railways' steam depots, each main Southern shed had its own code number, carried by its stud of locomotives on an oval plate affixed to their smokebox doors. During 1966/7, the sheds and their codes were:

70A	Nine Elms	
70B	Feltham	(no steam allocation remaining in 1967, but still a servicing and signing-on point)
70C	Guildford	
70D	Eastleigh	
70E	Salisbury	
70F	Bournemouth	
70G	Weymouth	
70H	Ryde	

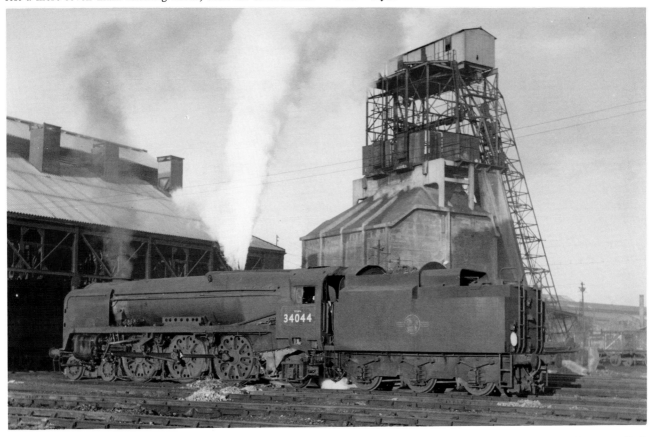

The majesty of steam at Nine Elms: surplus steam blows skywards as 'West Country' class No. 34044 *Woolacombe* waits its next call of duty. The shed's huge coaling tower made the depot a well known landmark.   *Derek Buckett*

111

EASTLEIGH DUTY NO. 280
4 MT (STANDARD) 75000 Class
MONDAY ONLY
Stabled off No. 280 SUN

	Weymouth Loco		11 40‖

MONDAY EXCEPTED
Stabled off No. 283

	Bmouth Loco		04 45‖
xx	Bmouth Cen.		05 15V
06 50	Weymouth	xx‖	
xx	Weymouth Loco		11 40‖

DAILY

xx	Weymouth		12 12P
13 39	Bournemouth Cen.		13 55‖
14 00	Bournemouth Loco		14 32‖
	(Coupled to No. 395 WX)		
15 00	Brockenhurst		16 15E
16 56	Eastleigh		17 05‖
17 10	Eastleigh Loco		18 15‖
18 35	Northam Yd.		19 04F
19 21	Eastleigh M. Yd.		19 40‖
19 45	Eastleigh		20 40V
23 00	Clapham Jn.		23 15‖
23 30	Nine Elms Loco		
	Work No. 281		

BOURNEMOUTH MEN
(1) 1st set (MX) on duty 03 45, work &
rlvd in depot, prepare & work No. 430
08 35‖ & relieved at Bournemouth Cen. 11 05
WEYMOUTH MEN
(2) 1st set on duty 10 40, work and perform
requirements for 14 32‖, relieve No. 433
at 16 28, work & relieved in depot.

BOURNEMOUTH MEN
(3) 2nd set on duty 14 12, work & assist
requirements for 18 15‖, to station,
relieve No. 432 at 19 48, work & relieved
in depot.
EASTLEIGH MEN
(4) 1st set on duty 17 15, perform requirements, work & rlvd at Eleigh 19 45, to depot,
work No. 461 & rlvd at Eleigh 00 45
NINE ELMS MEN
(5) Off No. 90 rlve at Eleigh 19 45 work
& rlvd at Clapham Jn. 23 00.
(6) Off No. 67 relieve at Clapham Jn.
23 00 work and dispose.

EASTLEIGH DUTY NO. 281
4 MT (STANDARD) 75000 Class
MO - Off No. 281 Saturday
MX - Off No. 280

	Nine Elms Loco		06 51‖
07 06	Waterloo		07 18P
10 09	Salisbury	xx‖	
xx	Salisbury Loco		13 30‖
13 35	Salisbury E. Sdgs.		
	Steam Heat		
	Salisbury E. Sdgs.		14 02E
14 05	Salisbury Stn.		
	Steam Heat 14 36 to Waterloo		
	Salisbury Stn.		14 30‖
14 35	Salisbury E. Sdgs.		
	Steam Heat		
	Salisbury E. Sdgs.	xxE	
xx	Salisbury		15 55P
17 16	Basingstoke	xx‖	
xx	Basingstoke Loco		
	Work No. 282		

NINE ELMS MEN
(1) 1st set - On duty 05 46, work and
relieved at Woking 07 57, pass to Basingstoke
relieve No. 464 at 09 00 work and dispose
GUILDFORD MEN
(2) 1st set on duty 07 07 pass 07 32 to
Woking rlve at 07 57 work and dispose,
home pass 12 35.
SALISBURY MEN
(3) No. 2 P. & D. Men prepare for 13 30‖
(4) 1st set on duty 13 15 work and dispose
relieve No. 464 at 18 28, work and relieved
at Salisbury 20 16.

A page from the locomotive and crew roster book for 1967, showing the duties to be worked by two of Eastleigh's class '4' 4-6-0s. Note that enginemen from six different sheds were involved in operating the two engines during the 24-hour period. In earlier years these diagram books were printed, but with the frequent changes of motive power as electrification approached, there were frequent duplicated reissues such as this example.

There were also other sheds with locomotive servicing facilities remaining, and still acting as crew signing-on points:
Basingstoke
Fratton
Southampton Terminus/Eastern Docks/Western Docks
Lymington
Swanage

Nine Elms

Nine Elms was the main locomotive depot of the Southern Railway, and continued its pre-eminence after nationalisation. Although it had been responsible for about 200 engines in its heyday at the turn of the century, this figure had been halved by the end of the 1950s. At the beginning of 1966, its run-down was nearing completion with an allocation of just 24 locomotives, less than Guildford, Bournemouth and Eastleigh. Strangely though, its fleet stabilised at that level so that on the final day of Southern Steam, it could still boast 24 on its books, which by then was the biggest total of all the Southern sheds!

Two dozen machines were a paltry total to house in such a sprawling and extensive site. The final rebuilding in 1910 had bequeathed a 25 road depot, with its two sections known as the 'Old' and 'New' sheds. The Old shed, the bigger of the two, had taken the brunt of German bombing during the war, and had never had its roofing fully replaced. This simply worsened in the post-war years and by the end of steam virtually all the Old shed was roofless, and had become little more than an open storage area for locomotives.

The unsatisfactory condition of the buildings was one of the reasons for the transfer to Weymouth of all the 'Merchant Navy' pacifics by 1965, although happily the survivors returned to Nine Elms for the final three months. By then the still standing New shed, was more than adequate to provide covered accommodation. The best overall view of the shed could be obtained from the blocks of flats to the south-east of the depot. Although enthusiasts were not popular with the residents, the flats gave a superb vista, with the turntable in the foreground and the twenty-five engine roads stretching beyond towards the shed. Dominating the sky-line from this vantage point was Battersea Power station, its tall chimneys belching smoke into the sky, in a repetition of the foreground scene where Bulleid pacifics and Standards were also contributing to London's pollution!

Architecturally, the shed's coaling plant was the supreme structure. This was a formidable concrete construction, ultra-modern when built in 1923. It was similar to the one that still survives in preservation at Carnforth, with a hoist to raise the loaded coal wagons to its peak, which were then inverted to tip coal into the hopper below. This could then be fed by gravity into a locomotive tender. Driver Bert Hooker recalls:

'On number one road pit, near the turntable, there was a water column, where the water ran very slowly. It would take twenty minutes to get half a tender of water! While you were waiting the fireman would be making up the fire and sorting out his coal. All the small stuff would go over the side and make a great big heap beside the track. As the day went on, when there was about half a wagon

load of the stuff deposited, the old grab would come along and pick it all up and drop it into a wagon, to be recycled into the hopper.'

Locomotives ready for duty would have to pass beside the New shed on one of the through roads, and could then head up for Waterloo. These movements were controlled by Loco Junction signalbox, which straddled the main lines, being carried on girders and supports.

The foreman's office, and those of the clerks and timekeepers were attached to the outside wall of the New shed, and all engines coming on shed would stop alongside, so that the driver could report in. A stand-by engine was often parked on the siding, the 'Store Road', alongside, ready to be summoned up to Waterloo in case of a failure. John Wickham who worked for a while with the list clerks recalls:

'I never saw such a filthy hole in all my life! It is hardly surprising it was closed down. Even the clerks had to wear long coats to protect their clothes. Once a month they used to get all the furniture out of the office and scrub it out. Because the atmosphere was so sooty, there were ruddy great weights on the doors, to make sure they shut as quickly as possible.'

Inevitably, with steam repairs ending and fewer and fewer engines left in service, drivers faced increasing difficulties towards the end. Jim Robinson was one of the older drivers, who had to come to terms with the decline of steam. 'Robbo' as he was always known to his colleagues, transferred to Nine Elms from Feltham in 1959 and was soon working his way up No. 1 link:

'The last two years, you wouldn't believe the state of the engines. One morning we were getting ready for the 08.30 to Bournemouth, and my mate did the usual business of putting his shovel in the firebox to see if there were any water drips coming

The 'Old' shed at Nine Elms with an assortment of Bulleid pacifics among the assorted debris.

E.J. Waters

A Standard class '5' awaits a main line duty (No. 145 in the diagram book according to the numbers pasted on the smokebox disc), while two Standard tanks await their next turns on Waterloo empty stock duties. The foreman's offices are to the right in this view of Nine Elms. *Doug Richards*

A view from the opposite side of the coaling tower with class '5' No. 73018 heading for the turntable, and 'West Country' class No. 34032 *Camelford* soon to follow on July 1st 1966. *Derek Buckett*

from the plugs. (A leaking plug was a serious matter, and was sufficient to have an engine failed, if the leak was not minor.) He found a leak, and the next two engines we were given as replacements were also leaking. Each time I had to tell the Inspector and he thought I was mad in the end! Finally we were given a Standard and that was alright!'

Another problem for all crews was the gradual disappearance of tools and equipment as lost items were not replaced, and the remainder hoarded by selfish (or prudent) men. Driver Robinson suffered like all the others:

'When you signed on there were no tools in the stores. The engine was stripped of everything, feeder, oil bottles, bucket, handbrush, coal pick, even the pep pipe. Things like the engine sanders would not be working. You'd book them in, but next morning they'd be just the same. Some of the men used to hide their oil feeders, and firemen hid their shovels in the coal stack! It was pathetic . . .'

However, some drivers managed to make arrangements. Bert Hooker says:

'At the end it was pretty grim, but we did have a toolman, a Pole called Stefan. He saw me alright . . . he always used to say don't worry, *Mr.* Hooker, I'll get you some tools."

Even that was no guarantee however. Doug Richards, Nine Elms list clerk remembers one desperate case:

'A driver and fireman had their engine ready, and left it to go for a cup of tea in the lobby. When they went back on board, to their amazement they found all the tools had been taken from the footplate while they were having their drink a few yards away!'

Although Nine Elms was much reduced in importance from its glory days, it was still a substantial source of employment. There were six 'links' of drivers, of declining seniority. In the No. 1 link were the prestige turns such as the 10.30 to Weymouth, the 'Royal Wessex' and the 'Bournemouth Belle' on Sundays. The second link contained men who were trained to drive Western region 'Warship' diesels that operated on the Salisbury–Exeter route. The last link comprised purely local duties. In addition there were the links of men who operated the Clapham Junction – Waterloo coaching stock turns, and the 'shed knockers', the preparation and disposal gangs. The latter would light up and raise steam and generally prepare main line locomotives, and then drive them up to Waterloo for men in No. 1 and 2 links to takeover for their passenger duties. In the lower links were the younger, less experienced, drivers, and also some nearing retirement who had opted for an easier life during their last five years.

Each driver was teamed with a regular fireman, but in the bottom links there was often a shortage of men. Towards the end this had to be made good by much overtime and rest day working, but even then it was necessary to borrow firemen from as far afield as Fratton and Salisbury. Doug Richards, who as a list clerk was responsible for allocating men to rosters, recalls that it was sometimes necessary to use three different firemen from Salisbury to cover one Nine Elms firing turn. This was due to the fact that a man's turn of duty had to be fitted into eight hours, including travelling time to and from his base. Needless to say the official complement of 26 cleaners just did not exist, so there was little or no evidence of clean engines at Nine Elms!

Apart from around 200 drivers and firemen, there were small numbers of assorted tradesmen. These included carpenters and fitters, as well as office staff. There were also ashmen, tube blowers, coalmen and turntable operators. There was even one man whose job was to paint the headcode discs white, and this he continued to do right up to the last day, working in a semi-derelict store room. There was a tremendous cosmopolitan atmosphere among the workers. Apart from immigrant West Indians, Pakistanis and Indians who had arrived during the preceding ten years, there were also many Czechs and Poles, who had settled during the War.

Despite its small allocation of locomotives, the shed was always busy with tank engines bustling about between turns of duty, and tender engines being coaled, taking water or turning on the table at the end of the yard. There were also ever increasing numbers of withdrawn or stored machines parked in the Old shed or the back of the New shed. A visitor, during 1967 would typically find close on thirty locomotives present, of which about half would be in steam.

In many ways it was the most dramatic of the surviving steam depots; the stark sombre shapes of uncleaned engines were relieved by the light which shafted in through roof ventilators. Their otherwise inanimate forms were brought to life by the acrid smoke that curled lazily skywards up through the steel girders of the roof supports, and the damp sweet smelling steam that issued forth from pipes and joints. The shed floor, black with soot and slippery from grime, was decorated with little patches of oily water condensed from the steam life blood of some Southern giant. It was not a beautiful place, yet the combination of light and shade, of noise and quiet, of men and machines, inspired many a photographer, film maker and artist.

Paul Barnes captured the movement and the sounds of the place superbly in his short colour film 'The Artist and the Engines'. His title referred, of course, to David Shepherd. The young painter, already well-known for his elephant studies, almost took up residence at Nine Elms in its final days, and committed its images to canvas, in a personal race against time. His classic 'Nine Elms, the final hours' is just one of the paintings he made which have immortalised the end of Southern Steam. David describes the memories of Nine Elms as vividly in words as in oils:

'Nine Elms had begun to cast its spell over me in the mid-sixties. On my journeys to London by train, I had always looked longingly to the right, down the slope towards the coaling stage, where the air seemed to be permanently filled with choking locomotive smoke. Finally the attraction became irresistible, and I made my first visit.

Every corner of the shed seemed to be a potential oil painting. Locomotives were everywhere, all dirty and most stripped of their nameplates. To me this was more exciting than seeing a lot of clean locomotives. Dirty engines have much more attraction to me as an artist. They talk to you, through their layers of grime and filth of their past experiences.

It seemed that engines were coming and going every few minutes from the great train shed at Waterloo up the line and all this contributed to the excitement and atmosphere. There was the inevitable scrap line . . . connecting rods and other bits and pieces were lying all over the place among the piles of ashes, twisted firing irons, old buckets and all the other rubbish. Growing everywhere, by a minor miracle, was that marvellous plant the willowherb. It was proving with dramatic effect that nature has the most amazing ability to clothe in a fleeting but nevertheless considerable beauty the most squalid and decrepit areas of industrial wasteland. For this was a wasteland. Our proud steam heritage was not going out in a blaze of glory. It was going out fast amongst all the degradation, and only the railwaymen and enthusiasts cared a damn.

The last days in these great steam sheds were a paradise for the painter such as myself. Shining locomotives, hurtling out of the canvas towards me, as in so many photographs, were not my choice. My subjects were the grimy workhorses in the twylight of their years, neglected, forlorn, but still working. In the gloomy depths of Nine Elms, I found intense beauty of a most dramatic kind if I searched for it through the dirt and grime. Lovely harmonies could be found in the cool greys and browns and mauves of the engines; and, on the connecting rods, one could detect the occasional glint of brilliant light where wet, slowly

dripping oil, caught the sun. There would always be the warm smell of engines and the murmur of gentle sound as they simmered in the gloom. If Rembrandt had been alive at this time, he would have loved it!'

Around the shed precincts, there was plenty for the photographer and artist to record and interpret. Ash was everywhere, dropped by engines and left to accumulate beyond the reach, or the willpower, of the driver of the travelling steam grab. The ash mingled with the heaps of coal, enough to trip the unwary, particularly in the hours of darkness. Lines of coal wagons stood on the sidings beside the coaling tower. Some were used just inside the shed yard to carry ash, and were designated accordingly on their body sides. The others, nominally grey steel but often rusted to a dirty orange, stood silently in untidy ranks. All over the place weeds grew healthily, between the tracks and beside them. For months the shed had been under sentence of death, with a 'Statement of Intent' to close the establishment from July 1967. Little wonder that the niceties of tidiness, repairs to breakages, and general cleanliness were overlooked.

Despite the evidence of imminent destruction of their work-base, the men soldiered on as if the battle would still go on for many a year. Jim Evans was one of those who lived through the last run-down of the shed:

'I had already experienced the closure of a great depot at Stewarts Lane, so nothing was going to be a surprise to *me*. The foot-platemen continued with their way of life as it had been for years. The great card schools that went on all day and night still reigned supreme; men who had just signed off waited to get a vacated seat to join in, while someone on a winning streak sat right through until his next turn of duty. If it wasn't cards, it was drink! Sessions in the nearby 'Brooklands Arms' continued around the back with three card brag, long after closing time.

The men's attitude to it all was that it wouldn't really happen, they would never take their steam engines away, they would be there forever. But, sadly, it was noticeable that you could now drop your engine down onto the pit road and find nothing else there, when a few months before you would have had to queue up behind half a dozen engines.

Occasionally I walked around the dead monsters, 'West Countries' and Standards, parked in the old shed, and saw the rust beginning to form on their pistons. Hand rails too turned reddish brown as eager hands no longer used them to climb aboard. Footplate controls were taking on the fixed positions of the dead, as the action of damp and cold locked metal against metal. These engines seemed to me to cry out to be used again, for great fires to be lit in their bellies, and the challenge of a fast run down to Bournemouth set before them. But in my head, if not my heart, I knew that it was not going to be, although it was still very hard to come to terms with.

As the final weeks drew near, things were noticeably winding down. No longer did you have to queue for oil at the stores, there was so little being used now you could go in and help yourself! Tucked behind the racks there were the nameplates and shields which had been rescued by the fitters from the Bulleid pacifics; alongside were the headboards of the 'Bournemouth Belle' and 'The Cunarder'. They were like jewels on display, but not to be worn. How could anyone possibly put a value on those things? Then one of the chutes on the coal hopper got blocked and so it was abandoned. At one time the coalmen would have struggled relentlessly to free a blockage, but no more, as long as one each side remained operative.

Outside the Elms, even the surrounding areas were being run down in unison. The typical Battersea houses of Brooklands Road were being flattened, although the actual pub remained standing proud above the rubble and ashes, a watering hole for the still thirsty footplate men. At least some things remained until the end, where I, and the others, could still sink the first pint before the landlord had returned with the change! The Brooklands Arms died with the shed: it too came to the end of the road, and was pulled down just a few days after Nine Elms closed . . .'

For all its dirt, squalor and dereliction, the shed was a real community of working men, and the combination of human wit and muscle with man's mechanical creations, threw up visions and voices which will never be recreated. In David Shepherd's words:

'In that great dramatic arena, the coaling stage was the central character . . . what a sight and what a memory for so many enthusiasts!

The line beneath it had sunk several inches into the ground through the years of heavy use, and more recent lack of maintenance. The sight (and sound) of several tons of coal crashing down into the bunker of a 'Merchant Navy' pacific was the prelude to a truly amazing scene. Wagner himself would have been inspired as the great beast tried to draw itself out from underneath the tower. Giant locomotives were trapped, often for many minutes at a time, as they struggled in torment, driving wheels spinning to be released from their smokey hell. Clouds of steam and sparks were hurled into the sky as the thunderous sound reverberated around the blocks of high-rise flats that created this amphitheatre.'

During the depot's final week of life, engines that were still steamable were prepared to be sent on their last runs down to Salisbury. It had been hoped to clear the shed out during the week, but so many engines returned unbidden, that Nine Elms eventually became the third collecting point for steam. Thus there were still 31 steam engines left at Nine Elms a fortnight after the end of steam, and it was weeks before the last was hauled away and demolition and clearance of the entire site begun.

The clerical staff stayed for a few weeks and were then transferred to Feltham. The drivers moved up to Waterloo. Most men transferred, some left the railway, some retired and some were made redundant, and now Nine Elms shed is just a memory, but certainly a very potent one.

Feltham

Feltham was a freight shed, opened in the 1920s, to service the new 'hump' marshalling yard beside the Twickenham to Staines line. It was a six-road straight-through shed of functional design, with an attached repair shed equipped with a 50 ton overhead crane. There was also a concrete mechanized coaling plant, similar to the one at Nine Elms.

In its heyday the shed had around 100 engines to call upon, for yard shunting, local 'trip' freights, and long-distance goods expresses to the West. Sometimes its freight engines, such as 'S15s' and 'H15s' were borrowed for relief passenger turns on Summer Saturdays. By 1966 the freight yard was already declining in importance, and local shunting had been turned over to

The characteristic exterior of Feltham shed is the location for this picture of the last active 'S15' class No. 30837. It is being oiled up ready for final rail tour duty, and it has been cleaned and polished to a superb standard. January 7th 1966.
John Scrace

diesels. The steam fleet had dwindled to just half a dozen standard 2-6-4Ts, and there was little rostered work for these. Four were withdrawn during the year and the two remaining, Nos. 80085 and 80140, transferred to Nine Elms in October. The shed's last booked steam working was a Waterloo – Reading parcels which went over to electro-diesel haulage in July.

As steam faded away, the newly built electro-diesels arrived on a weekly basis during the first half of the year. Together with other SR diesels, and visitors from other regions, such as WR 'Hymeks' and 'Westerns', the appearance of steam hauled freights to the Feltham yard became ever less common. However, the few steam engines arriving each day would go on shed to be serviced, and the overhead crane enabled minor repairs to be carried out there. The last 'S15', No. 30837, reminder of the shed's once large fleet of freight 4-6-0s, hung on in store well into the summer months of 1966. Sadly this magnificent machine was eventually towed away to the scrapyard.

After Christmas 1966, there was an unexpected revival of steam working, with two or three arrivals on some days, ranging from Ivatt tanks to 'Merchant Navies'. Indeed, on January 17th 1967, a *freight* turned up hauled by 'Battle of Britain' class No. 34090, carrying the 'Atlantic Coast Express' headboard, over two years after that famous passenger express ceased operating! Officially the depot closed to steam at the end of 1966, becoming a diesel depot under the Chief Mechanical and Electrical Engineer, Southern Region. However, this seemed to make little difference in practice to its continuing low-level steam useage.

A visit on January 11th revealed standard tanks Nos. 80016 and 80145 in the shed, together with a dozen assorted diesels and electro-diesels. The following month, it was host to two Bulleid pacifics which had incurred hot axle-boxes and needed repair. These were Nos. 34089 and 34100, the latter having run light to Feltham after failing on the LCGB tour of February 5th. During

March there were still two or three daily steam appearances, including the 11.08 Feltham – Kingston goods which was reported to be a regular 2-6-4T working. No. 34090 turned up again at Feltham with that turn on one occasion.

This pattern of infrequent steam operation to and from Feltham continued right up to the end of Southern steam. A visit to the shed on June 3rd found one locomotive in steam, Nine Elms No. 82019, together with Nos. 34047, 76058 and 80154 stored. The latter two had been withdrawn in the spring, and were to become the last two steam locomotives at Feltham, being photographed there on July 15th by David Druce. He later saw them at Gloucester Horton Road in August, being towed to Buttigieg's scrapyard at Newport.

Thus steam at Feltham quietly slipped away. Plans to build a diesel depot alongside never came to fruition, and there is now little evidence that Feltham shed, or the yard which gave rise to it, ever existed.

Guildford

Guildford shed was unusual among those of the Southern, in being designed on the roundhouse principal, with the shed buildings arranged around a central turntable. This was probably due to the cramped site, excavated from the chalk hillside, through which the Waterloo – Portsmouth route tunnelled alongside. For steam enthusiasts travelling towards London on the electrified main line, the emergence from the tunnel into daylight gave a fascinating prospect of a variety of steam engines simmering around the turntable. The locomotive allocation was always of the mixed traffic and tank variety, there being no express passenger responsibilities for Guildford.

The shed was originally built in 1887 by the LSWR, and was extended in 1896 to provide a straight shed on its southern

Class '4' 4-6-0 No. 75074 being turned on the Guildford turntable on June 17th 1967.

Derek Buckett

arm. It was not a true roundhouse, amounting to no more than a semi-circle, nevertheless the arrangement required the permanent attendance of a shed pilot to move dead engines about. This role was the preserve of various 0-4-0Ts in the 1950s, but towards the end of Southern steam, a 'USA' tank took over. The regular engine was No. 30072, which had its moment of glory as the last engine to leave the shed on July 9th 1967.

Although set on an electrified route, Guildford shed managed to boast an allocation of no less than 78 engines in 1947, and at the beginning of 1966 it still boasted 27. However, there were few rostered workings from the shed by this time; from January 1967 there were only five regular steam turns on weekdays. These were mainly van trains and a few secondary passengers, such as the 18.51 Bournemouth Central – Woking stopping train and the 16.51 Basingstoke – Salisbury. These requirements could be easily covered by the now depleted fleet of 12 assorted Standards.

However, Guildford's locomotives found most of their employment at night, and weekends, on engineers trains, many in connection with the electrification works.

Guildford enginemen did take their turn on main line work on occasions, even if their locomotives rarely had such opportunities. The long period of weekend diversions due to engineering works, brought Waterloo – Bournemouth expresses to the Guildford route, and also via Farnham and Alton over the Mid-Hants line. These workings often produced employment for Guildford crews, even on star turns such as the 'Bournemouth Belle'. On one Sunday, a Guildford crew arrived at Waterloo to take out the 'Belle' which had originally been booked to travel via Guildford. The Nine Elms crew which had brought the pacific in to head the Pullmans, said to the Guildford driver that they had put the boards (destination discs) up ready for departure. But the Guildford men looked up front and then said that they had got the wrong headcode. Hadn't they heard that the diversion was cancelled and they were now going to work the 'Belle' down the main line instead. The actual reply of the Nine Elms crew is not recorded, but they were certainly not amused at the thought of Guildford men doing their job. Such traditions were firmly held by many of the older drivers, about their status and responsibilities.

One of the Guildford drivers at the time was John Berryman. He recalls his highest speed with steam was working a diverted express down the Portsmouth line. They were touching 90 mph as they approached the Liss outer distant signal, which was interlocked with the Liss distant, and gave advance warning in case the level crossing gates ahead were closed. It was a matter of faith that the outer distant and the distant were both in the 'off' position. If not, there would have been every prospect of a Bulleid pacific passing Liss with level crossing gates wrapped around its buffers! Berryman turned to Inspector Bill Neil who was riding on the footplate and cheerily remarked, 'I hope the distant's off . . .' 'So do I . . .', replied the inspector laconically. Fortunately it was!

The engine crews at Guildford were divided into two gangs, each of twenty-four. The top gang contained the more senior men, whilst the 'boys' gang had the younger drivers. Although a steam depot, all drivers worked diesel and electric duties as well. This meant blue overalls one day and a green suit the next. The top gang had the Salisbury – Woking diesel unit runs, while the 'boys' were rostered to electric multiple unit (emu) trips. Both gangs also worked some of the Reading – Redhill line services, operated by 'Tadpole' demus. Other drivers were assigned to shunting diesels in the yards at Guildford and Woking, while others belonged to the shed duty teams or were on stand-by duties.

Although of lesser importance as a depot, Guildford still needed the services of a small detachment of 'back-up' men. Under the general direction of shedmaster Arthur Coe, they included half a dozen fitters and their mates, boilersmiths, boiler-washers, storesmen, toolmen and general labourers. Towards the end, as the depot was run down, some of these jobs were doubled up. Thus the storesman, apart from issuing materials such as oil and cloths, also acted as official timekeeper for the foreman. One or two of the drivers were also panelmen, which meant that they stood in as acting foremen when the need arose.

As mentioned in chapter three, Guildford shed began 1966 with three class 'Q1s', (Charlies) and four class 'U' 2-6-0s, as well as six class 'Ns'. These were well-liked, and made Guildford a popular place for photographers, as these were the last remnants of the old Southern. Although they had all been withdrawn by the middle of the year, they were part of that atmosphere which attracted David Shepherd to portray scenes there before his later work at Nine Elms.

'The evening of 9th September 1966 was a momentous one for me, the first time I walked into the shed. The shedmaster had gone home and no-one seemed to be about. At the end of the shed I could discern a wooden hut in the gloom, standing at the foot of the sheer chalk cliff. I walked between half a dozen locomotives, simmering away quietly, waiting to go out on ballasts to Woking and Aldershot. They were filthy and looked forlorn and unattended.

I opened the door and entered the hut. A couple of railwaymen were drinking tea and reading the 'Mirror'. The place was hardly a hive of activity. I only intended to stay a few minutes, but it became three hours!

The welcome was warm and in no time we were like old friends. I mentioned getting a permit to sketch in the shed. "You don't want to bother about things like that, mate", I was told, "just come in and see Mr. Coe tomorrow, and he'll fix you up." That was the start of many friendships forged with those great men, some of whom have since died and many left the railway. I was always assured of a warm welcome whenever I went there, for an all too brief few months.'

That really sums up Guildford: a small, friendly shed, with plenty to interest the enthusiast, right up to its very last day of existence. Sadly, all good things do have to end, and July 9th saw shed pilot No. 30072's departure, leaving Guildford steamless. The following year, David Shepherd's two engines passed by, whistling a salute, on their way to a temporary home on the Longmoor Military Railway. It is rather nice to record that David's move into steam preservation was in time to enable his engines, *Black Prince* and *The Green Knight*, to pass by the derelict shed where his interest was aroused, before it was demolished, having succumbed to the needs of car parking space.

Eastleigh

Eastleigh had little of the glamour or drama of Nine Elms, with which it should be compared in size and importance. It had never been responsible for the main express workings on the Bournemouth line, and so did not count 'Merchant Navies' among its allocation. However, it had always provided motive power for the Southampton Docks boat trains, and up until the early 'sixties, its 'Lord Nelsons' had been thus employed. It was essentially a functional place, a fifteen road straight through shed, with no frills. It had been clad in the ubiquitous corrugated asbestos sheeting in the post-war years, and was in reasonably good repair, never having the air of dilapidation or decay found elsewhere.

The corrugated asbestos clad elevations of Eastleigh shed play host to a mixture of diesel, electro-diesel and steam power on June 4th 1967. Steam is on the decline and only 'West Country' class Nos. 34024 *Tamar Valley* and 34093 *Saunton*, together with Standard class '4' No. 75076 are in evidence.

David M. Smith

At the beginning of 1966, Eastleigh was easily the most important depot handling steam on the Southern. Its allocation of seventy-six locomotives, included twenty-six Bulleid pacifics, over half of those then surviving. It also had five 'USA' tanks and four Ivatt '2' tanks, as well as seven of the large Standard '4' 2-6-4Ts. The rest of its fleet was a mixture of Standard tender engines, which performed most of the freight and local passenger work assigned to the depot. However, the year saw a dramatic decline in steam work at Eastleigh, and the January 1967 diagrams only contained nine weekday rosters for the shed.

These turns had no less than thirty-three machines to cover them, including twelve 'West Countries' and 'Battle of Britains', for which there was only one specific booked duty. That was No. 254, which started with the 10.52 passenger boat train from the Western Docks in Southampton up to Waterloo on Mondays only, and the 09.20 boat train from Waterloo to the Docks on Fridays, returning light engine later to work the 18.22 from Waterloo to Bournemouth. For the rest of the week, the locomotive on this turn was basically 'hanging around' away at Nine Elms, waiting for work. The other eleven Bulleids were likewise stand-bys, being called on for boat trains and special freights, and also being drafted in to cope with shortages elsewhere.

For the trainspotter much of Eastleigh's interest had always lain in the long lines of dead engines on the sidings behind the shed. There locomotives awaiting repair or scrapping in the nearby Works would be parked. Many a veteran had paused there before being towed across the road for its final appearance. However, by 1966 Eastleigh had virtually stopped cutting up locomotives; instead they were sold off to South Wales metal merchants such as Cashmore's of Newport, or the now famous emporium of Dai Woodham at Barry. Nevertheless withdrawn engines still stopped off at Eastleigh before being hauled

westwards, and there were usually a handful to be seen, coupling rods removed and stacked in the tender, looking suitably forlorn. One or two engines were actually cut up at the Shed, such as No. 80132 in the spring of 1966.

Apart from those machines about to face dismemberment, there were those others destined for repair and refurbishment. With its steam repair facilities, Eastleigh Works was host to various LMR types during 1966. Before overhaul and while running in, they were to be seen at Eastleigh shed. Thus class '5' 4-6-0 No. 45418 and '9F' class 2-10-0 No. 92213 were reported as being at the shed on April 2nd.

These foreign visitors became rarer as the year progressed and Eastleigh Works ceased steam repairs. One exception was No. 45222 which spent much of November and December in the shed awaiting repair after failing while on the Southern. It left eventually just before Christmas, working the 16.00 Salisbury – Basingstoke passenger on December 23rd and then on to the London Midland region the following day.

At Eastleigh, the main focus of activity was the ash pit, coal stage and watering point near the main entrance in Campbell Road. The scene was dominated by the massive water tank which stood astride the three storey brick building which housed offices and messing for the men. On the southern face of the tank, was affixed a gantry and a single solitary signal arm, which often puzzled the unknowing. Its existence had nothing to do with train control, but was a test arm for establishing the quality of a driver's vision. Many drivers made the trip to Eastleigh just for this medical reason; thus the famous Bert Hooker travelled down in 1966, to find out whether his footplate career would continue. The test was always conducted with another driver present as a witness. Happily, in Bert's case he passed satisfactorily, although he was warned that he would need glasses to drive electrics when Nine Elms closed.

Eastleigh's rostered work remained much the same up to the end of Southern steam. The visitor would find few engines actually in working order during 1967, however, and also it lacked the atmosphere of bustle and activity which was still to be found at Nine Elms even in the final months. When Frank Wakelam visited the shed on May 28th, he found the following position: In steam were Nos. 34013, 34023, 73093, 76031 and 80139, the latter being cleaned. Out of use were Nos. 30064, 30067, 73065, 75068, 75076, 76066 and 80138. Under repair was No. 34102, with its rear tender wheels removed. Withdrawn, ready to go for scrap, were Nos. 34044, 34071, 34077, 76033, 76063, 73115, 73117 and 80019. These observations were made at 21.00, and show that only five out of 21 steam locomotives present were actually in steam. Given that there were also 10 diesel shunters, and 12 diesel and electro-diesel locomotives present, it is clear that steam days at Eastleigh were drawing to a close.

During the final weekend, most of the Eastleigh steam fleet was sent off 'light engine' to Salisbury for storage prior to disposal. On Saturday, July 8th Bulleid pacifics Nos. 34089 and 34024 travelled together, while Standard tanks Nos. 80016, 80133 and 80146 made their final trips in steam singly. The

The speed of the onslaught on the shed building is largely explained by the fact that the area was required for servicing the new motive power, but it has also been suggested that it was to meet the long-standing demands of the owners of the adjacent Southampton Airport. The shed buildings had always been right under the descending flight path of aircraft, and instructions to minimise smoke emission had been issued as a result. The removal of the water tank building was probably well received by pilots as one less hazard to avoid.

Salisbury

When the Southern region controlled the main line from Waterloo to Exeter and the West Country beyond, Salisbury was a very important main line steam depot. With dieselisation and the take-over by the Western Region of all the track beyond Wilton South from September 1964, its *raison d'etre* disappeared almost completely. This was a great pity, as it had an excellent reputation, and the work of its drivers and firemen was second to none. By 1966, its once large allocation had dwindled to 23 engines, mainly Bulleid pacifics. These were retained to work the

An almost empty Salisbury shed on May 12th 1967, with Standard class '5' No. 73037 and '4' 76007 sharing the daylight with a Type '3' diesel. Within two months the depot filled again, with withdrawn steam locomotives heading for the Welsh scrapyards.
David M. Smith

'USA' tanks were also cleared out, with Nos. 30064 and 30071 forming one working and Nos. 30067 and 30069 the other, travelling by way of Chandler's Ford and Romsey. By the Sunday night the shed was nearly deserted. Just a handful of 'dead' engines remained to maintain Eastleigh's link with the world of steam for another few days. The survivors were 'West Country' class Nos. 34040, 34044 and 34102 and Standards Nos. 73085 and 76066.

When Mr. G. Wheeler made a sentimental visit to the shed on July 16th, he found that it was being demolished with great haste. The turntable and water tank were being cut up and all the windows had been removed from the offices. The coaling stage, which had been disused for some months, was being pulled down, and diesel multiple units were parked in the midst of the old steam shed. However, he did see Nos. 34040, 73085 and 76063 awaiting their final trip to Salisbury and thence South Wales. The other two, Nos. 34044 and 34102, had already left that day, but were destined to get no further than Romsey, where they were stopped with 'hot boxes'.

non-diesel services between Waterloo and Salisbury, as standbys for the not infrequent failures by 'Warship' diesels coming up from Exeter, and for local freight and parcels turns.

What it had lost in numbers and prestige, it gained in its reputation for having the cleanest and best maintained locomotives on the Southern. Every enthusiast who visited the Southern in 1966, soon noticed the difference. Salisbury engines were always clean, had their number and nameplates fitted, and often had extra embellishments too. Thus buffers, smokebox door hinges and lamp brackets were usually picked out in white paint. 'West Countries' such as *Bude, Okehampton, Appledore* and *Wincanton*, together with 'Battle of Britains' like *Biggin Hill, Croydon, Spitfire* and *602 Squadron*, were among the renowned products of the Salisbury cleaning brigade.

The clue to the depot's special character, lies in the shed-master Claud Dare. Known as 'Dan Dare' to his men, it is no coincidence that when he was transferred to a similar post at Eastleigh at the end of 1966, the same cleaning standards began there too. One of Salisbury's advantages was that it had no man-

Class '4' No. 76031 turns on the table at Salisbury beneath the enormous watertank which sat on the arched brick base.   *Paul Gibbons*

power shortages such as Nine Elms; it actually had *cleaners*, and plenty of firemen who were pleased to earn overtime by joining in too. Under the supervision of foreman cleaner Bob Bailey the work maintained Salisbury's long standing record for turning engines out smartly.

However, despite their superb external finish, the condition of the engines' out-of-sight regions was rather different. Whereas at one time, the underneath of a locomotive was kept clean, such niceties had long since been abandoned. Some drivers even used to dress up in oil-skins when they had to 'oil up' their engines from below! Others wore dirty old coats and kept a spare pair of shoes in their lockers just for that purpose.

With the staff shortages at Nine Elms in 1966/67, Salisbury men were called up for duty in London, as already mentioned. Doug Harding, who was a Salisbury fireman at the time recalls those days:

'What sticks in my mind was going over to Eastleigh and then towing dead steam engines up to Salisbury, owing to the shortage of staff going on loan to Nine Elms. In those last months, Salisbury men worked a lot of turns at Nine Elms, mainly on Waterloo to Clapham trips. This was because the London firemen were packing in the job, and others putting in for driving jobs 'on the juice'. At first we all looked forward to the coming of diesels and electrics. A nice clean job, with no more coal to shovel, seemed fine. But now, looking back we are so sad, our attitude has changed. The boredom of working on the new traction has killed our morale.'

By the early months of 1967, Salisbury had very little regular work left, and only a dozen engines remained. No wonder that the ten road shed, which had once been home to over eighty machines just before Nationalisation, now looked desolate and empty. Having a large staff and little work meant that the shed was kept tidy and well-maintained. The great piles of clinker which in its heyday had been up to cab height in places, no longer could be seen. The ash pits were emptied regularly and no piles of rubbish allowed to accumulate.

The shed was the last resting place of many of those precious nameplates removed from the Bulleid pacifics to prevent them from being stolen. A.E. Abbott, a famous Salisbury driver, and later one of the acting foremen, remembers their arrival:

'A box wagon came into the depot one afternoon, when the stores department was still in operation. The clerk, Fred Butcher, called me and showed me. The van was pushed onto the turntable to be taken into stores. When I looked inside it was like an Aladdin's cave, it was crammed full of 'Merchant Navy' and 'West Country' nameplates. They were then placed in the stores under lock and key, and remained there until they were disposed of, quite a treasure!'

Although the fitters at the shed carried on working right up until the last day, and all routine maintenance was carried out meticulously, there were increasing problems with mechanical failures. Mr. Abbott as a foreman had to make on the spot decisions of great importance:

'You might get told at the last minute that a lead plug was leaking. You had to decide if it was safe. On the wall in our office was a small mirror in a wooden surround. You would get a fireman's shovel and lay the mirror in it, and then put the shovel in over the throat of the firebox. By looking in the mirror you could see if it was leaking around the threads or through the fusible part. If it was the latter there was no question, otherwise you had to decide if it was okay to let her run.

You also used to get problems with the firebars. If the fireman was too keen cleaning the fire with the rocker grate, up would go the firebars and nine times out of ten they wouldn't come down again. It was a massive job to put right. The fire had to come out and cool down and then the boilersmith had to get in and reset the bars. With so few locos left it was a hell of a job to get another.'

For the last three months of steam, Salisbury only had three normal weekday rosters for steam. One of these involved the 167 mile round trip to Waterloo, with a seven hour lay-over in London. The second contained nothing more than a return freight trip to Basingstoke and a spot of carriage shunting. The third duty, No. 463, comprised a triangle of parcels workings, Salisbury to Basingstoke, Basingstoke to Fratton and Portsmouth back to Salisbury. That was the sum total of the depot's rostered work and little wonder that its steam fleet comprised only seven engines by May 1st, and a bare three for the final week of all.

From being almost completely empty, the shed ironically was soon to be filled to overflowing with steam engines, but only as a staging post on their way to scrap. Being at the western end of the region, and well away from the newly electrified services, it was a natural choice to house the redundant steamers on their way to scrapyards in South Wales. They began arriving towards the end of the last week of steam operation, sent 'light engine' from Nine Elms, Guildford and Eastleigh and Basingstoke. Doug Harding, like many of his colleagues felt a strong pull of nostalgia and sadness, as the engines arrived:

'Lots and lots of steam engines were coming to Salisbury. The shed was full to the brim by the Sunday night. They were mainly dirty, with little paint left on them. 'West Countries' and 'Channel Packets' with their nameplates missing, and most of the others with no number plates on their smokebox doors. Me and my close mates wanted to have a number plate or two, off the engines that had escaped the souvenir hunters. But we were told by the loco foreman to leave them alone so we had second thoughts! But some of the lads helped themselves to all sorts of bits like gauge glass covers, whistles, smokebox spanners and engine lamps.'

For A.E. Abbott, the last day was a bit of a nightmare and a very sombre experience. He was the last man on duty, working the 15.00 to 23.00 shift, and so he actually had the responsibility of closing the shed.

'When I signed on I was struck by all the biffing and banging going on in the shed. I discovered it was the noise of countless pieces being prised or pulled off the engines! It was an absolute waste of time trying to run round to stop all those people taking off shedplates and so on. The shed was absolutely choc-a-bloc, we couldn't get another loco in. I can still remember the sounds that evening of steam dying: the injectors and that, bubbling away, and the boilers just simmering after the fires had been thrown out, until they went cold. I couldn't believe it . . . it was a very sad day . . .'

This is a sentiment shared by Doug Harding:

'I remember taking my girlfriend (now my wife) down to the shed on the Sunday evening. She said, "Oh, what a sad thing this is, all these lovely engines going for scrap." That evening certainly did bring tears to my eyes. It was as if we were standing in a graveyard.'

The withdrawn engines were despatched in batches of a few at a time, to Newport and other destinations. The last three to leave were Nos. 34034, 35023 and 34102 which did not depart until March 30th, 1968! Shortly afterwards the shed was demolished, and the crews moved to their new base at Salisbury station. However, future industrial archaeologists might usefully carry out a 'dig' on the now completely cleared site. Apparently, although many of the unwanted steam spares were rounded up and sent away, the remainder were simply thrown into the engine pits and buried beneath the ash and rubble. So anyone wanting a genuine dart, pricker, clinker shovel or duck lamp from the later Southern steam era should consider excavating the wilderness that was once Salisbury shed!

Bournemouth

Bournemouth was a relatively small depot, situated at the west end of Central station. It was perfectly positioned for viewing by train spotters and photographers, as the station's unusually long 'down' platform was an excellent grandstand. Like Guildford, the site was fairly constricted, the yard being squeezed in between the running lines and adjacent housing development. This explains the prominent green enamel notice affixed to the yard wall which reminded enginemen to limit noise and smoke for the sake of the occupants of the villas beyond.

The shed possessed a 50 ton hoist which towered above the lifting road in front of the shed; beside it was the cylindrical form of the water softener, similar to the one at Eastleigh. Coaling of locomotives was carried out by a mobile crane which ran up and down the yard, between lines of coal wagons which provided the raw materials. There was a daily freight trip to Bournemouth Central Goods to take out the empties and bring in loaded wagons. At the east end of the yard was the large 65 foot turntable, and the Bournemouth breakdown train could usually be seen parked in the vicinity.

Despite its modest size, Bournemouth had a fairly large allocation of steam power, mainly for passenger work, both main line and branch. In 1965 it could boast nine of the 'Merchant Navy' class on its books, along with 30 other locomotives. At the beginning of 1966 it still had seven 'Merchant Navies' among its stud of thirty seven, giving it the second biggest allocation of the surviving steam depots. It also had the lion's share of the Ivatt class '2' tanks, with six on the books, which found employment on the Lymington and Swanage branches, as well as coaching stock duties at Branksome.

A year later the picture had changed; the 'Merchant Navies' had all left, leaving just six rebuilt 'West Countries' to represent express passenger types. Five of the Ivatts still remained, however, and ten Standards completed the picture, giving a total complement of twenty-one. There was little main line work left for these engines. The Bulleids had two duties, one of which involved an out and back to Basingstoke on the morning Poole – York train, while the other offered only menial local passenger work. There were also two diagrams for Ivatt '2' tanks, mainly employed at Branksome carriage sidings, with an overnight sojourn at Lymington thrown in. The Standards were also mainly involved in empty carriage duties to and from Branksome, although there was also the Ringwood line freight, and a few

Above: Only two locomotives visible on shed at Bournemouth as 'Merchant Navy' class No. 35028 *Clan Line* arrives at Bournemouth with the 11.18 Weymouth – Waterloo. The Bulleid pacific on the right is No. 34001 *Exeter.* Also in this May 26th 1967 view is one of the Brush Type '4' diesels loaned to the Southern at the time. *Author*

Left: A well-cleaned 'West Country' class No. 34004 *Yeovil* stands on Bournemouth shed turntable. Despite the missing nameplate and crest the locomotive looks in good order.
Mike Esau

more local passenger turns. With dieselisation of the Lymington branch from April 3rd, and also the Poole – York (in theory), steam duties declined still further.

Although quite a small shed, Bournemouth had its fair share of high status work. It had the prestige of providing the crews for the 'Bournemouth Belle' (except for Sundays), as well as a number of other Waterloo main line turns. By 1967 these were mainly worked by diesel power, or by emus after the April changeovers. There were fewer links of men than at, say, Nine Elms and these were being constantly reformed in 1966/67 as steam working contracted. This meant that some of the younger men finally got a look in; Bournemouth had always paid strict attention to age and seniority, while up at Nine Elms men in their late thirties had been getting into the top links for some time.

Bournemouth shed was virtually cleared of steam by the final weekend of July 8th/9th. All of its engines had departed by midnight on that last Sunday, mainly working down to Weymouth for storage. The shed building was demolished soon after, to make way for a car park. This was a sign of the success of the new electrics; not only had they swept away all vestiges of steam, but they had also encouraged London commuting by their speed and regularity, hence the increased need for car space.

70G Weymouth

Weymouth differed from all the other sheds described so far, in that it was originally a GWR shed, passing into Western Region control in 1948, on nationalisation. At that time the nearest Southern shed was at Dorchester, until that was closed down in 1957. The men from Dorchester were then transferred to the WR depot at Weymouth and responsibility for the shed then passed to the Southern. Thus its staff were a mixture of Western and Southern trained men, and right up to closure their duties involved turns up the Westbury line and up the Bournemouth line. Therefore they had to be prepared to drive Western engines such as 'Halls' and pannier tanks, and later 'Hymek' diesels and multiple units, as well as the Southern's pacifics and Standards.

The shed never had a large allocation; in 1957, before transfer to the Southern, it only had about two dozen on its books. They were an assortment of pannier tanks and the larger ex-GWR 2-6-2Ts, for local passenger and shunting duties. These included the Bridport branch, the Weymouth Quay and Portland lines, as well as stopping services via Maiden Newton to Westbury. The depot also had a handful of tender engines, including four 'Hall' class, for the more important passenger duties over the ex-GWR route. By 1961, the Western tender engines had gone, replaced by Standard '5' class 4-6-0s, but the pannier tanks remained on their traditional local duties. They then faded away too, replaced by Ivatt 2-6-2Ts and diesel shunters. The final twist was the transfer to Weymouth of a number of 'Merchant Navy' pacifics in September 1964 for Waterloo duties, when the conditions at Nine Elms became too dilapidated to cope with their servicing effectively.

At the beginning of 1966 Weymouth still had twenty engines at its disposal. These comprised nine 'Merchant Navies' from those transferred in 1964, and eight Standard '5s'. The tank engine brigade was now much reduced to just three 'Ivatt' tanks, following the complete closure of the Portland branch. During

A view of the yard at Weymouth shed, with Ivatt, Bulleid and Standard locomotives on view. The depot's Great Western origins are revealed by the design of water columns and the lower quadrant signal.
Derek Buckett

the year some of the 'Merchant Navies' were withdrawn but their places were taken by the transfer of the other survivors from Bournemouth bringing the tally up to ten. Withdrawals and transfers eliminated the Ivatts, and the Standard 4-6-0s were also depleted, leaving just four. Weymouth's duties were now much reduced, with the use of Brush Type '4' diesels on Waterloo services having commenced. There were just three diagrams booked to 'Merchant Navy' pacifics, involving the 13.30, 18.30 and 20.15 passenger departures from Waterloo, and balancing return workings. There was also one Class '5' turn, involving three local passenger trips between Dorchester South and Weymouth, and the banking of the 18.15 to Waterloo up Bincombe bank. It is no surprise, that with the further reduction of steam work from April, on the inauguration of electric working to Bournemouth, that these surviving steam duties ended also. The result was the transfer of all Weymouth's steam locomotives away to Nine Elms (the pacifics) and Guildford (the Standards).

No longer having an allocation did not, of course, mean the end of steam at Weymouth. Engines continued to work in regularly and retire to the shed for servicing or minor repairs. Like Salisbury, the depot filled up again at the end of steam, being chosen as the other reception point for withdrawn engines over the weekend of July 8th/9th. Weymouth men continued to work steam diagrams using other shed's locomotives right up to that final Sunday, and indeed two of them were responsible for the last Southern steam turn of all, as far as Bournemouth (see chapter nine).

Before the decline in useage, a typical turn of duty for top link Weymouth men would have been as follows:
'Book on at the shed at 14.50 and prepare the engine (Bulleid pacific). Run light to Weymouth Junction to take over the up 'Channel Island Boat Express' which would have been brought up from the Quay by an Ivatt tank or diesel shunter. Work the 12-coach train (400 tons) to Southampton Central where water is taken, and the crew relieved by men from Nine Elms, at about 18.00. Take a break for tea and refreshment, then relieve Nine Elms men on the 18.30 from Waterloo which arrives about 20.00. Again a 12-coach working to Bournemouth Central, where six coaches including the restaurant cars are detached to be taken to Bournemouth West sidings. Work the remaining part of the train semi-fast to Weymouth, where train is berthed by the station pilot. Then run 'light engine' back to the shed, dispose of engine and book off at 22.50.'

Dave Squibb who was a fireman in the top link in 1966/7 recalls the facilities for the men at Weymouth, which were actually better than some other sheds.

'The enginemen's cabin was built in the mid-fifties and was quite modern at the time. It was furnished with the standard wooden tables and benches, electric cooker, and hot water and central heating supplied by the stationary boiler in the fitting shop. I think the boiler was from an old 'Dean Goods' engine and had originally supplied power for the machinery in the fitting shop through a belt drive system. The fitters and shed staff had a similar cabin, but the coalmen and steam raisers had much more primitive facilities. They had a room under the coal stage with very old benches and tables, and a big stone sink with a single cold water tap. There was a large iron stove in the corner, and water for washing was heated in buckets placed on the stove!'

It seems hard to believe that such arrangements were acceptable just twenty years ago, and would certainly not be tolerated under current health and safety regulations. Yet despite the hardships and discomforts of the steam railway it is clear that Weymouth men, like all the others, miss the steam days badly. Dave Squibb puts it in a nutshell:

'Looking back to my time as a locoman, I realise that the job whilst being cleaner and physically easier, has been changed drastically. Instead of being the highly skilled 'art' of being part of a

living machine, it has been transformed into the boredom of pushing buttons and pulling handles on a lifeless diesel or electric train. We have allowed the driver's job to degenerate from the elite position it once enjoyed, to being just that of an ordinary employee, which could, with a little more technology, be replaced finally by a microchip!'

Ryde

The Isle of Wight railway system entered the British Railways era in 1948 with two running sheds, at Newport and at Ryde. The former had the larger allocation at the time, but when it was closed in 1957 all the engines on the Island were concentrated at Ryde. The two-road shed was built in 1930, replacing an earlier corrugated iron clad building situated in the middle of the goods yard. A curiosity of the new shed was the use of old LBSCR overhead electrification gantries as roof supports, yet another example of the re-use of mainland curios on the Wight system.

The shed provided covered accommodation for eight tank engines, and by 1966 it actually had fourteen class 'O2s' in residence. Alongside the shed building was a covered coal stage with two locomotive roads adjacent to it. The standard of operating on the Island is well-known and the men of Ryde shed maintained those fine traditions to the very end. Their story is more than adequately told in their own words in the several volumes of 'Once upon a line' edited by Andrew Britton (OPC). There was a tradition of each engine having its own regular driver and fireman, and it was no doubt this personal touch which ensured that the engines were so well kept. Right up to the very end the cleaners and crew at Ryde ensured that most of the engines were kept clean and sparkling. If standards did lapse a little as steam's finale approached, one need not be surprised. Even so, compared to most of their mainland brethren, the 'O2s' rarely looked unkempt.

After steam services ended on December 31st 1966, the shed was still occupied by the last two active 'O2s', Nos. 24 and 31, in the company of some of the newly delivered 'tube' trains to operate the electric services, and the solitary diesel shunter No. D2554. Subsequently, when the steam engines had gone, it was used for works purposes as a base for wagon conversions. It was eventually demolished during 1968, the new electrics being concentrated for maintenance purposes on the other side of the station at the Works.

Southampton Docks

The shunting engines based in Southampton Docks had their own shed, located in the Old Docks, or Eastern Docks, as they were renamed in 1965. In 1962 the shunting work had been dieselised with specially designed Ruston and Hornsby locomotives. Their arrival ended the domination by the 'USA' class 0-6-0Ts, and the entire class was transferred to Eastleigh. As described elsewhere, a number of these were then switched to departmental duties, and at least three others were assigned to shed and works pilot rosters at Eastleigh.

However, the fourteen new diesels were only just adequate to cover the shunting and trip haulage requirements of a then still busy port, and therefore the 'USAs' still found occasional employment right up to the end of Southern steam.

Officially the shed closed in January 1966, its allocation of diesels being transferred 'on paper' to Eastleigh also. In reality, it continued its separate existence, with its own shedmaster, Eddie Roberts, and a large staff of drivers and secondmen.

Architecturally, it was a simple shed with three roads, and was of brick construction, with a simple flat roof, rebuilt in place of a heavier looking predecessor in 1955. A novelty was the locomotive water facility, which comprised two pipes hanging down from within the shed roof, each with its own control wheel at the top of the 'bag'.

Alongside the shed was a small locomotive yard, and to the north side was the marine engineering works. There, fitters employed by the Shipping and Continental Department, could carry out running repairs on the engines. Thus the diesels could receive routine maintenance on site, and the steam shunters received their boiler wash-outs and also attention to valves and pistons.

The usual reason for 'USAs' to be called up for duty in 1966/7 was the arrival of a 'Elders and Fyffes' banana boat, such as the *Golfito*, from the West Indies. These berthed at the Empress Dock, usually arriving on a Sunday. It was then necessary to unload the cargo, under special conditions, as quickly as possible, for despatch to the markets. As Eddie Roberts recalls it was a very labour intensive exercise:

'The Fyffes banana vans were loaded with a bed of straw, and then steam heated. The 'USA' would shunt them round to the back of the Fyffes shed and bring them through for loading up. This was done one van at a time, and I must say there didn't seem to be many stems put into each van! Then the shunter drew them forward onto the weighbridge, so that each wagon could be assessed separately. Then they were drawn forward, before being propelled back into the three reception roads. Fyffes insisted that there was an engine available for each road, so that there was no delay. It could keep four engines busy during the Monday and the Tuesday, and usually two of these were steam.'

After this time of full employment, the 0-6-0Ts were not normally required for the rest of the week, and would sit 'dead' in the shed, or outside in the yard. If Eastleigh was short of power they would run back there for further duties, until needed again in the Docks. Once in a while, even in these last months, a 'USA' would stand in for a diesel and work a trip between the Eastern Docks and the Town Quay, or Western (New) Docks, but such events were extremely rare.

The last two 'USAs' left the Docks on Saturday July 8th, running 'light' together to Eastleigh and thence Salisbury, ending an association that had lasted for two decades.

Locomotives arriving in the Eastern Docks on boat trains did not use the shed facilities, which were purely for the shunters. However, in the Western Docks there were servicing arrangements, near the Millbrook entrance from the main line. These comprised a water column, coaling stage and offices, as well as a 70 foot turntable, large enough for the biggest visiting locomotives.

Also worthy of mention in this survey was the similar provision in the yard at Southampton Terminus. That resembled a miniature engine shed, with another 70 foot turntable, with three stabling roads radiating off it, and a coal stage and two water columns. Although it provided no covered accommodation it was regarded as a sub-depot of Eastleigh and was quite busy during the 1950s, when the Terminus station handled a considerable amount of local steam passenger traffic. By the time of the closure of the station in 1966, its useage had dwindled, although engines still turned on the table occasionally. Although derelict, the office building with its large green enamel sign 'QUIET PLEASE – SCHOOL', referring to the primary educational establishment behind, survived into the 1970s.

It is pleasing to record that the turntable from the Western Docks survives in preservation at Didcot, and that although the Dock railway system has been reduced considerably, there is still railway activity in the 1990s, and even the occasional boat train to recall former traditions.

'USA' class No. 30071 on a Fyffes banana van duty in Southampton Eastern Docks in 1967. These workings maintained the link between these American built locomotives and the Docks right through until the last weekend of steam.   *Klaus Marx*

A general view of Basingstoke shed in February 1967. Two class '4' Standard tender locomotives share the premises with a pair of what are now called class 33 diesels.

Author

Basingstoke

Basingstoke shed was built by the LSWR in 1905, providing accommodation for a small stud of about twenty locomotives. The brick-built shed with its pitched roof had just three roads, with turntable and coal stage in the yard outside. It was coded 70D, but in 1963 it ceased to have an independent existence and became just a crew signing-on point. However, it continued to act as a running shed, and there were usually ten or more engines to be found there during 1966 and 1967.

Situated beside the Waterloo – Weymouth and Waterloo – Salisbury – Exeter main lines, Basingstoke was an obvious provider of relief locomotives for ailing expresses. There were few instances of this in the last two years, despite the run down condition of the SR steam fleet. However, on July 3rd 1966, standard No. 73110 was called up to replace failed Warship diesel No. D810 *Kelly* on the 18.00 Waterloo – Exeter. This provided a most unusual spectacle for photographer Peter Harrod, as also on shed was Scottish region 'V2' class No. 60919. This had also failed, preventing it from working the LCGB 'Green Arrow' rail tour that day. After desperate attempts to repair it, it had eventually ended up rather forlornly at Basingstoke. There Mr. Harrod was able to photograph it, as its replacement for the day, No. 34002 *Salisbury* whisked by with the return working of the enthusiasts special.

Other foreign locomotives found their way to Basingstoke in connection with rail tour duty. Being situated at the junction of the SR lines and the cross-country link to Reading and the Midlands it was natural that new arrivals should come that way. On March 17th 1966, No. 77014 paused here in the course of its long trek from Cheshire to Guildford. Four days later streamlined 'A4' class pacific No. 60024 *Kingfisher* arrived with the 11.10 freight from Banbury. On September 10th famous 'A3' class No. 4472 *Flying Scotsman* was serviced at the depot after bringing in the 'Farnborough Flyer' from the Midlands, in connection with the Air Show. On that day the shed contained the following locomotives, showing how well-used it remained, although this was of course a Saturday with extra traffic for the Air Show specials.

'WCs'	34100, 34102
'5s'	73086, 73118, 73119
'4s'	76007, 76058, 76066
'4T'	80065
'BB'	34064 withdrawn, awaiting movement to scrapyard.

At the beginning of 1967, a number of the Waterloo – Basingstoke semi-fasts went over to electric working, bringing a further reduction in steam working. However, as late as June 4th, a visitor reported seven engines present, including No. 80152, which was by then a regular performer on the Andover – Ludgershall freight trip. This was part of Eastleigh Duty 313, which involved the tank being stabled at Basingstoke throughout the week. Also dumped on shed was sister engine No. 80151, which had failed while working on the same turn on April 28th as described in chapter two. The tank was withdrawn within a few days of that incident, with defective brake gear. A plea by Ron Cover that it should be repaired using parts taken from another locomotive was over-ruled.

Fratton

Fratton shed was square in plan, but organised on the roundhouse principal with a central turntable, serving the stabling roads, all under cover. Situated beyond the sidings at Fratton station, it was scarcely visible from passing passenger trains, although locomotives parked in the approach roads could be glimpsed. Officially Fratton had closed as a running shed in November 1959, but it continued as a signing-on point for steam crews right up to July 1967. For several years in the early 1960s it played host to several old Southern locomotives destined for preservation, such as No. 30850 *Lord Nelson* and No. 30777 *Sir Lamiel* following their withdrawal from active service.

Locomotives working into Portsmouth on the few steam hauled local passenger turns and on van trains were serviced and turned at Fratton, so that one or two standard 2-6-0s would be seen there during the day, together with the occasional visitor with a special working. Throughout the winter of 1965/66 the Plymouth – Brighton through train was steam hauled along the coast line to its destination, making a unique daily sight in normally steam free Sussex. The Bulleid pacific rostered for the working was shedded at Fratton overnight, running down light to Brighton at 06.00 and returning to Fratton at 20.00. This surprising working continued until April 30th 1966.

Although remaining in use until the summer of 1967, the shed presented a forlorn appearance in these declining months. It had lost most of its roof covering, and presented a general air of neglect and imminent demolition. In fact it was eventually laid waste in 1969 leaving just the office buildings as a reminder of its motive power functions for the previous eighty years.

Eastleigh Works

Although heavy repairs on steam locomotives had ended by 1965, Eastleigh Works continued to carry out steam overhauls until the end of 1966. Then came the end of its fifty-seven year association with steam, begun in 1909 when Dugald F. Drummond transferred the LSWR's locomotive department workshops from Nine Elms. Between then and 1950 over three hundred engines were constructed there, and far more were repaired or rebuilt. Situated at the south-western end of the station, between the lines to Portsmouth and the running shed complex, the locomotive works was the real reason for the existence of the town of Eastleigh. It was the major employer, taken together with the carriage and wagon works located at the east end of the station area. Eastleigh was, and to some extent still is, a 'railway town'. Not as famous as Swindon or Crewe in that respect, it is still a creation of the railway age, and fortunately the railway works remains today, albeit much reduced in size and function.

With the planned elimination of steam from the Southern Region, and the reduced needs for motive power that would result, Eastleigh Works could not avoid some scaling down. The impact of the 'Beeching Axe' in reducing the general level of rail services, the loss of the Salisbury to Exeter route to the Western region, and the run-down of Southampton Docks traffic also added to an air of uncertainty about Eastleigh's future in the 1963-4 period. This was not helped by the decision to carry out the building and rebuilding of the Bournemouth electrification stock at York and Crewe. In the event, Eastleigh survived, but

'West Country' class No. 34006 *Bude* under repair at Eastleigh Works on January 16th 1966. *John Scrace*

Above: Eastleigh Works yard with two of the 'USA' 0-6-0Ts on pilot duties. On the left is No. 30071, and with container wagons to the right is green liveried No. 30064. *John Fairman*

Left: The last locomotive repair at Eastleigh Works: Chief Erecting Shop Foreman, Harry Frith, plays a starring role for the TV film unit on October 6th 1966, as 'Battle of Britain' class No. 34089 *602 Squadron* is officially returned to traffic.
Harry Frith collection

only at the cost of the closure of the carriage works, and the integration of its work force with that of the locomotive works.

This contraction was carried out fairly painlessly, and with great skill, considering that the men had to changeover from steam maintenance work to diesels and electrics at the same time. This meant that old skills such as boiler making and copper-smithing had to die, whilst new techniques such as fibre-glass construction, electrical fitting and diesel power plant over-hauling were acquired. It also meant that sections of the works such as the brass foundry became redundant, while new sections had to be incorporated. Before the changeover, the locomotive work was concentrated in the erecting shop, where there were three bays for engines and a fourth, where tenders were worked on. Beyond these bays, which were dominated by overhead cranes capable of lifting 50 tons each, was the boiler shop. There, boilers were overhauled and tested often using components, such as tubes and pipework, which was fabricated in the adjacent coppersmiths shop. The main locomotive works building also housed the machine shop where iron and steel castings were engineered to precise dimensions, the smith shop for light steel manufacture and the brass shop where components such as injectors and gauges were machined and fitted.

Much of the work in these areas was carried out in condi-tions of considerable noise, dirt and some danger. The asbestos with which boilers were lagged, was suspected of being dangerous even then, but most workers did not take the dangers seriously. Indeed, one fitter recalls how they used to throw the material at their work-mates in horseplay! The noisiest and hottest area of the works was undoubtedly the iron foundry and the forge, which were part of a separate range of buildings west of the erecting shops. In the forge, giant steel hammers pounded away at the work of shaping and bending red hot steel components, such as axles and coupling rods. While in the heat of the iron foundry, up to a hundred tons of brake blocks, cylinders and axleboxes were cast from molten metal in sand moulds each week.

Obviously much of this activity was in decline by the beginning of 1966. There were no more general repairs, instead engines were 'half soled and heeled' in the words of the fitters. That meant that boilers were no longer lifted from their frames; instead new tubes were fitted as necessary, and as long as the boiler inspector felt they were alright for two years that was sufficient. Repairs to the motion were similarly restricted to what was deemed essential for the time remaining. New rings would have been fitted to the pistons and piston heads, the axle boxes serviced, and the tyres on the wheels turned. Rusted metal platework would be made good, but not by replacing large sections as formerly. Instead patches were welded over the offending areas, and this could be seen on several Bulleid pacific tenders during 1967.

Before the run-down of steam, the Works regularly had about thirty steam engines in at any one time, ranging from light casual repairs, through the intermediate overhauls, to the heavy general overhauls which in the case of a 'Merchant Navy' were scheduled to take twenty-two working days. As the diesels came in at the end of the 1950s, part of the erecting shop was cordoned off to provide clean conditions in which the special equipment for overhauling the new traction could be kept. By 1961 Eastleigh fitters were working on steam, electric and diesel repairs and maintenance, side by side in the same building.

The change in the type of work being carried out is illus-trated in Table 9, which is based on admissions to the Works during sample four week periods in the years shown:

Table 9

	Steam				Diesel		Electric	Electro-diesel	
	ExGWR	ExSR	ExLMR	STD.	Shunters	Locos	Locos	Locos	TOTAL
1960	1	26	1	11	3	0	2	0	35
1961	2	34	3	16	6	2	2	0	65
1962	0	15	1	9	4	4	0	0	33
1963	0	26	6	7	1	0	1	1	42
1964	0	6	1	9	2	0	0	0	18
1965	0	3	1	3	10	5	0	0	22
1966	0	2	0	2	3	8	0	0	15

Although the figures need to be treated with some caution, as they are not all based on admissions at the same time of the year, they do indicate trends fairly clearly. From 1965, steam locomotives formed the minority portion of the work carried out, and repairs to ex-Southern engines almost ground to a halt from 1964 onwards. Among the ex-LMR and Standard types recorded during the same period were a number actually based on the London Midland Region. These included class '4' 2-6-0s in the 43XXX series, class '5' 4-6-0s, class '8F' 2-8-0s, and a variety of Standards, including some '9F' 2-10-0s.

During 1966, steam overhauls were very few, and most work on the engines comprised casual running repairs to keep the survivors going. Some cannibalisation of condemned engines was practised to keep others going: On April 27th, for example, 'Merchant Navy' No. 35011 entered the Works for a day to have various useful parts removed. Visitors to the Works found steam engines very much in the minority as shown in Table 10.

Table 10
March 19th, 1966   Locomotives under repair
Steam: 34004, 35014
Diesel: D3671, D5236, D6521, D6526, D6557, D6570
Electric: E5010
Electro-diesel: E6002, E6003

August 9th 1966   Steam Locomotives under repair
34023, 76005, 76026
(under restoration) 2818, 30053, 30926

On August 25th the first redundancy notices were issued in connection with the end of steam repairs. These comprised 16 fit-ters, coppersmiths and platers, out of a total of about sixty anticipated job losses. It was hoped that 'natural wastage' could account for the majority of these. The last locomotive to receive classified repairs was 'Battle of Britain' No. 34089 which emerged from the Works on October 6th. Twenty-six year old Albert Smith drove the engine out of the yard, his first steam driving turn since qualifying! The yard was well-filled with men from the Works saying farewell to their last 'official' steam job. The late Harry Frith, much-loved contributor to steam preservation, was chief erecting shop foreman, and remembered the day well:

'Normally engines came out of the Works tender-first, but the TV cameras wanted a good picture. So we sent No. 34089 round the triangle at the back of the works, so she could face the right way for the press. It wasn't a really big thing for the men, but several of them spoke for the cameras.'

Harry Lethbridge, a charge-hand in the erecting shop, who had worked on steam for thirty-one years, was one of those inter-viewed. He probably spoke for most of his colleagues when he said that although they were sad, it was really just one of those things, progress that was inevitable. Although steam has a sentimental appeal in retrospect, the reality for the workers was rather different: Harry Frith recalls:

'All the erecting shop fitters were basically glad to see the back of steam. You have to think of all that heavy work they had to do, stripping the motion down and so on. And then there was the filth. You had to wash your hair practically every night, and your feet! . . . It wasn't all that brilliant really . . .'

After No. 34089's departure, a few steam engines did appear in the Works for running repairs, mainly for things like 'hot boxes'. But to all intents and purposes, the days of Eastleigh as a steam works had finished. Nevertheless, it is a great happiness to see the memory of Harry Frith and his fellow Eastleigh workers preserved in the superbly restored 'S15' class locomotive No.30828, which Harry and his team did so much to bring about as a permanent memorial to the town's railway heritage.

Ryde Works

Apart from Eastleigh, the only steam railway workshop still operating on the Southern in 1966 was at Ryde. Although only a small establishment it performed herculean tasks in keeping the Island's antique rolling stock in working order. The Works building, on the east side of Ryde St. Johns station, was basically an extension of the original engine shed. It comprised a carriage and wagon shop, carpenters' shop, machine shop and loco repair shop.

In its pre-War heyday the Works employed around forty staff, displaying a variety of trades, such as coppersmiths, boilermakers, fitters and painters.

Although a very cramped site, it was possible for the Works to handle all manner of repairs, to the engines, rolling stock and also much of the ancillary equipment, such as platform seats and sack trolleys. Outside the Machine shop on No. 4 road, was a set of shear legs, capable of lifting twenty-five tons, which had been sent to Ryde from Bournemouth shed in 1926, when it was

replaced there by an electric hoist. With the help of the shearlegs and the sweat of half a dozen men, it was possible to lift an 'O2' for maintenance purposes. Thus passengers on the station in February 1966 would have seen engine No. 16 suspended from its rear end, and without its bogie wheels. The last major steam repair followed in July when No. 27 was outshopped.

The normal procedure for overhauling an engine was to begin by stripping it down, outside in the yard. Items such as the Westinghouse pump would be removed and serviced separately as required. Using the lifting capacity of the shear legs, the boiler would be removed from the frames, and taken into the shops for overhaul. The frames and wheels would also be taken in for a thorough going over at the same time. It was a common practice to use parts from other engines as available, to speed up the overhaul time. Thus a newly outshopped 'O2' might well have little in common with the one that entered, apart from the main frames and, probably, the wheels! Up until 1965 overhauled engines were always turned out resplendent in lined mixed traffic black, lustrous in as many as ten coats of paint, offset by the splendid red backed brass nameplates. However, when No. 24 *Calbourne*, now preserved at Havenstreet, emerged after the last general overhaul in June 1965, it merited no more than a plain black finish, with no lining, no nameplates and no buffer beam numbers. It was a clear indication that steam days were nearly at an end. Nameplates were removed from the rest of the class by early 1966 to ensure that they did not get removed illegally, but to their credit the men of Ryde manufactured replacement ones from tin-plate. Intended as cheap substitutes they eventually became nearly as highly prized as the originals.

With the end of steam services at the end of 1966, Ryde Works was turned over to the repair and maintenance of the 'new' electric trains. It was fortunate that the Works staff had lifelong experiences of getting the best out of time-expired machinery, as the ex-tube stock they now had to work with was already forty years old!

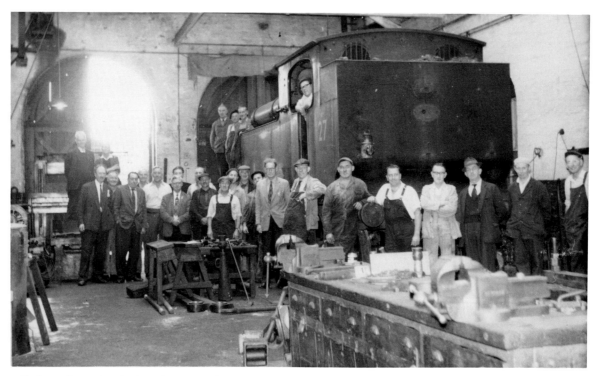

The last major repair at Ryde works is the cue for a staff line-up. No. 27 *Merstone* was the last to be outshopped, and ironically the first to be cut up at Newport a year later.

Dr. J. Mackett

Chapter Seven

Steam for Enthusiasts 1957-1967

Railway enthusiasts have existed in Britain for many decades, indeed the centenary of the founding of the *Railway Magazine*, celebrated in 1997, indicated the long-established credentials of what are sometimes derided as mere 'train spotters' or 'anoraks'! It is not absolutely clear when the first special train was chartered by railway lovers purely for the enjoyment of the ride, but it was probably the pioneering expedition from London to Peterborough by the Railway Correspondence and Travel Society (RCTS) in 1938.

After the end of the War, there was a blossoming of such activities, and by the late 1950s, railtours had become a regular and well patronised part of the railway scene. Apart from the RCTS, the Stephenson Locomotive Society (SLS) and the Locomotive Club of Great Britain (LCGB) were the most prolific organisers of special trains. Other regular organisers were the Southern Counties Touring Society (SCTS) and the Home Counties Railway Society (HCRS). Smaller groups such as the Plymouth Railway Circle (PRC) and the Railway Enthusiasts Club (REC) based in Farnborough, Hampshire played their part also. The latter society was very active, sponsoring a series of interesting tours which traversed little used lines with appropriate motive power.

Demand for rail tours proliferated as the end of steam approached. There was an understandable desire to organise 'the last trip' with a particular class of locomotive before its remaining survivors went to the scrapheap. However, there was also the wish to make last sentimental journeys along lines prior to their closure, and with so many miles of Britain's railways suffering that fate in the 1960s, there were plentiful opportunities for such commemorative specials. A third taste to be catered for was that of sheer speed of travel, and several specials were organised specifically to provide the possibility of high speed steam haulage.

On the Southern Region there were many examples of each of these types of tours in the period from 1957 onwards. Farewell was bade to the last 'H2' Atlantic No. 32424 *Beachy Head* on April 13th 1958, when it worked an RCTS special from Victoria to Newhaven. Likewise, a last trip with a 'Lord Nelson' 4-6-0 saw No. 30861 *Lord Anson* make a high speed run from Waterloo to Sidmouth Junction, and back from Exeter, for the Southern Counties Touring Society on September 2nd 1962. The last two Beattie class '0298' Well Tanks, finally redundant at Wadebridge in Cornwall, Nos. 30585 and 30587, returned to their London origins of the previous century to work tours to Hampton Court and Shepperton in December of the same year. In July 1964, 'M7' tank engine No. 30053 was resuscitated in order to have a last fling around the London suburbs.

Electrification of the remaining routes in Kent was marked by an LCGB tour, the 'South Eastern Limited' on June 11th 1961, using a wide variety of the locomotives which had been associated with the area. Representatives of the 'D1' and 'L1' 4-4-0s were used, as well as 'C' and 'O1' 0-6-0s. Tank engines were also used, one of the 'H' class, and two 'A1xs' for a last journey on the Kent and East Sussex Railway. There were also many specials to Devon and Cornwall between 1963 and 1965 to mourn the passing of Southern steam in its Western extremities.

Line closures provided excuses for many trips. The purpose of the 'Hayling Farewell' tour of November 3rd 1963 was self-

A memorable railtour began with the last passenger run for a Brighton 'Atlantic', between Victoria and Newhaven on an RCTS trip on April 13th 1958. Dick Riley was so overwhelmed by the occasion that he fired his shutter earlier than intended, but the result is still an evocative record of No. 32424 *Beachy Head* powering along in style at Star Lane.   *R. C. Riley*

One of the REC's many interesting railtours was on May 23rd 1959 and took an 'O1' 0-6-0 over the remains of the East Kent Railway from Shepherdswell. Locomotive No. 31258 is seen waiting to move off from the main line to ramble through the Kent coalfield. This must have been the only railtour of all time to include a box van in its formation, intended to carry the participants bicycles!   *R. C. Riley*

Marking the end of the majority of steam working in Kent and the demise of several branch lines, 'L1' 4-4-0 No. 31786 and 'D1' 4-4-0 No. 31749 pass Teston Crossing Halt with the LCGB's 'South Eastern Limited' on June 11th 1961.   *Mike Esau*

Passing Radipole Halt on the outskirts of Weymouth is 'A3' No. 60112 *St. Simon* with a railtour from Waterloo, which subsequently visited the Bridport branch before returning to Waterloo via Westbury and Salisbury. August 25th 1963. *C. L. Caddy*

explanatory, but it might be less obvious that the 'Hampshire Venturer' of April 18th 1964 was paying its respects to passenger services through Ringwood and Fordingbridge. Standard '3' 2-6-2T No. 82029 led the "Anton and Test Valley" tour of the LCGB up and down the Romsey to Andover line on the day of its closure in September 1964. A wide variety of engines were used on the same society's 'Wealdsman' trip in June 1965 which marked the withdrawal of passenger trains from part of the "Cuckoo" line and from the Horsham-Guildford route. Other tours brought 'foreign' locomotives to the Southern, notably 'A4' No. 60022 *Mallard*, the world speed record holder for steam, and another Gresley designed pacific, 'A3' No 60112 *St. Simon*, both of which normally graced the tracks of the Eastern Region.

My first acquaintance with railtours came on April 30th 1961. 1 had scarcely been aware of their existence up to that time, but I was tipped off by a colleague of my father's that it would be worth my while going down to Fareham on that particular Sunday morning. When I arrived it was to be greeted by a sight I could scarcely believe. Hundreds of men and youths of varying ages were scrambling around the platforms, walking on the tracks and had generally taken possession of the station. They had disgorged themselves from a set of fairly elderly Southern green carriages, which had been brought into the station by a beautiful 'T9' class 4-4-0 No. 30117. I found this unbelievably exciting, recalling the Sunday afternoons at Netley of four years before, which I have mentioned in Chapter One.

Even more incredible was the sight of two little black tank engines, No. 32694 which I thought to be the last survivor of the 'E1' class, and No. 30200 of the 'O2' class. They coupled on to the train, and everybody clambered back on board at the sound

of the whistle. I had never seen anything like it, and wondered where this strange odyssey was now heading. I asked someone on the platform to be told it was going to Gosport, down a line closed to passengers before I was even conscious that railways existed! This was absolute magic for a ten year old, and how I wished I was on board that train, or that I had brought the family box camera with me. Later on, I gathered that the train was going to venture up the Meon valley line, to Droxford. This was just too much for me. I had listened with envy to my father telling me of journeys he had made on that line, heading for Alton, prior to its closure. I would so much have liked to have made that journey, but sadly it was never to be, and no rail tour ever went up that part of the Meon valley again in future years.

The result of that Sunday morning was a permanent interest in rail tours, and over the next six years I endeavoured to photograph or travel on them whenever possible. Sadly, many of the Sunday trips were out of reach for a boy not yet in his teens, either too expensive or too difficult to join because of early starts from London. I can only dream as I look back at some of the exploits of the railway societies in those years. The 'Rother Valley Limited' run in October 1958 must have taken some beating with a journey on the Kent and East Sussex line with two 'Terrier' tanks, haulage by 4-4-0s of the 'E1' and 'Schools' classes to and from London, and an amble along the Sussex coast with another of my favourite types, the 'O1' class 0-6-0s.

Another outstanding special was the 'South Western Limited' of September 1960 when the LCGB brought together some of the more interesting Southern steam survivors for an excursion through the byways of Hampshire and then over the Somerset and Dorset line. It was an opportunity to travel

The railtour that first alerted me to the excitement of such activities was this LCGB 'Solent Limited' which I saw at Fareham before the train engines ('E1' No. 32694 and 'O2' No. 30200) whisked it off to the northern operational extremity of the Meon Valley line at Droxford. How necessary a jacket and tie was in the early 1960s to be an appropriately dressed railtourer! *Stanley Creer*

The last train to Hayling Island was the LCGB special run on Sunday November 3rd 1963, which was operated by 'A1x' 0-6-0Ts Nos. 32636 leading and 32670 trailing. The five coach formation is seen setting out from Havant for the short sunlit journey across to the island. *Author*

The LCGB's "Hampshire Venturer" tour is seen at Fullerton on the Romsey to Andover line on April 18th 1964, headed by 'Q' 0-6-0 N0. 30548.
Author

The last steam locomotive built for British Railways, Standard '9F' 2-10-0, although based on the Western, made a number of appearances on Southern territory during its short five-year operational life. One such occasion was on September 20th 1964 when it hauled the SCTS "Farewell to Steam" tour over the Mid-Hants line en route from London to the West of England. Its unprecedented appearance on this route is recorded by the photographer on the outskirts of Alresford on a bright Sunday morning.
Author

behind a class '700' goods engine beautifully cleaned for the occasion, an 'L' class 4-4-0 which hauled the special over what was to become the preserved 'Watercress' line from Alton, and to experience the bulk of a Maunsell 'H16' 4-6-2T, No. 30516, from Eastleigh down the branch line to Fawley. One of the S&D 2-8-0s, No. 53804 took over at Broadstone, and eventually brought the train into Salisbury, a rare visitor to that station.

By all accounts, one of the best tours to have travelled on for the enjoyment of speed and express steam action would have been the 'Exeter Flyer' organised by the SCTS as a last chance to travel to the LSWR's furthest outpost in the West Country by steam. 'Merchant Navy' No. 35022 worked from Waterloo to Exeter Central and back on two occasions, such was the demand for seats on the special. On the second trip, on October 3rd 1965, it covered the 88.1 miles from passing Salisbury to Exeter Central in under 79 minutes, and achieved an almost identical time in the return direction. Each journey involved one severe slowing, so the net times would have been several minutes less. The distinguishing feature of the running, admittedly with only eight coaches in tow, was not the downhill maxima achieved, but the high speeds maintained on the severe up-gradients, through the skilled work of Driver Hooper and Fireman Brown. Between the excitement of sustained high speed running, there was the opportunity to visit either Torrington or Ilfracombe, hauled by one of a pair of Standard '4MT' tanks, which split the train at Barnstaple Junction. These were the last steam workings to those destinations, adding an extra dimension to a very satisfying day for the participants.

A tour that I would have liked both to travel on, and yet also to be 'chasing' for photographic purposes, would have been one of the rather modest, but nevertheless personally significant efforts by the Railway Enthusiasts Club at Farnborough. On several occasions they hired an 'M7' class tank engine and a push-pull set and sent it round the Hampshire, Surrey, Berkshire borderlands, visiting every possible nook and cranny of disused or freight-only track. In particular they travelled up the siding from Alton to Treloar Hospital platform, to what was then a short remaining stub of the long since closed and rather eccentric Basingstoke and Alton Light railway. In so doing the tour would have crossed the road bridge, long since demolished,

which stood about two hundred yards away from where I am now sitting writing this text. If I had a capacity to time travel, I would certainly want to be standing on the pavement outside my house, camera poised, and the date to be October 15th 1960!

There were many other fascinating tours in the period 1957-1965, too numerous to describe fully in this book, but details of them are given in Appendix 2. It attempts to provide a complete record of the excursions for enthusiasts that took place, but some may have eluded the net, and I would welcome any additions or amendments to complete the summary. I am particularly grateful to Hugh Davies, and also to Peter Harrod, Roger Merry-Price, Klaus Marx and Bert Moody, for their help in compiling some of the details.

Despite the enormous variety of tours organised between 1957 and 1965, it was the last two years of Southern steam which provided the backdrop for a veritable explosion of such activity. Not only did the well-established clubs and societies arrange or propose more tours than ever before, but a whole range of new operators attempted to join the fray. Some of their plans reached fruition in the shape of well-organised events such as the Manchester Rail Travel Society's tour of Hampshire branch lines on March 25th 1967. Unfortunately other excursions appeared briefly in advertisements, raised false hopes among patrons and spectators, and were never heard of again.

One or two potentially interesting plans failed simply due to the sheer pressure of competition. A situation was being reached where the enthusiast market was being asked to support two, or even three, specials on the same day: this could not be realistic. One such casualty was the RCTS 'Vectis' tour scheduled for April 1st 1967. No doubt the date planned for the occurrence must have led some would-be participants to question its authenticity, particularly as the advertisements offered them travel from Waterloo to Portsmouth Harbour in underground trains! In fact, it was no joke: it had been planned to start the journey in the newly converted tube stock for the Isle of Wight electrification, some of which was still on the mainland awaiting shipment. If that wasn't an odd enough experience for the aspiring travellers, the rest of the day's meanderings were planned to take in the short branch into Portsmouth Dockyard, the Meon Valley line from Fareham up

Just a few yards from my home, a concrete platform that was once a halt for the Lord Mayor Treloar's Hospital lies buried in undergrowth, but on October 10th 1959 it could still be reached by rail, to enable the local goods working to bring in wagons of coal for the boilerhouse. It formed a short surviving section of the old Basingstoke and Alton light railway and class 'M7' No. 30328 has brought its REC tour as far as it was possible to venture.
Mike Esau

to Droxford, and the last remains of the old Bishops Waltham line, a few yards of siding at Botley! This would have been the first passenger train over those lines for at least six years but sadly this ambitious proposal had to be cancelled at short notice. The motive power for the steam section had been rostered for a pair of Ivatt '2' tanks, one at each end of the train, and what a splendid sight they would have made coming down the Meon Valley.

One reason for lack of support was undoubtedly the conflicting 'County of Hants' tour, announced for the very same day. That certainly did sound like an April Fools prank! The sponsor, a Mr. Turk, had previously advertised the expedition for the preceding September, but that too had been cancelled at a late stage. In its revised publicity the tour claimed to be bound from Romsey to Andover, over a line closed eighteen months previously, and was also to tour the Meon Valley line but this time the northern surviving section from Alton to Farringdon. If that was not sufficient to entice the customer, promised motive power included the class 'C' departmental shunters from Ashford Works, one of which was now being used as a stationary boiler, while the other was in the course of restoration! It was a nice idea but it bore little resemblance to possible reality. To complete the day there was a third enthusiasts' run planned using a 'Merchant Navy' and intended as a straight-forward Waterloo-Weymouth return trip with an emphasis on the locomotive performance. Its profits were to be donated to the

Southern Railwaymen's Home for Children at Woking, a worthy cause that benefitted from the operation of several other specials. As one might guess the end result of all these conflicting plans was that no rail tours ran on 1st April 1967!

No less than eighty Southern specials were planned sufficiently deeply to be advertised nationally for our period of review: no doubt dozens of others were conceived in the minds of hopeful organisers but never saw the pages of the railway press. (The figure of eighty includes specials planned to run over non-Southern lines but using the Region's motive power.) Not surprisingly twenty-two of those promoted did not materialise but the amazing fact is that fifty-eight did take place, an average of more than one every ten days.

The worst bout of cancellations was in the autumn of 1966. Southern-based or visiting steam power was scheduled for seventeen outings in the months of September and October but only seven of those actually ran. This may partly account for the dramatic decline in tours being advertised over the next four winter months. Only nine were publicised, and all but one of them took place. No doubt railway management had become very frustrated at the staff time being put into planning 'non-events'.

Among the autumn casualties were two potentially interesting propositions. The MRTS proposed to use a London Midland Region 'Crab' 2-6-0, and one of the ex-Crosti boilered '9F' standard 2-10-0s on a Waterloo-Weymouth-Yeovil-

Nicely cleaned Ivatt '2' 2-6-2T No. 41320 takes the Swanage branch at Worgret Junction on 25th March 1967 with the MRTS "Hants and Dorset Branch Line Flyer".   *Author*

Salisbury-Waterloo itinerary on 2nd October. A week later the same route was supposed to have been traversed by double-headed LMR 'Jubilee' 4-6-0s on behalf of the Metropolitan Railway Society. Each of these locomotive types was extremely rare on the Southern, and the appearance of any one of them would have been fascinating. In the event the only 'foreign' visitor that autumn was the evergreen *Flying Scotsman* which turned up at Basingstoke on 10th September with the 'Farnborough Flyer', running from the North and Midlands in connection with the International Air Show. Exactly one week later it was back on the Southern making its first ever visit to Sussex. Penetrating the 'non-steam' Central Division it worked from Victoria to Brighton, and then along the coast to Eastleigh, returning the same way later in the day. This event was organised by Mr. C.A.G. Spiller, who six months later brought another preserved LNER machine, *The Great Marquess*, down to run over the same path. The SR authorities were somewhat reluctant to authorise the use of this alien on their region, and then agreed subject to the train also having a Bulleid pacific attached. However, the mechanical report on the engine that they eventually received seems to have convinced them that it was quite capable of handling its train alone, and that proved to be the case. The working on 12th March was a great success, and No. 3442 provided some interesting photographic subject matter while being cleaned at Nine Elms before the event.

On the debit side, the cameramen must have been very upset at the non-running of the 'Wessex Merchantman' which would have taken a 'Britannia' from Waterloo to Weymouth, and on a smaller scale the failure to operate the 'Dock Tank Tour'. That would have made use of the then privately owned class 'B4' 0-4-0T No. 30096 *Corrall Queen* which was employed shunting coal wagons at Dibles Wharf in Southampton. The RCTS hoped to use it to take participants around the Southampton quaysides as part of an attractive all day sally through the southern counties. Alas, it was to no avail.

Dwelling no further on what might have been, there remained plenty of rail tours which did take place. Not surprisingly Bulleid pacifics were the most frequently used type of locomotive on 1966/67 specials. Eighteen different light pacifics were provided and nine of the remaining 'Merchant Navies'. However, the most intensively employed locomotive was undoubtedly 'U' Class 2-6-0 No. 31639, which was seen on seven different tours in just four months at the beginning of 1966. Another unsurprising favourite was the unique BR class '3' No. 77014, which found itself deployed five times after its arrival at Guildford in 1966. Also popular with tour organisers were the 'USA' class, with Nos. 30064 and 30073 being the most common choices. Guildford's shed pilot, No. 30072, also had a couple of mainline flings.

The second of these was most unusual: it conveyed members of the Railway Enthusiasts Club to their annual dinner at Deepdene. The little tank hauled its two coaches there from Guildford and then carried on to Redhill to be coaled and watered. Its other escape from its normal confines was on 9th October 1966, when it worked on a Southern Counties Touring Society train along the goods branch from Wimbledon to Tooting.

"The Marquess Goes S.S.W." Rail Tour of Loco Preservation (Sussex) Ltd, hauled by class 'K4' 2-6-0 N0. 3442 *The Great Marquess* speeds up the gradient towards Hassocks on the Victoria-Brighton main line, while making its first run on the Southern on 12th March 1967.   *Author*

As the different classes of locomotive based on the Southern dwindled, it became ever more difficult to attract patrons with an interesting motive power diet. However, the LCGB managed a bonanza of steam with its 'Hampshire Branch Lines' tour of 9th April 1967. It was worked by *ten* different locomotives, representing nine different classes including the 'USA' tank shown in the picture on this page. Only the standard '3' 2-6-2Ts did not participate in the haulage of the tour. In fact, it is interesting to note that the '3' class was not used on any of the multiplicity of railtours run in the last eighteen months of steam. The only other occasions of such use were in September 1964 on the LCGB 'Anton and Test Valley' railtour and on the last leg of the same Society's Steyning line special in December 1965.

The LCGB also takes the prize for the greatest number of locomotive changes during a special's journey. Its 'South West Suburban' of 5th February 1967 was notable anyway for being the Club's 100th railtour. Carrying a special headboard to denote the fact, and rostered in the weekly traffic notice as special duty No. 100, no effort was spared to make the most of the occasion.

For the journey to Fawley 'USAs' Nos. 30069/30064 took over. 'Eh, you, get back on the train' was the cry as last pictures were snatched during the photographic stop at Marchwood. *Author*

Standard class '4' No. 76058 negotiates the curved approaches to Reading Central goods depot with appropriate caution with the LCGB's 'South West Suburban' tour on 5th February 1967. *Author*

The final stroke of ingenuity was the use of the hundredth member of the smaller Bulleid pacific class to haul the train. Although No. 34100 *Appledore* was beautifully turned out unfortunately it succumbed to a 'hot box' after handling the Windsor to Staines section and had to retire to Feltham MPD for attention. This was to no avail, and a rather less clean class-mate, No. 34077, deputised.

Other sections of the tour involved standards Nos. 76033, 76058, 77014 and 80145, in an itinerary which involved no fewer than nine changes of engine as it rambled up and down the electrified branch lines of suburbia.

There was also a rare meander up the Western's Reading Central Goods siding, which was taken tender first by No. 76058. It also involved some complicated shunting in the goods yard to enable the locomotive to return to the front of the train.

Above: The improbable spectacle of the Army's 2-10-0 No. 600 *Gordon* heading down the Portsmouth main line at Woking junction, on April 16th 1966, with the RCTS tour to Longmoor. *Author*

Right: For the second RCTS 'Longmoor' rail tour on April 30th 1966, the weather was hot and dry, with the result that diesel power took over on the second trip around the LMR's Hollywater loop, due to fire hazard. Prior to that decision, 0-6-0ST No. 196 is seen near Hollywater Platform on the first run of the day, with a mixed ensemble in tow. *Roger Merry-Price*

Equally outstanding for locomotive variety and for simply being different were the two RCTS 'Longmoor' trips in April 1966. The highlight of these events was the use of War Department 2-10-0 No. 600 *Gordon*, now resident on the Severn Valley Railway. After much wrangling, the big blue locomotive was permitted to run on the Southern's tracks, and so it met the tour train at Woking, for haulage to Liss, and then transfer on to the Longmoor Military Railway. So popular was the idea that the trip had to take place twice, using much the same locomotives on each occasion.

The other aspect of the tour which rendered it so attractive was the opportunity for a last trip over the goods only Bordon-Bentley line which had closed completely on 4th April and by implication a last chance to run a railtour from one end of the Longmoor Military Railway to the other, using both BR connections.

Among the many participants was Klaus Marx, whose detailed recollections are included because they emphasise the sheer enjoyment and entertainment that was offered to rail tourists in the 1960s.

The first tour was a sell-out, not surprisingly at 30/- (£1.50); but I had booked early and made my way to Waterloo on Saturday, 16th April 1966, my hopes dampened somewhat by the murky weather. It was one of those rare Aprils with a heavy snowfall which had fallen the two preceding days and so there were still occasional small amounts to be seen amongst the lineside bushes in the countryside. The sky remained disappointingly overcast when there was the chance of some unique photographs for the taking, though the visual effects were more than dramatic. It was one of those dank calm days when escaping steam clung round each locomotive and where dense columns of smoke hung low in the air above the whole length of the train and beyond. The weather was unrelenting, and the afternoon mist lay over the handsome Hampshire landscape of birches and clustered firs and the broken ground of familiar yellow-grey sand. It was military country, rutted by the trails of tracked vehicles, punctuated every couple of miles or so by camps and depots with unbecoming sheds the size of hangars which shared the common link of the Longmoor Military Railway.

As the railtour went through its carefully planned motions and wended its roundabout route back to London, there must have been a certain feeling of disappointment all round that its magnificently scenic possibilities had not yielded their full delights. I shared that view for, though I had used a whole film, the majority of these proved quite unpresentable for any slide lecture. Walking down the platform at Waterloo I went up to the guard's compartment of the leading coach to commiserate with the organising team and thank them for their efforts. The reply came: 'We're hoping for a better day *next time*!' That was exciting news, there was to be another chance to obtain some memorable pictures.

'What about the chances of getting on this second trip?'

'Turn up at 9.30 am and if there are any unsold tickets we'll fix you up'. If this were to come off, the first trip would not have been in vain. I now knew every move, shunt, set back, engine change, run past and photogenic possibility, from which side to look out, how long to stay off the train and what to expect at any given point and moment. Needless to say I prayed for fine weather! When Saturday 30th April 1966, dawned bright and clear I needed no second bidding, and this time it was a gloriously hot, sunny and cloudless day.

All went as hoped for. I squeezed on board the repeat tour; alas even in a fortnight in railway history, the sands of time took their toll. Expecting to see as previously 'N' No. 31411 piloting 'U' No. 31639, the new pilot turned out to be 'U' No. 31791. We were to learn that there were now no surviving 'N's fit to work the train, and the sole surviving pair of 'U's were used, both polished up to a high pitch by their Guildford crews. However, even they were totally outshone by the splendidly turned out Army Department 2-10-0 *Gordon* which was standing across the platform in the 'down' bay at Woking, looking magnificent with its blue livery and several mechanical parts below the running plate picked out in red. There was an almost universal and frenzied rush across the platform to inspect this marvellous machine and then, as it reversed out past the platform ends, it was greeted by the railway enthusiasts' standing ovation, the clicking accompaniment of scores of camera shutters.

The official report stated:- 'The schedule allowed 43 minutes for the 27 mile non-stop run from Woking to Liss, and understandably no heroics were attempted.' But if memory serves me right, on one of the occasions, *Gordon* was held for a few minutes at Milford to allow a stopping electric ahead to get clear. On arrival in the 'down' platform at Liss (SR) I was off like a flash across the footbridge and down into the exchange sidings. I was so quick that I was able to photograph AD 0-6-0ST No. 195 which was waiting there before it backed on to the rear of the train. With a locomotive at each end the cavalcade proceeded into the LNM exchange sidings, reversing to set back into Liss (LNM). Here, *Gordon* ran round and coupled up tender first in front of the saddle tank. The 8-coach special stuck out far beyond the platforms of the LMR station, and the whole place was a seething mass of tour participants seeking to operate in a very restricted area. There were a few other photographers around the exchange sidings and at Liss Forest Road, but most enthusiasts of those days, myself included, had not yet attained to the ranks of the car owning plutocracy.

As the excursion drew into Longmoor Downs, waiting across the platform was the Hollywater Loop special, in the charge of AD 0-6-0ST No. 196 (now on the Mid-Hants). Only half the main train's complement could be accommodated so, whilst these toured the loop in an anti-clockwise direction, the other half were able to visit points of interest at Longmoor and then catch the second run with this train. According to the notice, 'A special feature of the Hollywater trips will be the two photographic stops, when the train will reverse and run through for photographers'. These took place in the cutting at Holm Hills and at the Hopkins Bridge site. Whilst a fortnight previously the first location provided a stirring smoke screen as the Austerity pounded up the cutting, the present assault on the bank was achieved with barely a wisp of smoke. Nothing quite so exciting happened at the second run past at Hopkins Bridge where the track had been much moved in relaying operations and the ground was potholed with deep puddles that caught many an enthusiast unawares. The train moved gingerly across the rickety and often unballasted track-work. Between the two 'run throughs' lay Hollywater's timber platform surrounded by forested glades in glorious silence. The main line was reached at Whitehill, where a triangle provided the only means, other than by crane, of turning locomotives and stock on the railway.

Those not on the train were able to photograph it leaving Longmoor Downs and alongside the road to Liphook, and again on its return approach past Woolmer yard, still the site of shunting and marshalling training. Here a third 'run through' took place, the participants alighting en masse to photograph the train as it ran past at speed. A fortnight before I had travelled on the second trip; this time having elected to do the same, I chose to capture the train pounding up the grade out of Longmoor Downs but at the last moment I saw a couple of enthusiasts dashing back to their car and cadged a brief lift with them. These were the precursors of today's train chasers for they overtook the train as the railway parallels the road for about a mile and photographed it on a further two occasions near Heifers Down and Griggs Green. I left them there as it was only a few hundred yards round the corner to Holm Hills where the train was now reversing back for its run pasts, following which I providentially joined it.

Though the locomotive had not been making any smoke, there was plenty billowing in the far background where it had started its dramatic assault which I feel sure exceeded the 15 mph restriction on the loop. Lineside fires had already taken root at Weaversdown on the main special's run up to Longmoor and nearly all the available troops at the

The RCTS 'Longmoor' special of April 30th 1966 approaches Farnham with LMR No 600 *Gordon* in charge for the section from Bordon to Staines.
Peter Harrod

camp must have been summoned to beat out the fires raging all round the Hollywater circuit. Orders came through for 0-6-0 diesel shunter No. 878 *Basra* to officiate on the second run. To offset the disappointment of no steam for the second lot of 'run throughs', the departure of the main train was advanced a quarter of an hour to allow for a run past at Woolmer, a small compensation for the unfortunates but an added bonus for those who had already taken their fill on the first train. *Gordon* was now at the rear of the train so as to be the right way round after the special reversed at Borden, and thoughtfully arranged to be at the head of the extra 'run through', a fact much appreciated by all with cameras.

Following the return of the second Hollywater circular, the main train left with No. 195 at the head and *Gordon* trailing at the rear and, so via Whitehill and the sharpest curve on the railway, to arrive in the goods road opposite the military platform at Bordon. There we were ready to move forward following reversal with *Gordon* now at the head, chimney first. Most passengers alighted whilst the saddletank was detached, and there was plenty of opportunity to photograph *Gordon* easing the train forward onto the BR line and then setting back into Bordon SR platform, still neat but its doom foretold by the armless signal posts and the rusted set of rails. They had seen their last regular passenger train on 16th September 1957, and final goods train almost a month previously on 4th April 1966. The station was never built for a train of this length, and *Gordon* stood out past the loop points. With photographic activity completed, the last passenger train left Bordon and, passing the silent intermediate Kingsley Halt, reached the Alton line at Bentley. Aware in advance of the briefest of stops, I obtained a surreptitious photograph from the edge of the 'up' platform.

The next portion of the tour took the special over the section from Ash Vale to Frimley junction, unusual in being single line and electrified, and so on through Ascot and Staines Central and into the 'up' loop opposite Staines exchange sidings so that engines could be changed clear of the main line. On 16th April the BR locomotive had been Standard Class '3' 2-6-0 No. 77014, and this was attached to the rear. A fortnight later it was declared unfit to work and Standard Class '5' 4-6-0 No. 73114 *Etarre* took over for the stretch to Windsor and Eton (Riverside), while *Gordon* took his leave, returning to Longmoor via Virginia Water, Woking and Liss.

At Windsor the pair of 'Moguls' were waiting to back on for the return to Waterloo via Staines and the Hounslow loop. The scene at Windsor was fairly dramatic, the bulk of train passengers who had alighted, cramped along the then island platform while numerous others, including locals and non-travelling enthusiasts viewing and photographing from the side, had to contend with a set of electric rails. Guard Bill Crawfurth, who relished railtours and somehow always got his name down for the most prominent ones on the Southern Region, weighed in with all his authority at the platform end and it was a marvel no-one ended up burnt to a frazzle!

The journey from Windsor behind Nos. 31411 and 31639 on 16th April via Staines and Brentford was uneventful apart from catching up a stopping electric train on the Hounslow loop. Excellent time was made from Barnes to Waterloo and, according to a report of the tour, 'an early arrival brought the day's proceedings to a fitting conclusion'. Arrival a fortnight later was 'on time', and all in all the tours represented a gratifying and highly successful outcome to months of patient negotiation and planning. We shall never see their like again.'

The Longmoor tour of 30th April was the last to use pre-War SR motive power, for the last 'U' and 'N' class locomotives were condemned the following month. Previously, on 3rd April, the last 'Q1', No. 33006, had taken its bow. Coupled with 'U' No. 31639 it worked the LCGB 'Wilts and Hants' special from Salisbury to Waterloo, by way of Southampton, Alresford and Woking. The pair put in a spirited performance with a top speed of 64 mph on the main line at Hersham and reached Waterloo about nine minutes early.

A fortnight earlier the 'Q1' had held the stage by itself, also for the LCGB. Although it had been withdrawn in January, No. 33006 had been specially retained to work these last two tours in the spring. I was an eager participant in the March 19th event, named the 'New Forester', since it gave me the last chance to travel behind steam along my local line. It was particularly apt timing, for the line from Netley to St. Denys had been opened on 5th March 1866, so this was an excellent way to commemorate the centenary. The only disappointment from my point of view

Above: Class 'U' No. 31639 and class 'N' No. 31411 near Ash with the LCGB 'Wilts and Hants' tour on April 3rd 1966.   *Peter Harrod*

Below: After a change of locomotives at Salisbury, class 'U' No. 31639 is now joined by 'Q1' No. 33006 for the return to Waterloo via the Mid-Hants line. The pair were photographed approaching Alresford and, for the 0-6-0, this was probably its very last run.   *Peter Harrod*

The last 'Q1'in service, No. 33006, captures the lenses of the cameramen at Gosport on 19th March 1967. Eastleigh shed has made a good job of cleaning up the freight locomotive for the tour, the LCGB's 'New Forester'

Author

was that there was no photographic stop arranged at Netley or any of the other intermediate stations after Fareham.

The special was scheduled to leave Eastleigh at 12.15, having made connections from London. This gave patrons a chance to visit Eastleigh Works and shed before departure. According to my notebook only two steam locomotives were receiving attention in the works, No. 34004 *Yeovil* and No. 35014 *Nederland Line*. They were easily outnumbered by diesel and electric machines. Outside the Works was the ex-GWR freight locomotive No. 2818 which was in for restoration, together with 'USA' No. 30067 and 'West Country' No. 34001 *Exeter*. I include my own recollections of that enjoyable day.

Over at the nearby Eastleigh engine sheds there was still some steam variety to see and photograph. The other two 'Q1s' which had survived into 1966 had reached Eastleigh on their way to scrapping at Newport, South Wales. They each looked forlorn, stripped of their number plates and coupling rods and emphasised our good fortune in having the use of No. 33006. Also outside the shed was 'M7' No. 30053 which had been withdrawn in May 1964, reinstated for a later LCGB tour, and then purchased for preservation in the USA. There it was to spend the next twenty years, before its happy return to Swanage in April 1987. Its restoration was carried out at Eastleigh Works before it set out on its trans-Atlantic journey, together with 'Schools' 4-4-0 No. 30926 *Repton* on 13th April 1967. Also present were some of the condemned 2-6-0s like No. 31809, and the usual Eastleigh selection of Bulleid pacifics, Ivatt tanks and 'Standards' of various sorts. Blowing off vigorously inside the shed were 'USA; tank Nos. 30073 and 30064, cleaned up ready to haul the 'New Forester' later in the day.

Returning to the station to await the start of the tour, we soon found No. 33006 coming into view at 12.09. It was propelling its train of seven green carriages into the 'down' loop platform, where around three hundred enthusiasts waited to board. For the first section of the trip the 'Q1' was to run tender-first. There was just time to notice that it had been nicely turned out for the occasion with white painted buffers, smokebox door hinges and coupling rods! The only pity was that the weather was rather dull and grey, which didn't breathe much life into the locomotive's sombre black livery.

Punctually, at 12.15, we set off, curving sharply left past the Locomotive Works on the line to Botley, and then followed the route through Funtley tunnels to Fareham. On this first section, our locomotive worked up to 45 mph which wasn't bad for a freight locomotive. A brief pause at Fareham station confirmed our route across to the Gosport branch which had been closed to passenger traffic in 1953, and had not seen many enthusiast specials since. This was something of a 'silly' season though, for this tour was the second of three to visit the branch in the space of a month. The line required sedate progress so that the five miles occupied nearly twenty minutes, with speed not exceeding 25 mph.

Some photographers had now begun to appear by the lineside to record the special, particularly at the intermediate station at Fort Brockhurst and from the various road over-bridges. A few seconds before 13.00 the 'Q1' rolled into Gosport, coming to a stand beneath the unglazed remains of the overall roof. The opportunity to inspect the classical features of Sir William Tite's station design occupied some, while others were anxious to record the locomotive movements. Once No. 33006

Left: What the photographers on the previous page saw! No. 33006 at the terminus of the freight-only Gosport branch. *Author*

Below: 'Q1' No. 33006 rattles over River Hamble bridge at Bursledon *en route* from Gosport to Southampton Terminus. *Paul Riley/IAL*

had installed itself at the head of the train, chimney leading, a throng of cameramen went into action. All this activity brought the Victorian terminus to life for an unreal fifteen minutes, before it returned to its normal undisturbed repose. Those taking pictures may have had mixed feelings about the front end of the engine. It was normal LCGB practice for their tours to carry a large headboard with the name of the particular special inscribed upon it, as well as a small rectangular plaque with the club's initials displayed. On this occasion only the latter board was carried, which to my mind left a far less cluttered locomotive to view.

Punctually, at 13.15, we set off again, once the participants had been persuaded to join the train. Another slow but purposeful saunter brought the train back to Fareham and then off onto the Netley line. Twenty minutes had been scheduled for the exacting 123/4 miles thence to St. Denys, with its severe speed restrictions at Bursledon and Woolston, and the sharp climbs up to Swanwick and Sholing. In the event No. 33006 exceeded the allowance by 21/2 minutes, with speeds mainly in the mid-40s, apart from a brief 50 mph in the dip west of Swanwick. From St. Denys the route took us through Northam to Southampton Terminus and the second reversal of the day.

Thus, within an hour, we were at rest within another of architect Tite's creations, built just before Gosport station in 1839, for the opening of the London and Southampton Railway. With No. 33006 confined by the buffer stops, our motive power was switched for the two 'USA' tanks. Unlike most railtours we set off again five minutes early, for a non-stop run through

Above: Now powered by a pair of green 'USA' tanks, Nos. 30073 and 30064, the LCGB's 'New Forester' pauses at Fawley, among the trappings of a great oil terminal. *Author*

Below: The conductor rails at Totton are rusty and as yet unelectrified, but they herald the end of Southern steam, including No. 33006, waiting to continue to Brockenhurst on 19th March 1966. *Author*

Southampton's Central station, albeit at a very restrained 15 mph! Then Nos. 30073 and 30064 led us on to Totton, and then left on to the Fawley branch. With its succession of ungated level crossings there was a genuine excuse for much use of the engine whistles, to the general satisfaction. A brief stop for photographs at Marchwood was marred by an excess of steam emananting from underneath No. 30073, which obscured the rest of the train. The 'New Forester' was soon on its way again, with the locomotives rattling along in fine style at about 25 mph.

Arrival at Fawley was on time at 15.15 and the locomotives each took water from the cylindrical water tower at the north end of the station. The passenger service on the line had been withdrawn just a month before on 14th February, and so the stations still looked as though they were 'in business' and provided pleasant backdrops for the photographers.

By now the sun was beginning to appear, giving a better impression of a spring day, and there were plenty of opportunities to snap the pair of green tanks as they fussed around the station area, before coupling up bunker-first ready for the return journey. This got under way after some twenty minutes spent at Fawley, and we then enjoyed another noisy return up the branch to Totton. There No. 33006 was waiting to resume as our motive power and posed on tracks where conductor rails were already installed, although rusty and as yet, unused. Our train waited as planned while the 'down' stopper passed by with No. 80085 in charge. Then we too set off westwards through the New Forest, with speed again hovering around the 45 mph mark. To allow the

'Q1' No., 33006 pauses at Brockenhurst with the "New Forester" tour on March 19th 1966 prior to making its trip down the branch to Lymington. *Author*

Nearing the end of an enjoyable tour, the 'Q1' runs round its seven carriages at Lymington Pier on 19th March 1966, and prepares to return to Brockenhurst as the 17.30 ordinary service, as well as the LCGB 'New Forester' excursion. *Author*

tour train on to the Lymington branch, it was actually necessary to cancel the regular passenger working to create a path on what was a fairly busy branch line. So now we were the 'New Forester' *and* the 17.00 Brockenhurst to Lymington Pier! Actually by my watch we left some 2¹/2 minutes early, so I hope that no ordinary passengers missed the train, or were deterred by its unusual clientele. The 'Q1' could not cope with the rather tight 14 minute schedule and lost a couple of minutes despite accelerating up to its preferred 45 mph running speed.

At the Pier station No. 33006's polished paintwork was at last shown off to advantage in the low evening sunlight as it ran

round its train ready to form the 17.30 return working to Brockenhurst. Once the Isle of Wight ferry *Farringford* had docked we were ready to depart. The final stage from Town station up to Brockenhurst was very slow but no-one seemed to mind for it had been a very pleasant and satisfying tour of the Solent byways. No-one could pretend that it was the most exciting Southern special during 1966 or 1967, but it had given participants almost their last chance to travel behind a 'Q1' class locomotive, had marked a centenary, the closing of a branch line and had taken passengers into two of the oldest stations in Hampshire.

Table 11. **The 'New Forester' rail tour, March 19th 1966.**

Locomotive No: 33006
Load: 7/230/250

Miles		Schedule	Actual	Speeds
00.00	EASTLEIGH	0	00.00	-/45
05.55	Botley		10.38	36
			sigs	
10.90	FAREHAM	18	23.14	-
	Fort Brockhurst		10.59	-/26
05.00	GOSPORT	20	19.15	-
	Fort Brockhurst		07.35	18
05.00	FAREHAM	20	20.00	-
03.65	Swanwick		09.09	39/50
05.65	Bursledon		11.52	42/45
07.20	Hamble Halt		13.54	43
07.90	Netley		14.44	46/40
10.30	Woolston		18.32	30★
11.05	Bitterne		21.14	45
12.60	St. Denys	20	22.34	15★
13.55	Northam junction	22	24.47	-
14.60	SOUTHAMPTON TERM.	26	27.21	-

Locomotives Nos: 30073/30064

Miles		Schedule	Actual	Speeds
00.00	SOUTHAMPTON TERM.	0	00.00	-
01.50	So'ton Central	5	08.07	15

Miles		Schedule	Actual	Speeds
04.25	Redbridge	14	16.04	23
04.90	Totton	17	18.05	20
08.50	MARCHWOOD	29	30.42	-
03.75	Frost Lane crossing		12.23	25
06.05	FAWLEY	23	19.46	-
02.30	Frost Lane	12	07.47	-/26
06.05	Marchwood	24	18.59	21
09.65	TOTTON	40	34.39	-

Locomotive No. 33006

Miles		Schedule	Actual	Speeds
00.00	TOTTON	0	00.00	-/32
02.90	Lyndhurst Road		08.04	36
05.60	Beaulieu Road		12.15	43/46
10.25	BROCKENHURST	15	19.57	-
00.95	Lymington Jct.	2¹/2	03.00	-/45
04.90	LYMINGTON TOWN	10	11.20	-
00.55	LYMINGTON PIER	2	02.50	-
00.55	LYMINGTON TOWN	2	02.35	-
03.95	Lymington Jct.	7¹/2	11.13	-
04.90	BROCKENHURST	9	13.26	-

★indicates permanent speed restriction.

Apart from the 'Q1' and 'N' and 'U' class Moguls, only one other pre-War Southern tender locomotive saw rail tour duty in 1966. This was the magnificent 4-6-0 No. 30837, the last survivor of Maunsell's 'S15' class. It had been especially retained after the withdrawal of the last few members of the class in the autumn of 1965, so that it could be used on an LCGB commemorative rail tour. In the event the demand for a last ride behind one of these locomotives was so great that the tour had to be run on consecutive Sundays in January 1966. The itinerary involved a Waterloo departure making for Bentley on the electrified Alton line. From there a trip over the Bordon branch was included, worked on each occasion by an immaculate class 'U' No. 31639. Continuing via the Mid-Hants line to Winchester with the 'S15', the next port of call was Eastleigh where a visit to the Works was laid on. The tour train was pulled into the works yard by green-liveried 'USA' No. 30073. The return to London was by way of Botley, Fareham, Havant and the Guildford line.

The first trip, on 9th January, was blessed with a magnificent cloudless winter day, and the bright sunshine brought out all the care with which No. 30837 had been prepared for its big day. Buffers and copper work were burnished and the locomotive's black livery well-polished. The following Sunday the weather changed, with snowfalls and dull overcast conditions. Not surprisingly the 'S15' was piloted over the steep climb from Alton to Medstead by No. 31639, making an attractive combination, thence to Eastleigh. After its final fling, No. 30837 was stored at Feltham for several months raising hopes for possible preservation, before it was despatched for scrap to South Wales. Nevertheless, it had been a most nostalgic experience, for which the participants were duty grateful.

Above: Class 'S15' No. 30837 departs from Alresford after a photographic stop with the LCGB's S15 Commemorative Railtour on January 9th 1966.   *Author*

Below: Class 'U' 2-6-0 No. 31639 pulls onto the Bordon branch at Bentley with the first S15 Commemorative Railtour on January 9th 1966.   *Author*

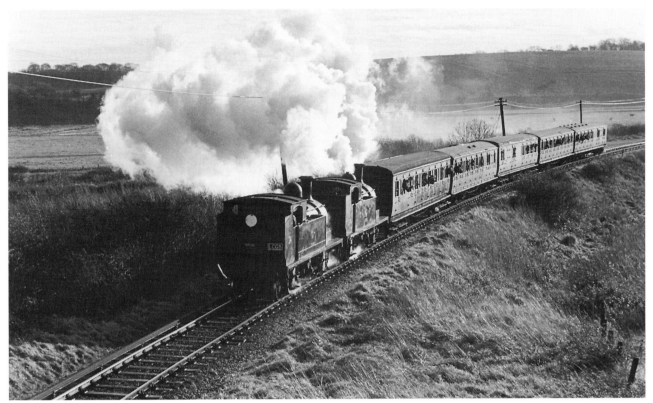

Above: The return from Shanklin on 31st December 1966 saw a change to clear blue skies. *Calbourne* and *Chale* parade before the golden spotlight at Brading.

Author

Below: Last day of lsle of Wight steam: the LCGB tour emerges from Ryde Tunnel with '02' Nos. 31 *Chale* and 24 *Calbourne* in charge.

By the end of 1966, the only pre-War Southern locomotives remaining in service were the 'O-2' tanks on the Isle of Wight. Steam services on the Island ended on 31 st December 1966 and the LCGB ran a last special over the Ryde Esplanade-Shanklin section, all that remained of the once extensive railway network. Over 500 enthusiasts travelled from Waterloo, and crammed the 5-coach train provided for them. It was worked by locomotives Nos. 24 *Calbourne* and 31 *Chale*, which completed the return trip under brilliant winter sunshine.

Whilst 'last runs' were a regular excuse for specials, for other enthusiasts excitement was a crucial ingredient: new routes, high speed or outstanding motive power interest being essentials. No wonder therefore that the railway societies started to bring 'foreign' locomotives down on to the Southern. The last twelve months of steam operation saw representatives of LNER classes 'A2', 'A4', 'K4' and 'V2' in the South, as well as a BR standard 'Britannia'. (The visits of 'A3' No. 4472 *Flying Scotsman* in September 1966 have already been recorded.) For the sake of completeness I should also refer to the use of two different LMSR Stanier '8F' 2-8-0s on Somerset and Dorset farewell tours in January and March 1966, which brought Nos. 48309 and 48706 down to the Bournemouth area.

Probably the most outstanding event was the LCGB's achievement in bringing 'A2' pacific No. 60532 *Blue Peter* all the way down from Scotland to haul just one special! That was a Waterloo-Exeter run on 14th August 1966, producing an unprecedented sight on the Southern. Sadly the crew did not seem to get the best out of their strange mount and after an undistinguished run down through Salisbury, Exeter Central was reached two hours late. After the fire was rebuilt at Exmouth junction, the return journey up the Western to Taunton and

Westbury was more vigorous, but lateness had by then reached a massive three hours! It had been planned for 'Britannia' No. 70004 *William Shakespeare* to haul the special to Salisbury, whilst No. 60532 went ahead to be turned and serviced. In retrospect it seems incredible that a 'Britannia' should have been brought from the North West just to carry out a 25 mile assignment. The LCGB obviously had much influence!

In view of *Blue Peter's* poor performance, No. 70004 was given the task of bringing the tour all the way home to Waterloo, which was finally reached a mere 80 minutes late! The 'A2' accordingly retired to Salisbury shed in semi-disgrace where it languished for a couple of days. I tried in vain to persuade the shed-foreman to allow me to photograph it lurking among the

Southern pacifics, and it eventually embarked light engine to Basingstoke and then on its long journey back to Scotland. On the other hand No. 70004's travels were not wasted by the Southern. Someone had the bright idea of rostering it to the 17.23 Waterloo to Southampton Docks boat train on 16th August, even putting in special stops at Winchester and Eastleigh for the convenience of any non-boat passengers who might just have wanted to get on board! It also worked a few local passenger trains from Basingstoke during its stay on the Southern, and then returned north on the 17th powering the 17.43 Southampton Docks to Crewe banana train.

Above: Having been brought specially down from Scotland, 'A2' No. 60532 Blue Peter is already looking to be in trouble as it approaches Basingstoke with the LCGB tour to Exeter on August 14th 1966.
Peter Harrod

Below: After the 'A2' had experienced an unhappy journey to the West Country, 'Britannia' No. 70004 *William Shakespeare* took over and is seen approaching Salisbury at dusk.
Author

This was not the only attempt by the LCGB to bring a locomotive from Scotland down to the other end of Britain. It organised the 'Green Arrow' railtour of 3rd July to allow a 'V2' to show off its paces. This was rather less unique because members of the class had been on loan to the region in 1953 during the temporary withdrawal of the entire 'Merchant Navy' class for investigation. Thus No. 60919 was despatched from Dundee on 25th June and five days later it reached Basingstoke having travelled down through the Midlands.

Unfortunately on the morning of the tour, the 'V2' was declared a failure at Nine Elms, and unrebuilt 'West Country' No. 34002 *Salisbury* was substituted. *Salisbury* gave an excellent showing as deputy on the run to Salisbury, with a top speed of 90 mph! It was hoped that during the course of the day repairs could be carried out to the 'V2' for it to be reunited with its train but this was not to happen.

While the tour train was wending its way around Wiltshire and Dorset the 'V2' had received attention at Nine Elms to its broken spring. It then ran 'light' down to Eastleigh with a view to carrying on to Bournemouth to take over haulage of the special. However, when it reached Eastleigh, in midafternoon, it was found that the right-hand water supply to the injector would not shut off. Bob Joy, the late chargehand fitter, repaired the fault, but then 'Control' would not let the locomotive carry on down the line because it might have delayed an express. It was then sent back up the line, but promptly suffered an overheated inside small end and so it had to be stopped at Basingstoke shed. There it lay when eventually No. 34002 went past, still standing in for the unfortunate Scottish visitor, heading for Waterloo.

Above: Despite many efforts to get the visiting 'V2' 2-6-2 into position and working order, it failed to fulfil its commitment to the passengers on the LCGB's "Green Arrow" tour. They did at least get a glimpse of the locomotive as their train, hauled by replacement locomotive No. 34002 *Salisbury*, passed the grounded No. 60919 at Basingstoke shed.
Peter Harrod

Below: The 'V2' should have powered the 'Green Arrow' tour to Salisbury on 3rd July 1966. As planned 'Black 5' No. 45493 and 'West Country' class No. 34100 *Appledore* took over at the Cathedral City for the next stage to Yeovil.
Author

'A4' No. 60024 *Kingfisher* passes Evershot on the Weymouth to Yeovil line with A4 Preservation Society Tour on March 26th 1966.   *Peter Harrod*

After its abortive mission, No. 60919 was sent back again on 6th July, once again making use of a banana van train heading for the Midlands, as its payload. It was a great pity that so little was achieved after a round trip of some 1000 miles, although the travellers on the 'Green Arrow' tour did get a refund as part compensation.

Other LNER visitors fared better than the 'A2' and the 'V2': the successful forays by Nos. 4472 and 3442 have already been recounted. Then in March 1966, one of the illustrious 'A4' class graced Southern metals. It was the streamlined form of No. 60024 *Kingfisher* which was chartered by the 'A4 Locomotive Preservation Society' from Waterloo to Weymouth and Yeovil, returning through Salisbury to London. Like its less happy counterparts it had to be summoned from Scotland, but it reached the South in fine fettle, by way of the 11.10 Banbury to Eastleigh freight on 22nd March. It then ran light up to Nine Elms to be prepared for the weekend. Learning of its journey south, the LCGB arranged to make use of it as well, despite the short notice. Thus it was also to be seen on a Waterloo to Exeter round trip on the 27th, possibly being the last steam locomotive to use the turntable at Exmouth junction shed before it was scrapped.

Both runs attracted enormous attention, the 'A4' performing very well on the Weymouth and Exeter routes. Even more excitement would have been generated if patrons of the 10.30 Waterloo to Weymouth had turned up to board their train on March 28th, to find it hauled by a class mate of the world famous *Mallard*! That was indeed the plan concocted in the diagram office at Wimbledon and was justified as being a way of getting the locomotive to Bournemouth so it could earn its keep on the way back to Scotland by hauling the following day's 'Pines Express'. Unfortunately it was not the adverse reaction from senior management, but rough track between Woking and Waterloo that prevented this romantic notion for vibrations to

the locomotive caused the brick arch to collapse. Despite considerable efforts the pacific could not be made ready in time and eventually it ran 'light' to Birmingham via Neasden, High Wycombe and Banbury.

A year later the 'A4' preservationists achieved their dream and purchased No. 60007 *Sir Nigel Gresley*. Restored to its LNER magnificence as No. 4498 it was soon setting supreme standards of performance on rail tour duty all over the north. Bringing it down to the Southern before steam's reign ended was too good an opportunity to miss, and so it was allowed to have two outings during the first weekend in June. On the 3rd it ran from Waterloo to Bournemouth and back to Southampton where the train continued to Salisbury in the care of another streamlined pacific, Bulleid's No. 34023 *Blackmore Vale* while the 'A4' ran 'light', ahead, via Redbridge and Romsey. No. 4498 then took over for the Salisbury to Waterloo leg. The following morning it was back at Waterloo, this time for a return trip to Weymouth, confirming its free running reputation, with speeds in excess of 90 mph achieved.

It must not be thought that the locomotive 'trade' was one-way only, however. The Southern also exported some of its locomotives for the benefit of clubs and societies. The most prolific traveller was 'Merchant Navy' class No. 35026 *Lamport and Holt Line* which began its wanderings on a weekend trip from Waterloo to Scotland on 24th June 1966. The locomotive worked overnight to Crewe, via Birmingham and Market Drayton, powering the first stage of the Warwickshire Railway Society's ambitious 'Aberdonian' tour. It then ran across to Doncaster to pick up the set of Southern coaches returning from Scotland, which it proceeded to haul by way of Newark, Dudley and Birmingham Snow Hill to Waterloo. In the Birmingham suburbs it was piloted by '9F' No. 92113, making a very unusual and powerful combination.

On June 3rd 1967, class 'A4' No. 4498 *Sir Nigel Gresley* accelerates past Woking with the special to Bournemouth. *Author*

No. 35026 clearly had an appetite for northern climes, because on 22nd October it powered the Altrinchamian Railway Excursion Society's 'Elizabethan' tour between York and Newcastle attaining a speed of 90 mph at Thirsk. That special was a history-maker already, because it had broken the steam embargo at Kings Cross with its *Flying Scotsman*-hauled first leg from the Capital. To confirm that the steam ban had been breached, the 'Merchant Navy' ran 'light' back down the East Coast main line and was actually stabled overnight at Finsbury Park depot.

A month later and *Lamport and Holt Line* was at it again, bidding farewell to familiar Basingstoke at the head of a special coaching stock working to Red Bank (Manchester). Its latest quest was to work a Williams Deacons Bank charter special to York on 20th November. It was based at Stockport Edgeley shed for cleaning before the outing, and was serviced at Doncaster on the day itself. After that expedition No. 35026 returned to the relatively banal life of the Waterloo-Weymouth line, and perhaps deprived of the freedom of the great northern plains, it expired and was condemned the following March!

Two other Bulleid pacifics travelled well off their normal tracks in the summer of 1966. 'West Country' No. 34002 *Salisbury* followed up its 'Green Arrow' success by working an RCTS special from Waterloo to Nottingham Victoria and then back to Marylebone on 13th August. The LCGB's version of the Great Central Railway's farewell was on that line's final weekend and involved No. 35030 *Elder Dempster Lines*.

If some of the more fanciful proposals had actually occurred, I would also be able to write about the visit of unrebuilt Bulleids to Aberdeen, or the Settle and Carlisle line. Ironically, in the preservation era, main line steam tours have produced just such surprises, which could never have been foreseen in the mid-1960s! However, it has not so far proved possible to carry out what the ARES was proposing in June and July 1966. The gullible could apply to take part in a brake-van tour of Wigan using 'SI5' No. 30837, or if that wasn't available, 'Q1' No. 33006. Both locomotives were condemned and heading for scrap by then, but other representatives of the two classes do survive, so perhaps one day even that might be arranged ... if enough brake-vans could be found to cope with the crowds!

If such ventures were optimistic to say the least, it might be thought that attempts to run steam tours over the electrified fines of the Southern's Central and Eastern divisions would also be fraught with problems. Although Mr. C.A.G. Spiller had managed to get steam to Brighton, the majority of East Sussex and Kent was forbidden territory to steam. It was therefore a major triumph when a society managed to steal a few miles travel over track which was not on the steam-easy Western division.

The Southern Counties Touring Society (SCTS) was particularly successful in that respect. Its 'Southdown Venturer' tour of 20th February 1966 saw 'West Country' class No. 34013 *Okehampton* starting out from Victoria and running by way of East Croydon, Edenbridge Town, Uckfield and Lewes to Brighton. Its return journey was via Portsmouth,

Right: 'West Country' 4-6-2 No. 34002 *Salisbury* finds itself in strange surroundings at Colwick shed while being serviced after working the RCTS tour from Waterloo to Nottingham Victoria on August 13th 1966. *Edwin Wilmshurst*

Below: The LCGB 'Hampshire Branch Lines' tour arrives at Romsey headed by 'Battle of Britain' No. 34057 *Biggin Hill*, sadly deprived of its nameplate by that time. *Author*

Guildford and West Croydon to terminate at London Bridge, where steam was a very rare visitor. Subsequently the SCTS operated a tour to the West Country on 13th November which used BR class '5' No. 73065, again with a Victoria departure. By travelling through Herne Hill and Crystal Palace to Norwood junction and thence Redhill, it became reputedly the first steam train over the Kent Coast line for over a year.

Not to be outdone, the LCGB's 'Reunion' Rail tour of 10th December saw BR class '4' 4-6-0 No. 75075 working a stage from Clapham junction to Herne Hill, East Croydon and down to East Grinstead (High Level) station and then on to Three Bridges. This involved considerable mileage over the Central division, including a rare steam visit to the Oxted line, as well as the brief wandering over the South Eastern sector between Brixton and Herne Hill. Subsequently the special traversed the Brighton to Victoria main line, in the care of 'Battle of Britain' class No. 34089 *602 Squadron*.

In due course the same two societies each offered final steam runs over the South Eastern division. The LCGB's 'Surrey Downsman' of 5th March 1967 took unrebuilt Bulleid No. 34102 *Lapford* from Nunhead through Lewisham and Woodside *en route* to Oxted, while a fortnight later the SCTS 'Southern Rambler' repeated the same path with rebuilt No. 34108 *Wincanton* in charge. This was advertised as a 'last steam ride over the SECR', which indeed it proved to be. Furthermore, the trip later ran from Brighton to Eastbourne, and then returned via Plumpton to Haywards Heath and Victoria. The pacific could not turn on the table at Eastbourne, so it had to run out to Pevensey and reverse on the triangle, returning through Polegate. This was certainly a memorable incursion into a normally steamless area, and a fitting finale to steam in Sussex.

Whilst the SCTS claim to have run the last steam train in the South East seems credible, its earlier claims to be promoting

Above: The last ever steam train on the Lymington branch was the LCGB special of April 9th 1967, which was headed by Standard '4MT' 2-6-4T No. 80151 seen approaching the town station.
Author

Left: Ivatt 2-6-2T No. 41320 at the rear of the LCGB tour covering the Brockenhurst to Lymington branch line on April 9th 1967.   *Author*

the 'Last steam train to Exeter' began to wear rather thin during 1966 for there were no less than **five** last steam runs down the old LSWR main line to Devon! The first, and presumed final trip, was a privately sponsored outing on 8th January, again for the benefit of the Woking Children's Home. It set out via Guildford and Fareham with the appropriately rostered 'West Country' pacific No. 34001 *Exeter* in charge as far as Salisbury. Unfortunately *Exeter* had already lost its nameplates by then. The engine change saw an absolutely resplendent unrebuilt No. 34015 *Exmouth* taking over, showing Salisbury depot's cleaning prowess to the full. Expectations were high of a true

Bulleid performance for this last excursion to the West, but sadly events proved otherwise. This led to the unusual step of the promoters issuing an apology through the columns of the railway press for the 'uncharacteristic locomotive performance', but at least the charity benefitted to the tune of £722.

Considering that Western Region lines were officially banned for steam working, apart from rights of transit between Banbury and Basingstoke, it is remarkable that a further five steam runs took place to Exeter. Even more remarkable, once the turntable at Exmouth Junction had been removed, the latter specials were routed over the Western's own Exeter to Westbury

The first 'last' steam train to Exeter of 1966. Immaculate 'West Country' class No. 34015 *Exmouth* storms away from Salisbury on 8th January.
Author

main line! Perhaps it was just Western Region locomotives that were anathema. This seems particularly likely when the other incursions by steam onto the Western's territory are considered. It was the Dorchester West-Yeovil-Westbury link which saw a number of steam hauled tours, but perhaps the most remarkable 'wandering' was by No. 34013 *Okehampton* on 6th March 1966. As part of the RCTS 'Somerset and Dorset' farewell tour it ran from Highbridge to Weston-super-Mare, Mangotsfield and Bristol.

The finality of the 8th January Exeter run, was soon dispelled by another unrebuilt 'West Country' hauled tour on 2nd April which took No. 34006 *Bude* to Sidmouth Junction, but more particularly by 'A4' No. 60024 *Kingfisher*'s sortie all the way to Exeter on 27th March. Nevertheless the SCTS's advertisement for its 26th June extravaganza duly and confidently proclaimed:

'LAST STEAM TRAIN TO EXETER ... This will be the LAST TO EXETER and WESTBURY by kind permission of Western Region before water columns scrapped and turntables removed Exeter. DON'T MISS your last ride as this definitely last beyond Salisbury . .

The 'telegram' style of the society's announcements made the drama of this run seem all the greater as a potential history maker. Certainly it was a very exciting day with 'Merchant Navy' No. 35023 *Holland Amerika Line* running from Salisbury to Exeter (St. Davids) then up the Western main line to Westbury, with some excellent uphill work and a maximum of 84 mph on the latter section. 'West Country' No. 34100 *Appledore* completed the day's entertainment taking the train onwards to Salisbury and Waterloo. Excellent trip though it was, it was definitely not the last steam train to Exeter! Seven weeks later *Blue Peter* made its unhappy struggle down to Exeter following the same route as No. 35023 and on 15th October No. 35026 *Lamport and Holt Line* performed the circuit in the opposite direction, again for the Woking charity. Without exceeding 78 mph, Driver Parsons achieved a net time of 75 minutes from Westbury to Exeter St. Davids, beating the schedule by sixteen minutes. That was a fine complement to Driver Hooker's 100 mph running on the initial Waterloo to Westbury section.

It would have been stretching everybody's credulity if the SCTS had attempted to promote yet another Exeter run on 13th November as the last, but ironically this is what it turned out to

Above: The last 'last' steam train to Exeter! Another unrebuilt 'West Country', this time No. 34019 *Bideford*, in ex-GWR territory leaving Westbury, 13th November 1966.   *Author*

Below: More steam on the Western: the LCGB's 'Shakespearian' tour changes engines at Reading General on 12th November, 1966. 'West Country' class No. 34015 *Exmouth* gives way to 'Merchant Navy' class No. 35023 *Holland-America Line*.   *John Fairman*

be. Publicity had studiously avoided any reference to it being the final one. A less than clean No. 34019 *Bideford* worked down from Westbury to Exeter and then back up the old SR line to Yeovil Junction and became the last steam passenger train over the Western lines until 1985 and the GWR 150 celebrations. As if the Western had not had enough of steam that weekend, the previous day, No. 34015 *Exmouth*, had hauled the LCGB's 'Shakespearian' tour into Reading General. There it had handed over to No. 35023 running thence to Didcot, Oxford and Banbury.

Fortunately the Southern motive power seems to have behaved itself on nearly all of its wanderings over Western metals and therefore the authorities had little to worry about. The only exception was the notorious 'Bridport Belle' of 22nd January 1967, when Ivatt tanks Nos. 41320 and 41295 contrived to become stuck fast on the steep climb back to Maiden Newton, and gave participants a succession of 'action replays' of a section of the line, as they made repeated, and unsuccessful, attempts to get going again. Eventually the 'rescue services' had to be called and after a long delay a Type '3' diesel was summoned from Weymouth to retrieve the stranded patrons. However, they had the bonus of steam haulage onwards to Yeovil with No. 35030 *Elder Dempster Lines* so the delay was probably worthwhile!

In the last few months before electrification, the scope for running steam specials was much reduced. The Southern Region management was planning its own programme of last steam

Above: The LCGB's last Southern steam tour, the "Dorset Coast Express", restarts from a photographic stop at Corfe Castle on May 7th 1967. The train engine is 'West Country' class No. 34023 *Blackmore Vale*, assisted at the rear by class '4' 2-6-4T No. 80011. *Author*

Below: Privately sponsored tour up from Weymouth to Waterloo on 3rd June 1967, with a very tidy 'Merchant Navy' class No. 35030 *Elder Dempster Lines* in charge, passing Woking. *Author*

trips, so all the private bodies had to be governed by the weekends that were left, when engineering works did not make pathing impossible. Thus the LCGB, for so long at the forefront of Southern special planning, had to be content with its last steam tour as early as 7th May. Its 'Dorset Coast Express' utilised three different Bulleid pacifics and three BR Standards. The highlight of the tour was the organising of two runs along the Swanage branch headed by unrebuilt No. 34023 *Blackmore Vale* enabling participants to alight at Corfe Castle to photograph one of the runs actually in motion. This was well before the more recent phenomenon of the 'run-past'. Because there were no longer run-round facilities at Swanage, each trip down the line had an engine at each end. *Blackmore Vale*'s companions were Nos. 76026 and 80011 respectively. The latter were grimy products of Bournemouth shed, but at least the tour had begun well with a specially cleaned 'West Country' No. 34021 *Dartmoor* setting out from Waterloo.

Apart from the *Sir Nigel Gresley* excursions on 3rd/4th June, there were three others during that month. The first was a privately arranged run on the 3rd, which unusually began from Weymouth, and involved a return trip to Waterloo. Immaculately turned out No. 35030 *Elder Dempster Lines* worked the train up, even having its nameplates restored. Unfortunately it failed in London, and a grimy No. 35007 *Aberdeen Commonwealth* substituted for the return journey.

The following weekend, a fairly steamless Sunday was enlivened by the efforts of the Warwickshire Railway Society. Their trip down from Birmingham brought the unusual scene

Above: The very rare pairing of rebuilt Bulleid pacifics is a very attractive one, as shown by 'West Country' No. 34108 *Wincanton* and 'Battle of Britain' No. 34089 *602 Squadron* passing Millbrook on the Southampton to Wareham stage of the RCTS tour on June 18th 1967.   *Peter Harrod*

Right: On the return leg from Weymouth, Nos. 34023 and 34108 attack Parkstone bank on the outskirts of Bourne-mouth.   *Author*

of LMR Mark II carriages in Inter City livery on to the Swanage branch. Also of interest was the use of steam power at Kensington Olympia station, double-headed into the bargain. Standard No. 73085 piloted No. 34004 Yeovil on the outward journey, and No. 34023 Blackmore Vale on the return.

It fell to the RCTS to have the honour of running the last society excursion over the Southern. It was a splendid event, begun with very clean locomotives Nos. 73029 (in green livery) and No. 34023 working from Waterloo down the Portsmouth line to Havant. It was another glorious sumnier's day and the local fire brigades were soon in action as the pair attacked the climbs south of Guildford with vigour, creating many sparks. From Havant they took the north side of the Cosham triangle to

Fareham where another well-groomed pacific, No. 34089 *602 Squadron*, was waiting. The single locomotive was needed due to weight restrictions at Bursledon and Bitterne, but at Southampton No. 34108 *Wincanton* was coupled in front to provide a splendid pairing. What a shame that it was not possible to restore the locomotives' nameplates for this trip. The two 4-6-2s worked through to Wareham, where No. 34089 combined with Standard No. 80146, at the rear, for a last steam run down to Swanage. Returning to the main line, No. 34089 continued single handed to Weymouth. After a delay to remove a defective coach, the return to London was commenced with unrebuilt No. 34023 *Blackmore Vale* and rebuilt No. 34108 *Wincanton* in charge. They continued to Salisbury where No. 35013 *Blue Funnel* made one of its rare

161

railtour appearances. It didn't disappoint those present, with speeds in the mid-80s, and a net time to Waterloo of 79 minutes.

Although that was the last fling by the enthusiast organisations, BR itself had widely publicised its own steam farewell specials. Initially five had been promoted, but the high cost of tickets and uninteresting nature of what was planned, combined to depress the market. Had they been arranged for the very last day, or a week later, as the LMR did in the North West the following year, things might have been different!

In the event only two trains ran on July 2nd, but both performed well in the charge of 'Merchant Navy' class locomotives, and provided a fitting finale to Southern specials. (Fuller details of the two trips are given in Chapter Nine.) So ended a frantic eighteen months of steam hauled delights on the Southern, the culmination of a regular weekend pastime for so many enthusiasts, which had been gathering momentum over the previous ten years. With the electrification programme to Bournemouth effective from July 10th, no more steam specials were allowed, and the general BR steam ban from 1968 merely confirmed the apparent impossibility of ever seeing steam on the Southern again. At the time, I never even dreamed that steam specials would one day return to nearly every part of the old Southern Region!... but that is definitely another story for a different book...

Top: The first BR special on 2nd July 1967 returns from Weymouth, double-headed by Nos. 35007 *Aberdeen Commonwealth* and 35008 *Orient Line*, seen here near Branksome.   *Author*

Above: Eighty-six minutes after leaving Waterloo, according to the Civic Centre clock, No. 35028 *Clan Line* rolls into Southampton Central with the second BR special.   *Author*

Chapter Eight

The Bournemouth Electrification Scheme

As discussed in chapter one, the motive power policies of the British Transport Commission in the 1950s were rather confused. Under the leadership of R.A. Riddles, who was responsible for Mechanical and Electrical Engineering, it was decided to design and order a range of new steam locomotives to standard designs, embodying the best of practice from the 'Big Four' private companies, following the experience gained in the Locomotive Exchanges.

However, it was already obvious that steam would come under strong competition from diesel and electric power and a committee was set up at the same time to review future traction policy. By the time it reported in 1951, there was no surprise that it advocated a programme of main line electrification based on the 25kV overhead system on major routes, and that diesel power should replace steam elsewhere. This was the background to the Modernisation Plan launched in December 1954, and intended to indicate the way forward right up to 1970. The end of steam locomotive construction was announced in the Plan, and it was suggested that the Southern's steam worked routes from Waterloo should be dieselised.

There were obvious advantages to using diesel locomotives since there would be no need for expensive electrical equipment along the track. Even existing rolling stock could be retained without replacement or conversion. On the other hand, the Southern was above all the 'Southern Electric' and there had been strong grounds for simply extending the third rail across as much of the region as possible. That had already happened in Kent in 1959 and 1961, and with enormous success in terms of increased passengers and revenue generated. However, there was a view that any new electrification schemes should adopt the high-voltage overhead wire system. It is not so surprising therefore, that the Bournemouth electrification was some long time in its gestation. The arguments for overhead electrification were eventually ruled out by the difficulty of running different types of electric trains side by side, and above all by the practical problems of installing the overhead equipment on the congested viaducts that carry the track between Waterloo and Clapham junction. Had that option been pursued, overhead electric cables would also have been installed from Worting Junction to Salisbury, and from Waterloo to Byfleet Junction via Richmond, Feltham and Chertsey.

An alternative case was made for introducing a new specification of 1500V dc, carried in a protected conductor rail. This would have reduced the capital costs of the electrification, as sub-stations could have been spaced further apart, but incompatibility with existing equipment seemed too great an obstacle. Thus, thinking gradually clarified in the shape of a straightforward extension of third-rail electrification. Then there was the question of putting up a viable economic argument to justify the capital outlay; it was likely to be some years before it would rank as a high priority. Therefore thoughts also had to be turned to maintaining a steam worked service in the interim. Although the rebuilt Bulleid pacifics were excellent and modern engines, there were plans to transfer the LMR 'Duchess' pacifics to the Southern, once they became redundant on their native territory. This prospect was scotched by clearance problems, at locations such as the Battledown flyover west of Basingstoke. It was an intriguing idea, but to the relief of Southern steam supporters it was never seriously canvassed.

Preliminary planning in the 1960s set the scene for the announcement of the Bournemouth electrification scheme in September 1964. Although a £15m project, it was really modernisation on the cheap. The Bournemouth - Weymouth and Basingstoke - Salisbury sections were excluded, and the bulk of the electric trains were to be converted from existing steam hauled carriages. The number of electric units was to be kept to the absolute minimum by ambitious diagramming which would require $3^1/_2$ Waterloo - Bournemouth round trips daily! This was setting almost impossible targets for machines and men, and an obvious store of future problems. However, it is unlikely that Government approval would have been obtained without such a cost-conscious package having been devised.

When the SR General Manager launched the scheme on September 29th at a press conference, he predicted that electrification would boost net receipts by some £2$^1/_2$m, which seemed a good return on a paper capital programme of only six times that amount. The novel feature of the electrification plan was the first British use of push-pull working on main lines, and at authorised speeds up to 90 mph. This followed extensive tests by the Southern in the previous three years which showed no operational problems in propelling carriages with a power source at the rear. Thus for the Bournemouth line it was planned to use high power electric units (4-REPs) pushing seven or eight carriages, again formed into sets (TC units). On arrival at Bournemouth, the non-powered TC sets would be diesel hauled by type '3' Bo-Bo locomotives on to Weymouth. In the 'up' direction the diesel would propel, eliminating run-round problems at Weymouth, and enabling rapid turning round of train sets. At Bournemouth the 'TC' set(s) would be buffered up to the waiting train to be '4-REP' hauled up to Waterloo. With line speeds of 90 mph, schedules of 100 minutes from London to Bournemouth were to be offered, including a brief Southampton stop.

Another ingenious aspect of the scheme was its great flexibility. A Type '3' diesel, an electric powered coaching unit, or one of the region's electro-diesel locomotives were equally useable with the 'TC' coaching sets. To accompany the electrification, it was also agreed to build some more of the existing electro-diesels bringing the class up to forty nine machines, some of which would replace Type '3' diesels on the Central and Eastern divisions, which could then be switched to the Bournemouth line. For boat train duties off the third rail, a new larger electro-diesel was planned, converted from the Southern's E5000 series straight electric locomotives. Ten of these were ordered, intended to be of similar power to the '4-REP' units when working on electric power.

Obviously a major object of the scheme was to eliminate all steam working, with a target date of June 1967 for implementation. Also to be replaced was the steam age semaphore signalling, with colour light equipment to be installed over virtually the whole route. That was essential for the slick operation of high speed train services. Fortunately the existing signalling was reckoned to be obsolete, so the cost of replacing it was not chargeable to the electrification programme itself. To improve the general level of amenity to passengers, it was also planned to reballast and relay the main lines throughout, installing continuous welded rail at the same time. Stations were to be extended to take 12-car trains, and the 'up' side buildings at

Above: The final days of the original 'up' side buildings at Southampton Central station. Bulldozers clear the rubble from the site, leaving only the clock tower to be dismantled. The classical features of this last remnant were rather more attractive than the severe modernity of the office block that rose in its place.   *Author*

Left: At Eastleigh it was the 'down' side buildings that were reduced to mounds of debris. On March 18th 1967 little was left of the old brick-built facilities. They were replaced with a two-storey pre-cast sectional office block, with passenger facilities below. Happily the famous platform tree was spared in the redevelopment.   *Author*

Track relaying had to take place while ordinary train services continued during the 1965 to 1967 period. This resulted in lengthy periods of single line working while the engineers worked on the track under possession. On October 31st 1966, class '5' No. 73113 *Lyonesse* crossed to the 'up' line at Sway to travel 'wrong line' to New Milton, with the 11.30 Waterloo – Weymouth.   *Author*

Southampton, distinguished by their clock tower, were to be demolished and replaced with a new '60s style office block, with passenger facilities incorporated.

Clearly this constituted a major upheaval, and a considerable engineering challenge. Work started almost immediately and during 1965, there were plentiful signs of what lay ahead. Bournemouth West station was closed and a new carriage shed built nearby. Elsewhere a start was made on the construction of new power signalboxes at Basingstoke and Eastleigh. To relay the track it was necessary to takeover complete sections at a time, so that the work could proceed without interruption. This started in earnest in the autumn of 1965, when one line between Brockenhurst and Beaulieu Road was taken out of use for replacement. This meant single line working over the other track for two months, a pattern that was repeated over all the other sections between Southampton and Bournemouth over the following months.

On the four-track sections, particularly between Woking and Basingstoke, it was possible to take out the fast through lines for engineers possessions for several weeks, while trains carried on running on the slow lines. This was not so likely to cause protracted delays as single line working, but it still added minutes to running times. To take into account these anticipated delays, all services were decelerated by about 15 minutes. This ended the pattern of express Waterloo – Bournemouth two-hour trains,

although as has been described in chapter three it was not the signal for steam working to become unexciting!

It was a coincidence that 1965 also saw the launch of the new British Rail image, with its emphasis on corporate identity. Therefore the renewal of stations, facilities and stock also saw the sweeping away of Southern green and its replacement by the rather bland black and white script, and rail blue and monastral grey theme colours. Another visual change resulted from the despatch to York of nearly one hundred BR green Mark 1 carriages, for conversion to the new electric stock. Their place was taken by transferred vehicles from other regions, mainly in maroon livery, but later in the new British Rail colours. By 1967 it was quite possible to see a typical steam hauled train in which each vehicle differed in colour to its neighbour, with a blend of pre-nationalisation Bulleid green stock, British Railways Mark 1s in green, maroon, and blue and grey, and even a Gresley buffet car, in maroon painted teak thrown in!

The new rolling stock began to appear slowly, and in the main, late. No. E6007, the first of the new batch of electro-diesels left its birthplace at Vulcan Foundry on October 13th 1965, and was followed at regular intervals by the rest of the build until No. E6049 was delivered in January 1967. Eastleigh Works built the first couple of specimen 'TC' trailer cars, by converting locomotive hauled carriages, and these were on view by the beginning of 1966. The publicity photographs hardly suggested a new age of luxury travel had dawned with the design ideas of the decade largely ignored. Comment in *Modern Railways* was particularly scathing:

> The refurbishing . . . is no better than face-lift standard. There is little evidence of the lessons learned from . . . the BRB's Design Panel consultants on rolling stock . . . this is regrettable and the results are frankly disappointing . . . (but) one should temper dissatisfaction that without such undoubted economies the Bournemouth scheme might never have got the 'green light'.

The production 'TC' sets were built at York, and the first unit arrived on the Southern in August 1966, for crew training and testing in the Bournemouth area. From the 15th of the month, a train set of 'TC' units entered service, with diesel Type '3' haulage, on a diagram which included the 09.30 Waterloo – Bournemouth. This was the first real visual evidence of the motive power transformation that was to follow. As further sets were delivered, more diesel worked diagrams were introduced. Meanwhile some Type '3s' were being converted for push-pull operation, and by December the first so equipped, No. D6521, was able to start the push-pull era on the Bournemouth line by propelling the 07.15 from Eastleigh up to Waterloo, then hauling the 09.30 back to Weymouth.

By January 1967, nearly all the 'TC' sets had been delivered, but by then it was obvious that the remaining traction requirements would not be available in time for the planned timetable launch in June. Already six Brush Type '4' diesels had been borrowed from the Western, the first, No. D1921, having arrived in early September, and these would have to stand in for the large electro-diesels whose conversion from electric locomotives was proving a headache. It was the misery of that venture which led the Southern's Chief Mechanical Engineer W.J. Sykes, to make his much quoted remark, "Never convert!". In the event, the cost of rebuilding the machines was as great (£90,000 each) as for brand new ones, and they proved very unreliable and were all withdrawn by 1977! Crewe finally managed to deliver the first of these, No. E6102, in November 1967, but its arrival was nearly twelve months late.

Similar delays beset the vital '4-REP' sets, which were to be the everyday workhorses of the Bournemouth run. Only eleven sets were authorised, allowing little more than one set to be out of use for repair or maintenance. With the immense annual mileages planned, this was an example of totally unrestrained optimism, and subsequently further sets were quietly added to stock! The first '4-REP' set appeared for test early in 1967, but it was March before trial running with the complete unit No. 3001 commenced.

The gradual extension of the 'juice' westwards had occupied the tail end of 1966. Conductor rails had started to appear in places during 1965, but their energising was systematic in a planned programme. Before the current was switched on, a special conductor rail test train was used to check the alignment and height of the 'live' rail. This was usually hauled by an electro-diesel, and involved engineers riding on a brakevan looking carefully at the pick-up shoes of an emu driving trailer following behind. Once the checks had been completed electric running could commence. Thus the current was switched on in the stages shown in Table 12.

Table 12
Extension of Electrification Westwards to Bournemouth

Section	Date Opened
Pirbright Junction – Northbrook (Micheldever)	December 12th 1966
Northbrook (Micheldever) – Swaythling	December 14th 1966
Swaythling – Lymington Junction	January 18th 1967
Lymington Junction – Bournemouth Central	March 6th 1967
Bournemouth Central – Branksome	March 28th 1967

Notice to BR staff proclaiming the energisation of the first section of the Bournemouth route, westwards from Brookwood. *G. Marks collection*

Above: It is hard to believe that examples of the class '47' diesel-electric locomotives, which were lent to the Southern Region in 1966/67 to assist the ailing steam fleet, were still in front-line use on Britain's railways thirty years later. The Bulleid and Standard steam locomotives they usurped were at most twenty-five years old, and in some cases less than fifteen! Here No. D1923 pauses at Southampton at dusk on Bonfire Night, 1966, with the down 'Royal Wessex'. *Author*

Right: Ancient and Modern . . . well, ancient and not quite so ancient really! Class '02' No. 24 on a clearance run from Ryde to Shanklin with one of the recently delivered 'VEC-TIS' trailers for the Isle of Wight electrification.

Dr. J. Mackett

Regrettable casualties of modernisation were the venerable signal gantries between Basingstoke and Woking, with their lower quadrant signals. The new colour light gantries are already in place as 'West Country' class No. 34032 *Camelford* canters Capital bound on September 10th 1966.   *Author*

The new signalling was controlled from purpose-built panelboxes, such as this one at Basingstoke. Alongside is one of the many traditional signal boxes rendered redundant in the process, Basingstoke 'C' Box.   *John Fairman*

In most cases test running with electric multiple units took place on the day of the current being switched on for the first time.

As a result of the electric conductor rail being activated, it was possible to begin electric services between Woking and Basingstoke on local trains from January 2nd 1967. By then, test emu running to Eastleigh had begun, and this was extended to Brockenhurst on January 18th. The first electric units were able to reach Bournemouth on March 6th, and thus it was possible to inaugurate electric services to Bournemouth from April 3rd. Had there been sufficient stock available, steam could have been dispensed with on passenger services from that date, subject to adequate trained crews being available too. As already explained, there was in fact a chronic shortage of stock, and by April moves had been made to assemble sufficient stock to operate the new timetable in July. This included borrowing stock from the Central and Eastern divisions which was of sufficiently modern construction, to operate on the Bournemouth line's slightly higher line voltage of 750.

The conversion of steam-age signalling to colour lights went ahead very smoothly in advance of the traction changes. As Table 13 shows, new signals were brought into use in phases, leaving very little semaphore signalling in use. The main exception was in the Southampton area, where the equipment was not yet life exired, and running speeds not high enough to cause problems. Thus the famous gantries of signal arms at St. Denys and Southampton Central stations were to survive until the late 1970s. The saddest demise was of the automatic semaphore signalling on the quadruple track section between Woking and Basingstoke which dated back to LSWR days; this was taken out of use at the end of October 1966 with the commissioning of Basingstoke new power signalbox. The resignalling programme resulted in the closing and demolition of numerous manual signalboxes, including the curiously named Woodfidley box in the New Forest, which was sufficiently isolated to require the daily delivery of fresh water in churns by the guard of a 'down' passenger train!

Table 13
Replacement of Semaphore Signalling by Colour Light System

Section	Date
Woking – Farnborough	June 5th 1966
Eastleigh – St. Denys (down line)	September 7th 1966
Northam Junction – Southampton Central	October 2nd 1966
Totton – Brockenhurst	October 23rd 1966
Farnborough – Basingstoke	October 30th 1966
Winchester City – Eastleigh (and to St. Denys, up line)	November 6th 1966
Winchester City – Wootton	November 13th 1966
Basingstoke – Wootton	November 20th 1966
Basingstoke – Overton	November 20th 1966
Pokesdown – Bournemouth Central	December 11th 1966
Bournemouth Central – Branksome	January 15th 1967
Overton – Andover	February 5th 1967
Lymington Junction – Christchurch	February 26th 1967

Note In most cases the last named location was not itself included in the change of signalling, the process stopping short with the elimination of the immediately preceding signalbox. The replacement programme left semaphore signalling in place between Surbiton and Working, and at isolated locations between St. Denys and Totton, at Brockenhurst and between Christchurch and Bournemouth Central.

Thus July 1967 was reached with much of the electrification programme carried out, particularly on the civil engineering side, and only in the field of rolling stock was there a serious shortfall. In these final weeks before steam's disappearance, passengers could travel in and behind a wide variety of train types. It was possible to travel behind steam, SR diesel-electric, BR Type '4' diesel-electric, SR electro-diesel, '4-REP' emu, WR 'Hymek' diesel hydraulics (on inter-regional trains) or locally operating emus and demus. It was of course possible that one's train would be propelled by one of the aforementioned types, apart from the steam and non-SR diesel types. It is doubtful whether such a variety of motive power types had ever been seen on any British railway before, in concurrent use!

From the steam point of view, these latter days gave drivers and firemen those modern operating conditions which enabled them to show what even run-down steam could do. Most of the heavy delays due to track modification work were over, the new track was suitable for 90/100 mph running, the signalling was likewise orientated, and it was only the limitations of the engines, or the crews, which precluded steam from having a colourful finale.

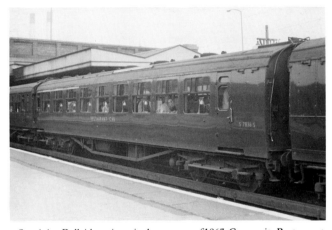

Surviving Bulleid carriages in the summer of 1967. Composite Restaurant Car No. S7836S was built in May 1949 and was originally paired with one of the infamous 'Tavern' cars, Kitchen buffets disguised as 'Olde English' inns. This coach's partner had carried the 'Jolly Tar" sign on its exterior. It was withdrawn in September 1967. *Author*

Until the end of 1965 Southern carriages were formed into permanent sets, with a number assigned to each, painted on the ends of the outermost carriages in the formation. It is very surprising to see that Corridor Brake Second No. S3977S still carried its set No. 833 on June 29th 1967, even though it was no longer coupled to the other four coaches which had made up that grouping. *Author*

Above: Type '3' later class '33/1', No. D6520 propels the 15.23 Bournemouth – Waterloo away from Southampton on March 15th 1967. The locomotive has been recently outshopped from Eastleigh after conversion to push-pull operation. Note also that the 'TC' units are in their original drab overall blue livery.

Author

Left: One of the first '4-REP' units to be tested on the Bournemouth line was No. 3003, seen passing Micheldever's newly installed island platform on March 18th 1967. The pick-up shoes which were to give so much trouble seem to be arcing well! *Author*

Left: The '4-VEP' emus intended for semi-fast and stopping services began to appear in May 1967. Nos. 7706 and 7705 pause at Millbrook on a 'down' test run on May 20th 1967. *Author*

Chapter Nine

The Final Week of Southern Steam

Steam should have finished on the Southern on June 11th 1967, but as explained in the previous chapter, this did not prove possible. However, there was to be only one postponement, and by Saturday July 1st everyone knew that the final days of Southern steam had arrived. There were few steam turns diagrammed that weekend; instead it was a time of preparation for disposing of the steam fleet to Salisbury and Weymouth, and getting rid of spares and tools and other salvageable materials from the sheds. For most drivers and firemen, there was probably more concern for learning what was required of them under the new electric services, than time to be very nostalgic about the end of steam. There were officially seventy-two locomotives left in service for the final week's operations, a number far in excess of actual requirements, in view of the small amount of steam working that remained.

During that penultimate weekend, there was steam working to be sampled however. The friends of steam on the 'inside' arranged for 'Merchant Navy' No. 35003 *Royal Mail* to be booked on the 08.30 Waterloo - Weymouth in place of the scheduled Brush Type '4'. Later, another of the class, No. 35030 *Elder Dempster Lines* set out westwards from Waterloo, this time with a rather unusual party special; for House of Commons members, for a return trip to Bournemouth. There was also steam on the 12.35 to Bournemouth, in place of another Type '4' diesel, in the shape of Standard No. 73093. A fourth Waterloo departure, a Southampton Docks boat train was rather underpowered with Standard 2-6-0 No. 76064, which not surprisingly caused delays to following trains by its sedate progress. The 09.24 Bournemouth - Waterloo was also unexpectedly steam worked with No. 34025, but the strangest working involved Standard class '4' No. 75074. It worked a return Portsmouth Harbour - Colne holiday excursion via Guildford all the way to Mitre Bridge junction, Willesden on the London Midland region!

The following day, Sunday July 2nd, was the official farewell to steam. The earlier plans of running five commemorative specials had wilted down to two, one to Bournemouth and one to Weymouth. To their credit, the Southern authorities turned out the two train engines in fabulous condition. The chosen locomotives were 'Merchant Navies' Nos. 35008 *Orient Line* and 35028 *Clan Line*, each cleaned to the highest standards, and with their nameplates refitted. It was also pleasing to the photographers that they had not been adorned with any fanciful headboards, although those travelling might have been disappointed that there was no special distinguishing feature for their train. *Clan Line*'s nameplate had been carefully prepared at Nine Elms by Doug Richards, who spent his spare time in the roster clerk's office touching it up with red enamel.

The first special with No. 35008 was booked out of Waterloo at 09.55 travelling to Weymouth. The high fare was some disincentive to travel; another was the 09.33 excursion to Bournemouth, which also offered steam haulage at normal charge, and haulage by 'West Country' class No. 34025 *Whimple*. However, participants on No. 35008's run had good value for money with a maximum speed of 88 mph on the 'down' journey and 90 mph in the 'up' direction. An unusual bonus for the photographers was the use of another 'Merchant Navy', No. 35007 *Aberdeen Commonwealth*, on the return journey as far as Bournemouth. This avoided the need for a banker on the climbs past Upwey and Parkstone, and provided a powerful, but rare,

spectacle. Dave Squibb was the fireman of No. 35007 and has an interesting recollection of the run:

'I was booked with Driver Gordon Brewer to work the assisting engine. It was usual for an assisting engine to come off at Dorchester but we were rostered to go right through. Gordon and I were joined on the footplate by a Motive Power Inspector. We had a good trip because both engines seemed to be as good as new. At that time Driver Brewer was the instructor of our mutual improvement class and was responsible for training firemen prior to their taking the driving exam. Not surprisingly he had a reputation for following the rules 100%. Therefore it was quite a surprise when we came off at Dorchester and roared over Rockly Sands bridge at about 60 mph. It wasn't until we had got to Bournemouth, and the inspector had left the footplate, that Gordon confessed that in an effort to rise to the occasion, he had completely forgotten the 30 mph restriction at the bridge for coupled 'Merchant Navies'! I can only assume that the Inspector was not aware of the restriction, or did not wish to spoil the fun either.'

The other special, with No. 35028, departed from Waterloo at 12.20, ten minutes ahead of the diesel-hauled 'Bournemouth Belle'. No. 35028 had a simple return trip to Bournemouth, with the customary water stop at Southampton, for which the patrons paid a return fare of £4. This seemed outrageously high at the time but allowing for inflation, was about the level now asked of enthusiasts for steam trips on British Rail.

Those who saved money by travelling on scheduled services probably fared better; not only did No. 34025 return with its excursion to Waterloo, but also No. 34037 *Clovelly* was turned out for the 19.36 from Bournemouth and was noted at Vauxhall near journey's end running 25 minutes early!

There was even steam penetration deep into the Western Region on July 2nd! It was reported that a 'West Country' worked the 18.45 Weymouth Quay - Bristol parcels via Yeovil (Pen Mill) to Westbury. In order to turn, it then had to carry on 'light engine' all the way to Limpley Stoke in order to cross over tracks before getting on to the Bradford Junction triangle. No. 34021 *Dartmoor* also reached Westbury that afternoon with a tomato train up from Weymouth.

Monday morning dawned and with it the last week of steam on the Southern Region. The weekday rosters offered rather more steam operation than over the previous two days. Also the Channel Island tomato traffic continued to require extra trips over the Western Region route to Westbury from Weymouth. Among the engines involved during the week were Nos. 34001, 34052, 34095, 35003, 73018 and 73092. Local passenger trips between Eastleigh and Weymouth also contributed a number of steam workings, as did the surviving non-diesel work between Waterloo and Salisbury. To that may be added the night-time mail and newspaper trains, a few of the main line express duties, and a sprinkling of freights and parcels, and so there was plenty of steam left to enjoy during this final chapter.

On the motive power front, there was a predominance of the rebuilt Bulleids and Standards, as of the two surviving original 'West Countries' little was seen. No. 34023 *Blackmore Vale* was already retired from the fray, perhaps to spare it from any over enthusiastic driver who might have thrashed it to extinction in the final week; it was necessary to ensure that it remained preservable, after all! The other unrebuilt left was No. 34102 *Lapford* which was stopped for minor repairs at Eastleigh. It reappeared on July 4th with workings from Weymouth to Bournemouth and thence to Waterloo, and was turned out for the

On July 5th 1967 the 'Bournemouth Belle' was steam worked for the last time. The 'down' run was taken by 'West Country' class No. 34024 *Tamar Valley* seen near Hersham.

Roy Bicknell

18.54 to Salisbury the following evening. Its last recorded passenger run was on the 06.49 Salisbury-Waterloo on July 5th. By all accounts it did not cover itself in glory, and was described by its driver as being "bloody rough". It then made its last journey in steam, heading the 11.38 Waterloo-Basingstoke parcels, and then running light to Eastleigh, where it finished the week at the back of the shed. It was one of the last engines to remain there, departing on July 16th to Newport for scrap.

The highlight of the week was undoubtedly the appearance of steam on the 'Bournemouth Belle' on two separate occasions. On the Monday, No. 34025 worked both 'up' and 'down' journeys: two days later, No. 34024 set out on the 'down' working. As it had already worked the 02.15 Waterloo - Bournemouth and returned on the 06.22 to London, it is not surprising that it did not make the 'up' 'Belle' too! Instead No. 34036 took up that working, the very last steam worked pullman on the Southern.

The 02.45 Waterloo - Bournemouth newspaper train enjoyed exuberant steam haulage each night, the lightweight train being driven in almost manic fashion, as described in chapter five. It is surprising that the steam fleet stood up so well to the excesses demanded of it by enthusiasts and drivers. However, the inevitable did happen on July 6th when No. 35007, on the 17.30 ex-Weymouth, met its 'Waterloo', rather sooner in the journey than expected! Having topped Roundwood summit at an excellent 71 mph, it had been hustled up to 98 mph near Woking when disaster struck. According to subsequent reports its valve cover blew off and it suffered an over-heated 'big end'. That did not stop the crew

from continuing at around 60 mph to the terminus, from where its approach was allegedly to be heard for at least 10 minutes!

Another 'last' notched up during the week was that of an ordinary steam passenger train at Reading. On July 4th the 09.40 Poole - Newcastle was most unusually steam powered, and that brought 'West Country' class No. 34095 *Brentor* into Reading General station, and it also powered the return working to Poole in the afternoon.

Off the main lines, the Clapham Junction - Kensington Olympia peak hour service remained in steam hands all week. Ivatt class '2' 2-6-2T No. 41319 was the regular performer, with a set of four green carriages that included the experimental fibre glass bodied vehicle No. S1000. The final run up from Kensington on July 7th was in the hands of Standard class '2' 2-6-2T No. 82019, although surprisingly, that was not to prove the last passenger duty by that class of locomotive.

Friday July 7th was also very special as the last weekday of steam operation. Many feared, with some reason, that there would be very little steam operation during the final weekend itself, so every movement on the 7th was of great importance.

All known passenger workings on that day, and for the other days of the final week, are shown in Table 14. Some parcels and van trains are also included, but not freight workings or light engine movements. The information is based on the observations made by a number of railway enthusiasts, and is as complete as possible, although further observations and amendments would be most welcome.

Table 14
Observations of Steam Workings during the Last Week of Steam Operation
July 2nd 1967 - July 9th 1967

DOWN WORKINGS	July 2nd	July 3rd	July 4th	July 5th	July 6th	July 7th	July 8th	July 9th
02.15 Waterloo-Weymouth				34024b?				
02.30 Waterloo-Portsmouth			73020	34060			34037	
02.30 Waterloo-Poole (Sun)								35030
02.45 Waterloo-Bournemouth			34001	35030	73029	73092	34095	
04.40 Waterloo-Woking		75074??		35008			76066	
07.08 Bournemouth-Weymouth		34037				73092		
05.48 Eastleigh-Bournemouth/Weymouth			34095					
07.50 Bournemouth-Weymouth(05.48 ex-Eastleigh)		76009	76006	76006	76006	76006		
05.30 Waterloo-Weymouth			34024					
07.56 Brockenhurst-Bournemouth						80011		
09.20 Bournemouth-Weymouth			76026	76026	76005	76005		
06.30 Woking-Salisbury		75074		35008??			76066	
07.18 Waterloo-Salisbury		73093	73065	73037?		34024	82029	
08.10 Waterloo-Weymouth Quay		34001	34087	34087	35030	35023		
08.20 (Q) Waterloo-Southampton East Docks					34021	34089		
08.30 Waterloo-Weymouth							35023	
08.35 Waterloo-Weymouth		35030a	35028	35007	35008	35003		
08.54 (Q) Waterloo- Southampton West Docks				34025	73092	34025		
10.43 Southampton-Bournemouth		76011	76011	34060	34036	75075	77014	
09.33 Waterloo-Bournemouth (Sun)	34025							
09.55 Waterloo-Weymouth SPL	35008							
10.02 Bournemouth-Weymouth (Sun)								73018
13.08 Bournemouth- Weymouth		76011	76011	34060	34036	75075		
11.20 (Q) Waterloo-Southampton West Docks					34037			
11.38 Waterloo-Basingstoke parcels		34060	35023??	34102	34093	34052		
12.20 Waterloo-Bournemouth SPL	35028							
12.30 Waterloo-Bournemouth (Bournemouth Belle)	D1926	34025		34024	D1925		D1903	D1924
15.01 Bournemouth-Weymouth		73020	35030	34001	34004	34095		
16.03 Brockenhurst-Christchurch		35030						
16.20 Southampton-Bournemouth			73029	76027	76066	73043		
16.51 Basingstoke-Salisbury		34095	73020		73043	73029		
17.20 Eastleigh -Fratton						76005?		
17.16 Southampton-Bournemouth		73037	75075	75075	75075	80016		
10.08 York-Poole			34095					
18.30 Southampton-Bournemouth		76026	76026	34093	76005	34004		
17.23 (Fri) Waterloo-Bournemouth						34093		
18.20 (Q) Waterloo-Southampton Docks							34037	
18.54 Waterloo-Salisbury			34102	34013	34087	34025		
20.50 Bournemouth-Weymouth vans			34037					77014
21.00 Bournemouth-Weymouth (18.30 ex-W'loo)		34021	35028	35007	35008	35003	34095	
19.06 Basingstoke-Eastleigh		34060	35023			34052		
20.15 Southampton-Bournemouth						34052		
Salisbury- Northam vans						77014		
22.35 Waterloo-Weymouth		34025						

The observations in this table are based upon records made at the time by the following: R.J. Addison, Nigel Bath, John Bird, Dr. Jim Boudreau, Mark Bradmore, David Druce, John Fairman, Paul Gibbons, Michael Hardy, D. Lusby, Geoff Smith, C. Stone, Peter R. Turnbull, K. Widdowson and R.J. Woollard.

UP WORKINGS	July 2nd	July 3rd	July 4th	July 5th	July 6th	July 7th	July 8th	July 9th
06.49 Salisbury-Waterloo		34060	35023	34102	34013	34052		
06.30 Fareham-Eastleigh						80016		
06.22 Bournemouth-Waterloo		34025		34024				
06.48 Bournemouth-Brockenhurst			80146			80011		
07.30 Portsmouth-Eastleigh			73020					
06.45 Poole-Bournemouth		34004	34004			73020		
06.43 Weymouth-Bournemouth		34102	34025	35028				
07.49 Weymouth-Waterloo			34021b			35008		
08.46 Bournemouth-Waterloo		34102		34013	34024			
08.27 Weymouth-Bournemouth		34021	34037		34087	73018		
11.26 Portsmouth-Colne SPL							34037	
09.40 Poole-York			34095					
09.47 Fratton-Clapham e.c.s.								73029
10.13 Weymouth-Bournemouth		73020	76031	73029		76066	34095	
10.20 Weymouth-Westbury (tomatoes)								34095
11.07 Bournemouth-Waterloo			34024					
Southampton Central-So'ton E. Docks boat train							80152	
11.18 Weymouth Bournemouth		76006	76006		76006	76006		
12.34 Bournemouth-Waterloo		35023	34021	35028	34087	35008		
Up Ocean Liner Express					73092		34021	
12.12 Weymouth-Bournemouth		76026	76026	76026	76005	76005	73092	
13.52 Bournemouth-Southampton		76026		76026		76005		
14.07 Weymouth-Waterloo								35030
14.20 Weymouth -Westbury (tomatoes)								34052
14.24 Weymouth-Eastleigh			7xxxx					
14.45 Weymouth-Westbury (tomatoes)			34001	35003	73018?			73092
15.55 Salisbury-Basingstoke		73093	73065		34xxx	34024		
16.30 Bournemouth-Waterloo SPL	35028							
16.37 Bournemouth-Waterloo (Bournemouth Belle)		34025		34036			D1903	D1924
16.00 Weymouth Quay-Waterloo		34001c	34087	35030	35003	35023d	35023	
16.15 (Fri) Weymouth Quay-Waterloo (note e)						34037		
Up Ocean Liner Express					34025			
16.47 Weymouth-Bournemouth		76011	76011	34060	73029	75075		
Weymouth-Waterloo SPL	35008f							
17.42 Bournemouth-Eastleigh		34093				34021		
18.38 Salisbury-Waterloo		75074	75074	35008	76011	73029		
17.30 Weymouth-Waterloo		35007	34025	35023	35007	34013		
17.49 Weymouth-Bournemouth		34021	35028	35007	35008	35003		
18.51 Bournemouth-Woking		76011	76011		73029	75075	D6521g	
18.15 Weymouth-Waterloo						34095		
19.35 Bournemouth-Waterloo		73020	35030	34001	34004			
19.36 (Sun) Bournemouth-Waterloo	34037							
19.59 (Sun) Bournemouth-Waterloo	34025							
21.20 Bournemouth-Eastleigh						73092		
23.32 Portsmouth-Eastleigh		80016						
22.13 Weymouth-Waterloo		34087h				34052?i		
Clapham-Kensington service a.m.						41319		
Clapham-Kensington service p.m.					82019	82019		
Waterloo station pilots		41319	41319		41298	41319	41298	41319
			82019			82019	41319	
							80015	
							82019	

Notes

a Replaced by 34021 at Bournemouth   **b** To Bournemouth only   **c** Banked by 41320 Poole-Branksome   **d** Banked by 41320 Poole-Branksome
e May have been an e.c.s. working   **f** Piloted by 35007 to Bournemouth   **g** Banked by 77014 Branksome-Bournemouth
h 76005 and D65xx worked Weymouth-Bournemouth, then D1926 to Southampton   **i** If working did occur, probably only to Bournemouth
? Working not fully confirmed   **??** Assumed to have worked it

The misfortune of having to attend school (why didn't I take the day off!) on the Friday meant that my participation in the day's events could not start until the evening. A must for me was to see what was likely to be the last steam train through my own local station at Netley. Every weekday, for the preceding year or more, there had been a steam-hauled evening parcels working passing through from Portsmouth to Salisbury. This was always worked by a Salisbury engine in all its glory, and for the rest of the week 'Battle of Britain' class No. 34052 *Lord Dowding* had been turned out with total regularity. Over tea I decided that seeing it was not enough; I wanted to *travel* on it. Being a parcels train that would not be easy! I decided the only strategy was to go down to Fareham, its last stop before Netley, and beg a cab ride from the driver. Surely he would not turn an enthusiast down so near the end of Southern steam?

At 19.30 I was standing patiently on Fareham 'up' plat-form, my heart beginning to pound in anticipation. Would the crew agree to my joining them? Would it be No. 34052 again, or might it be one of the last two unrebuilts by some extraordinary fluke? The approach signals were pulled off, and I waited for the first glimpse of the motive power as it swung round the sharp bend into the station.

Imagine my horror, therefore, to hear an unmistakable throbbing noise rather than the clank of coupling rods and the hiss of steam . . . that could only be a diesel coming. Sure enough, for the first time in a year or more, the parcels was diesel hauled, and for its final steam run! I could scarcely believe my ill-fortune, and what was almost worse, the prospect of being marooned for another half an hour at Fareham until the next passenger train could take me on to Southampton and some chance of seeing steam.

As the Type '3' rolled to a halt, I prepared to pour out my tale of woe to its driver. Fortunately he took pity on me, and offered me a cab ride to St. Denys. So I travelled on a parcels train through Netley in the cab of No. D6500; no doubt in years to come I will eventually treasure the memory of a cab ride in the prototype class '33' diesel, but on that evening it was certainly not the experience I had intended.

At St. Denys the driver slowed right down so that I could leap out and I was just in time to photograph No. 75075 departing on the 18.51 Bournemouth – Woking. Its smokebox was adorned with the chalked messages which were becoming a feature of the last weekend, as enthusiasts created impromptu tributes to their loved ones. I soon caught a local demu to Southampton and approaching Northam Junction I could see a steam train being held in the 'down' road awaiting the path ahead. To my surprise it turned out to be No. 34052, which I had expected to be travel-ling on through Netley. Somehow it had found itself on the 19.06 Basingstoke to Eastleigh, and was now heading for Southampton to form the 20.30 to Bournemouth. Ironically standing alongside, also held by signals, was No. D6500 with the parcels train it should have worked from Portsmouth!

During the day I had missed a number of interesting steam turns as engines were diagrammed so as to take them out to Weymouth or Salisbury for disposal. However, they were not staying west, but returning to London, so that Nine Elms was getting them back as fast as it sent them away, or so it seemed. At Southampton I saw several steam workings before dusk. These included No. 34095 on the 18.15 Weymouth – Waterloo and No. 34052 departing on the Bournemouth stopper. The most surprising appearance was Standard class '3' No. 77014 which had worked the 19.20 Salisbury – Northam vans and appeared at the Central station running 'light'.

I then retired to bed, while the real enthusiasts were preparing to pack the platforms at Waterloo to get a seat on the 02.45 newspaper train to Bournemouth, on which Driver

Porter's exploits have already been described. Other nocturnal travellers experienced the pleasure of riding behind No. 34037 *Clovelly* on the 02.30 newspaper train to Portsmouth, the start of a very busy day for that particular 'West Country'. Also in the small hours, No. 76066 set out on the 04.40 Waterloo – Woking, which then formed the 06.30 to Salisbury.

The next steam trip down to Salisbury provided the most unexpected working of the day. Apparently the booked engine failed, and the only locomotive Nine Elms could provide for the 07.18 departure was station pilot No. 82029. This was certainly the last passenger train to be hauled by a Standard tank engine of the 2-6-2T type on British Railways, while a few hours later probably the last passenger working of all by a tank engine took place.

Standard class '4' 2-6-4T No. 80152 lurked in the 'down' siding just outside Southampton tunnel mid-morning; its purpose was to detach a couple of carriages from the rear of the diesel worked 08.35 Waterloo – Weymouth. These were to form a through boat train working to Southampton Eastern Docks, which No. 80152 later hauled round the now lifted curve on the west side of the Northam triangle.

The most bizarre events of the day involved the 08.30 Waterloo – Weymouth. Not only had its diesel power been switched for 'Merchant Navy' class No. 35023 (a victory for a puffer-nutter) but it had also made an unscheduled stop at Woking, despite being officially non-stop to Southampton. This was arranged to rescue a large contingent of enthusiasts from impending disaster. They had travelled down to Southampton on the aforementioned 02.45 newspaper train, planning to return to Waterloo for the 08.30 to Weymouth. However, fate dealt a cruel blow to their plans when the 06.07 Southampton – Reading diesel broke down, resulting in the loss of the London connection at Basingstoke. The telephone wires were soon buzzing with urgent pleas to stop the 08.30 at Woking so that they could at least join the last steam express to Weymouth at some point on its journey. Their tactics paid off and they were able to join a fine run to Southampton, reached 7¾ minutes early, with a top speed of 94 mph before Winchester.

Another 'last' working that morning, was that of a Standard class '3' on a passenger train. No. 77014, which had reached Eastleigh the previous evening, was turned out for the 10.29 Eastleigh – Bournemouth. Its arrival at Bournemouth was quite an event for it was the driver's last steam turn, and he was resplendent in a top hat! He took No. 77014 across to the shed in a frenzy of whistling to round off his steam career.

Another steam stopper to arrive at Bournemouth was the 12.12 from Weymouth which was observed by Richard Adderson with No. 73092 in charge, its smoke box with the chalk inscrip-tions 'The Cunarder, Queen Mary' rather inappropriately emblazoned. Mr. Adderson then travelled on to Weymouth and recalls:

'There I found No. 35023 on the 'up' 'Channel Island Boat Express' banked away by what was to become a class '33'. Surrounded by dead locos in the shed yard was No. 80011 which had arrived earlier in the day and was gently simmering. No. 35030 was in steam as a standby and there was also a very shiny No. 34052, which I was told was being prepared to work the 22.13 mail train up to London.

On my return journey to London I noted No. 34093 was now on shed at Weymouth, and we passed a Standard tender engine near Moreton on a 'down' passenger train. No. 80134 was noted at Poole, and No. 77014 on carriage shunting at Branksome. On shed at Bournemouth I could see Nos. 41224, 73092 and 76026, together with 'West Country' class No. 34095. Later at Eastleigh I noticed No. 34021 looking exceptionally clean, and at Winchester we passed No. 34037 on a 'down' boat train.'

Above: Last days at Guildford shed: Standard class '3' No. 77014 and 'Battle of Britain' class No. 34060 *25 Squadron* stand over the ash-pits. The shed was in the distance behind the other Bulleid pacific. *Ray Ruffell*

Left: By July 7th No. 77014 had found its way across the Region, working the 19.20 Salisbury – Northam Yard parcels seen at Eastleigh.

John Fairman

Keith Lawrence's classic photograph of the Portsmouth line steam finale. Standard class '5' No. 73029 with smokebox front duly inscribed 'Farewell to Steam' and 'Play up Pompey', approaches Guildford with empty stock from Fratton to Clapham Junction. Shed pilot 'USA' class No. 30072 is being turned before departing for Salisbury and soon 'West Country' class No. 34018 *Axminster* will also depart, leaving the shed deserted forever.

K.P. Lawrence

Nearly the end at Basingstoke too . . . a time to stand and watch steam's dying rituals. Standard class '5' 4-6-0s Nos. 73065 and 73093 are the victims.

Rod Hoyle

And so they departed in sorrow . . . Nos. 73118 and 73155 performed final duties at Guildford and then set off together for their last run in steam. Heading down the main line to Salisbury they are between Woking and Brookwood on July 9th 1967. 'Still good for 50 years' proclaims the graffiti on the leading engine.
Brian Stephenson

The previous day other pairs of locomotives had made their way to Salisbury or Weymouth sheds. The discs on No. 80015 indicate that Salisbury is the final destination, for the Standard class '4' tank, and its smaller class '3' partner, No. 82019. They were passing Durnsford Road, Wimbledon at 11.33 according to the photographer.
Derek Buckett

Mention of that 'West Country' requires a description of its very busy day. As already mentioned it had reached Portsmouth about dawn on the newspaper train, and was then turned at Fratton, before being assigned to the 11.26 Portsmouth Harbour – Colne return holiday special. Travelling over the Guildford line, it achieved 88 mph near Witley, and worked on to the London Midland Region at Mitre Bridge Junction, before handing over to another locomotive. It then retired to Nine Elms for servicing, having been the last steam locomotive over the East Putney line and the West London line.

Its subsequent place in the history books is best described by Klaus Marx, who was to photograph it for posterity a few hours later:

'It was just my luck to have to spend nearly the whole of that last Saturday at a meeting in Bloomsbury. When I eventually managed to rush up to Waterloo just after 17.00 I found a large number of rather despondent looking men and boys. The truth was that there had been no main line steam all day, since the departure of the 08.30 to Weymouth. I had missed nothing after all!

I wandered to the end of Platform 11 looking optimistically for signs of steam, but with more hope than belief. Then miraculously a plume of steam could be discerned in the distance beyond the roof-tops. Before long the outline of a tender first 'West Country' appeared round the curves, obviously to back down on to the awaiting stock of the 18.20 boat train to Southampton Docks. As it came alongside, I could see that it was No. 34037 *Clovelly* with its empty, but red painted nameplate bracket.

The sun was shining brightly but there was no chance of a successful picture from my position on the platform. Like several other photographers, I suddenly decided to head for the flats which had been built a few years earlier, just to the north of Waterloo signalbox. I had seen some pictures published in the railway press which must have been taken from there, but the question now was could I get there in the fifteen minutes before departure. I took a calculated risk and rushed down the taxicab tunnel beneath the station. Coming out into daylight I was soon in front of the high-rise block, which was called Canterbury House.

I tore up eight flights of stairs, with scarcely a pause for breath, and my reward was a superb vantage point with five minutes to spare. However, a new problem now emerged; with the other photographers who had sped along with me, we were now the objects of a very hostile reception. The occupants of the flats had been on the receiving end of people like ourselves for too long, and we were subjected to much colourful verbal Cockney abuse.

As time was running out and the situation was becoming more fraught, I made a strategic withdrawal and descended one flight of steps to a more peaceful viewpoint. I was none too soon; there was a tower of black smoke sent skywards and the sound of steam being put to work reached my ears. Even better, some cloud which had been hiding the sun chose to pass by right on cue, leaving a brilliant scene. But could it be true? Now there was another potential mishap. A Richmond line '4-SUB' electric train was leaving the Windsor line platforms, and was threatening to catch up with *Clovelly* as the latter threaded its way out of the terminus. Fortunately, the 'West Country' just kept ahead long enough for me to press the shutter. An instant later and the electric had drawn alongside and obscured the view of the steam hauled train!'

Mr. Marx's classic colour-slide records the last daylight steam departure from Waterloo ever. So many other people had gone home in disgust by then that they missed that historic moment.

For those who waited, there was more to come. The 'Merchant Navy' which had gone down on the 08.30 to Weymouth, was now making back for the City on the 'up' boat train, that left the Quay at 15.55. In charge was No. 35023 with 'THE END, THE LAST ONE' chalked in large letters on the smokebox door. It swept through Clapham Junction some 3 minutes early, a satisfactory finale for a service that had provided steam power with a daily outing even in those sparse last months.

During much of Saturday, the other steam activities had been far more melancholy. They had comprised the movement singly or in pairs of workable steam locomotives to Weymouth and in particular, Salisbury. Thus Standard tanks Nos. 80015 and 82019 had gone down together in the late morning from Nine Elms, followed by Ivatt '2' No. 41312. At Eastleigh, the arrivals from Nine Elms were interspersed with movements from the local shed, making for the Chandler's Ford route across to Romsey and Salisbury. The last two 'USAs' from Southampton Docks came up in the morning, for a shuffle out to Salisbury. For the record they were Nos. 30067 and 30069. A similar pairing of Nos. 30064 and 30071 also made the journey, as did Bulleid pacifics Nos. 34024 and 34089. Making the final journey in steam in solitary state were Standard tanks Nos. 80016, 80133 and 80146. In fact with a number of other steam movements, including Standards Nos. 76005 and 80152 double-heading a stone train, Eastleigh was one of the best places to be on that Saturday.

Then it was Sunday, the very last day, well so they had said anyway. None of us could really believe that this was going to be the end. There would still be steam lurking at Eastleigh or Bournemouth the next day . . . surely? Ironically, the best place to see steam on the last day was not on the Southern but on the Western. The demands of the tomato crop required no less than three special freights from Weymouth up the Westbury line, and each was steam worked. The ubiquitous Nos. 34052 and 34095 powered the van trains, together with Standard No. 73092. The first and last of the trio were actually to be seen in Westbury station at the same time, waiting to run out 'light' to Bradford Junction to turn, before making their final journeys back to Weymouth and the scrap sidings.

Meanwhile, Guildford and Basingstoke were busy clearing the decks of steam. The latter's last departures were Nos. 73093 and 80139, leaving behind a dead shed scene. At 70C, there was considerable activity. Redundant materials such as papers, oil cans and hand cloths were being loaded up in a box van, while shed pilot 'USA' class No. 30072 was being prepared for its longest journey for months! But there was also work to perform, the usual Guildford task, ballast empties to Farnham. Standard No. 73155 had worked down there from Woking earlier in the morning, and was now back on shed in the company of the other remaining engine No. 73118. Later they set off 'light' for Woking and thence Salisbury. The box van and other wagons were removed to Woking by the penultimate steam survivor 'West Country' No. 34018, and that left just the little 'USA' tank to bid farewell to steam at Guildford.

A little earlier the scene had been rather different; at noon, with the four steamers grouped around the shed precincts, a whistle had heralded the surprise appearance of an 'up' steam train emerging from the tunnel mouth. This had proved to be No. 73029 on the 09.47 Fratton to Clapham Junction empty stock working, formed of ten coaches. The former WR-based Standard locomotive, with its lined green livery, had large chalked inscriptions on its smokebox 'FAREWELL TO STEAM' and less predictably 'PLAY UP POMPEY'. Not surprisingly, the writing was the work of a Portsmouth Football Club supporter. The previous day, young Mark Bradmore had played truant from the Founder's day service at school and wandered off to Fratton shed instead. There he had found No. 73029 and had made his mark on the locomotive that had already made a small claim to

The writing on the smokebox door says it all, although this is not quite the last steam train in fact. It was actually the last 'up' Channel Islands Boat train on the penultimate day of Southern steam, July 8th 1967. The relief enginemen wait by the water column as 'Merchant Navy' class No. 35023 *Holland-Afrika Line* draws to a halt at Southampton Central, and a throng of enthusiasts wait to clamber aboard for the run up to Waterloo.   *Author*

fame by working the last steam passenger train out of Salisbury, the 18.38 to Waterloo on Friday, July 7th. After No. 73029's unexpected addition to the steam scene at Guildford on that last Sunday, it was just a few hours until the final curtain fell.

By early afternoon, the only sound left on shed was that of No. 30072 steaming up for its last run. John Berryman, who was on duty, describes its departure:

'I was acting foreman on the last day, working an 08.00 until 16.00 shift. About a dozen of the lads were around to give our shed pilot a good send-off. They put down loads of detonators, and she rolled off the turntable up to the station in a blaze of glory. I think she had a Fratton crew and they set off whistling all the way. She ran down the main line to Havant then up to Eastleigh. In fact I passed her in the up road at Haslemere on my way home later in the afternoon. That was the end of steam at Guildford.'

On the Bournemouth line hundreds of cameramen and general spectators turned out to see the final 'Bournemouth Belle'. There had been rampant rumours during the week that it was going to be steam worked as a grand steam finale. Many gathered in misplaced optimism, but it can now be revealed that the rumour was well founded. John Wickham, of the Wimbledon diagram office had done his best to create the enthusiasts dream:

'I tried to put steam on the 'Belle' on the last day; I had what I thought was the perfect excuse, that there was no other working available to get the engine west for scrap! Unfortunately the top management were going to travel on the train, and apparently they wanted a more modern form of motive power. I had already told Nine Elms what was in mind and they had got a 'Merchant Navy' cleaned up specially. They'd even got the old headboard out, which would have been the first time it had been carried on the train for years. The senior driver at Nine Elms was going to do the working. It was going to be quite a day, but at the eleventh hour I had to cancel it. I had a hell of an argument with various blokes, and ended up with a bit of a carpeting!'

For the record, the chosen 'Merchant Navy' was No. 35023, fresh from its exploits on the previous day's 'Channel Island Boat Express'. Sadly, it was not to be.

Oblivious to the behind-the-scenes altercations, I stationed myself on the 'down' platform at Pokesdown in good time on that Sunday afternoon. I had heard the stories that the 'Belle' was going to bow out with a spectacular steam finale, and I wasn't going to miss out on that one. But despite the sort of clear summer sunshine that made Klaus Marx's picture at Waterloo, the previous evening, there was to be no steam delight; just a rather grimy Brush diesel No. D1924 at the head of nine pullman cars and two luggage vans.

Nevertheless the pundits at Bournemouth Central later that afternoon, were still confidently predicting that the return working would somehow materialise in the form of steam. The booking office was doing a brisk trade in supplementary Pullman tickets in consequence and I too made sure of my last Pullman ride on the 'Belle', even if it did prove to be diesel hauled again. For the next hour or so, like many others, I took advantage of it being 'open house' at Bournemouth shed. There was little steam to be seen there at this eleventh hour, but Ivatt tank No. 41224 was simmering in the yard and 2-6-0 No. 77014 was lurking within the shed.

Walking around the shed yard, over piles of ashes, and beside the water column with its still dripping bag, it was not yet possible to comprehend that steam's surrender to electricity and diesel oil was nigh. I talked to someone who claimed that there was nothing to worry about because a dozen or more Bulleid pacifics were to be retained for standby and boat train duties. This seems highly improbable in retrospect, but was a substantial straw to clutch at on that summer afternoon.

Those musings were suddenly disturbed by a whistling from the country end of the station, and the unmistakeable sounds of a steam train arriving. With only a single steam passenger working since dawn, the 10.02 to Weymouth hauled by Standard '5' No. 73018, the sight of an eastbound working at this stage of the last day must have seemed like an illusion. However, apparently some enthusiasts were not so surprised and must have had some prior warning of what was going to happen! The station loudspeaker confirmed that this was indeed the 14.07 ex-Weymouth bound for Waterloo, and up on the front was 'Merchant Navy' No. 35030. Surprise, surprise, there had been a diesel failure at Weymouth, and a steam engine had to be substituted! But now what a dilemma ... to ride behind steam, or to wait for the remote chance that steam might appear on the last

The last 'down' 'Bournemouth Belle' parades past Pokesdown with Brush Type '4' No. D1924 in charge, in its original two-tone green livery. It is travelling over the 'down' throughline, by-passing the 'Hampshire' demu forming a Southampton-Bournemouth stopping service.   *Author*

The last steam train to leave Southampton Docks crosses Canute Road behind 'West Country' class No. 34021 *Dartmoor*, on July 9th 1967. The flagman has a last look at Southern steam in action.
K. Withers

'up' 'Belle'. Most people like me went for the certainty, and abandoning their right to Pullman travel so recently purchased, leapt on to the Weymouth train. In fact, it was not such a certainty as it seemed. On the footplate, Driver Allen was accompanied by Weymouth fireman Len Groves, who recalls that there was some indecision on arrival at Bournemouth:

'I thought we were coming off the train at Bournemouth to return to our shed, so I ran the fire down as we got near there. When we stopped I uncoupled the engine, when an Inspector or somebody came up and said that she was going through. I said that she hadn't been coaled up, and the driver was there hopping about. So I was told to hook her back on again. There were spotters everywhere, and one bloke asked me for a lump of coal, so I knocked a lump down which shattered on the platform, and they scrambled to get a bit! Then the Inspector told me that the engine was coming off after all, but when I went to uncouple her again, he came back and told me not to bother as she was definitely running up to Waterloo. To put it mildly I was a bit fed up by then!'

Driver Ray Hardy had the distinction of working the train up to London which was to prove to be the last steam passenger run on the Southern in 1967. (The only other possible contender for the title would have been a boat train which was worked by an immaculate No. 34021, from Southampton Eastern Docks up to London. Its journey had been completed by lunchtime however, and already No. 34021 had run back down to fulfil its appointment with the Salisbury scrap lines.)

For what I felt certain was probable my last steam run on the Southern. I hoped for some suitably lively running. *Elder Dempster Lines* certainly began in the right vein, as the table shows.

Table 15
Bournemouth – Southampton

Date	July 9th 1967
Train	14.07 Weymouth – Waterloo
Locomotive No.	35030

Miles		Actual	Speeds
0.00	BOURNEMOUTH CENTRAL	0.00	—
	Boscombe	3.35	39
1.65	Pokesdown	4.24	50/62
3.60	Christchurch	6.18	63
6.90	Hinton Admiral	9.27	64
7.70	Milepost 100¼	10.15	60/64
9.45	New Milton	11.50	62/72
12.40	Sway	14.23	70
		sigs.	
14.25	Lymington Junction	16.03	40
15.20	Brockenhurst	17.19	50/65
	Woodfidley Box	20.31	53
19.85	Beaulieu Road	22.27	53
22.55	Lyndhurst Road	25.45	45/53
25.45	Totton	29.10	50
26.15	Redbridge	29.53	53
		sigs.	
27.80	Millbrook	33.44	16
		36.35	
	sig. stop	40.05	
28.70	SOUTHAMPTON CENTRAL	43.35	

The start out to Christchurch was of the highest standards, with the climb past Hinton Admiral started with speed well over

The arrival of the last steam hauled boat train at Waterloo on July 9th 1967. No. 34021 blows off gently at the buffer stops, as the enthusiasts stand in mourning.
Ray Ruffell

60 mph. The good running continued up the incline, with speed not dropping below 60 mph at the summit, and an acceleration to 72 mph beyond New Milton. I was confident that a personal record for the section to Southampton was in the offing, hopefully inside the 30 minute barrier. However, it was not to be; adverse signals were sighted before Lymington Junction which brought speed down to 50 mph, and a succession of further checks precluded any recovery. In the Southampton suburbs progress was progressively reduced to a crawl, and then a dead stand for signals beyond Millbrook. The final time into the Central station was a most unmemorable 43½ minutes, certainly my *slowest* non-stop run ever up from Bournemouth!

Ordinary passengers on the train really could not understand why the expected tranquility of Sunday afternoon travel up from Dorset, was being totally disrupted by an army of assorted railway enthusiasts. Their alarm was somewhat allayed by being assured that they were travelling on the very last steam train on the Southern Region, for that was by now the general consensus view. On arrival at Southampton the chalk artist struck again and covered the front of the engine with slogans during a few minutes frenzied scribbling, while the 'Merchant Navy' took water.

To my great regret I had to leave the train here, and so it was left to others to participate in the final steam arrival at Waterloo. It was well-photographed on its run up to London, as it

was only about 45 minutes ahead of the last 'Bournemouth Belle', for which many cameramen were waiting in a totally forlorn hope of steam traction. There was no such hope since it is alleged that instructions had gone out that if the diesel rostered were to 'fail', or be made to 'fail', then the 'Bournemouth Belle' was to be cancelled, rather than have a steam engine hauling it! At around 17.12 the last 'Belle' duly appeared at Platform 1 at Southampton Central, predictably hauled by the same No. D1924 which had worked it down from Waterloo earlier. We took our last pictures as the old image train lumbered off into the darkness of Southampton tunnel and so bade farewell to CAR No. 303, CAR No. 64, *Ursula*, *Phyllis*, *Lucille*, *Aquila* and the other Pullman carriages.

Meanwhile, No. 35030 was powering on towards Waterloo to give a competent performance to complete the inevitability of steam's defeat on the Southern. It reached the terminus 10 minutes early, and it was perhaps appropriate that the last of the 'Packets', as most enginemen called them, should have been the last steam engine to pull a passenger train on the Southern. At Waterloo Driver Hardy and his mate climbed off the footplate and the rostered disposal crew took over to steam No. 35030 on its very last short journey to Nine Elms shed. Richard Adderson, who rode up all the way from Bournemouth, recalls that the loco backed out of Waterloo at 18.24, whistling loudly round the bends out of the terminus.

This *is* the last one! 'Merchant Navy' class No. 35030 *Elder Dempster Lines* takes water at Southampton, while an impromptu tribute is chalked on the smokebox front by a young man believed to be one P.J. Odell of Bedford, subsequently Driver Odell at De Aar depot in South Africa! The inscription reads 'LAST STEAM. GRAND FINALE WEYMOUTH-WATERLOO 9-7-67 GUARANTEED BRISTOL-BEDFORD AND SUNDERLAND. The working was the 14.07 from Weymouth, and as described in the text, it was extremely uncertain whether the last Bulleid to be built would actually remain on the train all the way to Waterloo.
Author

One driver who had long harboured an ambition to drive the last steam train on the Southern was Jim Evans. That honour had now already passed to Ray Hardy, but at the controls of No. 35030 for the last steam departure from Waterloo, albeit only as a light engine, was none other than . . . Jim Evans! As he remembers, it came as a complete surprise for him, when he had given up hope of fulfilling his dreams:

'So the fateful day came, July 9th. I booked on for duty and one of my jobs for the day was to relieve the 'Brush' on the 'up' Weymouth at Waterloo. There were a few enthusiasts still gathered waiting in case any more steam turned up. I don't think they could believe this was the end, that tomorrow there would be no more steam. Then to my great surprise I could hear the unmistakeable 'clank clank' of worn coupling rod journals, as No. 35030 came coasting into Waterloo. No diesel! . . apparently it had failed. And so my dream was going to come true; the last

'Merchant' to be built, the last steam engine at Waterloo, and I was going to drive it! I never thought it would happen, and I certainly never even dreamt of it back in 1944 when I started on the very bottom of the ladder, which had brought me to main line driver.

So very sadly we left Waterloo for the last time, giving plenty of blasts on the whistle . . . well, wouldn't you? . . . and we trundled slowly down the local line and into Nine Elms. My fireman John Cottee religiously disposed of the engine as he had done hundreds of times before. I took out all the trimmings to conserve oil, we turned her off the turntable, and I left John to take her back into the engine sheds to join all her sisters to die. I waited to watch as the smokebox faded from view into the darkness of the shed building. There was a last mournful cry from her whistle, denied a full blast because already the steam of her life blood was ebbing away from the boiler, and then she was gone, absorbed into the blackness of the locomotive graveyard.'

Above: The last steam hauled freight train in the South was captured on film by Sid Nash on Sunday July 9th 1967 approaching Yeovil South Junction. It was the last of three steam worked Weymouth to Westbury consignments of perishable Channel Islands produce, mostly tomatoes, which operated on that day. Ironically these workings brought an unusual influx of steam onto the Western Region in the process, as the entire journey north of Dorchester was over WR territory. This final train was worked by green liveried Standard '5' 4-6-0 No.73092, still bearing its smokebox front inscriptions mentioning 'Queen Mary' and 'The Cunarder'. It had the honour of being the last steam train to leave Weymouth, departing at 15.00, some time after Merchant Navy No.35030 has set out with the famous final passenger train, the 14.07 to Waterloo.   *S.C.Nash*

Below: Ivatt '2MT' 2-6-2T No.41320 waits at Poole in the early evening of Sunday July 9th 1967, before performing its final duty, which was the penultimate steam operation on the Southern. At about 18.45 it buffered up to the rear of an eastbound empty coaching stock train hauled by an electro-diesel locomotive, and for the last time performed its familiar duty of banking up the steep climb to Parkstone and Branksome. It then ran light engine to Weymouth, for withdrawal and storage.   *Colin Stone*

But even Jim Evans cannot claim to have operated the very last steam locomotives active on the Southern, even though he has the honour of the last steam departure from Waterloo. It was at the other end of that last steam main line, from Bournemouth to Weymouth, that the very last revenue earning operations by steam were going to take place.

Ever since No. 35030 had left Bournemouth in the early afternoon, two other steam locomotives had remained on shed. These were Ivatt 2-6-2T No. 41224 which was simmering in the yard, and the unique Standard '3' 2-6-0 No. 77014, which had arrived at Bournemouth the previous day. Ironically, the Southern's most recent steam acquisition was destined to star in the final act, as it sat quietly a the back of the shed. No. 41224 duly set off light engine to Weymouth during the afternoon, to have its fire dropped and be stored. On the way it passed sister engine No. 41320 which was standing in the down siding at Poole. The second 'Ivatt' was waiting for its final duty, to bank an up empty carriage stock working to Branksome, which turned up at Poole hauled by one of the Southern's new electro-diesels.

So at about 18.50 the 'cock crow' was heard over the townscape of Poole for the last time as the little 2-6-2T gave the conquering form of motive power a mighty push up the hill towards Bournemouth. Its duty completed, No. 41320 followed No. 41224 on a final foray to the Weymouth gathering point.

And that left No. 77014, which by a strange twist of fate was now about to haul the Southern's very last steam train, a non-Southern locomotive and one that had spent less than a year in the South. There were few eye-witnesses left that summer evening as dusk descended. One was Mr. C. Stone who was standing on Parkstone station, quite unaware that there was any steam still to come. He recalls:

'At about 20.40 we heard a distant whistle and at 20.45 No. 77014, doing about 60 mph and whistling madly, tore down the bank towards Poole with a van train... a very quick moped ride took me to Poole where I found No. 77014 sitting in the down platform. She came off the vans, backed into the down bay and collected two more vans... station staff finished their work and at 21.25 I took my last photo of a steam loco at Poole as No. 77014, whistle sounding, barked off into the dusk to Weymouth. I watched her cross Holes Bay, heard her whistle a warning at Harnworthy, and that was it, definitely THE END ...'.

The final revenue earning steam train on the Southern Region, at 21.25 on the night of Sunday, July 9th 1967. Standard '3' 2-6-0 No.77014, the most recently arrived locomotive on the SR, has the honour as it leaves Poole with a van train from Bournemouth to Weymouth. As Mr Stone concedes, it was not his best photograph ever, but given the late hour, it is a creditable attempt to record an historic movement which few other enthusiasts witnessed.

Colin Stone

Chapter Ten

Post Mortem

Dawn broke on July 10th 1967 to a virtually steamless Southern Region. There were to be no more steam hauled trains in the South for the foreseeable future. The rumoured standby locomotives just did not exist; there were no Bulleids or Standards lurking furtively 'in light steam' at Bournemouth or Eastleigh, awaiting a call to duty. The revolution was complete, steam had indeed surrendered the previous night, and electrics and diesels were now in complete command. The only possible exception to this steam annihilation would be peripheral objects such as stationary boilers or breakdown cranes with steam power. It has been claimed that Nine Elms did keep one locomotive in steam right through the night, in case the breakdown train was called out, prior to its removal at 9 am on the Monday morn-

and delays and cancellations proved the order of the day. No less than 4,775 complaints were received from the public in the first two months of the new operation.

Not only did the new timetable demand extremely heavy utilisation of stock and slick operating at termini, but the situation was confounded by stock shortages. The power behind the Bournemouth electrics, the '4-REP' emus, was but recently delivered and the units were so heavily used that failures were inevitable, with no back-ups available. The converted large electro-diesels intended for boat train duties, which could have stepped into the breach, were nowhere near completion. In fact the first did not arrive until November and so this meant a protracted stay for the Brush Type '4' diesels. On one bleak

All quiet at Nine Elms. Steam days are over. No. 35030, the last arrival, has had some new messages chalked on the front, but now stands lifeless like all its brethren.   *John Fairman*

ing. If that was indeed the case, the likely engine involved was class '4' No. 75075.

Otherwise Nine Elms grew silent on the night of July 9th. No. 35030 came in as described in the previous chapter and quietly subsided into slumber. Also still warm was No. 35023, which apparently had been resurrected by some 'amateur' firebuilders who were determined not to let steam die. However, there was to be no halting the victory of modern traction, and no Southern engine turned a wheel in steam again that year.

Meanwhile, with the elder statesmen of railway traction retired to the back benches, the new image had a change to prove itself. The result was unmitigated chaos! The Southern Region had decided to link the Bournemouth electrification with a completely recast timetable affecting all its territories. The Monday morning was the first chance to test it out! Not surprisingly it proved difficult to operate without some practice and experience,

October day five of the eleven 'REP' sets were out of use making a mockery of the rosters. The most common failing was 'lost' or damaged electrical pick-up 'shoes', which could result in a unit becoming immobilised with consequent heavy delays to following trains.

Such were the hold-ups on the first Monday that even the VIP and press run was affected, resulting in unfavourable media coverage that evening. Was it only the sentimentalists who would have wished for steam to have stayed in the saddle for another few months until all the rolling stock was delivered and problems ironed out? Even a few standby engines and sets of coaching stock might have been appreciated on more than one occasion!

As far as the steam fleet was concerned, the task now was to dispose of it as efficiently as possible. The Southern was no longer cutting up withdrawn engines, and since 1964 they had been sold to private scrap yards. Thus it was necessary to invite

In the shadow of the Cathedral lies the locomotive graveyard at Salisbury. Examples of most of the classes to survive to the end can be seen waiting the call to the scrapyard. September 30th 1967.

Author

A closer view of the condemned machines: Nos. 34060, 76066 and 75077 look as though they could be brought back to life at any time, but this is August 1967, and their fate is sealed.

John Fairman

tenders for the purchase of the engines! While this was being negotiated, the task was to complete the assembling of the withdrawn locomotives at Salisbury and Weymouth, ready for haulage to the breakers. The few surviving engines at Eastleigh were soon removed, as described in chapter six. Feltham, Guildford and Bournemouth were also emptied, together with Basingstoke. It was just Nine Elms that retained a rather longer steam presence. Visitors in July and August 1967 found the New shed well-occupied with rusting engines being prepared for movement. When John Fairman made an inspection on July 22nd he found thirty-one steamers present, including Nos. 34023 and 35028 being worked on for preservation. The full list of stored engines is shown in Table 16.

Nine Elms was gradually cleared of locomotives; there were regular Sunday workings of dead engines, diesel hauled by Type '3' locomotives during August. On the 13th, Nos. 34034/47 made the journey for example but the former succumbed to a 'hot-box' at Surbiton and had to be detached. It made the journey two weeks later, but only as far as Basingstoke where it remained for several weeks. The last consignment of Bulleids left the Elms on September 10th when No. D6549 hauled Nos. 35023 and another to Salisbury.

The arrival of condemned engines at Salisbury kept the shed and yard there crammed with machines. Although there was a continuing series of departures to scrapyards, it no more than balanced newcomers. On August 6th fifty-five steam locomotives were present, which was probably as high a number as was seen at any time. Again recorded by John Fairman, the details are in Table 17.

As stated in chapter six, the last of the engines was not removed until the end of March, the following year! At the other disposal point, Weymouth, there were never so many to be seen,

but they still made an impressive if tragic sight, gathered in the sidings beside the shed. Twenty-six assorted Bulleids, Standards and Ivatts were to be found there on July 23rd, including No. 77014 which had worked the last steam train into Weymouth, and four Ivatt 2-6-2Ts from Bournemouth, two of which had been withdrawn back in the spring. The full list is shown in Table 18. These engines were also gradually dispersed to scrapyards all over the country, and by the end of the year Weymouth shed had been cleared of steam.

By the beginning of 1968, the electrified South Western division was beginning to settle down to normality. The winter months still saw failures and disruption, but as the summer approached the transformation was nearing completion. All the steam engines had departed. The Brush diesels were able to return to the Western, now that the large electro-diesels had entered traffic, and deliveries of 'REP', 'TC' and 'VEP' stock had reached an adequate level to actually operate the services. The stop-gap use of pairs of small electro-diesels hauling or propelling 'TC' sets could be brought to an end. It was also the signal to eliminate other curiosities, such as the use of ex-LNER Gresley buffet cars on some workings, mainly boat trains, and the continued existence of some thirty Bulleid carriages which had escaped the holocaust.

It should be noted that officialdom tried to eliminate as much of the steam image as quickly as possible. Perhaps this was from fear that it might encourage a resurrection of steam working in the light of the unreliability of the victors in the motive power battle. Earliest casualties were the water columns at stations, which were uprooted, or had their arms and bags removed, leaving only the ugly remains of the vertical columns. The sheds at Guildford and Bournemouth were demolished, together with those at Basingstoke, Weymouth and Salisbury, leaving scope for

It took a long time to rid Salisbury of the fifty or more engines stored there. The last to depart, hauled by 'Hymek' diesel No. D7045 on March 30th 1968, were Bulleid pacifics Nos. 34102, 35023 and 34034.

G. Marks

Table 16
Locomotives at Nine Elms Shed (70A) on July 22nd 1967
Observations by John Fairman

"Old Shed" (Roofless area)

Road Nos. 1	2	3	4	5	6
	34047	80012	73022	34057	35013
				34008	
41284	80145		76064	35007	

"New Shed"

Road Nos. 1	2	3	4	5	6	7	8	9
35012	34088	34002	34023	34015	80085	35028		
73037	34100	34019	34013	80140	34001	35023		73119
41298	34034	35008	75075		35030			

Outside Yard

41319

Table 18
Locomotives at Weymouth Shed on July 23rd 1967
Observations by John Fairman

Inside shed:	35026	35014				
Behind shed:	75076					
In shed yard:	41230	41295	76008	76009	80134	
	34036	34095	76026	41224	73092	41320
	34004	73020	34052	76069	75068	77014
	73002	73016	73018			
	35003	80011	34093			

TOTAL: 26

Table 17
Locomotives at Salisbury Shed on August 6th 1967
Observations by John Fairman

Inside Shed

Road Nos. 1	2	3	4	5	6	7	8	9	10
EMPTY	73065	76005	BREAKDOWN CRANE	34018	34102	80015			EMPTY
	80139	30067		73029	73115	82019			
	73093	30069		34021	73117	34087	76007	34104	
	73118	80143		34090		34089	76011	34098	
	73155	34037		75077		34024	34025	76031	
	73085	73043		76066		80146	76006	75074	
		76067		34060		30071	41312		
						80152	80133		

Outside Shed

80016	34056
80151	30064
	30072
	82029
	80012
	41319
	76064
34040	80145
41284	34044
73119	

TOTAL: 55

Below: No more engine arrangements for Standard 4-6-0 No. 73065 or the other fifty-five locomotives in store at Salisbury shed on August 15th, 1967.
David M. Smith

The morning after the night before at Weymouth. The summer sun shines on the assembled ranks of Southern and Standard designs on July 10th 1967.
C.L. Caddy

Two withdrawn 'West Country' class pacifics found themselves plucked from the scrapyard convoys to star in the Bristol Bath Road diesel depot open day on October 21st 1967. Nos. 34100 and 34013 still display the cleanliness of their days as Salisbury engines, as small boys get the chance to clamber over them for the last time. They were both cut up at Cashmore's in Newport the following month.   *Author*

The Southern's engine sheds were swiftly demolished after steam finished. This picture records the destruction of Guildford's coaling stage.

Ray Ruffell

Bulleid Open Second No. S1481S in the formation of an Exeter train at Waterloo in 1968. This vehicle was one of about a hundred to survive beyond July 1967, and was formed into a permanent eight-car set, with BR standard vehicles. It was withdrawn in August 1968 and eventually secured for preservation on the Bluebell Railway. Other Bulleid carriages were transferred to the Eastern and Scottish regions, the last not being withdrawn until 1970.

Author

car parking or commercial redevelopment. Eastleigh was the first to disappear within a matter of weeks, the others following during 1968.

It would be appropriate to attempt a brief appraisal of the overall impact of events during this 1966-68 period. Firstly, there can be little doubt that *eventually* electrification produced a vastly improved service for the public. The regular interval services up from Bournemouth and Southampton, with times pared down to as little as 96 minutes, were a great advance. Frequency and regularity were other benefits felt by the traveller. It is more debatable whether standards of comfort were greatly enhanced. Although the track was upgraded throughout, the riding of the electric stock was probably little better at 90-100 mph than that of Bulleid carriages at more sedate speeds. Many would argue that the new interiors of the rebuilt carriages, whilst bright and modern looking, were no comparison for the comfortable seats and homely veneered interiors of the Bulleids and BR steam stock that they replaced. The disappearance of Pullman travel, and full restaurant car services, must certainly be placed on the debit side of the account. However, the improvement in passenger numbers and receipts is adequate evidence that electrification was a definite success on balance.

A more critical look needs to be taken at the motive power policies however. The Southern possessed a fleet of excellent modern steam engines, many less than twenty years old, and in the case of the rebuilt Bulleids, virtually still in their infancy. These were a splendid asset, and in other circumstances could have been expected to have given satisfactory service at least up to the time of writing this book. Had they benefitted from a modest infrastructure investment programme, with spending on track and signalling to raise line speeds, could a high quality

steam service have been maintained for a few years? Clearly one of the biggest obstacles to such a proposition would have been the increasing difficulty of recruiting staff to service and operate steam trains. The rising affluence of the late fifties and the social changes of the sixties, made working on steam engines for modest rates of pay, an uninviting prospect, especially at a time of low unemployment.

The building of new steam depots, and the adoption of devices such as mechanical stokers or oil firing, could have alleviated some of the unattractive aspects of steam railway employment. Such a policy was never really considered of course. The Southern was not the region to perpetuate steam working when most of its services were already electric, and the decision to get rid of steam trains across the whole country was deeply rooted.

Eastleigh shed has lost its steam allocation, and a lone electro-diesel stands outside on July 25th 1967. Demolition of the site was already under way, and the shed was removed in a matter of weeks.
Author

This poignant photograph shows the very last working by an unmodified Bulleid pacific, No. 34102 *Lapford*, passing Weybridge, on the 12.38 Waterloo to Basingstoke van train on July 5th 1967. After completing its journey *Lapford* ran light engine to Eastleigh shed to drop its fire for the last time, before being hauled off to Wales and scrapping.
Keith Lawrence

Three 'West Country' class locomotives meet their fate at Buttigieg's scrapyard at Newport. The tender of No. 34017 is visible to the left, No. 34032 has been partly stripped and No. 34005 has been reduced to an 0-2-2! A coupling rod sticks out gauntly from the firebox door and in a matter of weeks these fine locomotives were reduced to piles of scrap.
Author

Given that steam had to go, it is still valid to argue that better use could have been made of the locomotive fleet. With overhauls continued for a further twelve months, engines could have been kept running into 1968, allowing time for the electric services to be introduced in a blaze of glory, instead of the near disaster that actually occurred. It would have been quite possible to have kept steam in operation until August 1968, the eventual national deadline for steam elimination, giving the Southern another twelve months to prepare for its electrification properly. Such views come easily with hindsight!

A last thought must be spared for the men. Steam work was hard, dirty and sometimes dangerous, yet while most were pleased to see it go, it was still a time of difficult adjustment. There were new skills to be learned, old ways to be forgotten – change is never easy, especially for a man who has given much of his life to a particular occupation. Even those who looked forward to the new clean, electric future, seem to have found instead boredom and a loss of status, and perhaps there lies a lesson for all of us in an era of technological advance!

The first day of full electric working on the Bournemouth line, July 10th 1967. A pair of electro-diesels haul a rake of 'TC' sets for Waterloo away from Southampton. Such working was necessary in the absence of sufficient '4-REP' electric multiple units.
Southern Newspapers

Appendix One SR Locomotive Fleet - Summer 1957

70A Nine Elms (Total 94)

700 class (0-6-0)-4
30692 30694 30699 30701
BB class (4-6-2)-4
34063 34064 34065 34090
E4 class (0-6-2T)-7
32486 32493 32497 32498 32500 32560 32563
H15 class (4-6-0)-12
30478 30482 30484 30486 30487 30488 30489 30491 30521 30522
30523 30524
LN class (4-6-0)-3
30858 30859 30860
M7 class (0-4-4T)-13
30123 30132 30133 30241 30242 30244 30245 30248 30249 30319
30320 30321 30322
MN class (4-6-2)-10
35005 35012 35014 35016 35017 35018 35019 35020 35029 35030
N15 class (4-6-0)-4
30763 30774 30778 30779
O2 class (0-4-4T)-1
30224
Ql class (0-6-0)-3
33015 33017 33038
Standard 5 class (4-6-0)-10
73110 73111 73112 73113 73114 73115 73116 73117 73118 73119
T9 class (4-4-0)-3
30338 30718 30719
U class (2-6-0)-4
31617 31621 31624 31634
V class (4-4-0)-5
30903 30904 30905 30906 30907
WC class (4-6-2)-11
34006 34007 34008 34009 34010 34011 34012 34018 34019 34020
34095

70B-Feltham (Total 60)

700 class (0-6-0)-6
30346 30352 30355 30687 30688 30696
G16 class (4-8-0T)-4
30492 30493 30494 30495
H16 class (4-6-2T)-5
30516 30517 30518 30519 30520
M7 class (0-4-4T)-4
30038 30041 30043 30243
O2 class (0-4-4T)-2
30177 30179
0395 class (0-6-0)-2
30567 30568
Ql class (0-6-0)-12
33006 33007 33008 33009 33010 33011 33012 33013 33016 33018
33026 33027
S15 class (4-6-0)-25
30496 30497 30498 30499 30500 30501 30502 30503 30504 30505
30506 30507 30508 30509 30510 30511 30512 30513 30514 30515
30833 30834 30838 30839 30840

70C-Guildford (Total 49)

700 class (0-6-0)-8
30308 30325 30326 30350 30693 30697 30698 30700
B4 class (0-4-0T)-1
30086
C class (0-6-0)-2
31722 31723
Dl class (4-4-0)-2
31145 31247
E4 class (0-6-2T)-3
32487 32505 32506

G6 class (0-6-0T)-2
30238 30349
M7 class (0-4-4T)-7
30026 30027 30109 30110 30124 30246 30675
0395 class (0-6-0)-1
30575
Ql class (0-6-0)-8
33001 33002 33003 33004 33005 33019 33022 33025
T9 class (4-4-0)-2
30337 30705
U class (2-6-0)-13
31616 31622 31625 31627 31628 31630 31631 31635 31636 31797
31798 31799 31800

70D-Basingstoke (Total 19)

700 class (0-6-0)-1
30368
G6 class (0-6-0T)-2
30160 30258
N15 class (4-6-0)-5
30455 30456 30457 30738 30748
Standard 4 class (4-6-0)-6
75074 75075 75076 75077 75078 75079
T9 class (4-4-0)-1
30724
U class (2-6-0)-4
31611 31612 31633 31806

70E-Reading South (Total 1)

G6 class (0-6-0T)-1
30277

70F-Fratton (Total 31)

AlX class (0-6-0T)-5
32640 32646 32650 32661 32677
C2X class (0-6-0)-3
32548 32549 32550
El class (0-6-0T)-2
32694 32139
E4 class (0-6-2T)-4
32479 32494 32495 32509
K class (2-6-0)-2
32337 32349
M7 class (0-4-4T)-3
30022 30039 30357
0395 class (0-6-0)-1
30578
T9 class (4-4-0)-4
30726 30729 30730 30732
U class (2-6-0)-7
31637 31638 31804 31805 31807 31808 31809

70G Newport, Isle of Wight (Total 12)

El class (0-6-0T)-2
3 4
02 class (0-4-4T)-10
26 27 28 29 30 31 32 33 35 36

70H Ryde, Isle of Wight (Total 9)

02 class (0-4-4T)-9
14 16 17 18 20 21 22 24 25

71A Eastleigh (Total 121)

Ivatt class 2MT(2-6-2T)-2
41293 41305

700 class (0-6-0)-2
30306 30316
757 class (0-6-0T)-1
30757
B4 class (0-4-0T)-2
30083 30096
C14 class (0-4-0T)-1
30588
E4 class (0-6-2T)-6
32491 32510 32556 32557 32559 32579
H15 class (4-6-0)-5
30473 30474 30475 30476 30477
LN class (4-6-0)-11
30850 30851 30852 30853 30854 30855 30856 30857 30861 30862 30863
M7 class (0-4-4T)-17
30028 30029 30030 30032 30033 30125 30130 30328 30356 30375
30376 30377 30378 30379 30479 30480 30481
N15 class (4-6-0)-10
30770 30784 30785 30786 30787 30788 30789 30790 30791 30792
O2 class (0-4-4T)-5
30212 30223 30229 30232 30233
0395 class (0-6-0)-1
30566
P class (0-6-0T)-1
31325
Q class (0-6-0)-7
30530 30531 30532 30535 30536 30542 30543
Ql class (0-6-0)-3
33020 33021 33023
Standard 3 class (2-6-2T)-4
82012 82014 82015 82016
Standard 4 class (4-6-0)-1
75070
Standard 4 class (2-6-0)-24
76007 76009 76010 76011 76012 76013 76014 76015 76016 76017
76018 76019 76025 76026 76027 76028 76029 76063 76064 76065
76066 76067 76068 76069
T9 class (4-4-0)-9
30117 30120 30283 30284 30285 30287 30288 30289 30300
U class (2-6-0)-9
31613 31618 31619 31620 31629 31639 31801 31802 31803

71B Bournemouth (Total 62)

700 class (0-6-0)-2
30690 30695
B4 class (0-4-0T)-3
30087 30093 30102
BB class (4-6-2)-2
34109 34110
G6 class (0-6-0T)-1
30260
LN class (4-6-0)-2
30864 30865
M7 class (0-4-4T)-16
30040 30057 30058 30059 30060 30104 30105 30106 30107 30108
30111 30112 30127 30128 30318 30324
MN class (4-6-2)-6
35010 35021 35022 35025 35026 35027
N15 class (4-6-0)-9
30764 30765 30771 30772 30773 30780 30781 30782 30783
Q class (0-6-0)-3
30539 30541 30548
T9 class (4-4-0)-4
30310 30706 30707 30727
U class (2-6-0)-3
31614 31615 31632
WC class (4-6-2)-11
34040 34041 34042 34043 34044 34093 34094 34105 34106 34107 34108

71G Bath Green Park (Total 44)

Ivatt 2MT class (2-6-2T)-3
41241 41242 41243
2P class (4-4-0)-4
40696 40697 40698 40700
3F class (0-6-0T)-6
47275 47316 47465 47496 47542 47557
4F class (0-6-0)-8
44096 44146 44422 44523 44558 44559 44560 44561
5MT class (4-6-0)-2
44917 45440
7F class (2-8-0)-11
53800 53801 53802 53803 53804 53805 53806 53807 53808 53809
53810
Sentinel (0-4-0T)-2
47190 47191
Standard 4 class (4-6-0)-3
75071 75072 75073
Standard 5 class (4-6-0)-5
73047 73049 73050 73051 73052

71H-Templecombe (Total 19)

Ivatt 2MT class (2-6-2T)-2
41248 41249
2P class (4-4-0)-5
40563 40564 40568 40569 40634
3F class (0-6-0)-7
43194 43216 43218 43248 43356 43419 43436
4F class (0-6-0)-3
44102 44417 44557
G 6 class (0-6-0T)-1
30274
Z class (0-8-0T)-1
30953

71I Southampton Docks (Total 20)

El class (0-6-0T)-3
32151 32689 32113
E2 class (0-6-0T)-3
32101 32108 32109
USA class (0-6-0T)-14
30061 30062 30063 30064 30065 30066 30067 30068 30069 30070
30071 30072 30073 30074

71J Highbridge (Total 4)

IP class (0-4-4T)-1
58086
Ivatt 2MT class (2-6-2T)-2
41296 41304
3F class (0-6-0)-1
43682

72A Exmouth Junction (Total 108)

lvatt 2MT class (2-6-2T)-2
41306 41307
700 class (0-6-0)-2
30315 30691
BB class (4-6-2)-12
34056 34057 34058 34059 34060 34061 34062 34069 34075 34076
34081 34086
EIR class (0-6-2T)-3
32124 32135 32697
M7 class (0-4-4T)-14
30021 30023 30024 30025 30044 30045 30046 30323 30374 30667
30668 30669 30670 30676
MN class (4-6-2)-8

35002 35003 35008 35009 35011 35013 35023 35024
N class (2-6-0)-20
31830 31831 31832 31833 31834 31835 31836 31837 31838 31839
31840 31841 31842 31843 31844 31845 31846 31847 31848 31849
O2 class (0-4-4T)-1
30199
0395 class (0-6-0)-1
30564
0415 class (4-4-2T)-3
30582 30583 30584
S15 class (4-6-0)-6
30841 30842 30843 30844 30845 30846
Standard 3 class (2-6-2T)-10
82010 82011 82013 82017 82018 82019 82022 82023 82024 82025
T9 class (4-4-0)-7
30708 30709 30710 30711 30712 30715 30717
WC class (4-6-2)-17
34002 34004 34014 34015 34016 34021 34022 34023 34024 34026
34028 34029 34030 34031 34032 34033 34034
Z class (0-8-0T)-2
30950 30956

72B Salisbury (Total 51)

700 class (0-6-0)-3
30309 30317 30327
BB class (4-6-2)-7
34049 34050 34051 34052 34053 34054 34055
G6 class (0-6-0T)-2
30266 30270
H15 class (4-6-0)-4
30331 30333 30334 30335
M7 class (0-4-4T)-2
30673 30674
MN class (4-6-2)-3
35004 35006 35007
N class (2-6-0)-2
31813 31814
N15 class (4-6-0)-7
30448 30449 30450 30451 30452 30453 30454
S15 class (4-6-0)-11
30823 30824 30825 30826 30827 30828 30829 30830 30831 30832
30847
Standard 4 class (2-6-0)-3
76005 76006 76008
T9 class (4-4-0)-5
30301 30304 30313 30702 30721
Z class (0-8-0T)-2
30954 30957

72C Yeovil Town (Total 13)

M7 class (0-4-4T)-2
30129 30131
O2 class (0-4-4T)-1
30182
U class (2-6-0)-10
31610 31623 31626 31790 31791 31792 31793 31794 31795 31796

72D Plymouth Friary (Total 21)

Ivatt class 2MT (2-6-2T)-5
41302 41315 41316 41317 41318
B4 class (0-4-0T)-2
30088 30089
G6 class (0-6-0T)-1
30162

M7 class (0-4-4T)-4
30034 30035 30036 30037
O2 class (0-4-4T)-5
30183 30192 30193 30216 30225
WC class (4-6-2)-4
34035 34036 34037 34038

72E Barnstaple Junction (Total 14)

Ivatt 2MT class (2-6-2T)-5
41294 41295 41297 41298 41314
M7 class (0-4-4T)-9
30247 30250 30251 30252 30253 30254 30256 30671 30255

72F Wadebridge (Total 5)

02 class (0-4-4T)-2
30200 30236
0298 class (2-4-0T)-3
30585 30586 30587

73A Sewarts Lane (Total 100)

Ivatt 2MT class (2-6-2T)-3
41290 41291 41292
4MT class (2-6-4T)-8
42074 42086 42087 42088 42089 42090 42091 42106
BB class (4-6-2)-6
34066 34067 34068 34087 34088 34089
C class (0-6-0)-8
31317 31575 31578 31581 31582 31583 31584 31719
Dl class (4-4 0)-3
31545 31743 31749
El class (4-4-0)-4
31019 31067 31504 31506
E2 class (0-6-0T)-4
32100 32102 32103 32106
E3 class (0-6-2T)-1
32455
H class (0-4-4T)-7
31261 31265 31266 31321 31550 31551 31552
MN class (4-6-2)-3
35001 35015 35028
N class (2-6-0)-10
31408 31409 31410 31411 31412 31413 31414 31810 31811 31812
N15 class (4-6-0)-7
30766 30767 30768 30769 30793 30794 30795
O1 class (0-6-0)-2
31048 31064
P class (0-6-0T)-3
31178 31557 31558
Standard 5 class (4-6-0)-10
73080 73081 73082 73083 73084 73085 73086 73087 73088 73089
Standard 7P6F class (4-6-2)-2
70004 70014
Ul class (2-6-0)-8
31894 31895 31897 31898 31904 31905 31906 31907
V class (4-4-0)-3
30908 30909 30915
W class (2-6-4T)-3
31914 31915 31921
WC class (4-6-2)-5
34005 34091 34092 34101 34102

73B Bricklayers Arms (Total 100)

Ivatt 2MT class (2-6-2T)-4
41299 41300 41301 41303

4MT class (2-6-4T)-3
42080 42081 42082
C class (0-6-0)-9
31068 31071 31086 31102 31267 31293 31461 31480 31717
C2X class (0-6-0)-8
32524 32525 32538 32539 32551 32552 32553 32554
Dl class (4-4-0)-3
31735 31739 31741
El class (4-4-0)-3
31165 31497 31507
E2 class (0-6-0T)-3
32104 32105 32107
E3 class (0-6-2T)-1
32454
E4 class (0-6-2-T)-6
32471 32472 32473 32474 32564 32565
E6 class (0-6-2T)-6
32408 32409 32410 32412 32415 32417
H class (0-4-4T)-5
31305 31306 31533 31540 31553
Ll class (4-4-0)-2
31783 31784
N class (2-6-0)-l5
31823 31824 31825 31826 31827 31828 31829 31851 31853 31870
31871 31872 31873 31874 31875
N15 class (4-6-0)-3
30799 30800 30801
Ul class (2-6-0)-6
31890 31891 31899 31900 31901 31902
V class (4-4-0)-17
30923 30924 30925 30926 30927 30928 30929 30930 30931 30932
30933 30934 30935 30936 30937 30938 30939
WC class (4-6-2)-6
34001 34003 34013 34017 34025 34027

73C Hither Green (Total 45)

C class (0-6-0)-18
31018 31033 31054 31059 31061 31253 31287 31573 31686 31688
31689 31690 31691 31692 31693 31694 31695 31721
N class (2-6-0)-8
31822 31855 31856 31857 31858 31859 31860 31861
Nl class (2-6-0)-5
31876 31877 31878 31879 31880
N15 class (4-6-0)-2
30796 30806
Ql class (0-6-0)-4
33014 33037 33039 33040
W class (2-6-4T)-8
31911 31912 31913 31916 31922 31923 31924 31925

73D Gillingham (Total 25)

C class (0-6-0)-15
31037 31112 31227 31229 31297 31495 31508 31510 31576 31579
31681 31682 31683 31684 31720
H class (0-4-4T)-5
31161 31308 31322 31512 31518
Ll class (4-4-0)-3
31785 31786 31787
N class (2-6-0)-2
31815 31816

73E Faversham (Total 27)

Ivatt class 2MT (2-6-2T)-6
41308 41309 41310 41311 41312 41313
C class (0-6-0)-8
31242 31255 31256 31268 31298 31481 31714 31715
Dl class (4-4-0)-3

31494 31505 31509
H class (0-4-4T)-1
31503
L class (4-4-0)-4
31765 31766 31767 31768
N class (2-6-0)-2
31850 31852
Ul class (2-6-0)-3
31892 31893 31903

74A Ashford (Total 45)

4MT class (2-6-4T)-6
42092 42095 42096 42098 42099 42100
C class (0-6-0)-6
31218 31219 31221 31223 31589 31593
Dl class (4-4-0)-2
31246 31727
H class (0-4-4T)-6
31005 31263 31276 31307 31319 31522
Ll class (4-4-0)-5
31756 31757 31758 31759 31782
N class (2-6-0)-9
31400 31401 31402 31403 31404 31405 31406 31407 31854
N15 class (4-6-0)-2
30802 30803
O1 class (0-6-0)-1
31370
Standard 2 class (2-6-2T)-5
84020 84021 84022 84023 84024
Z class (0-8-0T)-3
30951 30952 30955

74B Ramsgate (Total 42)

BB class (4-6-2)-8
34077 34078 34079 34080 34082 34083 34084 34085
C class (0-6-0)-5
31004 31245 31252 31271 31592
H class (0-4-4T)-3
31324 31326 31500
L class (4-4-0)-4
31764 31779 31780 31781
Standard 2 class (2-6-2T)-5
84025 84026 84027 84028 84029
V class (4-4-0)-12
30910 30911 30912 30913 30914 30916 30917 30918 30919 30920
30921 30922
WC class (4-6-2)-5
34096 34097 34098 34099 34100

74C Dover (Total 57)

4MT class (2-6-4T)-5
42075 42076 42077 42078 42079
B4 class (0-4-0T)-1
30084
BB class (4-6-2)-5
34070 34071 34072 34073 34074
C class (0-6-0)-4
31113 31150 31191 31243
H class (0-4-4T)-2
31328 31542
Ll class (4-4-0)-5
31753 31754 31755 31788 31789
N class (2-6-0)-4
31818 31819 31820 31821
N15 class (4-6-0)-7
30775 30776 30777 30797 30798 30804 30805
O1 class (0-6-0)-5

31065 31258 31425 31430 31434
P class (0-6-0T)-2
31027 31323
Rl class (0-6-0T)-l0
31010 31047 31069 31107 31128 31147 31174 31337 31339 31340
Standard 4 class (4-6-0)-5
75065 75066 75067 75068 75069
WC class (4-6-2)-2
34103 34104

74D Tonbridge (Total 45)

C class (0-6-0)-8
31244 31270 31272 31280 31585 31588 31590 31716
Dl class (4-4-0)-4
31470 31487 31489 31492
E3 class (0-6-2T)-1
32456
E4 class (0-6-2T)-2
32578 32580
H class (0-4-4T)-l0
31164 31177 31184 31193 31239 31259 31517 31523 31543 31548
L class (4-4-0)-6
31760 31762 31763 31770 31771 31772
Ql class (0-6-0)-10
33024 33028 33029 33030 33031 33032 33033 33034 33035 33036
Ul class (2-6-0)-4
31896 31908 31909 31910

74E St. Leonards (Total 17)

AlX class (0-6-0T)-3
32636 32670 32678
C class (0-6-0)-1
31498
H class (0-4-4T)-7
31162 31269 31274 31279 31295 31519 31520
L class (4-4-0)-3
31773 31774 31775
V class (4-4-0)-3
30900 30901 30902

75A Brighton (Total 63)

Al x class (0-6-0T)-2
32655 32662
C class (0-6-0)-2
31724 31725
C2x class (0-6-0)-7
32437 32440 32441 32442 32449 32521 32540
E3 class (0-6-2T)-2
32165 32166
E4 class (0-6-2T)-15
32467 32468 32475 32481 32484 32485 32502 32503 32504 32508
32512 32515 32562 32566 32577
H2 class (4-4-2)-1
32424
K class (2-6-0)-6
32338 32339 32340 32341 32342 32343
L class (4-4-0)-3
31776 31777 31778
M7 class (0-4-4T)-4
30031 30053 30054 30055
P class (0-6-0T)-1
31556
Standard 4 class (2-6-4T)-15
80010 80011 80031 80032 80033 80145 80146 80147 80148 80149
80150 80151 80152 80153 80154
WC class (4-6-2) 5
34039 34045 34046 34047 34048

75B Redhill (Total 25)

C2X class (0-6-0)-2
32450 32451
E4 class (0-6-2T)-1
32507
N class (2-6-0)-9
31817 31862 31863 31864 31865 31866 31867 31868 31869
S15 class (4-6-0)-3
30835 30836 30837
Standard 4 class (2-6-0)-10
76053 76054 76055 76056 76057 76058 76059 76060 76061 76062

75C Norwood Junction (Total 28)

C2X class (0-6-0)-10
32444 32445 32446 32447 32448 32543 32544 32545 32546 32547
E4X class (0-6-2T)-2
32466 32477
E6 class (0-6-2T)-4
32413 32414 32416 32418
E6X class (0-6-2T)-2
32407 32411
Q class (0-6-0)-6
30533 30534 30537 30538 30540 30549
W class (2-6-4T)-4
31917 31918 31919 31920

75D Horsham (Total 16)

C2X class (0-6-0)-3
32522 32526 32541
E4 class (0-6-2T)-4
32463 32469 32470 32480
M7 class (0-4-4T)-5
30047 30048 30049 30050 30051
Q class (0-6-0)-4
30544 30545 30546 30547

75E Three Bridges (Total 31)

Ivatt 2MT class (2-6-2T)-1
41319
4MT class (2-64T)-6
42066 42067 42068 42069 42070 42071
C2X class (0-6-0)-10
32438 32443 32523 32527 32528 32529 32532 32534 32535 32536
E4 class (0-6-2T)-1
32519
H class (0-4-4T)-2
31521 31530
K class (2-6-0)-9
32344 32345 32346 32347 32348 32350 32351 32352 32353
M7 class (0-4-4T)-2
30052 30056

75F Tunbridge Wells West (Total 21)

4MT class (2-6-4T)-5
42101 42102 42103 42104 42105
E4 class (0-6-2T)-2
32517 32581
H class (0-4-4T)-6
31278 31310 31327 31329 31544 31554
Standard 4 class (2-6-4T)-8
80012 80013 80014 80015 80016 80017 80018 80019

(Total Steam Locomotives in Southern Region Service -1,444)

Appendix Two
Southern Steam Specials 1957-1967

Includes all known rail tours operated on SR and/or using SR motive power on other regions.
(Tours nationally advertised but not actually operated shown in italics.)

Locomotive/s	Route	Tour/Operator
February 24th 1957		
69257/69319	Marylebone-Wembley-Kew East Jct	'Southern Counties
32424	Kew East Jct-Lewisham-East	Limited'/
	Grinstead-Horsted Keynes	LCGB
32437	Horsted Keynes-Brighton-	
	Preston Park	
80152	Preston Park-Havant	
32636/32650	Havant-Hayling Island-Havant	
80152	Havant-Portsmouth Harbour	
30929	Portsmouth Harbour-Waterloo	
April 28th 1957		
30453	Waterloo-Reading	'North Somerset'
3440	Reading-Bristol Temple Meads	RCTS
41202/41203	Bristol area branches	
3440/5528	Bristol-Radstock-Frome-	
	Westbury-Paddington	
May 19th 1957		
31545	Victoria-Margate-Ramsgate-	'Chatham and Dover'
	Shepherdswell	SLS
31425/31434	Shepherdswell-EKR-Dover Marine-	
	Folkestone Jct	
R1	Folkestone Harbour branch	
31545	Folkestone-Dover-Canterbury East-	
	Holborn Viaduct	
August 25th 1957		
3440	Birmingham-Eastleigh-Birmingham	SLS
October 5th 1957		
30051	Farnborough-Aldershot-Tongham-	'Compass Rose'/
	Guildford-Godalming Goods-Woking-	REC
	Ascot-Reading-Basingstoke-Farnborough	
October 5th 1957		
30687	Blackfriars-Brixton-Dudding Hill Jct	'London Freight lines'/
42686	Dudding Hill Jct.-Broad Street	RCTS
November 10th 1957		
3440	Greenford-Kew-Kensington	'Kentish Heights'
31064	Clapham Jct-Balham-Crystal Palace-	
	Dunton Green-Westerham-Norwood-	
	Selhurst-Kensington	
3440	Kensington-Greenford	
March 29th 1958		
31518		'London River'/
68646		RCTS
April 12th (10th) 1958		
3440/6313	Swindon-Eastleigh Works	Ian Allen
April 13th 1958		
32424	Victoria-Newhaven	'Brighton Atlantic
80154	Newhaven-Brighton	Farewell'/
30796	Brighton-Victoria	RCTS
May 11th 1958		
3440	Greenford-East Croydon	'Bluebell Special'
32342	East Croydon-Horsted Keynes-	
	Haywards Heath-East Croydon	
3440	East Croydon-Greenford	
June 7th 1958		
30107	Poole-Hamworthy Goods-Melcombe	'South Dorset'/
	Regis-Portland-Easton-Maiden	REC
	Newton-West Bay-Maiden Newton-	
	Bournemouth West	
June 8th 1958		
30549	London-Midhurst	'West Sussex
80154		Downsman'

Locomotive/s	Route	Tour/Operator
September 20th 1958		
35017	Waterloo-Exeter	Ian Allan
30712/30726	Exeter-Okehampton-Plymouth	
35023	Plymouth-Paddington	
October 4th 1958		
30120	Waterloo-Liss	'The Sapper'/
WD400	Liss-LMR-Bordon	RCTS
30120	Bordon-Aldershot-Waterloo	
October 4th 1958		
30585	Wadebridge-Wenford Bridge-Wadebridge	LCGB
October 19th 1958		
31019	Paddington-Kensington-Crystal	'Rother Valley Ltd'/
	Palace-Oxted-Tonbridge-Robertsbridge	LCGB
377S/32678	Robertsbridge-Tenterden and return	
31019	Robertsbridge-Bexhill West-Crowhurst	
377S/32678	Crowhurst-Hastings	
31258	Hastings-Lewes-Newhaven Harbour	
30905	Newhaven Harbour-Victoria	
January 25th 1959		
30567	Victoria-Cobham-Goldalming-Guildford	'Portsmouth Direct
30350	Guildford-Gosport-Guildford	Line Centenarian'/
March 7th 1959		
30111	Portsmouth Harbour-Emsworth-	BLS
	Chichester-Lavant-Havant-Bishops	
	Waltham-Knowle-Droxford-	
	Gosport-Fareham-Portsmouth	
March 21st 1959		
69614	Liverpool Street-Canonbury	'London and North
69504	Canonbury-East Finchley-	Kent'/
	Finsbury Park	RCTS
68987	Finsbury Park-Snow Hill-Blackfriars	
31507	Blackfriars-Gravesend West-Hither Green	
D8401	Hither Green-Liverpool Street	
May 2nd 1959		
7001	Paddington-Saltash	'Brunel Centenarian
6420	Saltash-Plymouth Friary-Plymstock	and Plymouth
30182	Plymstock-Turnchapel and return	District'/
6420	Plymstock-Plymouth	RCTS
5069	Plymouth-Paddington	
May 23rd 1959		
31258	Shepherdswell-EKR station-	REC
	Tilmanstone-Kearnsey-Deal-	
	Betteshanger-Minster-Richborough	
	Port Sidings-Kearnsey	
July 12th 1959		
32535	Tonbridge-East Grinstead-Horsted	'Bluebell Special'/
	Keynes-Haywards Heath-Lewes-	
	Uckfield-Tonbridge	
September 20th 1959		
K	*Farnborough-Staines-Kew-Willesden-*	*'Thames and*
L1	*Clapham Jct-New Beckenham-Slade Green-*	*Medway Rambler'/*
E500x	*Chatham Dockyard-Woking-Farnborough*	*REC*
October 3rd 1959		
31193		'London River No.2'/
		RCTS
October 10th 1959		
30328	Ash-Alton-Treloars Siding-Butts Jct-	REC
	Farringdon-Alton-Ash	
January 3rd 1960		
120	Southampton-Reading West-	Privately Sponsored
	Swindon-Reading-Southampton	
May 14th 1960		
6384	Mangotsfield-Bath	'Severn and Wessex'/
53807	Bath Green Park-Bournemouth West	Ian Allan
35008	Bournemouth West-Waterloo	
May 14th 1960		
3440	Gloucester-Cheltenham-Swindon-	GRS
	Andover-Eastleigh-Southampton Docks-	
	Winchester Chesil-Newbury-Gloucester	

May 14th 1960

11227	Plymouth Friary-Cattewater-Plymouth	PRC & RCTS
30193	Plymouth-Stonehouse Pool-Plymouth	

May 22nd 1960

31069	London Bridge-Streatham-Wimbledon-Reading-Newbury-Eastleigh-Reading-Wokingham-London	'North Hampshire Downsman'/ REC

August 14th 1960

31768	Waterloo-Salisbury	'The Greyhound'/
30718	Salisbury-Yeovil-Weymouth	RCTS
3737	Weymouth-Easton-Weymouth	
30718	Weymouth-Broadstone-Fordingbridge-Salisbury	
31768	Salisbury-Waterloo	

September 11th 1960

53804	Bath-Templecombe-Bath	SLS

September 11th 1960

1000	Nottingham Victoria-Banbury-Oxford	'East Midlander
7317	Oxford-Basingstoke-Eastleigh	No. 4'/
76006	Eastleigh-Eastleigh Works	RCTS
7317	Eastleigh Works-Andover-Swindon Works	
1000	Swindon Works-Oxford-Nottingham	

September 18th 1960

30339	Cannon Street-Ludgate Hill-Ascot	'South Western Ltd'/
31768	Ascot-Alton-Eastleigh	LCGB
30516	Eastleigh-Fawley-Totton	
30782	Totton-Ringwood-Broadstone	
53804	Broadstone-Templecombe-Salisbury	
30729	Salisbury-Waterloo	

September 24th 1960

31512	Gravesend Central-All Hallows-Grain-Hoo Junction	REC
31177	Hoo Jct-Strood-Gillingham	
D3721/31177	Gillingham-Chatham Dockyard & return	
31177	Gillingham-Sheerness-on-Sea-Gravesend	

October 15th 1960

30028	Farnborough-Aldershot Government Sidings-Bordon-Alton Treloar's Siding-Farringdon-Frimley-Farnborough	'North Hampshire' REC

March 19th 1961

30582	Waterloo-Twickenham-Windsor-Staines-Woking-Guildford-Leatherhead-Waterloo	'LSWR Suburban'/ REC

April 22nd 1961

32418/32503	Brighton-Horsham-Three Bridges	'Bluebell Special
32564/32503	Three Bridges-East Grinstead-Oxted-Eridge-Polegate	No 2'/
32564/32479	Polegate-Lewes-Haywards Heath-Horsted Keynes-Brighton	

April 30th 1961

30856	Waterloo-Portsmouth Harbour	'Solent Ltd'/
30117	Portsmouth Harbour-Fareham	LCGB
32694/30200	Fareham-Droxford-Gosport-Fareham	
30117	Fareham-Netley-Southampton Ctl	
30073	Southampton-Docks-Eastleigh Works	
30117	Eastleigh Works-Newbury	
31786	Newbury-Reading-Ascot-Waterloo	

June 11th 1961

31749/31786	Victoria-Maidstone West-Paddock Wood	'South Eastern Ltd'/
31065/31592	Paddock Wood-Hawkhurst-Tonbridge	LCGB
31308/31749	Tonbridge-Robertsbridge	
32662/32670	Robertsbridge-Tenterden and return	
31749/31786	Robertsbridge-Tonbridge-London Bridge	

September 10th 1961

5306	Swindon-Ludgershall-Andover Jct Swindon Town-Cheltenham Spa-Gloucester-Swindon	'MSWJR'/ RCTS

September 10th 1961

7808	Birmingham-Swindon-Andover Jct and return	SLS

January 7th 1962

30901	Eastleigh-Salisbury-Westbury-Swindon Works-Reading-Eastleigh	

February 25th 1962

30782	Victoria-Chatham-Margate-Dover-Ashford	'Kentish Venturer'/ LCGB
31263/31690	Ashford-New Romney-Appledore	
30926	Ashford-Tonbridge-Orpington-Charing Cross	

March 25th 1962

30199	Waterloo-Twickenham-Shepperton-Richmond-Twickenham-Norwood Junction-Selhurst-Victoria	REC

April 1st 1962

1247	London Bridge-Haywards Heath-Sheffield Park-London Bridge	'Blue Belle'/

May 13th 1962

30925/40646	Nottingham Victoria-Darlington	'East Midlander'/
90348	Shunt to Works and shed	RCTS
30925/40646	Darlington-York-Nottingham	

June 24th 1962

120	Waterloo-Guildford-Horsham	'Sussex Coast
32417/32503	Horsham-Midhurst-Pulborough	Limited'/
32353	Pulborough-Bognor Regis-Haywards Heath	LCGB
120	Haywards Heath-Eastbourne	
30055/120	Eastbourne-Rotherfield	
120	Rotherfield-East Grinstead-London Bridge	

June 24th 1962

30850	Paddington-Swindon	

July 8th 1962

120	*Waterloo-Southampton Docks-So'ton Terminus-Fareham*	*'Clausentum'/ RCTS*
M7s or O2s	*Fareham-Gosport-Droxford-Portsmouth Harbour*	
120	*Portsmouth-Guildford-Waterloo*	

September 2nd 1962

30861	Waterloo-Sidmouth Jct	'South Western Ltd'/
30024/30025	Sidmouth Jct-Exmouth-Exeter	SCTS
30861	Exeter-Salisbury-Andover Jct	
30309	Andover-Romsey-Eastleigh	
30770	Eastleigh-Waterloo	

September 8th 1962

30587	Wadebridge-Wenford Bridge-Wadebridge	LCGB

September 22nd 1962

34050	Paddington-Weymouth	Ian Allan
53808	Weymouth-Bath Green Park	
4932	Bath Green Park-London	

September 30th 1962

34064	Waterloo-Ringwood-Broadstone	'Somerset & Dorset'/
53808	Broadstone-Evercreech Jct	LCGB
3210	Evercreech-Burnham-on-Sea-Evercreech Jct	
53808	Evercreech-Bath Green Park	
44558	Bath-Bristol Temple Meads	
4707	Bristol-Badminton-Didcot	
1007	Didcot-Paddington	

October 7th 1962

30925	London Bridge-Brighton	'Sussex Coast'/
32418/32636	Brighton-Seaford-Brighton	RCTS
32353	Brighton-Steyning-Epsom-London Bridge	

October 21st 1962

120	Victoria-Haywards Heath	'Blue Belle'
488/55	Haywards Heath-Sheffield Park	
120	Haywards Heath-Victoria	

November 11th 1962

120/30926	Waterloo-Eastleigh	HCRS
76011	Eastleigh-Eastleigh Works	
30062/30072	Eastleigh-Southampton Docks-Eastleigh	
120/30926	Eastleigh-Havant-Guildford-Waterloo	

December 2nd 1962

30585/30587	Waterloo-Hampton Court-Wimbledon	'South West
30517	Wimbledon-Chessington South-Wimbledon	Suburban'/
		RCTS &SLS
30585/30587	Wimbledon-Shepperton-Waterloo	

December 16th 1962

30585/30587	Waterloo-Hampton Court-Wimbledon	'South West
30517	Wimbledon-Chessington South-Wimbledon	Suburban'/
		RCTS & SLS
30585/30587	Wimbledon-Shepperton-Waterloo	

January or Febrary 1963

V(Schools)	*Waterloo-Cosham-So'ton-B'mth-Waterloo*	*RCTS & LCGB*

February 24th 1963

60022	Waterloo-Exeter Central	'West Countryman'/
4591/5564	Exeter-Thorverton-Tiverton Jct	LCGB
1450	Tiverton Jct-Hemyock-Tiverton Jct	
60022	Tiverton Jct-Taunton-Paddington	

March 9th 1963

30096	Winchester Chesil-So'ton Ocean Terminal-Eastleigh Works-Winchester City	'B4 Dock Tank'/ LCGB

March 10th 1963

120	Victoria-Andover Junction-Salisbury	'Hampshire
33039	Bulford branch-Salisbury	Venturer'/
120	Salisbury-Southampton Docks	SCTS
30073	Southampton-Fawley-Eastleigh	
30510	Eastleigh-Waterloo	

March 17th 1963

60022	Southampton-Bristol-Swindon-Westbury-Southampton	

March 23rd 1963

30108	Farnborough-Basingstoke Thorneycrofts Siding-Andover Jct-Bulford-Grateley-Salisbury-Southampton-Winchester Chesil-Newbury-Reading Ctl Goods-Farnborough	'Rambling Rose'/ REC

March 31st 1963

80084/473	Victoria-Haywards Heath	'Blue Belle'/
488/473	Haywards Heath-Horsted Keynes-Haywards Heath	
80084	Haywards Heath-Victoria	

April 6th 1963

30096	Winchester Chesil-So'ton Ocean Terminal-Eastleigh Works-Winchester City	'B4 Dock Tank'/ LCGB

April 17th 1963

34031	St.Pancras-Derby and return	Ian Allan

April 18th 1963

34031	St. Pancras-Derby and return	Ian Allan

April 27th 1963

120	Exeter Central-Wadebridge	'North Cornishman
1369	Wadebridge-Wenford Bridge & return	& Camel Valleyman'/
120	Wadebridge-Padstow-Exeter Central	RCTS

May 11th 1963

34006	St. Pancras-Derby	'North Midlands'/
61004	Derby-Buxton-Burton	LCGB & RCTS
34006	Burton-Coalville-St.Pancras	

May 12th 1963

34094	Birmingham New Street-Doncaster-Birmingham	WRS

May 18th 1963

4472	Gainsborough-Lincoln-Leicester-Banbury-Southampton-Banbury-Derby-Worksop	

June 16th 1963

Q	*London Bridge-Caterham*	*'Surrey'/*
M7	*Caterham-Tattenham Corner-Vicotria*	*RCTS*

August 25th 1963

60112	Waterloo-Hamworthy Junction	
30052	Hamworthy Goods branch	
60112	Hamworthy Jct-Weymouth-Maiden Newton	
4689/7782	Maiden Newton-West Bay-Maiden Newton	
60112	Maiden Newton-Westbury-Salisbury-Waterloo	

September 15th 1963

123/120	Victoria-Haywards Heath	'Blue Belle'/
488/473	Haywards Heath-Sheffield Park-Haywards Heath	
123/120	Haywards Heath-Victoria	

September 28th 1963

34064	Paddington-Banbury-Wolverhampton-Shrewsbury-Ruabon	TRPS
78xxs	Ruabon-Towyn-Shrewsbury	
34064	Shrewsbury-Reading-Paddington	

October 6th 1963

45552	Paddington-Bristol	HCRS
4103/6148	Bristol-Cheddar-Westbury	
Std 5/uWC	Westbury-Salisbury-Waterloo	

October 6th 1963

120	*Bristol-Salisbury-Eastleigh-*	*BDRS*
Standard	*Bournemouth-Bath-Bristol*	

October 12th 1963

120/31790	Waterloo-East Putney-Ascot-Banbury-Woodford Halse	'Thames, Avon & Severn'/
6368/2246	Woodford Halse-Stratford-on-Avon-Worcester Shrub Hill	LCGB
45552	Worcester-Birmingham-Cheltenham Spa	
7005	Cheltenham Spa-Swindon-Paddington	

October 19th 1963

4472	Paddington-Bath-Taunton	Ian Allan
7317/7332	Taunton-Ilfracombe-Exeter Central	
4472	Exeter Ctl-Waterloo	

October 20th 1963

120	*Waterloo-Bournemouth-Evercreech*	
4F	*Evercreech-Highbridge-Bath*	
7F	*Bath-Templecombe*	
120	*Templecombe-Waterloo*	

October 27th 1963

55/473	Brighton-Horsted Keynes-Brighton	'Brighton Blue Belle'/

November 3rd 1963

30512	Waterloo-Alton-Eastleigh-Fratton	'Hayling Farewell'/
34088/31791	Fratton-Portsmouth Dockyard	LCGB
31791	Portsmouth Dockyard-Havant	
32636/32670	Hayling Island-Havant and return	
30531/30543	Havant-Chichester-Lavant-Horsham-Three Bridges-Victoria	

February 16th 1964

35030	Waterloo-Yeovil Jct	'Quantock Flyer'/
4593/9663	Yeovil Jct-Yeovil Pen Mill-Taunton-Minehead-Taunton-Chard Jct	LCGB
35030	Chard Jct-Templecombe-Waterloo	

March lst 1964

35003	St. Pancras-Leicester-Derby	HCRS

March 8th 1964

70020	Waterloo-Ascot-Reading-Andover-Ludgershall-Salisbury	'South Western Rambler'/
92209	Salisbury-Templecombe-Hamworthy Junction-Bournemouth Central	SCTS
70020	Bournemouth Ctl-Waterloo	

March 14th 1964

M7	Farnborough North-Aldershot-Alton-Farringdon-Winchester-Newbury-Didcot-Reading-Farnborough	'Hampshire Hog'/ REC

March 22nd 1964

33027	Waterloo-Epsom-Guildford-Horsham	"Sussex Downsman'/
31411	Horsham-Steyning-Hove-Three Bridges	LCGB & RCTS
33027	Three Bridges-Tunbridge Wells West	
34066	Tunbridge Wells-Heathfield-Pevensey	
31411	Pevensey-Lewes-Brighton	
41287	Brighton-Kemp Town-Brighton	
34066	Brighton-Uckfield-Oxted-Victoria	

April 3rd 1964

92220	Paddington-Eastleigh	Ian Allan
76062	Southampton Docks-Fareham-Horsham-Three Bridges	
92220	Three Bridges-Paddington	

April 18th 1964

30548	Portsmouth and Southsea-Eastleigh	'Hampshire
30073	Eastleigh-Eastleigh Works and return	Venturer'/
30548	Eastleigh-Romsey-Andover Jct-Salisbury-Fordingbridge-Hamworthy Goods-Poole-Ringwood-Southampton Central	LCGB

May 3rd 1964

2887	Exeter St Davids-Plymouth	'Cornubian'/
34002	Plymouth-Penzance-Plymouth	PRC & RCTS
2887	Plymouth-Exeter St Davids	

May 9th 1964

46251	Nottingham-Banbury-Didcot	'East Midlander
34038	Didcot-Newbury-Eastleigh	No.7'/
30071	Eastleigh-Eastleigh Works and return	RCTS
34038	Eastleigh-Swindon	
46251	Swindon-Banbury-Nottingham	

June 7th 1964

MN	London-Bournemouth Central	'Somerset and
53807/44558	Bournemouth-Highbridge-Evercreech-Bath	Dorset'/ HCRS
7023	Bath-Mangotsfield-Gloucester-Stroud-London	

June 13th 1964

35012	Leeds-Carnforth	'Solway Ranger'/
45394	Carnforth shunt	RCTS
35012	Carnforth-Shap-Penrith	
46426/46458	Penrith-Workington	
dmmu	Workington-Carlisle	
49/123	Carlisle-Silloth-Carlisle	
35012	Carlisle-Ais Gill-Leeds	

June 14th 1964

34079	Birmingham NS-Derby-Crewe-B'ham

July 5th 1964

30053	Waterloo-Shepperton	'Surrey Wanderer'/
78038	Shepperton-Epsom Downs-Tulse Hill-Beckenham Jct-Caterham	LCGB
30053	Caterham-Tattenham Corner-Victoria	

August 16th 1964

4472	Sheffield-Derby-Birmingham-Swindon-Eastleigh and return	WRS

September 6th 1964

82029	Winchester Chesil-Romsey-Andover-Ludgershall-Andover-Romsey-Eastleigh	'Anton & Test Valley'/ LCGB

September 12th 1964

4472	Sheffied Midland-Birmingham-Banbury-Basingstoke-and return-	'Farnborough Flyer'/ Alan Pegler

September 19th 1964

61572	*Paddington-Devizes-Bristol-Bath-Bournemouth-Evercreech-Highbridge-Chippenham-Paddington*	*MGNJRS*
other locos		

September 19th 1964

1369	Wadebridge-Wenford Bridge-Wadebridge	'Wenford'/ PRC/RCTS

September 20th 1964

92220	Victoria-Wimbledon-Alton-Southampton-Salisbury-Yeovil-Yeovil-Axminster	'Farewell to Steam'/ SCTS
	Lyme Regis and Seaton branches	
	Seaton Jct-Chertsey-Victoria	

October 4th 1964

33026	Waterloo-Virginia Water-Aldershot-Guildford	'Vectis'/ LCGB
70000	Guildford-Reading-Basingstoke-Fareham-Portsmouth Harbour	
14	Ryde Pier Head-Ventnor-Ryde	
28	Ryde-Newport-Ryde Pier Head	
70000	Portsmouth Harbour-Waterloo	

October 11th 1964

35007	Birminham-Derby-Doncaster-York and return	WRS

October 18th 1964

30839	Waterloo-Ascot-Bagshot-Woking	'Midhurst Belle'/
30064	Woking-Guildford-Christs Hospital	RCTS & LCGB
30530	Christs Hospital-Midhurst-Pulborough-Littlehampton	
35007	Littlehampton-Brighton	
30530	Brighton-Kemp Town-Brighton	
35007	Brighton-Victoria	

October 31st 1964

1369	Wadebridge-Wenford Bridge-Wadebridge

December 6th 1964

70020	Broad Street-Kensington-Havant-Fareham	HCRS
34079	Fareham-Southampton Docks	
30069/30073	Southampton Docks-Eastleigh	
70020	Eastleigh-Broad Street	

December 11th 1964

34007	Exeter-Meldon Quarry-Exeter(brake vans)	EURS

January 3rd 1965

31639	Waterloo-Wimbledon-	'Maunsell
30545/31639	Wimbledon-Tooting Goods-Wimbledon	Commemorative'/
31639	Wimbledon-VirginiaWater-Staines	LCGB
30545	Staines-Reading South	
31831	Reading-Guildford-Redhill-	
31411	Redhill-Tonbridge-Oxted-London Bridge	

February 28th 1965 and March 7th 1965

35022	Waterloo-Sidmouth Jct-	'East Devon'/
41206/41291	Axminster-Lyme Regis-Axminster-Seaton Jct	LCGB
80041	Seaton Jct-Seaton-Seaton Jct-Sidmouth Jct	
4666	Sidmouth Jct-Sidmouth Tipton St Johns	
41291	Sidmouth Jct-Sidmouth Tipton St Johns	
4666/41291	Tipton St Johns-Exmouth-Exeter Ctl	
35022	Exeter Ctl-Waterloo	

March 7th 1965

31639/33006	Paddington-Fenny Compton-Stratford upon Avon-Rugby-Wellingborough-Oxford-Paddington	'Six Counties'/ HCRS

March 27th 1965

41324/41284	Melcombe Regis-Portland-Easton	SWRS

March 27th 1965

41206/41291	Exeter St.Davids-Torrington-Barnstaple-Braunton-Mortehoe-Ilfracombe	'Exmoor Ranger'/ RCTS & PRC
3205	(banker) Braunton-Mortehoe	
3205	Ilfracombe-Mortehoe (41206/41291 bankers)	
3205	Mortehoe-Barnstaple-Taunton-Exeter	

March 28th 1965

73022	Victoria-Dorking North-Fareham-Bournemouth-Templecombe	'Southern Wanderer'/
44560	Templecombe-Highbridge-Templecombe	SCTS
35023	Templecombe-Salisbury-Victoria	

April 4th 1965

30837	Waterloo-Reading General-	'Wessex
6963	Reading-Devizes-Bristol Temple Meads	Downsman'/
D7007/44466	Bristol-Mangotsfield	LCGB
44466	Mangotsfield-Bath Green Park	
48309	Bath Green Park-Bournemouth West	
34051	Bournemouth West-Waterloo	

April 21st 1965

Loco	Route	Tour
35028	Paddington-Swindon-Eastleigh-London	Ian Allan

May 2nd 1965

Loco	Route	Tour
30837	Waterloo-Reading General	'Wessex Downsman'/ LCGB
6963	Reading-Devizes-Bristol Temple Meads	
44264	Bristol-Mangotsfield-Bath Green Park	
48309	Bath Green Park-Bournemouth West	
34051	Bournemouth West-Waterloo	

May 23rd 1965

Loco	Route	Tour
34051	Birmingham Snow Hill-Leamington Spa-Reading-Salisbury	SLS
35017	Salisbury-Exeter-Bristol-Westbury	
7029	Westbury-Birmingham	

May 23rd 1965 (originally advertised for May 30th)

Loco	Route	Tour
35005	Waterloo-Eastleigh-Salisbury-Swindon-Paddington	'Southern Pacific'/ WRS

May 29th 1965

Loco	Route	Tour
4472	Nottingham-Leicester-Clapham Jct-Richmond-Reading-Swindon-Gloucester-Derby-Nottingham	'East Midlander No. 8'/ RCTS

May 30th 1965

Loco	Route	Tour
Unrebuilt WC	Victoria-Brighton-Portsmouth Portsmouth-Woking-Waterloo	'Isle of Wight'/ HCRS
O2	Ryde-Cowes-Ryde-Ventnor-Ryde	

June 12th 1965

Loco	Route	Tour
44777	Birmingham-Gloucester-Bath	'Somerset & Dorset'/ WRS
92238	Bath-Bournemouth Central	
34097	Bournemouth-Basingstoke-	
6967	Oxford-Birmingham	

June 12th 1965

Loco	Route	Tour
33006	Guildford-Horsham-Guildford	REC

June 13th 1965

Loco	Route	Tour
34050	Waterloo-Horsham-Three Bridges	'Wealdsman'/ LCGB
31803/31411	Three Bridges-Heathfield-Hastings-Eastbourne-Haywards Heath	
34050	Haywards Heath-Steyning-Horsham	
33027/33006	Horsham-Guildford-Cobham-Waterloo	

July 25th 1965

Loco	Route	Tour
46509	Waterloo-Twickenham-Herne Hill-Crystal Palace-Kensington Olympia	'Thames Valley'/ LCGB & REC
6106	Kensington-Greenford-Southall	
9773	Southall-Staines-Windsor	
6106	Windsor-Twyford-Henley-Reading	
80154	Reading-Ascot-Waterloo	

August 1st 1965

Loco	Route	Tour
Bl	Nottingham-Birmingham-Banbury-Haywards Heath-Guildford-Reading-Nottingham	Ten Counties'/ WRS

August 15th 1965

Loco	Route	Tour
75066	Waterloo-Reading General	'Western Ranger'/ LCGB
3863	Reading-Swindon-Radley	
9773	Radley-Abingdon-Witney-Yarnton	
6126	Yarnton-Bicester-Oxford	
75075	Oxford-Thame-Maidenhead-Clapham Jct.	

September 5th 1965 (was advertised as A4 throughout)

Loco	Route	Tour
60145	Birmingham-Banbury	'Hants and Dorset'/ WRS
7029	Banbury-Basingstoke	
73085	Basingstoke-Eastleigh	
34019	Eastleigh-Weymouth	
60145	Banbury-Birmingham	

September 5th 1965

Loco	Route	Tour
3205	Exeter-Okehampton-Launceston-Halwill-Bude	GWS

September 12th 1965

Loco	Route	Tour
35022	Waterloo-Exeter	'Exeter Flyer'/ SCTS
80039/80043	Exeter-Barnstaple Junction-Torrington/Ilfracombe	
80039	Barnstaple-Torrington-Barnstaple	
80043	Barnstaple Jct-Ilfracombe	
80039/80043	Barnstaple Jct-Exeter	
35022	Exeter-Salisbury-Waterloo	

September 12th 1965

Loco	Route	Tour
4472	Waterloo-Weymouth-Yeovil-Paddington	GMRS

September 18th 1965

Loco	Route	Tour
4472	Waterloo-Reading-Birmingham-Shrewsbury-Cheadle Heath	'High Peak'/ LCGB
45705	Cheadle Heath-Derby-Aston	
45114	Aston-Berkswell-Leamington Spa	
6853/6861	Leamington Spa-Bicester-Paddington	

October 3rd 1965

Loco	Route	Tour
35022	Waterloo-Exeter	'Exeter Flyer'/ SCTS
80039/80043	Exeter-Barnstaple Junction	
80039	Barnstaple-Torrington-Barnstaple	
80043	Barnstaple Jct- Ilfracombe	
80039/80043	Barnstaple Jct-Exeter	
35022	Exeter-Salisbury-Waterloo	

October 3rd 1965

Loco	Route	Tour
34002	Waterloo-Horsham-Chichester	'Vectis Farewell'/ LCGB
33027/33020	Lavant Branch	
34002	Chichester-Portsmouth Harbour	
24	Ryde Pier Head-Cowes-Ryde Pier Head	
24/14	Ryde Pier Head-Ventnor-Ryde Pier Head	
73155	Portsmouth Harbour-Waterloo	

November 27th 1965

Loco	Route	Tour
35022	Waterloo-Aylesbury-Rugby-Nuneaton-	'The Midlander'/ WRS
Britannia	Walsall-Wolverhampton-Crewe-Shrewsbury-Birmingham-Banbury-Paddington	

December 5th 1965

Loco	Route	Tour
31866	Waterloo-Horsham-Steyning-Brighton-Steyning-Sutton-Streatham	'Steyning Line'/ LCGB
82006	Streatham-Sutton-Victoria	

December 12th 1965

Loco	Route	Tour
34100	Waterloo-Basingstoke	'Cross Countryman'/ LCGB
34015	Basingstoke-Reading West-Cholsey	
9773	Wallingford Branch	
34015	Cholsey-Oxford	
48309	Oxford-Bedford-Oxford	
34015	Oxford-Thame-Greenford-Victoria	

January 1st 1966

Loco	Route	Tour
35011	Waterloo-Bournemouth-Templecombe	'Mendip Merchantman'/ RCTS
41307/41283	Templecombe-Highbridge	
92243	Highbridge-Bristol-Mangotsfield	
48760/92243	Mangotsfield-Bath Green Park	
48309/48760	Bath-Templecombe	
35011	Templecombe-Waterloo	

January 2nd 1966

Loco	Route	Tour
48309	Bath Green Park-Bournemouth and return	SLS

January 2nd 1966

Loco	Route	Tour
35011	Waterloo-Broadstone	RCTS
31639/34015	Broadstone-Bath Green Park	
48309	Bath-Bristol-Highbridge	
41283/41307	Highbridge-Templecombe	
35011	Templecombe-Waterloo	

January 8th 1966

Loco	Route	Tour
34001	Waterloo-Guildford-Fareham-Salisbury	Privately Sponsored
34015	Salisbury-Exeter Ctl-Salisbury	
34001	Salisbury-Waterloo	

January 9th 1966

Loco	Route	Tour
30837	Waterloo-Bentley	'S15 Commemorative'/ LCGB
31639	Borden branch	
30837	Bentley-Eastleigh	
30073	Eastleigh Works	
30837	Eastleigh-Fareham-Havant-Waterloo	

January 16th 1966

Loco	Route	Tour
30837	Waterloo-Bentley	'S15 Commemorative'/ LCGB
31639	Bordon branch	
30837	Bentley-Alton	
30837/31639	Alton-Eastleigh	
30073	Eastleigh Works	
30837	Eastleigh-Havant-Waterloo	

February 20th 1966

34013	Victoria-Oxted-Uckfield-Lewes-Brighton-Fareham	'Southdown Venturer'/ SCTS
31411	Fareham-Gosport-Portsmouth Hbr.	
34013	Portsmouth H-Guildford-London Bdg	

February 27th 1966

35028	Waterloo-Alton-Wareham	'Dorset Belle'/
41301/41284	Swanage branch	LCGB
35028	Wareham-Weymouth	
41301/41284	Weymouth-Bridport-Yeovil Jct.	
34057	Yeovil Jct.-Waterloo	

March 5th 1966

48706	Bath Green Park-Bournemouth-Bath	GW Society

March 5th 1966

35028	Waterloo-Templecombe	'Somerset & Dorset"/
41307/41249	Templecombe-Highbridge-E'creech	LCGB
34006/34057	Evercreech-Bath-Bournemouth	
35028	Bournemouth-Waterloo	

March 6th 1966

48706/80043	Bath G.P.-Bournemouth & return	SLS

March 6th 1966

35028	Waterloo-Staines-Woking-Broadstone-Templecombe	RCTS
41283/41249	Templecombe-Highbridge	
34013	Highbridge-Bristol-Mangotsfield	
D7014	Mangotsfield Nth. Jct.-Bath G.P.	
34013/34057	Bath-Templecombe	
35028	Templecombe-Waterloo	

March 12th 1966

(Britannia)	*Birmingham-Woking-Alton*	'Hampshireman'/
(N/Q1)	*Alton-Eastleigh*	WRS
(N)	*Eastleigh Works*	
(Q1)	*Eastleigh-Gosport & return*	
(Unrebuilt WC)	*Eastleigh-Salisbury-Yeovil Jct.*	
(Warship)	*Yeovil Jct.-Swindon-Banbury*	
(Britannia)	*Banbury-Birmingham*	

March 19th 1966

33006	Eastleigh-Gosport-Southampton Terminus	'New Forester'/ LCGB
30064/30073	So'ton Term.-Fawley-Totton	
33006	Totton-Lymington Pier-Brockenhurst	

March 20th 1966

34089	Waterloo-Salisbury	'Solent'/
75070	Salisbury-So'ton Ocean Terminal	RCTS
30064/30073	So'ton Docks-Fawley-So'ton Terminus	
75070	So'ton Terminus-Fareham	
31639	Gosport branch	
31639/75070	Fareham-Guildford-East Putney-Waterloo	

March 26th 1966

60024	Waterloo-Weymouth-Yeovil-Salisbury-Waterloo	A4 Locomotive Preservation Society
73114	(Banker up from Weymouth)	

March 27th 1966

60024	Waterloo-Salisbury-Exeter St. Davids-Exeter Ctl-Salisbury-Waterloo	'A4 Commemorative'/ LCGB
D7048	(Banker at Exeter)	

April 2nd 1966

34006	Waterloo-Sidmouth Jct.-Waterloo	Privately Sponsored
D70xx	Sidmouth Jct.-Exmouth & return	

April 3rd 1966

31639/31411	Waterloo-Twickenham-Clapham Jct.-Crystal Palace-East Croydon-Redhill-Basingstoke-Salisbury	'Wilts and Hants'/ LCGB
31639/33006	Salisbury-Southampton-Alton-Waterloo	

April 16th 1966

31411/31639	Waterloo-Woking	'Longmoor'/RCTS
WD600	Woking-Liss (BR)	
WD600/WD195	Liss-Longmoor	
WD195/WD600	Longmoor-Bordon (BR)	
WD600	Bordon-Bentley-Ascot-Staines	
77014	Staines-Windsor and Eton	
31411/31639	Windsor-Brentford-Waterloo	

April 30th 1966

31791/31639	Waterloo-Woking	'Longmoor'/RCTS
WD600	Woking-Liss	
WD600/WD195	Liss-Longmoor	
WD195/WD600	Longmoor-Bordon	
WD600	Bordon-Bentley-Staines	
73114	Staines-Windsor and Eton	
31791/31639	Windsor-Waterloo	

May 21st 1966

30073	So'ton Central-Fawley-Totton	'Hampshire Explorer'/
77014	Totton-Blandford Forum-Broadstone	BYTS
34006	Broadstone-Ringwood-Bournemouth-Southampton	

June 5th 1966

35028	Victoria-Redhill-Guildford-Clapham-Kensington Olympia	'Surrey Rambler'/ SCTS
80154	Kensington-Clapham-Norwood Jct.	
34089	Norwood-Epsom Downs-Wimbledon-Victoria	

June 24th-26th 1966

35026	Waterloo-Neasden-Banbury-Birmingham-Market Drayton-Crewe	'Aberdonian'/WRS
(other motive power to Scotland and return)		
35026	Doncaster-Newark-Dudley	
92113/35026	Dudley-Birmingham (Snow Hill)	
35026	Birmingham (SH)-Banbury-Waterloo	

June 25th 1966

(S15, Q1, N or U)	*Wigan area, brake van tour*	ARES

June 26th 1966

34002	Waterloo-Salisbury	'Last steam to Exeter'/
35023	Salisbury-Exeter St Davids-Westbury Westbury-Salisbury-Waterloo	SCTS 34100

July 3rd 1966

(34064)	*Manchester-Birmingham-Hellifield*	'Shap and Gill Climber'/
(S15, Q1, U or N)	*-Tebay-Carlisle-Settle-Manchester*	ARES

July 3rd 1966

34002	Waterloo-Salisbury	'Green Arrow'/
45493/34100	Salisbury-Yeovil-Weymouth	LCGB
41298	Weymouth Quay	
45493/34100	Weymouth-Bournemouth	
34002	Bournemouth-Waterloo	

July 31st 1966

(MN)	*Victoria-Brighton-Eastleigh*	C.A.G. Spiller
(Std 5)	*Eastleigh-Southampton Ctl*	
(BB)	*Southampton-Havant-Hove-Victoria*	

August 7th 1966

(MN)	*Waterloo-Eastleigh-Weymouth-*	'Wessex Merchantman'/
(Britannia)	*Yeovil-Salisbury-Waterloo*	MNLPS

August 13th 1966

34002	Waterloo-Neasden-Nottingham Victoria	RCTS
(other motive power around the Midlands)		
34002	Nottingham Victoria-Waterloo	

August 14th 1966

60532	Waterloo-Salisbury-Exeter St Davids-Taunton-Westbury	'A2 Commemorative'/ LCGB
70004	Westbury-Salisbury-Waterloo	

September 3rd 1966

35030	Waterloo-Neasden-Nottingham Victoria	'Great Central'/
(other motive power around the Midlands)		LCGB
35030	Nottingham Victoria-Waterloo	

September 3rd 1966

(MN)	*Nottingham-Marylebone and return*	North Dorset Loco Society

September 10th 1966

4472	Doncaster-Woking-Farnborough and return	'Farnborough Flyer'

September 11th 1966

(MN)	Waterloo-Horsham-Littlehampton-	'B4 Dock Tank'/
(Std 5)	Botley-Eastleigh-Southampton	RCTS
(LMS 5)	Docks-Brockenhurst-Lymington-	
(B4)	Poole-Hamworthy Goods	
(Std 4)	Southampton-Staines-Waterloo	

September 17th 1966

4472	Victoria-Brighton-Eastleigh	'Scotsman goes
80152/80016	Eastleigh-Salisbury-Eastleigh	South'/
4472	Eastleigh-Brighton-Victoia	C.A.G. Spiller

September 24th 1966

(Unrblt WC)	Waterloo-Guildford-Fareham-	'County of Hants/
(Ivatt 2Ts)	Gosport	A. Turk
(USAs)	Totton-Fawley-Lymington-Eastleigh-	
(LMS 5)	S'bury-Reading-G'ford-W'loo	

October 1966 (date unknown)

(Britannia)	Waterloo- Weymouth	'Wessex Merchantman'/
(MN)	Weymouth-Yeovil-S'bury W'loo	MNLPS

October 2nd 1966

(LMS Crab)	Waterloo-Eastleigh	MRTS
(Crosti 9F)	Eastleigh-Weymouth-Salisbury	
(LMS Crab)	Salisbury-Waterloo	

October 2nd 1966

?	Waterloo-Portsmouth-and Isle	Putney Railway
	of Wight lines	Society

October 9th 1966

80154	London Bridge-Wimbledon	'Four Counties'/
80154/30072	Wimbledon-Tooting-Merton Park	SCTS
30072	Merton Park-Wimbledon	
34052	Wimbledon-Epsom-Guildford-	
	Eastleigh-Salisbury	
35023	S'bury-Andover-Ludgershall-	
	Basingstoke-Reading-Redhill-	
	Victoria	

October 9th 1966

(Jubilees)	Waterloo- Weymouth-	'Dorsetonian/
	Salisbury-Waterloo	Metropolitan
		Railway Society

October 9th 1966

(Unrblt WC)	Glasgow-Aberdeen-Glasgow	'Bulleid
		Commemorative'/
		Glasgow Loco Club

October 15th 1966

35023	Waterloo,-Westbury	Privately Sponsored
35026	W'bury-Exeter St Davids-S'bury	
35023	Salisbury-Waterloo	

October 16th 1966

34019/34023	Waterloo-Guildford-Fareham	'Dorset & Hants'/
34023	Fareham-So'ton-Broadstone	LCGB
77014/76026	B'stone-Ringwood-Blandford Forum-	
	Hamworthy Goods-Hamworthy Jct.	
34019/34023	Hamworthy Jct.-Waterloo	

October 22nd 1966

4472	Kings Cross-York	'Elizabethan'/ARES
35026	York-Newcastle-York	
4472	York-Kings Cross	

October 22nd 1966

?	Waterloo-Windsor-Guildford	RCTS and SLS
	suburban area	

October 30th 1966

(Unrblt WC)	Manchester-Crewe-Derby-	Buckley Wells
	Manchester	Railway Enthusiasts

November 5th 1966

(Urlrblt WC,	Crewe-Southport-Hellifield-Settle-	'North Briton'/ARES
U or USAs)	Carlisle-Newcastle-Manchester-Crewe	

November 12th 1966

34015	Waterloo-Feltham-Ascot-Reading	'Shakespearian'/
35023	Reading General-Banbury	LCGB
7029	Midlands lines	
70004	Midlands lines	
35023	Banbury-High Wycombe-Victoria	

November 13th 1966

73065	Victoria-Herne Hill-Norwood Jct.-	'West Country'/
	Redhill-Reading-Westbury	SCTS
34019	W'bury-Exeter St Davids-Yeovil Jct.	
35023	Yeovil Jct.-Waterloo	

November 20th 1966

35026	Manchester-York and return	Williams Deacons
		Bank

December 10th 1966

34089	Waterloo-Twickenham-Hounslow-	'Reunion'/LCGB
	Clapham Jct.	
75075	Clapham Jct.-East Croydon-Three	
	Bridges	
34089	Three Bridges-Brighton	
34089	Three Bridges-Preston Park	
Diesel Shunter	Preston Park-Brighton	
E6006/E6017	Kemp Town branch	
34089	Brighton-Victoria	

December 31st 1966

73065/73043	Waterloo-Portsmouth Harbour	'Vectis Farewell'/
31/24 & 17	Ryde Esplanade-Ryde St. Johns Road	LCGB
31/24	Ryde St. Johns Road-Shanklin	
24/31	Shanklin-Ryde St. Johns Road	
24/31 &22	Ryde St. Johns Road-Ryde Esplanade	
34013	Portsmouth Harbour-Horsham-Waterloo	

January 22nd 1967

34102/34057	Waterloo-Twickenham-Chertsey-	'Bridport Belle'/
	Salisbury	LCGB
34057	Salisbury-Westbury	
34013	Westbury-Maiden Newton	
41320/41295	Maiden Newton-Bridport-Toller	
D6541/41320/		
41295	Toller-Maiden Newton	
35030	Maiden Newton-Yeovil-Salisbury	
34102/34057	Salisbury-Waterloo	

February 2nd 1967

30072	Guildford-Deepdene-Redhill-G'ford	REC

February 5th 1967

77014	Waterloo-Chessington Sth-	'South West
	Wimbledon Park	Suburban'
80145	W'don Pk-Wimbledon-Shepperton	LCGB
34100	Shepperton-Twickenham	
77014	Twickenham-Windsor and Eton	
34100	Windsor and Eton-Staines	
76033	Staines-Reading General	
76058	R'dng G-Reading Central Goods-	
	Virginia Water	
34077	V- Water-Chertsey-Surbiton	
77014	Surbiton-Hampton Court	
34077	Hampton Court-Waterloo	

March 5th 1967

34087	W'loo-Staines-Weybridge-Cl.Jct.	'Surrey Downsman'/
34102	Clapham Jct.-Brixton-Sanderstead-	LCGB
	Oxted	
75077	Oxted-Norwood Jct.	
34087	N.Jct.-Redhill-G'ford-East Putney-	
	Clapham Jct.-Kensington Olympia	
75077	Kensington Olympia-Tulse Hill	
34102	Tulse Hill-Forest Hill-London Bridge	
75077	London Bridge-Peckham Rye-Victoria	

March 12th 1967

3442	Victoria-Redhill-Brighton-Chichester	
D6544	Lavant branch	The Marquess goes
3442	Chichester-Havant-Southampton	south south west'/
80151	So'ton-Lymington Pier-Eastleigh	Locomotive
3442	Eastleigh-Chichester-E Croydon	Preservation
D65xx	East Croydon-Victoria	(Sussex) Ltd.

March 19th 1967

34108	Victoria-Lewisham-Selsdon	'Southern Rambler'
E6016	Selsdon-East Croydon	SCTS
34108	East Croydon-Brighton-Eastbourne-	Plumpton-Victoria

March 25th 1967

30064	So'ton Ctl-Fawley-Totton	'Hants and Dorset
80151	Totton-Lym. Pier-Brockenhurst	Branch Flyer'/MRTS
41320	B'hurst-Blandford Forum-Swanage-Bournemouth	
34004	Bournemouth-Southampton	

April 1st 1967

(MN)	*Waterloo-Weymouth and return*	*Privately Sponsored*

April 1st 1967

(VEC-TIS emu, Unrblt WC, Ivatts)	*Waterloo-Portsmouth Hb, Pmouth Hbr.-Dockyard-Fareham-Droxford-Bishops Waltham branch-Chichester-Lavant-Havant-Guildford-Waterloo*	*RCTS*

April 1st 1967

(Unrblt WC, USAs, C, 01, Ivatts, 77014)	*Victoria Stewarts Lane-Clapham Jct.-Southfields-Alton-Farringdon-Botley-Droxford-Gosport-Soton Termninus-Fawley-Romsey-Andover-Waterloo*	*Pivately Sponsored*

April 9th 1967

35023	Waterloo-Salisbury	'Hampshire Branch
34057	Salisbury-Eastleigh-Southampton	Lines'/LCGB
30069/30064	So'ton-Fawley-Totton	
80151	Totton-Brockenhurst	
80151/41320	Lymington Branch	
34025	B'hurst-Reading-Ascot	
76031	Ascot-Camberley-Aldershot	
77014	Aldershot-Guildford	
73093	G'ford-Byfleet-Addlestone-Virginia Water-Waterloo	

April 16th 1967

?	*W'loo-Ascot-Reading-Basingstoke-So'ton-Salisbury-Westbury S'bury-Andover-Victoria*	*Glasgow Locomotive Club*

April 29th 1967

(Unrblt WC, Std 4)	*W'loo-Ascot-Alton-Farringdon-Treloars Siding-Guilford-Havant-So'ton Ocean Terminal-Salisbury-Andover-Ludgershall-Waterloo*	*REC*

May 7th 1967

34021	Waterloo-Havant-So'ton-Warcham	'Dorset Coast
34023/76026	Swanage branch, first run	Express'/LCGB
34023/80011	Swanage branch, second run	
34023	Wareham-Weymouth	
76026/73029	Weymouth-Bournemouth	
35003	Bournemouth-Waterloo	

June 3rd 1967

34034/35030	Weymouth-Bournemouth	Privately Sponsored
35030	Bournemouth-Waterloo	
35007	Waterloo-Weymouth	

June 3rd 1967

4498	Waterloo-B'mouth-Southampton	A4 Locomotive
34023	Southampton-Salisbury	Preservation Society
4498	Salisbury-Waterloo	

June 4th 1967

4498	Waterloo-Weymouth-Waterloo	A4 Locomotive Preservation Society

June 10th 1967

(4472, Unrblt WC)	*W'loo-Bournemouth-Weymouth-Eastleigh-Salisbury-Waterloo*	*ARES*

June 11th 1967

E31xx	B'ham New St.-Bletchley-Mitre Bridge	WRS
73085/34004	Mitre Bridge-Clapham Jct.-Woking	
34004	Woking-Wareham	
34004/80146	Swanage branch	
34004	Wareham-Weymouth	
35013/35030	Weymouth-Dorchester	
35030	Dorchester-Poole-Salisbury	
34023	Salisbury-Basingstoke	
73085/34023	Basingstoke-Clap.Jct.-Willesden Jct.	
E31xx	Return to Birmingham	

June 18th 1967

73029/34023	Waterloo-Guildford-Fareham	RCTS
34089	Fareham-Southampton	
34108/34089	So'ton-Bournemouth-Wareham	
34089/80146	Swanage Branch	
34089	Wareham-Weymouth	
34023/34108	Weymouth-Eastleigh-Salisbury	
35013	Salisbury-Waterloo	

June 25th 1967

(Unrblt WC)	*Crewe-Carlisle-Settle-Stoke*	*BPPS*

July 2nd 1967

35008	Waterloo-Weymouth	'Farewell to Southern Steam, No 1'/
35007/35008	Weymouth-Bournemouth	BR
35008	Bournemouth-Waterloo	

July 2nd 1967

35028	Waterloo-Bournemouth-Waterloo	'Farewell, No 2'/BR

July 2nd 1967

(?)	*Waterloo-Weymouth-Waterloo*	*'Farewell No 3'/BR*

July 2nd 1967

(?)	Bournemouth-Waterloo	*'Farewell No 4'/BR*
(emu)	*Waterloo-Bournemouth*	

Abbreviations

ARES	Altrinchamian Railway Excursion Society
BPPS	Bulleid Pacific Preservation Society
BYTS	British Young Travellers Society
BDRS	Bristol and District Railway Society
BLS	Branch Line Society
EURS	Exeter University Railway Society
GMRS	Gainsborough Model Railway Society
GRS	Gloucestershire Railway Society
HCRS	Home Counties Railway Society
LCGB	Locomotive Club of Great Britain
MRTS	Manchester Rail Travel Society
MGNJRS	Midland and Great Northern Joint Railway Society
PRC	Plymouth Railway Circle
REC	Railway Enthusiasts Club
SCTS	Southern Counties Touring Society
SLS	Stephenson Locomotive Society
SWRS	South and West Railway Society
TRPS	Talyllyn Railway Preservation Society
WRS	Warwickshire Railway Society

Acknowledgements

I am most grateful to the many people who have assisted me in compiling this account of the last ten years of Southern Steam. In particular I would like to thank Roger Hardingham for originally encouraging me to tackle the period between 1966 and 1967, Peter Turnbull and others for prompting me to extend coverage to the years before 1966, and Stephen Mourton of *Runpast Publishing* for his continuous support and guidance.

Like any author, I have found that writing a book can only be achieved with the help and tolerance of those nearest and dearest. To my wife. Marian, and my sons, Peter and Matthew, I owe a special debt. My only sadness is that my eldest son, John David, a great companion on many a railway expedition, died too young to cast a critical eye over his dad's handiwork. However, I have no doubt that he has been keeping a watchful eye on me from his place of peace.

Sadly too, a number of the many generous contributors, who freely gave of their time and memories while I was carrying out research, have also passed on. To them, and to all the others who have lent photographs, notebooks and items from their railwayana collections, or simply answered my requests for information, I wish to express my sincere thanks.

The following list records, with gratitude, all who have assisted me in any way:
A.E. Abbott, R.J. Adderson, Nigel Bath, Martin Beckett, John Berryman, Roy Bicknell, Michael R. Bonavia, Dr. Jim Boudreau, Mark Bradmore, Tony Brentnall, Miss J. A. Browne, Derek Buckett, C.L. Caddy, Gilbert Chudleigh, Peter Cooper, J. Corkill, Ron Cover, Stan Coxhead, D.M. Cox, Stanley Creer, Claud Dare, Hugh Davies, C.C. Deamer, David Druce, A. Dumpleton, Peter Dyson, Graham Earl, Tim Edmonds, Les Elsey, Mike Esau, Jim Evans, Bert Farley, John Fairman, R.W. Fletcher, Mike Foster, Harry Frith, Paul Gibbons, Ray Glassey, Alan Gosling, F.W. Goudie, Len Groves, Douglas Harding, Roger Hardingham, Clern Harris, Peter Harrod, Peter Hay, J.C. Haydon, Colin Hogg, Bert Hooker, Rod Hoyle, H.N. James, Nigel Kendall, Keith Lawrence, Ron Lumber, D. Lusby, P.J. Lynch, Dr. John Mackett, G. Marks, John Marshall, Klaus Marx, Roger Merry-Price, C.J. Mills, Bert Moody, G.M. Moon, S.C. Nash, Gordon Nicholson, Dr. L.A. Nixon, Joseph Paddick, Ian Partridge, Andrew Philip, Ray Philips, Ivan J. Prior, Len Renwick, Doug Richards, R.C. Riley, Geoff Rixon, Jim Robinson, Ray Ruffell, E.H. Sawford, John Scrace, Tony Sedgwick, D. Sheather, David Shepherd, Gerald Siviour, Peter J.C. Skelton, David M. Smith, G.A. Smith, Roger Sherlock, Dave Squibb, Brian Stephenson, Colin Stone, R.J. Sweet, D.Swetham, Keith Taylor, Nigel J.Tilly, S.C. Townroe, Frank Wakelam, Johnny Walker, E.J. Waters, Lyn Weaver, Michael Welch, A.G. Westlake, K. Widdowson, Edwin Wilmshurst, D.W. Winkworth, Len Witt, R.J.C. Woollard, Andrew P.M. Wright, Keith Withers, D.J. Wroe, Eric Youlden.
The Editors and reporters of the Alton Gazette, Alton Herald, Bournemouth Evening Echo, Dorset Evening Echo, Eastleigh Weekly News, Kentish Messenger, Lymington Times, Salisbury Journal and Times, Southern Evening Echo, BBC Solent, County Sound Radio.

Bibliography

Books and Pamphlets
Allen, G. Freeman *The Southern since 1948* Ian Allan 1987
Anglian Locomotive Group *80151* 1977
Arlett, Mike & Lockett, David *Southern Steam in the South and West* OPC 1992
Ballantyne, Hugh *Southern Steam in Colour* Jane's Publishing Company 1985
Bird, John H. *Southern Steam Surrender* Kingfisher Railway Productions 1987
Body, Geoffrey *Railways of the Southern Region* PSL 1984
Bolger, Paul *BR Steam Motive Power Depots, SR* Ian Allan 1983
Bonavia, Michael R. *The History of the Southern Railway* Unwin Hyman 1987
Bradley, D.L. *Locomotives of the Southern Railway (Parts 1 and 2)* RCTS 1975/6
Bradley, D.L. *A Locomotive History of the Railways on the Isle of Wight* RCTS 1982
Britton, A. *Once Upon a Line (Volumes 1 and 2)* OPC 1983, 1984
Cooper, B.K. *Electric Trains in Britain* Ian Allan 1979
Cousins, S and Berrow, J *After the Rhinoceros* LTVAS 1983
Fereday Glenn, D. *Roads, Rails and Ferries of the Solent Area 1919-1969* Ian Allan 1980
Gammell, C.J. *Southern Region Engine Workings* Oxford Publishing Co. 1994
Gough, Terry *British Railways Past and Present No 18 Surrey and West Sussex* Silver Link Publishing 1993
Grafton, P. (Ed.) *Man of the Southern: Jim Evans looks back* G. Allen & Unwin 1980
Griffiths, Roger *Southern Sheds in Camera* Oxford Publishing Company 1989
Hawkins, C and Reeve, G. *An Historical Survey of Southern Sheds* OPC 1979
Hay, Peter *Steaming through Surrey* Middleton Press 1986
Kichenside, G.M. *Isle of Wight Album* Ian Allan 1967
Maggs, Colin G. *Rail Centres: Exeter* Ian Allan 1985
Dendy Marshall, C.F. and Kidner, R.W. *History of the Southern Railway* Ian Allan 1963
Mitchell, David *British Railways Past and PresentNo 8 Devon* Silver Link Publishing 1991
Mitchell, David *British Railways Past and Present No 17 Cornwall* Silver Link Publishing 1993
Mitchell, Vic and Smith, Keith *Branch Line to Lyme Regis* Middleton Press 1987
Mitchell, Vic and Smith, Keith *Guildford to Redhill* Middleton Press 1989
Mitchell, Vic and Smith, Keith *Reading to Guildford* Middleton Press 1988
Moody, G.T. *Southern Electric 1909-1979* Ian Allan 1979
Morrison, Brian and Beer, Brian *British Railways Past and Present No 20 Kent and East Sussex* Silver Link Publishing 1994
Paye, P and Paye, K *Steam on the Isle of Wight (1956-1966)* OPC 1977
Robbins, M. *The Isle of Wight Railways* Oakwood Press 1981
Robertson, Kevin *The last days of steam in Berkshire* Alan Sutton 1987
Rogers, Col. H.C.B. *Transition from Steam* Ian Allan 1980
Rogers, J. and Hardingham, R. *Southern Region Locomotive Shed Allocations 1953* Kingfisher 1981
Russell, J.H. *A Pictorial Record of Southern Locomotives* Oxford Publishing Co. 1991
Smith, Martin *An Illustrated History of Plymouth's Railways* Irwell Press 1995
Southern Railways Group *Nonsuch Notebook of Railways and Models* undated
Stephenson, Brian and Russell, Patrick *Specials in Steam* Ian Allan 1968
Stubbs, W.T. and Boddy, M.G. (compilers) *Locomotive StockBook 1960* RCTS
Teal, Paul *BR Motive Power Allocations 1959-1968 Part 1* Ian Allan 1985
Trevena, Nigel *Steam for Scrap (Vols. 1 and 2)* Atlantic 1985
Welbourn, Nigel *Lost Lines, Southern* Ian Allan 1996
Welch, M.S. *Bluebell Steam in Retrospect* BRPS 1980
White, H.P.A. *Regional History of the Railways of Great Britain (Vol. 2)* Phoenix House 1961
Winkworth, D.W. *Bulleid's Pacifics* G. Allen & Unwin 1974
Williams, H.L. *Docks and Ports:Southampton* Ian Allan 1984

Magazines and Periodicals

Modern Railways
Monthly Bulletin LCGB
Railway Magazine
Railway World
Railway Observer RCTS
Steam Days (various issues) Redgauntlet Publications
Trains Illustrated Ian Allan

Newspapers

Eastleigh Weekly News
Lymington Times
Southern Evening Echo
The News, Portsmouth
The Times

Various British Railways, Southern Region publications, internal and public, held in private collections.